THE
HARVARD CLASSICS

Registered Edition

◆

Signing the Declaration of Independence
From the painting by Charles E. A. Dumaresq

THE HARVARD CLASSICS
EDITED BY CHARLES W. ELIOT, LL.D.

American Historical Documents

1000-1904

With Introductions *and* Notes

P. F. Collier & Son Corporation
NEW YORK

CONTENTS

I

INTRODUCTORY NOTE

No final history of the United States of America has been written, or is likely to be written. Research is constantly bringing to light new facts that correct details or modify the traditional view of larger questions; and the most impartial historian is subject to personal or sectional bias which leads to his works being regarded as imperfect by another generation, or as unfair by the people of parts of the country other than his own. In such a series as the present, then, it is unwise to represent the story of the growth of this nation by the summary of any one scholar.

The alternative has been to place before the reader a selection of the most important documents which record in contemporary terms the great events in the history of the country. Beginning with the personal records of the earliest discoverers of the continent, the selection goes on to present the first attempts at organizing a machinery of government made by the first settlers of the New England colonies; proceeds to the landmarks of the struggle for independence and the formation of the Constitution; shows the laying of the foundation of national policies and of the interpretation of the Constitution; indicates by the texts of the treaties themselves the acquisition of each successive increase of territory; and reveals by the original state papers the main causes and effects of the wars in which the country has from time to time been engaged. Read in succession, these documents afford a condensed view of the political progress of the American people; freed from any prejudice save that which swayed the makers of the history themselves.

AMERICAN
HISTORICAL DOCUMENTS

THE VOYAGES TO VINLAND
(c. 1000)

[The following account of the discovery of North America by Leif Ericsson is contained in the *"Saga of Eric the Red"*; and the present translation is that made by A. M. Reeves from the version of the Saga in the *Flateyar-bók,* compiled by Jón Thórdharson about 1387. The part of the coast where Leif landed is much in dispute, the most recent investigations tending to the southern part of the coast of Labrador, though many scholars believe Vinland to have been on the New England shore.]

LEIF THE LUCKY BAPTIZED

AFTER that sixteen winters had lapsed, from the time when Eric the Red went to colonize Greenland, Leif, Eric's son, sailed out from Greenland to Norway. He arrived in Drontheim in the autumn, when King Olaf Tryggvason was come down from the North, out of Halagoland. Leif put into Nidaros with his ship, and set out at once to visit the king. King Olaf expounded the faith to him, as he did to other heathen men who came to visit him. It proved easy for the king to persuade Leif, and he was accordingly baptized, together with all of his shipmates. Leif remained throughout the winter with the king, by whom he was well entertained.

BIARNI GOES IN QUEST OF GREENLAND

HERIULF was a son of Bard Heriulfsson. He was a kinsman of Ingolf, the first colonist. Ingolf allotted land to Heriulf between Vág and Reykianess, and he dwelt at first at Drepstokk. Heriulf's wife's name was Thorgerd, and their son, whose name was Biarni, was a most promising man. He formed an inclination for voyaging while he was still young, and he prospered both in property and public esteem. It was his custom to pass his winters alternately abroad and with his father. Biarni soon became the owner of a trading-ship;

5

and during the last winter that he spent in Norway [his father] Heriulf determined to accompany Eric on his voyage to Greenland, and made his preparations to give up his farm. Upon the ship with Heriulf was a Christian man from the Hebrides, he it was who composed the Sea-Roller's Song, which contains this stave:

. "Mine adventure to the Meek One,
Monk-heart-searcher, I commit now;
He, who heaven's halls doth govern,
Hold the hawk's-seat ever o'er me!"

Heriulf settled at Heriulfsness, and was a most distinguished man. Eric the Red dwelt at Brattahlid, where he was held in the highest esteem, and all men paid him homage. These were Eric's children: Leif, Thorvald, and Thorstein, and a daughter whose name was Freydis; she was wedded to a man named Thorvard, and they dwelt at Gardar, where the episcopal seat now is. She was a very haughty woman, while Thorvard was a man of little force of character, and Freydis had been wedded to him chiefly because of his wealth. At that time the people of Greenland were heathen.

Biarni arrived with his ship at Eyrar [in Iceland] in the summer of the same year, in the spring of which his father had sailed away. Biarni was much surprised when he heard this news, and would not discharge his cargo. His shipmates inquired of him what he intended to do, and he replied that it was his purpose to keep to his custom, and make his home for the winter with his father; "and I will take the ship to Greenland, if you will bear me company." They all replied that they would abide by his decision. Then said Biarni, "Our voyage must be regarded as foolhardy, seeing that no one of us has ever been in the Greenland Sea." Nevertheless, they put out to sea when they were equipped for the voyage, and sailed for three days, until the land was hidden by the water, and then the fair wind died out, and north winds arose, and fogs, and they knew not whither they were drifting, and thus it lasted for many "dœgr." Then they saw the sun again, and were able to determine the quarters of the heavens; they hoisted sail, and sailed that "dœgr" through before they saw land. They discussed among themselves what land it could be, and Biarni said that he did not believe that it could be Greenland.

They asked whether he wished to sail to this land or not. "It is my counsel" [said he] "to sail close to the land." They did so, and soon saw that the land was level, and covered with woods, and that there were small hillocks upon it. They left the land on their larboard, and let the sheet turn toward the land. They sailed for two "dœgr" before they saw another land. They asked whether Biarni thought this was Greenland yet. He replied that he did not think this any more like Greenland than the former, "because in Greenland there are said to be many great ice mountains." They soon approached this land, and saw that it was a flat and wooded country. The fair wind failed them then, and the crew took counsel together, and concluded that it would be wise to land there, but Biarni would not consent to this. They alleged that they were in need of both wood and water. "Ye have no lack of either of these," says Biarni,—a course, forsooth, which won him blame among his shipmates. He bade them hoist sail, which they did, and turning the prow from the land they sailed out upon the high seas, with south-westerly gales, for three "dœgr," when they saw the third land; this land was high and mountainous, with ice mountains upon it. They asked Biarni then whether he would land there, and he replied that he was not disposed to do so, "because this land does not appear to me to offer any attractions." Nor did they lower their sail, but held their course off the land, and saw that it was an island. They left this land astern, and held out to sea with the same fair wind. The wind waxed amain, and Biarni directed them to reef, and not to sail at a speed unbefitting their ship and rigging. They sailed now for four "dœgr," when they saw the fourth land. Again they asked Biarni whether he thought this could be Greenland or not. Biarni answers, "This is likest Greenland, according to that which has been reported to me concerning it, and here we will steer to the land." They directed their course thither, and landed in the evening, below a cape upon which there was a boat, and there, upon this cape, dwelt Heriulf, Biarni's father, whence the cape took its name, and was afterward called Heriulfsness. Biarni now went to his father, gave up his voyaging, and remained with his father while Heriulf lived, and continued to live there after his father.

HERE BEGINS THE BRIEF HISTORY OF THE GREENLANDERS

NEXT to this is now to be told how Biarni Heriulfsson came out from Greenland on a visit to Earl Eric, by whom he was well received. Biarni gave an account of his travels [upon the occasion] when he saw the lands, and the people thought that he had been lacking in enterprise, since he had no report to give concerning these countries; and the fact brought him reproach. Biarni was appointed one of the Earl's men, and went out to Greenland the following summer. There was now much talk about voyages of discovery. Leif, the son of Eric the Red, of Brattahlid, visited Biarni Heriulfsson and bought a ship of him, and collected a crew, until they formed altogether a company of thirty-five men. Leif invited his father, Eric, to become the leader of the expedition, but Eric declined, saying that he was then stricken in years, and adding that he was less able to endure the exposure of sea life than he had been. Leif replied that he would nevertheless be the one who would be most apt to bring good luck, and Eric yielded to Leif's solicitation, and rode from home when they were ready to sail. When he was but a short distance from the ship, the horse which Eric was riding stumbled, and he was thrown from his back and wounded his foot, whereupon he exclaimed, "It is not designed for me to discover more lands than the one in which we are now living, nor can we now continue longer together." Eric returned home to Brattahlid, and Leif pursued his way to the ship with his companions, thirty-five men. One of the company was a German, named Tyrker. They put the ship in order; and, when they were ready, they sailed out to sea, and found first that land which Biarni and his shipmates found last. They sailed up to the land, and cast anchor, and launched a boat, and went ashore, and saw no grass there. Great ice mountains lay inland back from the sea, and it was as a [tableland of] flat rock all the way from the sea to the ice mountains; and the country seemed to them to be entirely devoid of good qualities. Then said Leif, "It has not come to pass with us in regard to this land as with Biarni, that we have not gone upon it. To this country I will now give a name, and call it Helluland." They returned to the ship, put out to sea, and found a second land. They sailed again to the land, and came to anchor, and launched the boat, and went ashore. This was a level wooded land; and there were broad stretches of white sand where they went, and the land was level by the sea. Then said Leif, "This land shall have a name after its nature; and we will call it Markland." They returned to the ship forthwith, and sailed away upon the main with north-east winds, and were out two "dœgr" before they sighted land. They sailed toward this land, and came to an island which lay to the northward off the land. There they went ashore and looked about them, the weather being fine, and they observed that there was dew upon the grass, and it so happened that they touched the dew with their hands, and touched their hands to their mouths, and it seemed to them that they had never before tasted anything so sweet as this. They went aboard their ship again and sailed into a certain sound, which lay between the island and a cape, which jutted out from the land on the north, and they stood in westering past the cape. At ebb-tide, there were broad reaches of shallow water there, and they ran their ship aground there, and it was a long distance from the ship to the ocean; yet were they so anxious to go ashore that they could not wait until the tide should rise under their ship, but hastened to the land, where a certain river flows out from a lake. As soon as the tide rose beneath their ship, however, they took the boat and rowed to the ship, which they conveyed up the river, and so into the lake, where they cast anchor and carried their hammocks ashore from the ship, and built themselves booths there. They afterward determined to establish themselves there for the winter, and they accordingly built a large house. There was no lack of salmon there either in the river or in the lake, and larger salmon than they had ever seen before. The country thereabouts seemed to be possessed of such good qualities that cattle would need no fodder there during the winters. There was no frost there in the winters, and the grass withered but little. The days and nights there were of more nearly equal length than in Greenland or Iceland. On the shortest day of winter, the sun was up between "eykarstad" and "dagmalastad." When they had completed their house, Leif said to his companions, "I propose now to divide our company into two groups, and to set about an exploration of the country. One-half of our party shall remain at home at the house, while the other half shall investigate the land; and they must not go beyond a point from which they can return home the same evening, and are not to separate [from each other]. Thus they did for a time. Leif, himself, by turns joined the exploring party, or remained behind at the house. Leif was a large and powerful man, and of a most imposing bearing, —a man of sagacity, and a very just man in all things.

Leif the Lucky Finds Men Upon a Skerry at Sea

It was discovered one evening that one of their company was missing; and this proved to be Tyrker, the German. Leif was sorely troubled by this, for Tyrker had lived with Leif and his father for a long time, and had been very devoted to Leif when he was a child. Leif severely reprimanded his companions, and prepared to go in search of him, taking twelve men with him. They had proceeded but a short distance from the house, when they were met by Tyrker, whom they received most cordially. Leif observed at once that his foster-father was in lively spirits. Tyrker had a prominent forehead, restless eyes, small features, was diminutive in stature, and rather a sorry-looking individual withal, but was, nevertheless, a most capable handicraftsman. Leif addressed him, and asked, "Wherefore art thou so belated, foster-father mine, and astray from the others?" In the beginning Tyrker spoke for some time in German, rolling his eyes and grinning, and they could not understand him; but after a time he addressed them in the Northern tongue: "I did not go much further [*than you*], and yet I have something of novelty to relate. I have found vines and grapes." "Is this indeed true, foster-father?" said Leif. "Of a certainty it is true," quoth he, "for I was born where there is no lack of either grapes or vines." They slept the night through, and on the morrow Leif said to his shipmates, "We will now divide our labors, and each day will either gather grapes or cut vines and fell trees, so as to obtain a cargo of these for my ship." They acted upon this advice, and it is said that their after-boat was filled with grapes. A cargo sufficient for the ship was cut, and when the spring came they made their ship ready, and sailed away; and from its products Leif gave the land a name, and called it Wineland. They sailed out to sea, and had fair winds until they sighted Greenland and the fells below the glaciers. Then one of the men spoke up

and said, "Why do you steer the ship so much into the wind?" Leif
answers: "I have my mind upon my steering, but on other matters
as well. Do ye not see anything out of the common?" They replied
that they saw nothing strange. "I do not know," says Leif, "whether
it is a ship or a skerry that I see." Now they saw it, and said that it
must be a skerry; but he was so much keener of sight than they that
he was able to discern men upon the skerry. "I think it best to tack,"
says Leif, "so that we may draw near to them, that we may be able
to render them assistance if they should stand in need of it; and,
if they should not be peaceably disposed, we shall still have better
command of the situation than they." They approached the skerry,
and, lowering their sail, cast anchor, and launched a second small
boat, which they had brought with them. Tyrker inquired who was
the leader of the party. He replied that his name was Thori, and
that he was a Norseman; "but what is thy name?" Leif gave his
name. "Art thou a son of Eric the Red of Brattahlid?" says he. Leif
responded that he was. "It is now my wish," says Leif, "to take you
all into my ship, and likewise so much of your possessions as the
ship will hold." This offer was accepted, and [with their ship] thus
laden they held away to Ericsfirth, and sailed until they arrived at
Brattahlid. Having discharged the cargo, Leif invited Thori, with
his wife, Gudrid, and three others, to make their home with him,
and procured quarters for the other members of the crew, both for
his own and Thori's men. Leif rescued fifteen persons from the
skerry. He was afterwards called Leif the Lucky. Leif had now
goodly store both of property and honor. There was serious illness
that winter in Thori's party, and Thori and a great number of his
people died. Eric the Red also died that winter. There was now
much talk about Leif's Wineland journey; and his brother, Thorvald, held that the country had not been sufficiently explored. Thereupon Leif said to Thorvald, "If it be thy will, brother, thou mayest
go to Wineland with my ship; but I wish the ship first to fetch the
wood which Thori had upon the skerry." And so it was done.

THORVALD GOES TO WINELAND

Now Thorvald, with the advice of his brother, Leif, prepared to
make this voyage with thirty men. They put their ship in order,

and sailed out to sea; and there is no account of their voyage before
their arrival at Leifs-booths in Wineland. They laid up their ship
there, and remained there quietly during the winter, supplying themselves with food by fishing. In the spring, however, Thorvald said
that they should put their ship in order, and that a few men should
take the after-boat, and proceed along the western coast, and explore
[the region] thereabouts during the summer. They found it a fair,
well-wooded country. It was but a short distance from the woods to
the sea, and [there were] white sands, as well as great numbers of
islands and shallows. They found neither dwelling of man nor
lair of beast; but in one of the westerly islands they found a wooden
building for the shelter of grain. They found no other trace of
human handiwork; and they turned back, and arrived at Leifs-booths
in the autumn. The following summer Thorvald set out toward
the east with the ship, and along the northern coast. They were met
by a high wind off a certain promontory, and were driven ashore
there, and damaged the keel of their ship, and were compelled to
remain there for a long time and repair the injury to their vessel.
Then said Thorvald to his companions, "I propose that we raise the
keel upon this cape, and call it Keelness"; and so they did. Then they
sailed away to the eastward off the land and into the mouth of the
adjoining firth and to a headland, which projected into the sea there,
and which was entirely covered with woods. They found an anchorage for their ship, and put out the gangway to the land; and Thorvald and all of his companions went ashore. "It is a fair region here,"
said he; "and here I should like to make my home." They then
returned to the ship, and discovered on the sands, in beyond the
headland, three mounds: they went up to these, and saw that they
were three skin canoes with three men under each. They thereupon
divided their party, and succeeded in seizing all of the men but one,
who escaped with his canoe. They killed the eight men, and then
ascended the headland again, and looked about them, and discovered
within the firth certain hillocks, which they concluded must be
habitations. They were then so overpowered with sleep that they
could not keep awake, and all fell into a [heavy] slumber from
which they were awakened by the sound of a cry uttered above them;
and the words of the cry were these: "Awake, Thorvald, thou and

all thy company, if thou wouldst save thy life; and board thy ship with all thy men, and sail with all speed from the land!" A countless number of skin canoes then advanced toward them from the inner part of the firth, whereupon Thorvald exclaimed, "We must put out the war-boards on both sides of the ship, and defend ourselves to the best of our ability, but offer little attack." This they did; and the Skrellings, after they had shot at them for a time, fled precipitately, each as best he could. Thorvald then inquired of his men whether any of them had been wounded, and they informed him that no one of them had received a wound. "I have been wounded in my arm-pit," says he. "An arrow flew in between the gunwale and the shield, below my arm. Here is the shaft, and it will bring me to my end. I counsel you now to retrace your way with the utmost speed. But me ye shall convey to that headland which seemed to me to offer so pleasant a dwelling-place: thus it may be fulfilled that the truth sprang to my lips when I expressed the wish to abide there for a time. Ye shall bury me there, and place a cross at my head, and another at my feet, and call it Crossness forever after." At that time Christianity had obtained in Greenland: Eric the Red died, however, before [the introduction of] Christianity.

Thorvald died; and, when they had carried out his injunctions, they took their departure, and rejoined their companions, and they told each other of the experiences which had befallen them. They remained there during the winter, and gathered grapes and wood with which to freight the ship. In the following spring they returned to Greenland, and arrived with their ship in Ericsfirth, where they were able to recount great tidings to Leif.

Thorstein Ericsson Dies in the Western Settlement

In the mean time it had come to pass in Greenland that Thorstein of Ericsfirth had married, and taken to wife Gudrid, Thorbrion's daughter, [she] who had been the spouse of Thori Eastman, as has been already related. Now Thorstein Ericsson, being minded to make the voyage to Wineland after the body of his brother, Thorvald, equipped the same ship, and selected a crew of twenty-five men of good size and strength, and taking with him his wife, Gudrid, when all was in readiness, they sailed out into the open ocean, and out of sight of land. They were driven hither and thither over the sea all that summer, and lost all reckoning; and at the end of the first week of winter they made the land at Lysufirth in Greenland, in the Western settlement. Thorstein set out in search of quarters for his crew, and succeeded in procuring homes for all of his ship-mates; but he and his wife were unprovided for, and remained to-gether upon the ship for two or more days. At this time Christianity was still in its infancy in Greenland. [Here follows the account of Thorstein's sickness and death in the winter.] . . . When he had thus spoken, Thorstein sank back again; and his body was laid out for burial, and borne to the ship. Thorstein, the master, faithfully performed all his promises to Gudrid. He sold his lands and live stock in the spring, and accompanied Gudrid to the ship, with all his possessions. He put the ship in order, procured a crew, and then sailed for Ericsfirth. The bodies of the dead were now buried at the church; and Gudrid then went home to Leif at Brattahlid, while Thorstein the Swarthy made a home for himself on Ericsfirth, and remained there as long as he lived, and was looked upon as a very superior man.

Of the Wineland Voyages of Thorfinn and His Companions

That same summer a ship came from Norway to Greenland. The skipper's name was Thorfinn Karlsefni. He was a son of Thord Horsehead, and a grandson of Snorri, the son of Thord of Höfdi. Thorfinn Karlsefni, who was a very wealthy man, passed the winter at Brattahlid with Leif Ericsson. He very soon set his heart upon Gudrid, and sought her hand in marriage. She referred him to Leif for her answer, and was subsequently betrothed to him; and their marriage was celebrated that same winter. A renewed discussion arose concerning a Wineland voyage; and the folk urged Karlsefni to make the venture, Gudrid joining with the others. He determined to undertake the voyage, and assembled a company of sixty men and five women, and entered into an agreement with his shipmates that they should each share equally in all the spoils of the enterprise. They took with them all kinds of cattle, as it was their intention to settle the country, if they could. Karlsefni asked Leif for the house in Wineland; and he replied that he would lend it, but not give it.

They sailed out to sea with the ship, and arrived safe and sound at Leifs-booths, and carried their hammocks ashore there. They were soon provided with an abundant and goodly supply of food; for a whale of good size and quality was driven ashore there, and they secured it, and flensed it, and had then no lack of provisions. The cattle were turned out upon the land, and the males soon became.very restless and vicious: they had brought a bull with them. Karlsefni caused trees to be felled and to be hewed into timbers wherewith to load his ship, and the wood was placed upon a cliff to dry. They gathered somewhat of all of the valuable products of the land,— grapes, and all kinds of game and fish, and other good things. In the summer succeeding the first winter Skrellings were discovered. A great troop of men came forth from out the woods. The cattle were hard by, and the bull began to bellow and roar with a great noise, whereat the Skrellings were frightened, and ran away with their packs, wherein were gray furs, sables, and all kinds of peltries. They fled towards Karlsefni's dwelling, and sought to effect an entrance into the house; but Karlsefni caused the doors to be defended [against them]. Neither [people] could understand the other's language. The Skrellings put down their bundles then, and loosed them, and offered their wares [for barter], and were especially anxious to exchange these for weapons; but Karlsefni forbade his men to sell their weapons, and, taking counsel with himself, he bade the women carry out milk to the Skrellings, which they no sooner saw than they wanted to buy it, and nothing else. Now the outcome of the Skrellings' trading was that they carried their wares away in their stomachs, while they left their packs and peltries behind with Karlsefni and his companions, and, having accomplished this [exchange], they went away. Now it is to be told that Karlsefni caused a strong wooden palisade to be constructed and set up around the house. It was at this time that Gudrid, Karlsefni's wife, gave birth to a male child, and the boy was called Snorri. In the early part of the second winter the Skrellings came to them again, and these were now much more numerous than before, and brought with them the same wares as at first. Then said Karlsefni to the women, "Do ye carry out now the same food which proved so profitable before, and nought else." When they saw this, they cast their packs in over the palisade. Gudrid was sitting within, in the doorway, beside the cradle of her infant son, Snorri, when a shadow fell upon the door, and a woman in a black namkirtle entered. She was short in stature, and wore a fillet about her head; her hair was of a light chestnut color, and she was pale of hue, and so big-eyed that never before had eyes so large been seen in a human skull. She went up to where Gudrid was seated, and said, "What is thy name?" "My name is Gudrid, but what is thy name?" "My name is Gudrid," says she. The housewife Gudrid motioned her with her hand to a seat beside her; but it so happened that at that very instant Gudrid heard a great crash, whereupon the woman vanished, and at that same moment one of the Skrellings, who had tried to seize their weapons, was killed by one of Karlsefni's followers. At this the Skrellings fled precipitately, leaving their garments and wares behind them; and not a soul, save Gudrid alone, beheld this woman. "Now we must needs take counsel together," says Karlsefni; "for that I believe they will visit us a third time in great numbers, and attack us. Let us now adopt this plan. Ten of our number shall go out upon the cape, and show themselves there; while the remainder of our company shall go into the woods and hew a clearing for our cattle, when the troop approaches from the forest. We will also take our bull, and let him go in advance of us." The lie of the land was such that the proposed meeting-place had the lake upon the one side and the forest upon the other. Karlsefni's advice was now carried into execution. The Skrellings advanced to the spot which Karlsefni had selected for the encounter; and a battle was fought there, in which great numbers of the band of the Skrellings were slain. There was one man among the Skrellings, of large size and fine bearing, whom Karlsefni concluded must be their chief. One of the Skrellings picked up an axe; and, having looked at it for a time, he brandished it about one of his companions, and hewed at him, and on the instant the man fell dead. Thereupon the big man seized the axe; and, after examining it for a moment, he hurled it as far as he could out into the sea. Then they fled helter skelter into the woods, and thus their intercourse came to an end. Karlsefni and his party remained there throughout the winter; but in the spring Karlsefni announces that he is not minded to remain there longer, but will return to Greenland. They now made ready for the voyage, and carried away with them much booty in vines and grapes and peltries. They sailed out upon the high seas, and brought their ship safely to Ericsfirth, where they remained during the winter.

Freydis Causes the Brothers to be Put to Death

There was now much talk about a Wineland voyage, for this was reckoned both a profitable and an honorable enterprise. The same summer that Karlsefni arrived from Wineland a ship from Norway arrived in Greenland. This ship was commanded by two brothers, Helgi and Finnbogi, who passed the winter in Greenland. They were descended from an Icelandic family of the East-firths. It is now to be added that Freydis, Eric's daughter, set out from her home at Gardar, and waited upon the brothers, Helgi and Finnbogi, and invited them to sail with their vessel to Wineland, and to share with her equally all of the good things which they might succeed in obtaining there. To this they agreed, and she departed thence to visit her brother, Leif, and ask him to give her the house which he had caused to be erected in Wineland; but he made her the same answer [as that which he had given Karlsefni], saying that he would lend the house, but not give it. It was stipulated between Karlsefni and Freydis that each should have on ship-board thirty able-bodied men, besides the women; but Freydis immediately violated this compact by concealing five men more [than this number], and this the brothers did not discover before they arrived in Wineland. They now put out to sea, having agreed beforehand that they would sail in company, if possible, and, although they were not far apart from each other, the brothers arrived somewhat in advance, and carried their belongings up to Leif's house. Now, when Freydis arrived, her ship was discharged and the baggage carried up to the house, whereupon Freydis exclaimed, "Why did you carry your baggage in here?" "Since we believed," said they, "that all promises made to us would be kept." "It was to me that Leif loaned the house," says she, "and not to you." Whereupon Helgi exclaimed, "We brothers cannot hope to rival thee in wrong dealing." They thereupon carried their baggage forth, and built a hut, above the sea, on the bank of the lake, and put all in order about it; while Freydis caused wood to be felled, with which to load her ship. The winter now set in, and the brothers suggested that they should amuse themselves by playing games. This they did for a time, until the folk began to disagree, when dissensions arose between them, and the games came to an end, and the visits between the houses ceased; and thus it continued far into the winter. One morning early Freydis arose from her bed and dressed herself, but did not put on her shoes and stockings. A heavy dew had fallen, and she took her husband's cloak, and wrapped it about her, and then walked to the brothers' house, and up to the door, which had been only partly closed by one of the men, who had gone out a short time before. She pushed the door open, and stood silently in the doorway for a time. Finnbogi, who was lying on the innermost side of the room, was awake, and said, "What dost thou wish here, Freydis?" She answers, "I wish thee to rise and go out with me, for I would speak with thee." He did so; and they walked to a tree, which lay close by the wall of the house, and seated themselves upon it. "How art thou pleased here?" says she. He answers, "I am well pleased with the fruitfulness of the land; but I am ill-content with the breach which has come between us, for, methinks, there has been no cause for it." "It is even as thou sayest," says she, "and so it seems to me; but my errand to thee is that I wish to exchange ships with you brothers, for that ye have a larger ship than I, and I wish to depart from here." "To this I must accede," says he, "if it is thy pleasure." Therewith they parted; and she returned home and Finnbogi to his bed. She climbed up into bed, and awakened Thorvard with her cold feet; and he asked her why she was so cold and wet. She answered with great passion: "I have been to the brothers," says she, "to try to buy their ship, for I wished to have a larger vessel; but they received my overtures so ill that they struck me and handled me very roughly; what time thou, poor wretch, wilt neither avenge my shame nor thy own; and I find, perforce, that I am no longer in Greenland. Moreover I shall part from thee unless thou wreakest vengeance for this." And now he could stand her taunts no longer, and ordered the men to rise at once and take their weapons; and this they yield. And they then proceeded directly to the house of the brothers, and entered it while the folk were asleep, and seized and bound them, and led each one out when he was bound; and, as they came out, Freydis caused each one to be slain In this wise all of the men were put to death, and only the women were left; and these no one would kill. At this Freydis exclaimed, "Hand me an axe." This was done; and she fell upon the five women, and left them dead. They returned home after this dreadful deed; and it was very evident that Freydis was well content with her work. She addressed her companions, saying, "If it be ordained for us to come again to Greenland, I shall contrive the death of any man who shall speak of these events. We must give it out that we left them living here when we came away." Early in the spring they equipped the ship which had belonged to the brothers, and freighted it with all of the products of the land which they could obtain, and which the ship would carry. Then they put out to sea, and after a prosperous voyage arrived with their ship in Ericsfirth early in the summer. Karlsefni was there, with his ship all ready to sail, and was awaiting a fair wind; and people say that a ship richer laden than that which he commanded never left Greenland.

Concerning Freydis

FREYDIS now went to her home, since it had remained unharmed during her absence. She bestowed liberal gifts upon all of her companions, for she was anxious to screen her guilt. She now established herself at her home; but her companions were not all so close-mouthed concerning their misdeeds and wickedness that rumors did not get abroad at last. These finally reached her brother, Leif, and he thought it a most shameful story. He thereupon took three of the men, who had been of Freydis' party, and forced them all at the same time to a confession of the affair, and their stories entirely agreed. "I have no heart," says Leif, "to punish my sister, Freydis, as she deserves, but this I predict of them, that there is little prosperity in store for their offspring." Hence it came to pass that no one from that time forward thought them worthy of aught but evil. It now remains to take up the story from the time when Karlsefni made his ship ready, and sailed out to sea. He had a successful voyage, and arrived in Norway safe and sound. He remained there during the winter, and sold his wares; and both he and his wife were received with great favor by the most distinguished men of Norway. The following spring he put his ship in order for the voyage to Iceland; and when all his preparations had been made, and his ship was lying at the wharf, awaiting favorable winds, there came to him a Southerner, a native of Bremen in the Saxonland, who wished to buy his "house-neat." "I do not wish to sell it," says he. "I will give thee half a 'mörk' in gold for it," says the Southerner. This Karlsefni thought a good offer, and accordingly closed the bargain. The Southerner went his way with the "house-neat," and Karlsefni knew not what wood it was, but it was "mösur," come from Wineland.

Karlsefni sailed away, and arrived with his ship in the north of Iceland, in Skagafirth. His vessel was beached there during the winter, and in the spring he bought Glaumbœiar-land, and made his home there, and dwelt there as long as he lived, and was a man of the greatest prominence. From him and his wife, Gudrid, a numerous and goodly lineage is descended. After Karlsefni's death Gudrid, together with her son Snorri, who was born in Wineland, took charge of the farmstead; and, when Snorri was married, Gudrid went abroad, and made a pilgrimage to the South, after which she returned again to the home of her son Snorri, who had caused a church to be built at Glaumbœr. Gudrid then took the veil and became an anchorite, and lived there the rest of her days. Snorri had a son, named Thorgeir, who was the father of Ingveld, the mother of Bishop Brand. Hallfrid was the name of the daughter of Snorri, Karlsefni's son: she was the mother of Runolf, Bishop Thorlak's father. Biorn was the name of [another] son of Karlsefni and Gudrid: he was the father of Thorunn, the mother of Bishop Biorn. Many men are descended from Karlsefni, and he has been blessed with a numerous and famous posterity; and of all men Karlsefni has given the most exact accounts of all these voyages, of which something has now been recounted.

THE LETTER OF COLUMBUS

TO LUIS DE SANT ANGEL
ANNOUNCING HIS DISCOVERY
(1493)

[The following letter was written by Columbus, near the end of his return voyage, to Luis de Sant Angel, Treasurer of Aragon, who had given him substantial help in fitting out his expedition. This announcement of his discovery of the West Indies was evidently intended for the eyes of Ferdinand and Isabella. The text of the present translation is taken from American History Leaflets, edited by Professors Hart and Channing.]

SIR:

AS I know you will be rejoiced at the glorious success that our Lord has given me in my voyage, I write this to tell you how in thirty-three days I sailed to the Indies with the fleet that the illustrious King and Queen, our Sovereigns, gave me, where I discovered a great many islands, inhabited by numberless people; and of all I have taken possession for their Highnesses by proclamation and display of the Royal Standard without opposition. To the first island I discovered I gave the name of San Salvador, in commemoration of His Divine Majesty, who has wonderfully granted all this. The Indians call it Guanaham. The second I named the Island of Santa Maria de Concepcion; the third, Fernandina; the fourth, Isabella; the fifth, Juana; and thus to each one I gave a new name. When I came to Juana, I followed the coast of that isle toward the west, and found it so extensive that I thought it might be the mainland, the province of Cathay; and as I found no towns nor villages on the sea-coast, except a few small settlements, where it was impossible to speak to the people, because they fled at once, I continued the said route, thinking I could not fail to see some great cities or towns; and finding at the end of many leagues that nothing new appeared, and that the coast led northward, contrary to my wish, because the winter had already set in, I decided to make for the south, and as the wind also was against my proceeding, I determined not to wait there longer, and turned back to a certain harbor whence I sent two men to find out whether there was any king or large city. They explored for three days, and found countless small communities and people, without number, but with no kind of government, so they returned.

I heard from other Indians I had already taken that this land was an island, and thus followed the eastern coast for one hundred and seven leagues, until I came to the end of it. From that point I saw another isle to the eastward, at eighteen leagues' distance, to which I gave the name of Hispaniola. I went thither and followed its northern coast to the east, as I had done in Juana, one hundred and seventy-eight leagues eastward, as in Juana. This island, like all the others, is most extensive. It has many ports along the sea-coast excelling any in Christendom—and many fine, large, flowing rivers. The land there is elevated, with many mountains and peaks incomparably higher than in the centre isle. They are most beautiful, of a thousand varied forms, accessible, and full of trees of endless varieties, so high that they seem to touch the sky, and I have been told that they never lose their foliage. I saw them as green and lovely as trees are in Spain in the month of May. Some of them were covered with blossoms, some with fruit, and some in other conditions, according to their kind. The nightingale and other small birds of a thousand kinds were singing in the month of November when I was there. There were palm trees of six or eight varieties, the graceful peculiarities of each one of them being worthy of admiration as are the other trees, fruits and grasses. There are wonderful pine woods, and very extensive ranges of meadow land. There is honey, and there are many kinds of birds, and a great variety of fruits. Inland there are numerous mines of metals and innumerable people. Hispaniola is a marvel. Its hills and mountains, fine plains and open country, are rich and fertile for planting and for pasturage, and for building towns and villages. The seaports there are incredibly fine, as also the magnificent rivers, most of which bear gold. The trees, fruits and grasses differ widely from those in Juana. There are many spices and vast mines of gold and other metals in this island. They have no iron, nor steel, nor weapons, nor are they

fit for them, because although they are well-made men of commanding stature, they appear extraordinarily timid. The only arms they
have are sticks of cane, cut when in seed, with a sharpened stick at
the end, and they are afraid to use these. Often I have sent two or
three men ashore to some town to converse with them, and the
natives came out in great numbers, and as soon as they saw our men
arrive, fled without a moment's delay although I protected them
from all injury.

At every point where I landed, and succeeded in talking to them,
I gave them some of everything I had—cloth and many other things
—without receiving anything in return, but they are a hopelessly
timid people. It is true that since they have gained more confidence
and are losing this fear, they are so unsuspicious and so generous
with what they possess, that no one who had not seen it would believe it. They never refuse anything that is asked for. They even
offer it themselves, and show so much love that they would give
their very hearts. Whether it be anything of great or small value,
with any trifle of whatever kind, they are satisfied. I forbade worthless things being given to them, such as bits of broken bowls, pieces
of glass, and old straps, although they were as much pleased to get
them as if they were the finest jewels in the world. One sailor was
found to have got for a leathern strap, gold of the weight of two and
a half castellanos, and others for even more worthless things much
more; while for a new *blancas* they would give all they had, were
it two or three castellanos of pure gold or an arroba or two of spun
cotton. Even bits of the broken hoops of wine casks they accepted,
and gave in return what they had, like fools, and it seemed wrong
to me. I forbade it, and gave a thousand good and pretty things that
I had to win their love, and to induce them to become Christians,
and to love and serve their Highness and the whole Castilian
nation, and help to get for us things they have in abundance, which
are necessary to us. They have no religion, nor idolatry, except that
they all believe power and goodness to be in heaven. They firmly
believed that I, with my ships and men, came from heaven, and with
this idea I have been received everywhere, since they lost fear of me.
They are, however, far from being ignorant. They are most ingenious men, and navigate these seas in a wonderful way, and

describe everything well, but they never before saw people wearing clothes, nor vessels like ours. Directly I reached the Indies in the first isle I discovered, I took by force some of the natives, that from them we might gain some information of what there was in these parts; and so it was that we immediately understood each other, either by words or signs. They are still with me and still believe that I come from heaven. They were the first to declare this wherever I went, and the others ran from house to house, and to the towns around, crying out, "Come! come! and see the men from heaven!" Then all, both men and women, as soon as they were reassured about us, came, both small and great, all bringing something to eat and to drink, which they presented with marvellous kindness. In these isles there are a great many canoes, something like rowing boats, of all sizes, and most of them are larger than an eighteen-oared galley. They are not so broad, as they are made of a single plank, but a galley could not keep up with them in rowing, because they go with incredible speed, and with these they row about among all these islands, which are innumerable, and carry on their commerce. I have seen some of these canoes with seventy and eighty men in them, and each had an oar. In all the islands I observed little difference in the appearance of the people, or in their habits and language, except that they understand each other, which is remarkable. Therefore I hope that their Highnesses will decide upon the conversion of these people to our holy faith, to which they seem much inclined. I have already stated how I sailed one hundred and seven leagues along the sea-coast of Juana, in a straight line from west to east. I can therefore assert that this island is larger than England and Scotland together, since beyond these one hundred and seven leagues there remained at the west point two provinces where I did not go, one of which they call Avan, the home of men with tails. These provinces are computed to be fifty or sixty leagues in length, as far as can be gathered from the Indians with me, who are acquainted with all these islands. This other, Hispaniola, is larger in circumference than all Spain from Catalonia to Fuentarabia in Biscay, since upon one of its four sides I sailed one hundred and eighty-eight leagues from west to east. This is worth having, and must on no account be given up. I have taken possession of all these islands, for their Highnesses, and all may be more extensive than I know, or can say, and I hold them for their Highnesses, who can command them as absolutely as the kingdoms of Castile. In Hispaniola, in the most convenient place, most accessible for the gold mines and all commerce with the mainland on this side or with that of the great Khan, on the other, with which there would be great trade and profit, I have taken possession of a large town, which I have named the City of Navidad. I began fortifications there which should be completed by this time, and I have left in it men enough to hold it, with arms, artillery, and provisions for more than a year; and a boat with a master seaman skilled in the arts necessary to make others; I am so friendly with the king of that country that he was proud to call me his brother and hold me as such. Even should he change his mind and wish to quarrel with my men, neither he nor his subjects know what arms are, nor wear clothes, as I have said. They are the most timid people in the world, so that only the men remaining there could destroy the whole region, and run no risk if they know how to behave themselves properly. In all these islands the men seem to be satisfied with one wife, except they allow as many as twenty to their chief or king. The women appear to me to work harder than the men, and so far as I can hear they have nothing of their own, for I think I perceived that what one had others shared, especially food. In the islands so far, I have found no monsters, as some expected, but, on the contrary, they are people of very handsome appearance. They are not black as in Guinea, though their hair is straight and coarse, as it does not grow where the sun's rays are too ardent. And in truth the sun has extreme power here, since it is within twenty-six degrees of the equinoctial line. In these islands there are mountains where the cold this winter was very severe, but the people endure it from habit, and with the aid of the meat they eat with very hot spices.

As for monsters, I have found no trace of them except at the point in the second isle as one enters the Indies, which is inhabited by a people considered in all the isles as most ferocious, who eat human flesh. They possess many canoes, with which they overrun all the isles of India, stealing and seizing all they can. They are not worse looking than the others, except that they wear their hair long like

women, and use bows and arrows of the same cane, with a sharp
stick at the end for want of iron, of which they have none. They are
ferocious compared to these other races, who are extremely cowardly;
but I only hear this from the others. They are said to make treaties
of marriage with the women in the first isle to be met with coming
from Spain to the Indies, where there are no men. These women
have no feminine occupation, but use bows and arrows of cane like
those before mentioned, and cover and arm themselves with plates
of copper, of which they have a great quantity. Another island, I am
told, is larger than Hispaniola, where the natives have no hair, and
where there is countless gold; and from them all I bring Indians
to testify to this. To speak, in conclusion, only of what has been
done during this hurried voyage, their Highnesses will see that I
can give them as much gold as they desire, if they will give me a
little assistance, spices, cotton, as much as their Highnesses may command to be shipped, and mastic as much as their Highnesses choose
to send for, which until now has only been found in Greece, in the
isle of Chios, and the Signoria can get its own price for it; as much
lign-aloe as they command to be shipped, and as many slaves as
they choose to send for, all heathens. I think I have found rhubarb
and cinnamon. Many other things of value will be discovered by the
men I left behind me, as I stayed nowhere when the wind allowed
me to pursue my voyage, except in the City of Navidad, which I
left fortified and safe. Indeed, I might have accomplished much
more, had the crews served me as they ought to have done. The
eternal and almighty God, our Lord, it is Who gives to all who
walk in His way, victory over things apparently impossible, and in
this case signally so, because although these lands had been imagined
and talked of before they were seen, most men listened incredulously
to what was thought to be but an idle tale. But our Redeemer has
given victory to our most illustrious King and Queen, and to their
kingdoms rendered famous by this glorious event, at which all
Christendom should rejoice, celebrating it with great festivities and
solemn Thanksgivings to the Holy Trinity, with fervent prayers for
the high distinction that will accrue to them from turning so many
peoples to our holy faith; and also from the temporal benefits that
not only Spain but all Christian nations will obtain. Thus I record

what has happened in a brief note written on board the *Caravel*, off the Canary Isles, on the 15th of February, 1493.

Yours to command,
THE ADMIRAL.

Postscript within the letter

Since writing the above, being in the Sea of Castile, so much wind arose south southeast, that I was forced to lighten the vessels, to run into this port of Lisbon to-day which was the most extraordinary thing in the world, from whence I resolved to write to their Highnesses. In all the Indies I always found the temperature like that of May. Where I went in thirty-three days I returned in twenty-eight, except that these gales have detained me fourteen days, knocking about in this sea. Here all seamen say that there has never been so rough a winter, nor so many vessels lost. Done the 14th day of March.

This letter Columbus sent to the Chancellor of the Exchequer, from the Islands discovered in the Indies, enclosed in another to their Highnesses.

AMERIGO VESPUCCI'S ACCOUNT OF HIS FIRST VOYAGE

(1497)

[Amerigo Vespucci was born in Florence in 1452 and died in Seville in 1512. He was employed in the latter city in the business house which fitted out Columbus's second expedition. The following letter gives his own account of the first of the four voyages which he claimed to have made to the New World. He seems to have touched the mainland a few weeks before Cabot, and some fourteen months before Columbus. The suspicions which long clouded his title to fame have been largely dissipated by modern investigation; and it seems to have been not without reason that Waldseemuller in 1507 proposed to call the new continent by his name.

The present translation is made from Vespucci's Italian (published at Florence in 1505–6) by "M. K.," for Quaritch's edition, London, 1885.]

LETTER OF AMERIGO VESPUCCI TO PIER SODERINI, GONFALONIER
OF THE REPUBLIC OF FLORENCE

MAGNIFICENT Lord. After humble reverence and due commendations, etc. It may be that your Magnificence will be surprised by (*this conjunction of*) my rashness and your customary wisdom, in that I should so absurdly bestir myself to write to your Magnificence the present so-prolix letter: knowing (*as I do*) that your Magnificence is continually employed in high councils and affairs concerning the good government of this sublime Republic. And will hold me not only presumptuous, but also idly-meddlesome in setting myself to write things, neither suitable to your station, nor entertaining, and written in barbarous style, and outside of every canon of polite literature: but my confidence which I have in your virtues and in the truth of my writing, which are things (*that*) are not found written neither by the ancients nor by modern writers, as your Magnificence will in the sequel perceive, makes me bold. The chief cause which moved (*me*) to write to you, was at the request of the present bearer, who is named Benvenuto Benvenuti our Florentine (*fellow-citizen*), very much, as it is proven,

28

your Magnificence's servant, and my very good friend: who happening to be here in this city of Lisbon, begged that I should make communication to your Magnificence of the things seen by me in divers regions of the world, by virtue of four voyages which I have made in discovery of new lands: two by order of the king of Castile, King Don Ferrando VI., across the great gulf of the Ocean-sea, towards the west: and the other two by command of the puissant King Don Manuel King of Portugal, towards the south; telling me that your Magnificence would take pleasure thereof, and that herein he hoped to do you service: wherefore I set me to do it: because I am assured that your Magnificence holds me in the number of your servants, remembering that in the time of our youth I was your friend, and now (*am your*) servant: and (*remembering our*) going to hear the rudiments of grammar under the fair example and instruction of the venerable monk friar of Saint Mark Fra Giorgio Antonio Vespucci: whose counsels and teaching would to God that I had followed: for as saith Petrarch, I should be another man than what I am. Howbeit soever I grieve not: because I have ever taken delight in worthy matters: and although these trifles of mine may not be suitable to your virtues, I will say to you as said Pliny to Mæcenas, you were sometime wont to take pleasure in my prattlings: even though your Magnificence be continuously busied in public affairs, you will take some hour of relaxation to consume a little time in frivolous or amusing things: and as fennel is customarily given atop of delicious viands to fit them for better digestion, so may you, for a relief from your so heavy occupations, order this letter of mine to be read: so that they may withdraw you somewhat from the continual anxiety and assiduous reflection upon public affairs: and if I shall be prolix, I crave pardon, my Magnificent Lord. Your Magnificence shall know that the motive of my coming into this realm of Spain was to traffic in merchandise: and that I pursued this intent about four years: during which I saw and knew the inconstant shiftings of Fortune: and how she kept changing those frail and transitory benefits: and how at one time she holds man on the summit of the wheel, and at another time drives him back from her, and despoils him of what may be called his borrowed riches: so that, knowing the continuous toil which man undergoes to win them, submitting himself to so many anxieties and risks, I resolved to abandon trade, and to fix my aim upon something more praiseworthy and stable: whence it was that I made preparation for going to see part of the world and its wonders: and herefor the time and place presented themselves most opportunely to me: which was that the King Don Ferrando of Castile being about to despatch four ships to discover new lands towards the west, I was chosen by his Highness to go in that fleet to aid in making discovery: and we set out from the port of Cadiz on the 10th day of May 1497, and took our route through the great gulf of the Ocean-sea: in which voyage we were eighteen months (*engaged*): and discovered much continental land and innumerable islands, and great part of them inhabited: whereas there is no mention made by the ancient writers of them: I believe, because they had no knowledge thereof: for, if I remember well, I have read in some one (*of those writers*) that he considered that this Ocean-sea was an unpeopled sea: and of this opinion was Dante our poet in the xxvi. chapter of the Inferno, where he feigns the death of Ulysses, in which voyage I beheld things of great wondrousness, as your Magnificence shall understand. As I said above, we left the port of Cadiz four consort ships: and began our voyage in direct course to the Fortunate Isles which are called to-day *la gran Canaria,* which are situated in the Ocean-sea at the extremity of the inhabited west, (*and*) set in the third climate: over which the North Pole has an elevation of 27 and a half degrees beyond their horizon[1] and they are 280 leagues distant from this city of Lisbon, by the wind between *mezzo di* and *libeccio:*[2] where we remained eight days, taking in provision of water, and wood and other necessary things: and from here, having said our prayers, we weighed anchor, and gave the sails to the wind, beginning our course to westward, taking one quarter by south-west:[3] and so we sailed on till at the end of 37 days we reached a land which we deemed to be a continent: which is distant westwardly from the isles of Canary about a thousand leagues beyond the inhabited region[4] within the

[1] That is, *which are situate at 27½ degrees north latitude.*

[2] South-south-west. It is to be remarked that Vespucci always uses the word *wind* to signify the course in which it blows, not the quarter from which it rises.

[3] West and a quarter by south-west.

[4] This phrase is merely equivalent to a repetition of *from the Canaries,* these islands having been already designated *the extreme western limit of inhabited land.*

torrid zone: for we found the North Pole at an elevation of 16 degrees above its horizon,[5] and (*it was*) westward, according to the shewing of our instruments, 75 degrees from the isles of Canary: whereat we anchored with our ships a league and a half from land; and we put out our boats freighted with men and arms: we made towards the land, and before we reached it, had sight of a great number of people who were going along the shore: by which we were much rejoiced: and we observed that they were a naked race: they shewed themselves to stand in fear of us: I believe (*it was*) because they saw us clothed and of other appearance (*than their own*): they all withdrew to a hill, and for whatsoever signals we made to them of peace and of friendliness, they would not come to parley with us: so that, as the night was now coming on, and as the ships were anchored in a dangerous place, being on a rough and shelterless coast, we decided to remove from there the next day, and to go in search of some harbour or bay, where we might place our ships in safety: and we sailed with the maestrale wind,[6] thus running along the coast with the land ever in sight, continually in our course observing people along the shore: till after having navigated for two days, we found a place sufficiently secure for the ships, and anchored half a league from land, on which we saw a very great number of people: and this same day we put to land with the boats, and sprang on shore full 40 men in good trim: and still the land's people appeared shy of converse with us, and we were unable to encourage them so much as to make them come to speak with us: and this day we laboured so greatly in giving them of our wares, such as rattles and mirrors, beads, *spalline,* and other trifles, that some of them took confidence and came to discourse with us: and after having made good friends with them, the night coming on, we took our leave of them and returned to the ships: and the next day when the dawn appeared we saw that there were infinite numbers of people upon the beach, and they had their women and children with them: we went ashore, and found that they were all laden with their worldly goods[7] which are suchlike as, in its (*proper*) place, shall be related: and before we reached the land, many of them jumped into the sea and came swim-

[5] That is, 16 degrees north latitude.   [6] North-west.

[7] *Mantenimenti*. The word "all" (*tucte*) is feminine, and probably refers only to the women.

ming to receive us at a bowshot's length (*from the shore*), for they
are very great swimmers, with as much confidence as if they had for
a long time been acquainted with us: and we were pleased with this
their confidence. For so much as we learned of their manner of
life and customs, it was that they go entirely naked, as well the
men as the women. . . . They are of medium stature, very well proportioned: their flesh is of a colour that verges into red like a lion's
mane: and I believe that if they went clothed, they would be as
white as we: they have not any hair upon the body, except the hair
of the head which is long and black, and especially in the women,
whom it renders handsome: in aspect they are not very good-looking,
because they have broad faces, so that they would seem Tartar-like:
they let no hair grow on their eyebrows, nor on their eyelids, nor
elsewhere, except the hair of the head: for they hold hairiness to be a
filthy thing: they are very light footed in walking and in running,
as well the men as the women: so that a woman recks nothing of
running a league or two, as many times we saw them do: and herein
they have a very great advantage over us Christians: they swim
(*with an expertness*) beyond all belief, and the women better than
the men: for we have many times found and seen them swimming
two leagues out at sea without anything to rest upon. Their arms are
bows and arrows very well made, save that (*the arrows*) are not
(*tipped*) with iron nor any other kind of hard metal: and instead
of iron they put animals' or fishes' teeth, or a spike of tough wood,
with the point hardened by fire: they are sure marksmen, for they
hit whatever they aim at: and in some places the women use these
bows: they have other weapons, such as fire-hardened spears, and
also clubs with knobs, beautifully carved. Warfare is used amongst
them, which they carry on against people not of their own language, very cruelly, without granting life to any one, except (*to
reserve him*) for greater suffering. When they go to war, they take
their women with them, not that these may fight, but because they
carry behind them their worldly goods, for a woman carries on her
back for thirty or forty leagues a load which no man could bear:
as we have many times seen them do. They are not accustomed to
have any Captain, nor do they go in any ordered array, for every
one is lord of himself: and the cause of their wars is not for lust of

dominion, nor of extending their frontiers, nor for inordinate covet-
ousness, but for some ancient enmity which in by-gone times arose
amongst them: and when asked why they made war, they knew
not any other reason to give than that they did so to avenge the
death of their ancestors, or of their parents: these people have neither
King, nor Lord, nor do they yield obedience to any one, for they live
in their own liberty: and how they be stirred up to go to war is (*this*)
that when the enemies have slain or captured any of them, his oldest
kinsman rises up and goes about the highways haranguing them
to go with him and avenge the death of such his kinsman: and so
are they stirred up by fellow-feeling: they have no judicial system,
nor do they punish the ill-doer: nor does the father, nor the mother
chastise the children: and marvellously (*seldom*) or never did we
see any dispute among them: in their conversation they appear
simple, and they are very cunning and acute in that which concerns them: they speak little and in a low tone: they use the same
articulations as we, since they form their utterances either with the
palate, or with the teeth, or on the lips:[8] except that they give different names to things. Many are the varieties of tongues: for in
every 100 leagues we found a change of language, so that they are
not understandable each to the other. The manner of their living
is very barbarous, for they do not eat at certain hours, and as often-
times as they will: and it is not much of a boon to them[9] that the
will may come more at midnight than by day, for they eat at all
hours: and they eat upon the ground without a table-cloth or any
other cover, for they have their meats either in earthen basins which
they make themselves, or in the halves of pumpkins: they sleep in
certain very large nettings made of cotton, suspended in the air:
and although this their (*fashion of*) sleeping may seem uncomfortable, I say that it is sweet to sleep in those (*nettings*) : and we slept
better in them than in the counterpanes. They are a people smooth
and clean of body, because of so continually washing themselves as
they do. . . . Amongst those people we did not learn that they had
any law, nor can they be called Moors nor Jews, and (*they are*)

[8] He means that they have no sounds in their language unknown to European
organs of speech, all being either palatals or dentals or labials.

[9] I have translated *"et non si da loro molto"* as "it is not much of a boon to
them," but may be "it matters not much to them."

worse than pagans: because we did not observe that they offered any sacrifice: nor even had they a house of prayer: their manner of living I judge to be Epicurean: their dwellings are in common: and their houses (*are*) made in the style of huts, but strongly made, and constructed with very large trees, and covered over with palm-leaves, secure against storms and winds: and in some places (*they are*) of so great breadth and length, that in one single house we found there were 600 souls: and we saw a village of only thirteen houses where there were four thousand souls: every eight or ten years they change their habitations: and when asked why they did so: (*they said it was*) because of the soil which, from its filthiness, was already unhealthy and corrupted, and that it bred aches in their bodies, which seemed to us a good reason: their riches consist of birds' plumes of many colours, or of rosaries which they make from fishbones, or of white or green stones which they put in their cheeks and in their lips and ears, and of many other things which we in no wise value: they use no trade, they neither buy nor sell. In fine, they live and are contented with that which nature gives them. The wealth that we enjoy in this our Europe and elsewhere, such as gold, jewels, pearls, and other riches, they hold as nothing; and although they have them in their own lands, they do not labour to obtain them, nor do they value them. They are liberal in giving, for it is rarely they deny you anything: and on the other hand, liberal in asking, when they shew themselves your friends. . . . When they die, they use divers manners of obsequies, and some they bury with water and victuals at their heads: thinking that they shall have (*whereof*) to eat: they have not nor do they use ceremonies of torches nor of lamentation. In some other places, they use the most barbarous and inhuman burial, which is that when a suffering or infirm (*person*) is as it were at the last pass of death, his kinsmen carry him into a large forest, and attach one of those nets, of theirs, in which they sleep, to two trees, and then put him in it, and dance around him for a whole day: and when the night comes on they place at his bolster, water with other victuals, so that he may be able to subsist for four or six days: and then they leave him alone and return to the village: and if the sick man helps himself, and eats, and drinks, and survives, he returns to the village, and his (*friends*) receive him with ceremony: but few are they who escape: without receiving any further visit they die, and that is their sepulture: and they have many other customs which for prolixity are not related. They use in their sicknesses various forms of medicines,[10] so different from ours that we marvelled how any one escaped: for many times I saw that with a man sick of fever, when it heightened upon him, they bathed him from head to foot with a large quantity of cold water: then they lit a great fire around him, making him turn and turn again every two hours, until they tired him and left him to sleep, and many were (*thus*) cured: with this they make use of dieting, for they remain three days without eating, and also of blood-letting, but not from the arm, only from the thighs and the loins and the calf of the leg: also they provoke vomiting with their herbs which are put into the mouth: and they use many other remedies which it would be long to relate: they are much vitiated in the phlegm and in the blood because of their food which consists chiefly of roots of herbs, and fruits and fish: they have no seed of wheat nor other grain: and for their ordinary use and feeding, they have a root of a tree, from which they make flour, tolerably good, and they call it Iuca, and another which they call Cazabi, and another Ignami: they eat little flesh except human flesh: for your Magnificence must know that herein they are so inhuman that they outdo every custom (*even*) of beasts; for they eat all their enemies whom they kill or capture, as well females as males with so much savagery, that (*merely*) to relate it appears a horrible thing: how much more so to see it, as, infinite times and in many places, it was my hap to see it: and they wondered to hear us say that we did not eat our enemies: and this your Magnificence may take for certain, that their other barbarous customs are such that expression is too weak for the reality: and as in these four voyages I have seen so many things diverse from our customs, I prepared to write a common-place-book which I name LE QUATTRO GIORNATE: in which I have set down the greater part of the things which I saw, sufficiently in detail, so far as my feeble wit has allowed me: which I have not yet published, because I have so ill a taste for my own things that I do not relish those which I have

[10] That is, "medical treatment."

written, notwithstanding that many encourage me to publish it: therein everything will be seen in detail: so that I shall not enlarge further in this chapter: as in the course of the letter we shall come to many other things which are particular: let this suffice for the general. At this beginning, we saw nothing in the land of much profit, except some show of gold: I believe the cause of it was that we did not know the language: but in so far as concerns the situation and condition of the land, it could not be better: we decided to leave that place, and to go further on, continuously coasting the shore: upon which we made frequent descents, and held converse with a great number of people: and at the end of some days we went into a harbour where we underwent very great danger: and it pleased the Holy Ghost to save us: and it was in this wise. We landed in a harbour, where we found a village built like Venice upon the water: there were about 44 large dwellings in the form of huts erected upon very thick piles, and they had their doors or entrances in the style of drawbridges: and from each house one could pass through all, by means of the drawbridges which stretched from house to house: and when the people thereof had seen us, they appeared to be afraid of us, and immediately drew up all the bridges: and while we were looking at this strange action, we saw coming across the sea about 22 canoes, which are a kind of boats of theirs, constructed from a single tree: which came towards our boats, as they had been surprised by our appearance and clothes, and kept wide of us: and thus remaining, we made signals to them that they should approach us, encouraging them with every token of friendliness: and seeing that they did not come, we went to them, and they did not stay for us, but made to the land, and, by signs, told us to wait, and that they should soon return: and they went to a hill in the background, and did not delay long: when they returned, they led with them 16 of their girls, and entered with these into their canoes, and came to the boats: and in each boat they put 4 of the girls. That we marvelled at this behavior your Magnificence can imagine how much, and they placed themselves with their canoes among our boats, coming to speak with us: insomuch that we deemed it a mark of friendliness: and while thus engaged, we beheld a great number of people advance swimming towards us across the sea, who came from the houses: and as they were drawing near to us without any apprehension: just then there appeared at the doors of the houses certain old women, uttering very loud cries and tearing their hair to exhibit grief: whereby they made us suspicious, and we each betook ourselves to arms: and instantly the girls whom we had in the boats, threw themselves into the sea, and the men of the canoes drew away from us, and began with their bows to shoot arrows at us: and those who were swimming each carried a lance held, as covertly as they could, beneath the water: so that, recognizing the treachery, we engaged with them, not merely to defend ourselves, but to attack them vigorously, and we overturned with our boats many of their almadie or canoes, for so they call them, we made a slaughter (*of them*), and they all flung themselves into the water to swim, leaving their canoes abandoned, with considerable loss on their side, they went swimming away to the shore: there died of them about 15 or 20, and many were left wounded: and of ours 5 were wounded, and all, by the grace of God, escaped (*death*): we captured two of the girls and two men: and we proceeded to their houses, and entered therein, and in them all we found nothing else than two old women and a sick man: we took away from them many things, but of small value: and we would not burn their houses, because it seemed to us (*as though that would be*) a burden upon our conscience: and we returned to our boats with five prisoners: and betook ourselves to the ships, and put a pair of irons on the feet of each of the captives, except the little girls: and when the night came on, the two girls and one of the men fled away in the most subtle manner possible: and next day we decided to quit that harbour and go further onwards: we proceeded continuously skirting the coast, (*until*) we had sight of another tribe distant perhaps some 80 leagues from the former tribe: and we found them very different in speech and customs: we resolved to cast anchor, and went ashore with the boats, and we saw on the beach a great number of people amounting probably to 4000 souls: and when we had reached the shore, they did not stay for us, but betook themselves to flight through the forests, abandoning their things: we jumped on land, and took a pathway that led to the forest: and at the distance of a bow-shot we found their tents, where they had made very large fires, and two (*of them*) were cooking their victuals, and roasting several animals, and fish of many kinds: where we saw that they were roasting a certain animal which seemed to be a serpent, save that it had no wings, and was in its appearance so loathsome that we marvelled much at its savageness: Thus went we on through their houses, or rather tents, and found many of those serpents alive, and they were tied by the feet and had a cord around their snouts, so that they could not open their mouths, as is done (*in Europe*) with mastiff-dogs so that they may not bite: they were of such savage aspect that none of us dared to take one away, thinking that they were poisonous: they are of the bigness of a kid, and in length an ell and a half:[11] their feet are long and thick, and armed with big claws: they have a hard skin, and are of various colours: they have the muzzle and face of a serpent: and from their snouts there rises a crest like a saw which extends along the middle of the back as far as the tip of the tail: in fine we deemed them to be serpents and venomous, and (*nevertheless, those people*) ate them: we found that they made bread out of little fishes which they took from the sea, first boiling them, (*then*) pounding them, and making thereof a paste, or bread, and they baked them on the embers: thus did they eat them: we tried it, and found that it was good: they had so many other kinds of eatables, and especially of fruits and roots, that it would be a large matter to describe them in detail: and seeing that the people did not return, we decided not to touch nor take away anything of theirs, so as better to reassure them: and we left in the tents for them many of our things, placed where they should see them, and returned by night to our ships: and the next day, when it was light, we saw on the beach an infinite number of people: and we landed: and although they appeared timorous towards us, they took courage nevertheless to hold converse with us, giving us whatever we asked of them: and shewing themselves very friendly towards us, they told us that those were their dwellings, and that they had come hither for the purpose of fishing: and they begged that we would visit their dwellings and villages, because they desired to receive us as friends: and they engaged in such

---

[11] This animal was the iguana.

friendship because of the two captured men whom we had with us, as these were their enemies: insomuch that, in view of such importunity on their part, holding a council, we determined that 28 of us Christians in good array should go with them, and in the firm resolve to die if it should be necessary: and after we had been here some three days, we went with them inland: and at three leagues from the coast we came to a village of many people and few houses, for there were no more than nine (*of these*): where we were received with such and so many barbarous ceremonies that the pen suffices not to write them down: for there were dances, and songs, and lamentations mingled with rejoicing, and great quantities of food: and here we remained the night: . . . and after having been here that night and half the next day, so great was the number of people who came wondering to behold us that they were beyond counting: and the most aged begged us to go with them to other villages which were further inland, making display of doing us the greatest honour: wherefore we decided to go: and it would be impossible to tell you how much honour they did us: and we went to several villages, so that we were nine days journeying, so that our Christians who had remained with the ships were already apprehensive concerning us: and when we were about 18 leagues in the interior of the land, we resolved to return to the ships: and on our way back, such was the number of people, as well men as women, that came with us as far as the sea, that it was a wondrous thing: and if any of us became weary of the march, they carried us in their nets very refreshingly: and in crossing the rivers, which are many and very large, they passed us over by skilful means so securely that we ran no danger whatever, and many of them came laden with the things which they had given us, which consisted in their sleeping-nets, and very rich feathers, many bows and arrows, innumerable popinjays of divers colours: and others brought with them loads of their household goods, and of animals: but a greater marvel will I tell you, that, when we had to cross a river, he deemed himself lucky who was able to carry us on his back: and when we reached the sea, our boats having arrived, we entered into them: and so great was the struggle which they made to get into our boats, and to come to see our ships, that we marvelled (*thereat*):

and in our boats we took as many of them as we could, and made our way to the ships, and so many (*others*) came swimming that we found ourselves embarrassed in seeing so many people in the ships, for there were over a thousand persons all naked and unarmed: they were amazed by our (*nautical*) gear and contrivances, and the size of the ships: and with them there occurred to us a very laughable affair, which was that we decided to fire off some of our great guns, and when the explosion took place, most of them through fear cast themselves (*into the sea*) to swim, not otherwise than frogs on the margins of a pond, when they see something that frightens them, will jump into the water, just so did those people: and those who remained in the ships were so terrified that we regretted our action: however we reassured them by telling them that with those arms we slew our enemies: and when they had amused themselves in the ships the whole day, we told them to go away because we desired to depart that night, and so separating from us with much friendship and love, they went away to land. Amongst that people and in their land, I knew and beheld so many of their customs and ways of living, that I do not care to enlarge upon them: for Your Magnificence must know that in each of my voyages I have noted the most wonderful things, and I have indited it all in a volume after the manner of a geography: and I entitle it LE QUATTRO GIORNATE: in which work the things are comprised in detail, and as yet there is no copy of it given out, as it is necessary for me to revise it. This land is very populous, and full of inhabitants, and of numberless rivers, (*and*) animals: few (*of which*) resemble ours, excepting lions, panthers, stags, pigs, goats, and deer: and even these have some dissimilarities of form: they have no horses nor mules, nor, saving your reverence, asses nor dogs, nor any kind of sheep or oxen: but so numerous are the other animals which they have, and all are savage, and of none do they make use for their service, that they could not be counted. What shall we say of others (*such as*) birds? which are so numerous, and of so many kinds, and of such various-coloured plumages, that it is a marvel to behold them. The soil is very pleasant and fruitful, full of immense woods and forests: and it is always green, for the foliage never drops off. The fruits are so many that they are numberless and entirely different from ours. This land is within the torrid zone, close to or just under the parallel described by the Tropic of Cancer: where the pole of the horizon has an elevation of 23 degrees, at the extremity of the second climate.[12] Many tribes came to see us, and wondered at our faces and our whiteness: and they asked us whence we came: and we gave them to understand that we had come from heaven, and that we were going to see the world, and they believed it. In this land we placed baptismal fonts, and an infinite (number of) people were baptised, and they called us in their language Carabi, which means men of great wisdom. We took our departure from that port: and the province is called Lariab: and we navigated along the coast, always in sight of land, until we had run 870 leagues of it, still going in the direction of the maestrale (north-west) making in our course many halts, and holding intercourse with many peoples: and in several places we obtained gold by barter but not much in quantity, for we had done enough in discovering the land and learning that they had gold. We had now been thirteen months on the voyage: and the vessels and the tackling were already much damaged, and the men worn out by fatigue: we decided by general council to haul our ships on land and examine them for the purpose of stanching leaks, as they made much water, and of caulking and tarring them afresh, and (then) returning towards Spain: and when we came to this determination, we were close to a harbour the best in the world: into which we entered with our vessels: where we found an immense number of people: who received us with much friendliness: and on the shore we made a bastion[13] with our boats and with barrels and casks, and our artillery, which commanded every point: and our ships having been unloaded and lightened, we drew them upon land, and repaired them in everything that was needful: and the land's people gave us very great assistance: and continually furnished us with their victuals: so that in this port we tasted little of our own, which suited our game well: for the stock of provisions which we had for our return-passage was little and of sorry kind: where (i.e., there) we remained 37 days: and went many times to their villages: where they paid us the greatest honour: and (now) desiring to

[12] That is, 23 degrees north latitude.   [13] Fort or barricade.

depart upon our voyage, they made complaint to us how at certain times of the year there came from over the sea to this their land, a race of people very cruel, and enemies of theirs: and (*who*) by means of treachery or of violence slew many of them, and ate them: and some they made captives, and carried them away to their houses, or country: and how they could scarcely contrive to defend themselves from them, making signs to us that (*those*) were an island-people and lived out in the sea about a hundred leagues away: and so piteously did they tell us this that we believed them: and we promised to avenge them of so much wrong: and they remained overjoyed herewith: and many of them offered to come along with us, but we did not wish to take them for many reasons, save that we took seven of them, on condition that they should come (*i.e., return home*) afterwards in (*their own*) canoes because we did not desire to be obliged to take them back to their country: and they were contented: and so we departed from those people, leaving them very friendly towards us: and having repaired our ships, and sailing for seven days out to sea between northeast and east: and at the end of the seven days we came upon the islands, which were many, some (*of them*) inhabited, and others deserted: and we anchored at one of them: where we saw a numerous people who called it Iti: and having manned our boats with strong crews, and (*taken ammunition for*) three cannon-shots in each, we made for land: where we found (*assembled*) about 400 men, and many women, and all naked like the former (*peoples*). They were of good bodily presence, and seemed right warlike men: for they were armed with their weapons, which are bows, arrows, and lances: and most of them had square wooden targets: and bore them in such wise that they did not impede the drawing of the bow: and when we had come with our boats to about a bowshot of the land, they all sprang into the water to shoot their arrows at us and to prevent us from leaping upon shore: and they all had their bodies painted of various colours, and (*were*) plumed with feathers: and the interpreters who were with us told us that when (*those*) displayed themselves so painted and plumed, it was to betoken that they wanted to fight: and so much did they persist in preventing us from landing, that we were compelled to play with our artillery: and when they heard the explosion, and saw one of them fall dead, they all drew back to the land: wherefore, forming our council, we resolved that 42 of our men should spring on shore, and, if they waited for us, fight them: thus having leaped to land with our weapons, they advanced towards us, and we fought for about an hour, for we had but little advantage of them, except that our arbalasters and gunners killed some of them, and they wounded certain of our men: and this was because they did not stand to receive us within reach of lance-thrust or sword-blow: and so much vigour did we put forth at last, that we came to sword-play, and when they tasted our weapons, they betook themselves to flight through the mountains and the forests, and left us conquerors of the field with many of them dead and a good number wounded: and for that day we took no other pains to pursue them, because we were very weary, and we returned to our ships, with so much gladness on the part of the seven men who had come with us that they could not contain themselves (*for joy*): and when the next day arrived, we beheld coming across the land a great number of people, with signals of battle, continually sounding horns, and various other instruments which they use in their wars: and all (*of them*) painted and feathered, so that it was a very strange sight to behold them: wherefore all the ships held council, and it was resolved that since this people desired hostility with us, we should proceed to encounter them and try by every means to make them friends: in case they would not have our friendship, that we should treat them as foes, and so many of them as we might be able to capture should all be our slaves: and having armed ourselves as best we could, we advanced towards the shore, and they sought not to hinder us from landing, I believe from fear of the cannons: and we jumped on land, 57 men in four squadrons, each one (*consisting of*) a captain and his company: and we came to blows with them: and after a long battle (*in which*) many of them (*were*) slain, we put them to flight, and pursued them to a village, having made about 250 of them captives, and we burnt the village, and returned to our ships with victory and 250 prisoners, leaving many of them dead and wounded, and of ours there were no more than one killed, and 22 wounded, who all escaped (*i.e., recovered*), God be thanked. We arranged our departure, and seven men, of whom five were wounded, took an island-canoe, and with seven prisoners that we gave them, four women and three men, returned to their (*own*) country full of gladness, wondering at our strength: and we thereon made sail for Spain with 222 captive slaves: and reached the port of Calis (*Cadiz*) on the 15th day of October, 1498, where we were well received and sold our slaves. Such is what befell me, most noteworthy, in this my first voyage.

JOHN CABOT'S DISCOVERY OF NORTH AMERICA

(1497)

[Giovanni Caboto (John Cabot) was a native of Genoa and a citizen of Venice, who obtained letters-patent from Henry VII. of England in 1496, for a voyage of discovery. In the summer of 1497, he crossed the Atlantic and discovered the mainland of North America—probably the Labrador coast. On this achievement was based the claim of England to North America. The following three documents contain all the evidence from contemporary witnesses whose information may have come from John Cabot himself. The text followed is from the Hakluyt Society's edition of Columbus's Journal.]

LETTER FROM LORENZO PASQUALIGO TO HIS BROTHERS ALVISE AND FRANCESCO.[1]

LONDON, 23rd August, 1497.

OUR Venetian, who went with a small ship from Bristol to find new islands, has come back, and says he has discovered, 700 leagues off, the mainland of the country of the Gran Cam, and that he coasted along it for 300 leagues, and landed, but did not see any person. But he has brought here to the king certain snares spread to take game, and a needle for making nets, and he found some notched trees, from which he judged that there were inhabitants. Being in doubt, he came back to the ship. He has been away three months on the voyage, which is certain, and, in returning, he saw two islands to the right, but he did not wish to land, lest he should lose time for he was in want of provisions. This king has been much pleased. He says that the tides are slack, and do not make currents as they do here. The king has promised for another time, ten armed ships as he desires, and has given him all the prisoners, except such as are confined for high treason, to go with him, as he has requested; and has granted him money to amuse himself till then. Meanwhile, he is with his Venetian wife and his

---

[1] *Calendar of State Papers* (Venice), i. p. 262, No. 752.

sons at Bristol. His name is Zuam Talbot,[2] and he is called the Great Admiral, great honour being paid to him, and he goes dressed in silk. The English are ready to go with him, and so are many of our rascals. The discoverer of these things has planted a large cross in the ground with a banner of England, and one of St. Mark, as he is a Venetian; so that our flag has been hoisted very far away.

First Despatch of Raimondo di Soncino to the Duke of Milan.[3] (Extract.)

24th AUGUST, 1497.

Some month afterwards His Majesty sent a Venetian, who is a distinguished sailor, and who was much skilled in the discovery of new islands, and he has returned safe, and has discovered two very large and fertile islands, having, it would seem, discovered the seven cities 400 leagues from England to the westward. These successes led His Majesty at once to entertain the intention of sending him with fifteen or twenty vessels.

Second Despatch of Raimondo di Soncino to the Duke of Milan.[4]

18th DECEMBER, 1497.

My most illustrious and most excellent Lord,

Perhaps amidst so many occupations of your Excellency it will not be unwelcome to learn how this Majesty has acquired a part of Asia without drawing his sword. In this kingdom there is a certain Venetian named Zoanne Caboto, of gentle disposition, very expert in navigation, who, seeing that the most serene Kings of Portugal and Spain had occupied unknown islands, meditated the achievement of a similar acquisition for the said Majesty. Having obtained royal privileges securing to himself the use of the dominions he might discover, the sovereignty being reserved to the Crown, he entrusted his fortune to a small vessel with a crew of 18 persons, and set out from Bristo, a port in the western part of this kingdom. Having passed Ibernia, which is still further to the west, and then

[2] A misprint: "T" for "C."

[3] *Calendar of State Papers* (Venice), iii. p. 260, No. 750.

[4] *Annuario Scientifico*, Milan, 1866, p. 700; *Archiv d'Etat Milan*, reprinted by Harrisse in his *John Cabot*, p. 324, from the *Intorno* of Desimoni, and translated from his text for the Hakluyt Society, with his permission

shaped a northerly course, he began to navigate to the eastern part, leaving (during several days) the North Star on the right hand; and having wandered thus for a long time, at length he hit upon land, where he hoisted the royal standard, and took possession for his Highness, and, having obtained various proofs of his discovery, he returned. The said Messer Zoanne, being a foreigner and poor, would not have been believed if the crew, who are nearly all English, and belonging to Bristo, had not testified that what he said was the truth. This Messer Zoanne has the description of the world on a chart, and also on a solid sphere which he has constructed, and on which he shows where he has been; and, proceeding towards the east, he has passed as far as the country of the Tanais. And they say that there the land is excellent and (the climate?) temperate, suggesting that brasil and silk grow there. They affirm that the sea is full of fish, which are not only taken with a net, but also with a basket, a stone being fastened to it in order to keep it in the water; and this I have heard stated by the said Messer Zoanne.

The said Englishmen, his companions, say that they took so many fish that this kingdom will no longer have need of Iceland, from which country there is an immense trade in the fish they call stock-fish. But Messer Zoanne has set his mind on higher things, for he thinks that, when that place has been occupied, he will keep on still further towards the east, where he will be opposite to an island called Cipango, situated in the equinoctial region, where he believes that all the spices of the world, as well as the jewels, are found. He further says that he was once at Mecca, whither the spices are brought by caravans from distant countries; and having inquired from whence they were brought and where they grow, they answered that they did not know, but that such merchandize was brought from distant countries by other caravans to their home; and they further say that they are also conveyed from other remote regions. And he adduced this argument, that if the eastern people tell those in the south that these things come from a far distance from them, presupposing the rotundity of the earth, it must be that the last turn would be by the north towards the west; and it is said that in this way the route would not cost more than it costs now, and I also believe it. And what is more, this Majesty, who is wise and not prodigal, reposes such trust in him because of what he has already achieved, that he gives him a good maintenance, as Messer Zoanne has himself told me. And it is said that before long his Majesty will arm some ships for him, and will give him all the malefactors to go to that country and form a colony, so that they hope to establish a greater depot of spices in London than there is in Alexandria. The principal people in the enterprise belong to Bristo. They are great seamen, and, now that they know where to go, they say that the voyage thither will not occupy more than 15 days after leaving Ibernia. I have also spoken with a Burgundian, who was a companion of Messer Zoanne, who affirms all this, and who wishes to return because the Admiral (for so Messer Zoanne is entitled) has given him an island, and has given another to his barber of Castione,[5] who is a Genoese, and both look upon themselves as Counts; nor do they look upon my Lord the Admiral as less than a Prince. I also believe that some poor Italian friars are going on this voyage, who have all had bishopricks promised to them. And if I had made friends with the Admiral when he was about to sail, I should have got an archbishoprick at least; but I have thought that the benefits reserved for me by your Excellency will be more secure. I would venture to pray that, in the event of a vacancy taking place in my absence, I may be put in possession, and that I may not be superseded by those who, being present, can be more diligent than I, who am reduced in this country to eating at each meal ten or twelve kinds of victuals, and to being three hours at table every day, two for love of your Excellency, to whom I humbly recommend myself. London, 18 Dec. 1497, your Excellency's most humble servant,   RAIMUNDUS.

5 Perhaps Castiglione, near Chiavari.

FIRST CHARTER OF VIRGINIA

(1606)

[This charter, granted by King James I. on April 10, 1606, to the oldest of the English colonies in America, is a typical example of the documents issued by the British government, authorizing "Adventurers" to establish plantations in the New World. The name "Virginia" was at that time applied to all that part of North America claimed by Great Britain.]

*I*JAMES, by the Grace of God, King of *England, Scotland, France* and *Ireland,* Defender of the Faith, &c. WHEREAS our loving and well-disposed Subjects, Sir *Thomas Gates,* and Sir *George Somers,* Knights, *Richard Hackluit,* Prebendary of *Westminster,* and *Edward-Maria Wingfield, Thomas Hanham,* and *Ralegh Gilbert,* Esqrs. *William Parker,* and *George Popham,* Gentlemen, and divers others of our loving Subjects, have been humble Suitors unto us, that We would vouchsafe unto them our Licence, to make Habitation, Plantation, and to deduce a Colony of sundry of our People into that Part of *America,* commonly called VIRGINIA, and other Parts and Territories in *America,* either appertaining unto us, or which are not now actually possessed by any *Christian* Prince or People, situate, lying, and being all along the Sea Coasts, between four and thirty Degrees of *Northerly* Latitude from the Equinoctial Line, and five and forty Degrees of the same Latitude, and in the main Land between the same four and thirty and five and forty Degrees, and the Islands thereunto adjacent, or within one hundred Miles of the Coasts thereof;

II. And to that End, and for the more speedy Accomplishment of their said intended Plantation and Habitation there, are desirous to divide themselves into two several Colonies and Companies; The one consisting of certain Knights, Gentlemen, Merchants, and other Adventurers, of our City of *London* and elsewhere, which are, and from time to time shall be, joined unto them, which do desire to begin their Plantation and Habitation in some fit and convenient Place, between four and thirty and one and forty Degrees of the

49

said Latitude, along the Coasts of *Virginia* and Coasts of *America* aforesaid; And the other consisting of sundry Knights, Gentlemen, Merchants, and other Adventurers, of our Cities of *Bristol* and *Exeter,* and of our Town of *Plimouth,* and of other Places, which do join themselves unto that Colony, which do desire to begin their Plantation and Habitation in some fit and convenient Place, between eight and thirty Degrees and five and forty Degrees of the said Latitude, all alongst the said Coast of *Virginia* and *America,* as that Coast lyeth:

III. We, greatly commending, and graciously accepting of, their Desires for the Furtherance of so noble a Work, which may, by the Providence of Almighty God, hereafter tend to the Glory of his Divine Majesty, in propagating of *Christian* Religion to such People, as yet live in Darkness and miserable Ignorance of the true Knowledge and Worship of God, and may in time bring the Infidels and Savages, living in those Parts, to human Civility, and to a settled and quiet Government; DO, by these our Letters Patents, graciously accept of, and agree to, their humble and well-intended Desires;

IV. And do therefore, for Us, our Heirs, and Successors, GRANT and agree, that the said Sir *Thomas Gates,* Sir *George Somers, Richard Hackluit,* and *Edward-Maria Wingfield,* Adventurers of and for our City of *London,* and all such others, as are, or shall be, joined unto them of that Colony, shall be called the *first Colony;* And they shall and may begin their said first Plantation and Habitation, at any Place upon the said Coast of *Virginia* or *America,* where they shall think fit and convenient, between the said four and thirty and one and forty Degrees of the said Latitude; And that they shall have all the Lands, Woods, Soil, Grounds, Havens, Ports, Rivers, Mines, Minerals, Marshes, Waters, Fishings, Commodities, and Hereditaments, whatsoever, from the said first Seat of their Plantation and Habitation by the Space of fifty Miles of *English* Statute Measure, all along the said Coast of *Virginia* and *America,* towards the *West* and *Southwest,* as the Coast lyeth, with all the Islands within one hundred Miles directly over against the same Sea Coast; And also all the Lands, Soil, Grounds, Havens, Ports, Rivers, Mines, Minerals, Woods, Waters, Marshes, Fishings, Commodities, and

Hereditaments, whatsoever, from the said Place of their first Plantation and Habitation for the space of fifty like *English* Miles all
alongst the said Coast of *Virginia* and *America*, towards the *East
and Northeast*, or towards the *North*, as the Coast lyeth, together
with all the Islands within one hundred Miles, directly over against
the said Sea Coast; And also all the Lands, Woods, Soil, Grounds,
Havens, Ports, Rivers, Mines, Minerals, Marshes, Waters, Fishings,
Commodities, and Hereditaments, whatsoever, from the same fifty
Miles every way on the Sea Coast, directly into the main Land by the
Space of one hundred like *English* Miles; And shall and may inhabit
and remain there; and shall and may also build and fortify within
any the same, for their better Safeguard and Defence, according to
their best Discretion, and the Discretion of the Council of that
Colony; And that no other of our Subjects shall be permitted, or
suffered, to plant or inhabit behind, or on the Backside of them,
towards the main Land, without the Express License or Consent of
the Council of that Colony, thereunto in Writing first had and
obtained.

V. And we do likewise, for Us, our Heirs, and Successors, by these
Presents, GRANT and agree, that the said *Thomas Hanham,* and
Ralegh Gilbert, William Parker, and *George Popham,* and all
others of the Town of *Plimouth* in the County of *Devon,* or elsewhere, which are, or shall be, joined unto them of that Colony, shall
be called the *second Colony;* And that they shall and may begin
their said Plantation and Seat of their first Abode and Habitation,
at any Place upon the said Coast of *Virginia* and *America,* where
they shall think fit and convenient, between eight and thirty Degrees
of the said Latitude, and five and forty Degrees of the same Latitude; And that they shall have all the Lands, Soils, Grounds, Havens,
Ports, Rivers, Mines, Minerals, Woods, Marshes, Waters, Fishings,
Commodities, and Hereditaments, whatsoever from the first Seat of
their Plantation and Habitation by the Space of fifty like *English*
Miles as is aforesaid, all alongst the said Coast of *Virginia* and
America, towards the *West* and *Southwest,* or towards the *South,*
as the Coast lyeth, and all the Islands within one hundred Miles,
directly over against the said Sea Coast; And also all the Lands,
Soils, Grounds, Havens, Ports, Rivers, Mines, Minerals, Woods,

Marshes, Waters, Fishings, Commodities, and Hereditaments, what-soever, from the said Place of their first Plantation and Habitation for the Space of fifty like Miles, all alongst the said Coast of *Virginia* and *America*, towards the *East* and *Northeast*, or towards the *North*, as the Coast lyeth, and all the Islands also within one hundred Miles directly over against the same Sea Coast; And also all the Lands, Soils, Grounds, Havens, Ports, Rivers, Woods, Mines, Minerals, Marshes, Waters, Fishings, Commodities, and Hereditaments, what-soever, from the same fifty Miles every way on the Sea Coast, directly into the main Land, by the Space of one hundred like *English* Miles; And shall and may inhabit and remain there; and shall and may also build and fortify within any the same for their better Safeguard, according to their best Discretion, and the Discretion of the Council of that Colony; And that none of our Subjects shall be permitted, or suffered, to plant or inhabit behind, or on the back of them, towards the main Land, without the express License of the Council of that Colony, in Writing thereunto first had and obtained.

VI. Provided always, and our Will and Pleasure herein is, that the Plantation and Habitation of such of the said Colonies, as shall last plant themselves, as aforesaid, shall not be made within one hundred like *English* Miles of the other of them, that first began to make their Plantation, as aforesaid.

VII. And we do also ordain, establish, and agree, for Us, our Heirs, and Successors, that each of the said Colonies shall have a Council, which shall govern and order all Matters and Causes, which shall arise, grow, or happen, to or within the same several Colonies, according to such Laws, Ordinances, and Instructions, as shall be, in that behalf, given and signed with Our Hand or Sign Manual, and pass under the Privy Seal of our Realm of *England;* Each of which Councils shall consist of thirteen Persons, to be ordained, made, and removed, from time to time, according as shall be directed, and comprised in the same instructions; And shall have a several Seal, for all Matters that shall pass or concern the same several Councils; Each of which Seals shall have the King's Arms en graven on the one Side thereof, and his Portraiture on the other And that the Seal for the Council of the said first Colony shall have engraven round about, on the one side, these Words; *Sigillum Regi*

Magnæ Britanniæ, Franciæ, & Hiberniæ; on the other Side this Inscription, round about; *Pro Concilio primæ Coloniæ Virginiæ.* And the seal for the Council of the said second Colony shall also have engraven, round about the one Side thereof, the aforesaid Words; *Sigillum Regis Magnæ, Britanniæ, Franciæ, & Hiberniæ;* and on the other Side; *Pro Concilio secundæ Coloniæ Virginiæ:*

VIII. And that also there shall be a Council established here in *England,* which shall, in like Manner, consist of thirteen Persons, to be, for that Purpose, appointed by Us, our Heirs and Successors, which shall be called our *Council of Virginia;* And shall, from time to time, have the superior Managing and Direction, only of and for all Matters, that shall or may concern the Government, as well of the said several Colonies, as of and for any other Part or Place, within the aforesaid Precincts of four and thirty and five and forty Degrees, abovementioned; Which Council shall, in like manner, have a Seal, for Matters concerning the Council of Colonies, with the like Arms and Portraiture, as aforesaid, with this Inscription, engraven round about on the one Side; *Sigillum Regis Magnæ Britanniæ, Franciæ, & Hiberniæ;* and round about the other side, *Pro Concilio suo Virginiæ.*

IX. And moreover, we do GRANT and agree, for Us, our Heirs and Successors, that the said several Councils, of and for the said several Colonies, shall and lawfully may, by Virtue hereof, from time to time, without any Interruption of Us, our Heirs, or Successors, give and take Order, to dig, mine, and search for all Manner of Mines of Gold, Silver, and Copper, as well within any part of their said several Colonies, as for the said main Lands on the Backside of the same Colonies; And to HAVE and enjoy the Gold, Silver, and Copper, to be gotten thereof, to the Use and Behoof of the same Colonies, and the Plantations thereof; YIELDING therefore, to Us, our Heirs and Successors, the fifth Part only of all the same Gold and Silver, and the fifteenth Part of all the same Copper, so to be gotten or had, as is aforesaid, without any other Manner or Profit or Account, to be given or yielded to Us, our Heirs, or Successors, for or in Respect of the same:

X. And that they shall, or lawfully may, establish and cause to be made a Coin, to pass current there between the People of those several Colonies, for the more Ease of Traffick and Bargaining between and amongst them and the Natives there, of such Metal, and in such Manner and Form, as the said several Councils there shall limit and appoint.

XI. And we do likewise, for Us, our Heirs, and Successors, by these Presents, give full Power and Authority to the said Sir *Thomas Gates,* Sir *George Somers, Richard Hackluit, Edward-Maria Wingfield, Thomas Hanham, Ralegh Gilbert, William Parker,* and *George Popham,* and to every of them, and to the said several Companies, Plantations, and Colonies, that they, and every of them, shall and may, at all and every time and times hereafter, have, take, and lead in the said Voyage, and for and towards the said several Plantations and Colonies, and to travel thitherward, and to abide and inhabit there, in every the said Colonies and Plantations, such and so many of our Subjects, as shall willingly accompany them, or any of them, in the said Voyages and Plantations; With sufficient Shipping and Furniture of Armour, Weapons, Ordinance, Powder, Victual, and all other things, necessary for the said Plantations, and for their Use and Defence there: PROVIDED always, that none of the said Persons be such, as shall hereafter be specially restrained by Us, our Heirs, or Successors.

XII. Moreover, we do, by these Presents, for Us, our Heirs, and Successors, GIVE AND GRANT Licence unto the said Sir *Thomas Gates,* Sir *George Somers, Richard Hackluit, Edward-Maria Wingfield, Thomas Hanham, Ralegh Gilbert, William Parker,* and *George Popham,* and to every of the said Colonies, that they, and every of them, shall and may, from time to time, and at all times for ever hereafter, for their several Defences, encounter, expulse, repel, and resist, as well by Sea as by Land, by all Ways and Means whatsoever, all and every such Person and Persons, as without the especial Licence of the said several Colonies and Plantations, shall attempt to inhabit within the said several Precincts and Limits of the said several Colonies and Plantations, or any of them, or that shall enterprise or attempt, at any time hereafter, the Hurt, Detriment, or Annoyance, of the said several Colonies or Plantations.

XIII. Giving and granting, by these Presents, unto the said Sir *Thomas Gates,* Sir *George Somers, Richard Hackluit, Edward-*

Maria Wingfield, and their Associates of the said first Colony, and unto the said *Thomas Hanham, Ralegh Gilbert, William Parker,* and *George Popham,* and their Associates of the said second Colony, and to every of them, from time to time, and at all times for ever hereafter, Power and Authority to take and surprise, by all Ways and Means whatsoever, all and every Person and Persons, with their Ships, Vessels, Goods and other Furniture, which shall be found trafficking, into any Harbour or Harbours, Creek or Creeks, or Place, within the Limits or Precincts of the said several Colonies and Plantations, not being of the same Colony, until such time, as they, being of any Realms or Dominions under our Obedience, shall pay, or agree to pay, to the Hands of the Treasurer of that Colony, within whose Limits and Precincts they shall so traffick, two and a half upon every Hundred, of any thing, so by them trafficked, bought, or sold; And being Strangers, and not Subjects under our Obeysance, until they shall pay five upon every Hundred, of such Wares and Merchandise, as they shall traffick, buy, or sell, within the Precincts of the said several Colonies, wherein they shall so traffick, buy, or sell, as aforesaid, WHICH Sums of Money, or Benefit, as aforesaid, for and during the Space of one and twenty Years, next ensuing the Date hereof, shall be wholly emploied to the Use, Benefit, and Behoof of the said several Plantations, where such Traffick shall be made; And after the said one and twenty Years ended, the same shall be taken to the Use of Us, our Heirs, and Successors, by such Officers and Ministers, as by Us, our Heirs, and Successors, shall be thereunto assigned or appointed.

XIV. And we do further, by these Presents, for Us, our Heirs, and Successors, GIVE AND GRANT unto the said Sir *Thomas Gates,* Sir *George Somers, Richard Hackluit,* and *Edward-Maria Wingfield,* and to their Associates of the said first Colony and Plantation, and to the said *Thomas Hanham, Ralegh Gilbert, William Parker,* and *George Popham,* and their Associates of the said second Colony and Plantation, that they, and every of them, by their Deputies, Ministers and Factors, may transport the Goods, Chattels, Armour, Munition, and Furniture, needful to be used by them, for their said Apparel, Food, Defence, or otherwise in Respect of the said Plantations, out of our Realms of *England* and *Ireland,* and all other our Dominions,

from time to time, for and during the Time of seven Years, next
ensuing the Date hereof, for the better Relief of the said several
Colonies and Plantations, without any Custom, Subsidy, or other
Duty, unto Us, our Heirs, or *Successors,* to be yielded or paid for
the same.

XV. Also we do, for Us, our Heirs, and Successors, DECLARE, by
these Presents, that all and every the Persons, being our Subjects,
which shall dwell and inhabit within every or any of the said
several Colonies and Plantations, and every of their children, which
shall happen to be born within any of the Limits and Precincts of the
said several Colonies and Plantations, shall HAVE and enjoy all
Liberties, Franchises, and Immunities, within any of our other
Dominions, to all Intents and Purposes, as if they had been abiding
and born, within this our Realm of *England,* or any other of our
said Dominions.

XVI. Moreover, our gracious Will and Pleasure is, and we do,
by these Presents, for Us, our Heirs, and Successors, declare and set
forth, that if any Person or Persons, which shall be of any of the
said Colonies and Plantations, or any other, which shall traffick to
the said Colonies and Plantations, or any of them, shall, at any time
or times hereafter, transport any Wares, Merchandises, or Commodities, out of any of our Dominions, with a Pretence to land, sell,
or otherwise dispose of the same, within any the Limits and Precincts of any the said Colonies and Plantations, and yet nevertheless, being at Sea, or after he hath landed the same within any of
the said Colonies and Plantations, shall carry the same into any
other Foreign Country, with a Purpose there to sell or dispose of
the same, without the Licence of Us, our Heirs, and Successors, in
that Behalf first had and obtained; That then, all the Goods and
Chattels of such Person or Persons, so offending and transporting,
together with the said Ship or Vessel, wherein such Transportation
was made, shall be forfeited to Us, our Heirs, and Successors.

XVII. Provided always, and our Will and Pleasure is, and we
do hereby declare to all *Christian* Kings, Princes, and States, that
if any Person or Persons, which shall hereafter be of any of the said
several Colonies and Plantations, or any other, by his, their or any of
their Licence and Appointment, shall, at any time or times hereafter,

rob or spoil, by Sea or by Land, or do any Act of unjust and unlawful Hostility, to any the Subjects of Us, our Heirs, or Successors, or any the Subjects of any King, Prince, Ruler, Governor, or State, being then in League or Amity with Us, our Heirs, or Successors, and that upon such Injury, or upon just Complaint of such Prince, Ruler, Governor, or State, or their Subjects, We, our Heirs, or Successors, shall make open Proclamation, within any of the Ports of our Realm of *England,* commodious for that Purpose, That the said Person or Persons, having committed any such Robbery or Spoil, shall, within the Term to be limited by such Proclamations make full Restitution or Satisfaction of all such Injuries done, so as the said Princes, or others, so complaining, may hold themselves fully satisfied and contented; And that, if the said Person or Persons, having committed such Robbery or Spoil, shall not make, or cause to be made, Satisfaction accordingly, within such Time so to be limited, That then it shall be lawful to Us, our Heirs, and Successors, to put the said Person or Persons, having committed such Robbery or Spoil, and their Procurers, Abetters, or Comforters, out of our Allegiance and Protection; And that it shall be lawful and free, for all Princes and others, to pursue with Hostility the said Offenders, and every of them, and their and every of their Procurers, Aiders, Abetters, and Comforters, in that Behalf.

XVIII. And finally, we do, for Us, our Heirs, and Successors, GRANT and agree, to and with the said Sir *Thomas Gates,* Sir *George Somers, Richard Hackluit,* and *Edward-Maria Wingfield,* and all others of the said first Colony, that We, our Heirs, and Successors, upon Petition in that Behalf to be made, shall, by Letters-patent under the Great Seal of *England,* GIVE and GRANT unto such Persons, their Heirs, and Assigns, as the Council of that Colony, or the most Part of them, shall, for that Purpose nominate and assign, all the Lands, Tenements, and Hereditaments, which shall be within the Precincts limited for that Colony, as is aforesaid, TO BE HOLDEN OF Us, our Heirs, and Successors, as of our Manor at *East-Greenwich* in the County of *Kent,* in free and common Soccage only, and not in Capite:

XIX. And do, in like Manner, Grant and Agree, for Us, our Heirs, and Successors, to and with the said *Thomas Hanham,*

Ralegh Gilbert, William Parker, and *George Popham,* and all others of the said second Colony, That We, our Heirs, and Successors, upon Petition in that Behalf to be made, shall, by Letters-patent under the Great Seal of *England,* GIVE and GRANT unto such Persons, their Heirs, and Assigns, as the Council of that Colony, or the most Part of them, shall, for that Purpose, nominate and assign, all the Lands, Tenements, and Hereditaments, which shall be within the Precincts limited for that Colony, as is aforesaid To BE HOLDEN OF Us, our Heirs, and Successors, as of our Manour of *East-Greenwich* in the County of *Kent,* in free and common Soccage only, and not in Capite.

XX. All which Lands, Tenements, and Hereditaments, so to be passed by the said several Letters-patent, shall be sufficient Assurance from the said Patentees, so distributed and divided amongst the Undertakers for the Plantation of the said several Colonies, and such as shall make their Plantations in either of the said several Colonies, in such Manner and Form, and for such Estates, as shall be ordered and set down by the Council of the said Colony, or the most Part of them, respectively, within which the same Lands, Tenements, and Hereditaments shall lye or be; Although express Mention of the true yearly Value or Certainty of the Premises, or any of them, or of any other Gifts or Grants, by Us or any of our Progenitors or Predecessors, to the aforesaid Sir *Thomas Gates,* Knt. Sir *George Somers,* Knt. *Richard Hackluit, Edward-Maria Wingfield, Thomas Hanham, Ralegh Gilbert, William Parker,* and *George Popham,* or any of them, heretofore made, in these Presents, is not made; Or any Statute, Act, Ordinance, or Provision, Proclamation, or Restraint, to the contrary hereof had, made, ordained, or any other Thing, Cause, or Matter whatsoever, in any wise notwithstanding. In Witness whereof we have caused these our Letters to be made Patents; Witness Ourself at *Westminster,* the tenth Day of *April,* in the fourth Year of our Reign of *England, France,* and *Ireland,* and of *Scotland* the nine and thirtieth.

THE MAYFLOWER COMPACT

(1620)

[From the History of Plymouth Plantation by William Bradford (1590–1657), second governor of Plymouth.]

IN the name of God, Amen. We, whose names are underwritten, the loyal subjects of our dread sovereigne Lord, King James, by the grace of God, of Great Britaine, France, and Ireland king, defender of the faith, etc., having undertaken, for the glory of God, and advancement of the Christian faith, and honour of our king and country, a voyage to plant the first colony in the Northerne parts of Virginia, doe, by these presents, solemnly and mutually in the presence of God, and one of another, covenant and combine ourselves together into a civill body politick, for our better ordering and preservation and furtherance of the ends aforesaid; and by virtue hereof to enacte, constitute, and frame such just and equall laws, ordinances, acts, constitutions, and offices, from time to time, as shall be thought most meete and convenient for the generall good of the Colonie unto which we promise all due submission and obedience. In witness whereof we have hereunder subscribed our names at Cap-Codd the 11. of November, in the year of the raigne of our sovereigne lord, King James, of England, France, and Ireland, the eighteenth, and of Scotland the fiftie-fourth. Anno. Dom. 1620.

THE FUNDAMENTAL ORDERS
OF CONNECTICUT

(1639)

[These "Orders" were adopted by a popular convention of the three towns of Windsor, Hartford, and Wethersfield, on January 14, 1639. They form, according to historians, "the first written constitution, in the modern sense of the term, as a permanent limitation on governmental power, known in history, and certainly the first American constitution of government to embody the democratic idea."]

FORASMUCH as it hath pleased the Almighty God by the wise disposition of his diuyne prouidence so to Order and dispose of things that we the Inhabitants and Residents of Windsor, Harteford and Wethersfield are now cohabiting and dwelling in and vppon the River of Conectecotte and the Lands thereunto adioyneing; And well knowing where a people are gathered togather the word of God requires that to mayntayne the peace and vnion of such a people there should be an orderly and decent Gouerment established according to God, to order and dispose of the affayres of the people at all seasons as occation shall require; doe therefore assotiate and conioyne our selues to be as one Publike State or Comonwelth; and doe, for our selues and our Successors and such as shall be adioyned to vs att any tyme hereafter, enter into Combination and Confederation togather, to mayntayne and presearue the liberty and purity of the gospell of our Lord Jesus which we now professe, as also the disciplyne of the Churches, which according to the truth of the said gospell is now practised amongst vs; As also in our Ciuell Affaires to be guided and gouerned according to such Lawes, Rules, Orders and decrees as shall be made, ordered & decreed, as followeth:—

1. It is Ordered, sentenced and decreed, that there shall be yerely two generall Assemblies or Courts, the on the second thursday in Aprill, the other the second thursday in September, following; the first shall be called the Courte of Election, wherein shall be yerely

Chosen from tyme to tyme soe many Magestrats and other publike
Officers as shall be found requisitte: Whereof one to be chosen
Gouernour for the yeare ensueing and vntill another be chosen,
and noe other Magestrate to be chosen for more than one yeare;
prouided allwayes there be six chosen besids the Gouernour; which
being chosen and sworne according to an Oath recorded for that
purpose shall haue power to administer iustice according to the
Lawes here established, and for want thereof according to the rule
of the word of God; which choise shall be made by all that are admitted freemen and haue taken the Oath of Fidellity, and doe co-
habitte within this Jurisdiction, (hauing beene admitted Inhabitants.
by the maior part of the Towne wherein they liue,) or the mayor
parte of such as shall be then present.

2. It is Ordered, sentensed and decreed, that the Election of the
aforesaid Magestrats shall be on this manner: euery person present
and quallified for choyse shall bring in (to the persons deputed to
receaue them) one single paper with the name of him written in yt
whom he desires to haue Gouernour, and he that hath the greatest
number of papers shall be Gouernor for that yeare. And the rest
of the Magestrats or publike Officers to be chosen in this manner:
The Secretary for the tyme being shall first read the names of all
that are to be put to choise and then shall seuerally nominate them
distinctly, and euery one that would haue the person nominated to
be chosen shall bring in one single paper written vppon, and he that
would not haue him chosen shall bring in a blanke: and euery one
that hath more written papers then blanks shall be a Magistrat for
that yeare; which papers shall be receaued and told by one or more
that shall be then chosen by the court and sworne to be faythfull
therein; but in case there should not be six chosen as aforesaid,
besids the Gouernor, out of those which are nominated, then he or
they which haue the most written papers shall be a Magestrate or
Magestrats for the ensueing yeare, to make vp the foresaid number.

3. It is Ordered, sentenced and decreed, that the Secretary shall
not nominate any person, nor shall any person be chosen newly into
the Magestracy which was not propownded in some Generall Courte
before, to be nominated the next Election; and to that end yt shall
be lawfull for ech of the Townes aforesaid by their deputyes to

nominate any two whom they conceaue fitte to be put to election; and the Courte may ad so many more as they iudge requisitt.

4. It is Ordered, sentenced and decreed that noe person be chosen Gouernor aboue once in two yeares, and that the Gouernor be always a member of some approued congregation, and formerly of the Magestracy within this Jurisdiction; and all the Magestrats Freemen of this Comonwelth: and that no Magestrate or other publike officer shall execute any parte of his or their Office before they are seuerally sworne, which shall be done in the face of the Courte if they be present, and in case of absence by some deputed for that purpose.

5. It is Ordered, sentenced and decreed, that to the aforesaid Courte of Election the seuerall Townes shall send their deputyes, and when the Elections are ended they may proceed in any publike searuice as at other Courts. Also the other Generall Courte in September shall be for makeing of lawes, and any other publike occation, which conserns the good of the Comonwelth.

6. It is Ordered, sentenced and decreed, that the Gouernor shall, ether by himselfe or by the secretary, send out sumons to the Constables of euery Towne for the cauleing of these two standing Courts, on month at lest before their seuerall tymes: And also if the Gouernor and the gretest parte of the Magestrats see cause vppon any spetiall occation to call a generall Courte, they may giue order to the secretary soe to doe within fowerteene dayes warneing; and if vrgent necessity so require, vppon a shorter notice, giueing sufficient grownds for yt to the deputyes when they meete, or els be questioned for the same; And if the Gouernor and Mayor parte of Magestrats shall ether neglect or refuse to call the two Generall standing Courts or ether of them, as also at other tymes when the occations of the Comonwelth require, the Freemen thereof, or the Mayor parte of them, shall petition to them soe to doe: if then yt be ether denyed or neglected the said Freemen or the Mayor parte of them shall haue power to giue order to the Constables of the seuerall Townes to doe the same, and so may meete togather, and chuse to themselues a Moderator, and may proceed to do any Acte of power, which any other Generall Courte may.

7. It is Ordered, sentenced and decreed that after there are warrants giuen out for any of the said Generall Courts, the Con-

stable or Constables of ech Towne shall forthwith give notice distinctly to the inhabitants of the same, in some Publike Assembly or by goeing or sending from howse to howse, that at a place and tyme by him or them lymited and sett, they meet and assemble them selues togather to elect and chuse certen deputyes to be att the Generall Courte then following to agitate the afayres of the comonwelth; which said Deputyes shall be chosen by all that are admitted Inhabitants in the seuerall Townes and haue taken the oath of fidellity; prouided that non be chosen a Deputy for any Generall Courte which is not a Freeman of this Comonwelth.

The foresaid deputyes shall be chosen in manner following: euery person that is present and quallified as before expressed, shall bring the names of such, written in seuerall papers, as they desire to haue chosen for that Imployment, and these 3 or 4, more or lesse, being the number agreed on to be chosen for that tyme, that haue greatest number of papers written for them shall be deputyes for that Courte; whose names shall be endorsed on the backe side of the warrant and returned into the Courte, with the Constable or Constables hand vnto the same.

8. It is Ordered, sentenced and decreed, that Wyndsor, Hartford and Wethersfield shall haue power, ech Towne, to send fower of their freemen as deputyes to euery Generall Courte; and whatsoeuer other Townes shall be hereafter added to this Jurisdiction, they shall send so many deputyes as the Courte shall judge meete, a resonable proportion to the number of Freemen that are in the said Townes being to be attended therein; which deputyes shall have the power of the whole Towne to giue their voats and alowance to all such lawes and orders as may be for the publike good, and unto which the said Townes are to be bownd.

9. It is ordered and decreed, that the deputyes thus chosen shall haue power and liberty to appoynt a tyme and a place of meeting togather before any Generall Courte to aduise and consult of all such things as may concerne the good of the publike, as also to examine their owne Elections, whether according to the order, and if they or the gretest parte of them find any election to be illegall they may seclud such for present from their meeting, and returne the same and their resons to the Courte; and if yt proue true, the

Courte may fyne the parte or partyes so intruding and the Towne, if they see cause, and giue out a warrant to goe to a newe election in a legall way, either in parte or in whole. Also the said deputyes shall haue power to fyne any that shall be disorderly at their meetings, or for not coming in due tyme or place according te appoyntment; and they may returne the said fynes into the Courte if yt be refused to be paid, and the tresurer to take notice of yt, and to estreete or levy the same as he doth other fynes.

10. It is Ordered, sentenced and decreed, that euery Generall Courte, except such as through neglecte of the Gouernor and the greatest parte of Magestrats the Freemen themselues doe call, shall consist of the Gouernor, or some one chosen to moderate the Court, and 4 other Magestrats at lest, with the mayor part of the deputyes of the seuerall Townes legally chosen; and in case the Freemen or mayor parte of them, through neglect or refusall of the Gouernor and mayor parte of the magestrats, shall call a Courte, yt shall consist of the mayor parte of Freemen that are present or their deputyes, with a Moderator chosen by them: In which said Generall Courts shall consist the supreme power of the Comonwelth, and they only shall haue power to make laws or repeale them, to graunt leuyes, to admitt of Freemen, dispose of lands vndisposed of, to seuerall Townes or persons, and also shall haue power to call ether Courte or Magestrate or any other person whatsoeuer into question for any misdemeanour, and may for just causes displace or deale otherwise according to the nature of the offence; and also may deale in any other matter that concerns the good of this comon welth, excepte election of Magestrats, which shall be done by the whole boddy of Freemen.

In which Courte the Gouernor or Moderator shall haue power to order the Courte to giue liberty of spech, and silence vnceasonable and disorderly speakeings, to put all things to voate, and in case the vote be equall to haue the casting voice. But non of these Courts shall be adiorned or dissolued without the consent of the maior parte of the Court.

11. It is ordered, sentenced and decreed, that when any Generall Courte vppon the occations of the Comonwelth haue agreed vppon any sume or somes of mony to be leuyed vppon the seuerall Townes

within this Jurisdiction, that a Comittee be chosen to sett out and appoynt what shall be the proportion of euery Towne to pay of the said leuy, provided the Comittees be made vp of an equall number out of each Towne.

14th January, 1638,[1] the 11 Orders abouesaid are voted.

THE OATH OF THE GOUERNOR, FOR THE [PRESENT.]

I, 𝕹.𝖂. being now chosen to be Gouernor within this Jurisdiction, for the yeare ensueing, and vntil a new be chosen, doe sweare by the greate and dreadfull name of the everliueing God, to promote the publicke good and peace of the same, according to the best of my skill; as also will mayntayne all lawfull priuiledges of this Comonwealth; as also that all wholsome lawes that are or shall be made by lawfull authority here established, be duly executed; and will further the execution of Justice according to the rule of Gods word; so helpe me God, in the name of the Lo: Jesus Christ.

THE OATH OF A MAGESTRATE, FOR THE PRESENT.

I, 𝕹.𝖂. being chosen a Magestrate within this Jurisdiction for the yeare ensueing, doe sweare by the great and dreadfull name of the euerliueing God, to promote the publike good and peace of the same, according to the best of my skill, and that I will mayntayne all the lawfull priuiledges thereof, according to my vnderstanding, as also assist in the execution of all such wholesome lawes as are made or shall be made by lawfull authority heare established, and will further the execution of Justice for the tyme aforesaid according to the righteous rule of Gods word; so helpe me God, etc.

[1] 1638, old style; 1639, new style.

THE BODY OF LIBERTIES

(1641)

[The Massachusetts "Body of Liberties," the first code of laws established in New England, was compiled by Nathaniel Ward (c. 1578–1652) a leading English Puritan minister, who had been trained as a lawyer. He came to the colony in 1634, and was for a time pastor at Ipswich. The "Liberties" were established by the Massachusetts General Court in December, 1641.]

THE LIBERTIES OF THE MASSACHUSETS COLLONIE IN NEW ENGLAND, 1641

THE free fruition of such liberties, Immunities, and priveledges as humanitie, Civilitie, and Christianitie call for as due to every man in his place and proportion, without impeachment, and infringement, hath ever bene and ever will be the tranquillitie and Stabilitie of Churches and Commonwealths. And the deniall or deprivall thereof, the disturbance if not the ruine of both.

We hould it therefore our dutie and safetie whilst we are about the further establishing of this Government to collect and expresse all such freedomes as for present we foresee may concerne us, and our posteritie after us, And to ratify them with our sollemne consent.

Wee doe therefore this day religiously and unanimously decree and confirme these following Rites, liberties, and priveledges concerneing our Churches, and Civill State to be respectively, impartiallie, and inviolably enjoyed and observed throughout our Jurisdiction for ever.

1. No mans life shall be taken away, no mans honour or good name shall be stayned, no mans person shall be arested, restrayned, banished, dismembred, nor any wayes punished, no man shall be deprived of his wife or children, no mans goods or estaite shall be taken away from him, nor any way indammaged under colour of law or Countenance of Authoritie, unlesse it be by vertue or equitie

of some expresse law of the Country waranting the same, established by a generall Court and sufficiently published, or in case of the defect of a law in any partecular case by the word of God. And in Capitall cases, or in cases concerning dismembring or banishment according to that word to be judged by the Generall Court.

2. Every person within this Jurisdiction, whether Inhabitant or forreiner, shall enjoy the same justice and law, that is generall for the plantation, which we constitute and execute one towards another without partialitie or delay.

3. No man shall be urged to take any oath or subscribe any articles, covenants or remonstrance, of a publique and Civill nature, but such as the Generall Court hath considered, allowed, and required.

4. No man shall be punished for not appearing at or before any Civill Assembly, Court, Councell, Magistrate, or Officer, nor for the omission of any office or service, if he shall be necessarily hindred by any apparent Act or providence of God, which he could neither foresee nor avoid. Provided that this law shall not prejudice any person of his just cost or damage, in any civill action.

5. No man shall be compelled to any publique worke or service unlesse the presse be grounded upon some act of the generall Court, and have reasonable allowance therefore.

6. No man shall be pressed in person to any office, worke, warres, or other publique service, that is necessarily and suffitiently exempted by any naturall or personall impediment, as by want of yeares, greatnes of age, defect of minde, fayling of sences, or impotencie of Lymbes.

7. No man shall be compelled to goe out of the limits of this plantation upon any offensive warres which this Comonwealth or any of our friends or confederats shall volentarily undertake. But onely upon such vindictive and defensive warres in our owne behalfe or the behalfe of our freinds and confederats as shall be enterprized by the Counsell and consent of a Court generall, or by authority derived from the same.

8. No mans Cattel or goods of what kinde soever shall be pressed or taken for any publique use or service, unlesse it be by warrant grounded upon some act of the generall Court, nor without such

reasonable prices and hire as the ordinarie rates of the Countrie do afford. And if his Cattel or goods shall perish or suffer damage in such service, the owner shall be suffitiently recompenced.

9. No monopolies shall be granted or allowed amongst us, but of such new Inventions that are profitable to the Countrie, and that for a short time.

10. All our lands and heritages shall be free from all fines and licenses upon Alienations, and from all hariotts, wardships, Liveries, Primer-seisins, yeare day and wast, Escheates, and forfeitures, upon the deaths of parents or Ancestors, be they naturall, casuall or Juditiall.

11. All persons which are of the age of 21 yeares, and of right understanding and meamories, whether excommunicate or condemned shall have full power and libertie to make there wills and testaments, and other lawfull alienations of theire lands and estates.

12. Every man whether Inhabitant or fforreiner, free or not free shall have libertie to come to any publique Court, Councel, or Towne meeting, and either by speech or writeing to move any lawfull, seasonable, and materiall question, or to present any necessary motion, complaint, petition, Bill or information, whereof that meeting hath proper cognizance, so it be done in convenient time, due order, and respective manner.

13. No man shall be rated here for any estaite or revenue he hath in England, or in any forreine partes till it be transported hither.

14. Any Conveyance or Alienation of land or other estaite what so ever, made by any woman that is married, any childe under age, Ideott or distracted person, shall be good if it be passed and ratified by the consent of a generall Court.

15. All Covenous or fraudulent Alienations or Conveyances of lands, tenements, or any heriditaments, shall be of no validitie to defeate any man from due debts or legacies, or from any just title, clame or possession, of that which is so fraudulently conveyed.

16. Every Inhabitant that is an howse holder shall have free fishing and fowling in any great ponds and Bayes, Coves and Rivers, so farre as the sea ebbes and flowes within the presincts of the towne where they dwell, unlesse the free men of the same Towne

or the Generall Court have otherwise appropriated them, provided that this shall not be extended to give leave to any man to come upon others proprietie without there leave.

17. Every man of or within this Jurisdiction shall have free libertie, notwithstanding any Civill power to remove both himselfe, and his familie at their pleasure out of the same, provided there be no legall impediment to the contrarie.

Rites, Rules, and Liberties concerning Juditiall proceedings

18. No mans person shall be restrained or imprisoned by any authority whatsoever, before the law hath sentenced him thereto, if he can put in sufficient securitie, bayle or mainprise, for his appearance, and good behaviour in the meane time, unlesse it be in Crimes Capitall, and Contempts in open Court, and in such cases where some expresse act of Court doth allow it.

19. If in a general Court any miscariage shall be amongst the Assistants when they are by themselves that may deserve an Admonition or fine under 20 sh. it shall be examined and sentenced amongst themselves, If amongst the Deputies when they are by themselves, it shall be examined and sentenced amongst themselves, If it be when the whole Court is togeather, it shall be judged by the whole Court, and not severallie as before.

20. If any which are to sit as Judges in any other Court shall demeane themselves offensively in the Court, The rest of the Judges present shall have power to censure him for it, if the cause be of a high nature it shall be presented to and censured at the next superior Court.

21. In all cases where the first summons are not served six dayes before the Court, and the cause breifly specified in the warrant, where appearance is to be made by the partie summoned, it shall be at his libertie whether he will appeare or no, except all cases that are to be handled in Courts suddainly called, upon extraordinary occasions, In all cases where there appeares present and urgent cause any assistant or officer apointed shal have power to make our attaichments for the first summons.

22. No man in any suit or action against an other shall falsely pretend great debts or damages to vex his adversary, if it shall

appeare any doth so, The Court shall have power to set a reasonable fine on his head.

23. No man shall be adjudged to pay for detaining any debt from any Crediter above eight pounds in the hundred for one yeare, And not above that rate proportionable for all somes what so ever, neither shall this be a coulour or countenance to allow any usurie amongst us contrarie to the law of god.

24. In all Trespasses or damages done to any man or men, If it can be proved to be done by the meere default of him or them to whome the trespasse is done, It shall be judged no trespasse, nor any damage given for it.

25. No Summons pleading Judgement, or any kinde of proceeding in Court or course of Justice shall be abated, arested or reversed upon any kinde of cercumstantiall errors or mistakes, If the person and cause be rightly understood and intended by the Court.

26. Every man that findeth himselfe unfit to plead his owne cause in any Court shall have Libertie to imploy any man against whom the Court doth not except, to helpe him, Provided he give him noe fee or reward for his paines. This shall not exempt the partie him selfe from Answering such Questions in person as the Court shall thinke meete to demand of him.

27. If any plantife shall give into any Court a declaration of his cause in writeing, The defendant shall also have libertie and time to give in his answer in writeing, And so in all further proceedings betwene partie and partie, So it doth not further hinder the dispach of Justice then the Court shall be willing unto.

28. The plantife in all Actions brought in any Court shall have libertie to withdraw his Action, or to be nonsuited before the Jurie hath given in their verdict, in which case he shall alwaies pay full cost and chardges to the defendant, and may afterwards renew his suite at an other Court if he please.

29. In all actions at law it shall be the libertie of the plantife and defendant by mutual consent to choose whether they will be tryed by the Bensh or by a Jurie, unlesse it be where the law upon just reason hath otherwise determined. The like libertie shall be granted to all persons in Criminall cases.

30. It shall be in the libertie both of plantife and defendant, and

likewise every delinquent (to be judged by a Jurie) to challenge any of the Jurors. And if his challenge be found just and reasonable by the Bench, or the rest of the Jurie, as the challenger shall choose it shall be allowed him, and tales de cercumstantibus impaneled in their room.

31. In all cases where evidences is so obscure or defective that the Jurie cannot clearly and safely give a positive verdict, whether it be a grand or petit Jurie, It shall have libertie to give a non Liquit, or a spetiall verdict, in which last, that is in a spetiall verdict, the Judgement of the cause shall be left to the Court, And all Jurors shall have libertie in matters of fact if they cannot finde the maine issue, yet to finde and present in their verdict so much as they can, If the Bench and Jurors shall so suffer at any time about their verdict that either of them cannot proceede with peace of conscience the case shall be referred to the Generall Court, who shall take the question from both and determine it.

32. Every man shall have libertie to replevy his Cattell or goods impounded, distreined, seised, or extended, unlesse it be upon execution after Judgement, and in paiment of fines. Provided he puts in good securitie to prosecute his replevin, And to satisfie such demands as his Adversary shall recover against him in Law.

33. No mans person shall be arrested, or imprisoned upon execution or judgment for any debt or fine, If the law can finde competent meanes of satisfaction otherwise from his estaite, and if not his person may be arrested and imprisoned where he shall be kept at his owne charge, not the plantife's till satisfaction be made, unlesse the Court that had cognizance of the cause or some superior Court shall otherwise provide.

34. If any man shall be proved and Judged a common Barrator vexing others with unjust frequent and endlesse suites, It shall be in the power of Courts both to denie him the benefit of the law, and to punish him for his Barratry.

35. No mans corne nor hay that is in the feild or upon the Cart, nor his garden stuffe, nor any thing subject to present decay, shall be taken in any distresse, unles he that takes it doth presently bestow it where it may not be imbesled nor suffer spoile or decay, or give securitie to satisfie the worth thereof if it come to any harme.

36. It shall be in the libertie of every man cast condemned or sentenced in any cause in any Inferior Court, to make their appeale to the Court of Assistants, provided they tender their appeale and put in securitie to prosecute it, before the Court be ended wherein they were condemned, And within six dayes next ensuing put in good securitie before some Assistant to satisfie what his Adversarie shall recover against him; And if the cause be of a Criminall nature for his good behaviour, and appearance, And everie man shall have libertie to complaine to the Generall Court of any Injustice done him in any Court of Assistants or other.

37. In all cases where it appeares to the Court that the plantife hath wilingly and witingly done wronge to the defendant in commencing and prosecuting an action or complaint against him, They shall have power to impose upon him a proportionable fine to the use of the defendant or accused person, for his false complaint or clamor.

38. Everie man shall have libertie to Record in the publique Rolles of any Court any Testimony given upon oath in the same Court, or before two Assistants, or any deede or evidence legally confirmed there to remaine in perpetuam rei memoriam, that is for perpetuall memoriall or evidence upon occasion.

39. In all actions both real and personall betweene partie and partie, the Court shall have power to respite execution for a convenient time, when in their prudence they see just cause so to doe.

40. No conveyance, Deede, or promise whatsoever shall be of validitie, If it be gotten by Illegal violence, imprisonment, threatening, or any kinde of forcible compulsion called Dures.

41. Everie man that is to Answere for any criminall cause, whether he be in prison or under bayle, his cause shall be heard and determined at the next Court that hath proper Cognizance thereof, And may be done without prejudice of Justice.

42. No man shall be twise sentenced by Civill Justice for one and the same Crime, offence, or Trespasse.

43. No man shall be beaten with above 40 stripes, nor shall any true gentleman, nor any man equall to a gentleman be punished with whipping, unles his crime be very shamefull, and his course of life vitious and profligate.

44. No man condemned to dye shall be put to death within fower dayes next after his condemnation, unles the Court see spetiall cause to the contrary, or in case of martiall law, nor shall the body of any man so put to death be unburied 12 howers unlesse it be in case of Anatomie.

45. No man shall be forced by Torture to confesse any Crime against himselfe nor any other unlesse it be in some Capitall case, where he is first fullie convicted by cleare and suffitient evidence to be guilty, After which if the cause be of that nature, That it is very apparent there be other conspiratours, or confederates with him, Then he may be tortured, yet not with such Tortures as be Barbarous and inhumane.

46. For bodilie punishments we allow amongst us none that are inhumane Barbarous or cruel.

47. No man shall be put to death without the testimony of two or three witnesses or that which is equivalent thereunto.

48. Every Inhabitant of the Countrie shall have free libertie to search and veewe any Rooles, Records, or Regesters of any Court or office except the Councell, And to have a transcript or exemplification thereof written examined, and signed by the hand of the officer of the office paying the appointed fees therefore.

49. No free man shall be compelled to serve upon Juries above two Courts in a yeare, except grand Jurie men, who shall hould two Courts together at the least.

50. All Jurors shall be chosen continuallie by the freemen of the Towne where they dwell.

51. All Associates selected at any time to Assist the Assistants in Inferior Courts, shall be nominated by the Townes belonging to that Court, by orderly agreement amonge themselves.

52. Children, Idiots, Distracted persons, and all that are strangers, or new comers to our plantation, shall have such allowances and dispensations in any cause whether Criminal or other as religion and reason require.

53. The age of discretion for passing away of lands or such kinde of herediments, or for giveing, of votes, verdicts or Sentence in any Civill Courts or causes, shall be one and twentie yeares.

54. Whensoever any thing is to be put to vote, any sentence to be

pronounced, or any other matter to be proposed, or read in any Court of Assembly, If the president or moderator thereof shall refuse to performe it, the Major parte of the members of that Court or Assembly shall have power to appoint any other meete man of them to do it, And if there be just cause to punish him that should and would not.

55. In all suites or Actions in any Court, the plaintife shall have libertie to make all the titles and claims to that he sues for he can. And the Defendant shall have libertie to plead all the pleas he can in answere to them, and the Court shall judge according to the intire evidence of all.

56. If any man shall behave himselfe offensively at any Towne meeting, the rest of the freemen then present, shall have power to sentence him for his offence. So be it the mulct or penaltie exceede not twentie shilings.

57. Whensoever any person shall come to any very suddaine untimely and unnaturall death, Some assistant, or the Constables of that Towne shall forthwith sumon a Jury of twelve free men to inquire of the cause and manner of their death, and shall present a true verdict thereof to some neere Assistant, or the next Court to be helde for that Towne upon their oath.

Liberties more peculiarlie concerning the free men

58. Civill Authoritie hath power and libertie to see the peace, ordinances and Rules of Christ observed in every church according to his word, . , it be done in a Civill and not in an Ecclesiastical way.

59. Civill Authoritie hath power and libertie to deale with any Church member in a way of Civill Justice, notwithstanding any Church relation, office or interest.

60. No church censure shall degrade or depose any man from any Civill dignitie, office, or Authoritie he shall have in the Commonwealth.

61. No Magestrate, Juror, Officer, or other man shall be bound to informe present or reveale any private crim or offence, wherein there is no perill or danger to this plantation or any member thereof, when any necessarie tye of conscience binds him to secresie grounded upon the word of god, unlesse it be in case of testimony lawfully required.

62. Any Shire or Towne shall have libertie to choose their Deputies whom and where they please for the Generall Court. So be it they be free men, and have taken there oath of fealtie, and Inhabiting in this Jurisdiction.

63. No Governor, Deputy Governor, Assistant, Associate, or grand Jury man at any Court, nor any Deputie for the Generall Court, shall at any time beare his owne chardges at any Court, but their necessary expences shall be defrayed either by the Towne or Shire on whose service they are, or by the Country in generall.

64. Everie Action betweene partie and partie, and proceedings against delinquents in Criminall causes shall be briefly and destinctly entered on the Rolles of every Court by the Recorder thereof. That such actions be not afterwards brought againe to the vexation of any man.

65. No custome or prescription shall ever pervaile amongst us in any morall cause, our meaneing is maintaine anythinge that can be proved to be morrallie sinfull by the word of god.

66. The Freemen of every Towneship shall have power to make such by laws and constitutions as may concerne the wellfare of their Towne, provided they be not of a Criminall, but onely of a prudential nature, And that their penalties exceede not 20 sh. for one offence. And that they be not repugnant to the publique laws and orders of the Countrie. And if any Inhabitant shall neglect or refuse to observe them, they shall have power to levy the appointed penalties by distresse.

67. It is the constant libertie of the free men of this plantation to choose yearly at the Court of Election out of the freemen all the General officers of this Jurisdiction. If they please to dischardge them at the day of Election by way of vote. They may do it without shewing cause. But if at any other generall Court, we hould it due justice, that the reasons thereof be alleadged and proved. By Generall officers we meane, our Governor, Deputy Governor, Assistants, Treasurer, Generall of our warres. And our Admirall at Sea, and such as are or hereafter may be of the like generall nature.

68. It is the libertie of the freemen to choose such deputies for the Generall Court out of themselves, either in their owne Towne or elsewhere as they judge fitest. And because we cannot foresee

what varietie and weight of occasions may fall into future consideration, And what counsells we may stand in neede of, we decree. That
the Deputies (to attend the Generall Court in the behalfe of the
Countrie) shall not any time be stated or inacted, but from Court to
Court, or at the most but for one yeare, that the Countrie may have
an Annuall libertie to do in that case what is most behoofefull for
the best welfaire thereof.

69. No Generall Court shall be desolved or adjourned without
the consent of the Major parte thereof.

70. All Freemen called to give any advise, vote, verdict, or sentence in any Court, Counsell, or Civill Assembly, shall have full freedome to doe it according to their true judgements and Consciences,
So it be done orderly and inofensively for the manner.

71. The Governor shall have a casting voice whensoever an Equi
vote shall fall out in the Court of Assistants, or generall assembly,
So shall the presedent or moderator have in all Civill Courts or
Assemblies.

72. The Governor and Deputy Governor Joyntly consenting or
any three Assistants concurring in consent shall have power out of
Court to reprive a condemned malefactour, till the next quarter or
generall Court. The generall Court onely shall have power to pardon
a condemned malefactor.

73. The Generall Court hath libertie and Authoritie to send out
any member of this Comanwealth of what qualitie, condition or
office whatsoever into forreine parts about any publique message or
Negotiation. Provided the partie sent be acquainted with the affaire
he goeth about, and be willing to undertake the service.

74. The freemen of every Towne or Towneship, shall have full
power to choose yearly or for lesse time out of themselves a convenient number of fitt men to order the planting or prudentiall occasions of that Towne, according to Instructions given them in writeing, Provided nothing be done by them contrary to the publique laws
and orders of the Countrie, provided also the number of such select
persons be not above nine.

75. It is and shall be the libertie of any member or members of
any Court Councell or Civill Assembly in cases of makeing or executing any order or law, that properlie concerne religion, or any

cause capitall, or warres, or Subscription to any publique Articles or Remonstrance, in case they cannot in Judgement and conscience consent to that way the Major vote or suffrage goes, to make their contra Remonstrance or protestation in speech or writeing, and upon request to have their dissent recorded in the Rolles of that Court. So it be done Christianlie and respectively for the manner. And their dissent onely be entered without the reasons thereof, for the avoiding of tediousnes.

76. Whensoever any Jurie of trialls or Jurours are not cleare in their Judgments or consciences conserneing any cause wherein they are to give their verdict, They shall have libertie in open Court to advise with any man they thinke fitt to resolve or direct them, before they give in their verdict.

77. In all cases wherein any freeman is to give his vote, be it in point of Election, makeing constitutions and orders or passing sentence in any case of Judicature or the like, if he cannot see reason to give it positively one way or an other, he shall have libertie to be silent, and not pressed to a determined vote.

78. The Generall or publique Treasure or any parte thereof shall never be exspended but by the appointment of a Generall Court, nor any Shire Treasure, but by the appointment of the freemen therof, nor any Towne Treasurie but by the freemen of that Township.

Liberties of Women

79. If any man at his death shall not leave his wife a competent portion of his estaite, upon just complaint made to the Generall Court she shall be relieved.

80. Everie marryed woeman shall be free from bodilie correction or stripes by her husband, unlesse it be in his owne defence upon her assalt. If there be any just cause of correction complaint shall be made to Authoritie assembled in some Court, from which onely she shall receive it.

Liberties of Children

81. When parents dye intestate, the Elder sonne shall have a doble portion of his whole estate reall and personall, unlesse the Generall Court upon just cause alleadged shall judge otherwise.

82. When parents dye intestate haveing noe heires males of their bodies their Daughters shall inherit as Copartners, unles the Generall Court upon just reason shall judge otherwise.

83. If any parents shall wilfullie and unreasonably deny any childe timely or convenient mariage, or shall exercise any unnaturall severitie towards them, such children shall have free libertie to complaine to Authoritie for redresse.

84. No Orphan dureing their minoritie which was not committed to tuition or service by the parents in their life time, shall afterwards be absolutely disposed of by any kindred, freind, Executor, Towneship, or Church, nor by themselves without the consent of some Court, wherein two Assistants at least shall be present.

Liberties of Servants

85. If any servants shall flee from the Tiranny and crueltie of their masters to the howse of any freeman of the same Towne, they shall be there protected and susteyned till due order be taken for their relife. Provided due notice thereof be speedily given to their maisters from whom they fled. And the next Assistant or Constable where the partie flying is harboured.

86. No servant shall be put of for above a yeare to any other neither in the life time of their maister nor after their death by their Executors or Administrators unlesse it be by consent of Authoritie assembled in some Court or two Assistants.

87. If any man smite out the eye or tooth of his man-servant, or maid servant, or otherwise mayme or much disfigure him, unlesse it be by meere casualtie, he shall let them goe free from his service. And shall have such further recompense as the Court shall allow him.

88. Servants that have served deligentlie and faithfully to the benefitt of their maisters seaven yearse, shall not be sent away emptie. And if any have bene unfaithfull, negligent or unprofitable in their service, notwithstanding the good usage of their maisters, they shall not be dismissed till they have made satisfaction according to the Judgement of Authoritie.

Liberties of Forreiners and Strangers

89. If any people of other Nations professing the true Christian Religion shall flee to us from the Tiranny or oppression of their persecutors, or from famyne, warres, or the like necessary and compulsarie cause, They shall be entertayned and succoured amongst us, according to that power and prudence, god shall give us.

90. If any ships or other vessels, be it freind or enemy, shall suffer shipwrack upon our Coast, there shall be no violence or wrong offerred to their persons or goods. But their persons shall be harboured, and relieved, and their goods preserved in safety till Authoritie may be certified thereof, and shall take further order therein.

91. There shall never be any bond slaverie, villinage or Captivitie amongst us unles it be lawfull Captives taken in just warres, and such strangers as willingly selle themselves or are sold to us. And these shall have all the liberties and Christian usages which the law of god established in Israell concerning such persons doeth morally require. This exempts none from servitude who shall be Judged thereto by Authoritie.

Off the Bruite Creature

92. No man shall exercise any Tirranny or Crueltie towards any bruite Creature which are usuallie kept for man's use.

93. If any man shall have occasion to leade or drive Cattel from place to place that is far of, so that they be weary, or hungry, or fall sick, or lambe, It shall be lawful to rest or refresh them, for competant time, in any open place that is not Corne, meadow, or inclosed for some peculiar use.

94. Capitall Laws

I.

If any man after legall conviction shall have or worship any other god, but the lord god, he shall be put to death.[1]

[1] Deut. xiii. 6, 10. Deut. xvii. 2, 6. Ex. xxii. 20.

2.

If any man or woeman be a witch, (that is hath or consulteth with a familiar spirit,) they shall be put to death.[2]

3.

If any person shall Blaspheme the name of god, the father, Sonne or Holie Ghost, with direct, expresse, presumptuous or high handed blasphemie, or shall curse god in the like manner, he shall be put to death.[3]

4.

If any person committ any wilfull murther, which is manslaughter, committed upon premeditated malice, hatred, or Crueltie, not in a mans necessarie and just defence, nor by meere casualtie against his will, he shall be put to death.[4]

5.

If any person slayeth an other suddaienly in his anger or Crueltie of passion, he shall be put to death.[5]

6.

If any person shall slay an other through guile, either by poysoning or other such divelish practice, he shall be put to death.[6]

7.

If any man or woeman shall lye with any beaste or bruite creature by Carnall Copulation, They shall surely be put to death. And the beast shall be slaine, and buried and not eaten.[7]

8.

If any man lyeth with mankinde as he lyeth with a woeman, both of them have committed abhomination, they both shall surely be put to death.[8]

[2] Ex. xxii. 18. Lev. xx. 27. Deut. xviii. 10.
[3] Lev. xxiv. 15, 16.
[4] Ex. xxi. 22. Numb. xxxv. 13, 14, 30, 31.
[5] Numb. xxv. 20, 21. Lev. xxiv. 17.   [6] Ex. xxi. 14.
[7] Lev. xx. 15, 16.   [8] Lev. xx. 13.

9.

If any person committeth Adultery with a maried or espoused wife, the Adulterer and Adulteresse shall surely be put to death.[9]

10.

If any man stealeth a man or mankinde, he shall surely be put to death.[10]

11.

If any man rise up by false witnes, wittingly and of purpose to take away any mans life, he shall be put to death.[11]

12.

If any man shall conspire and attempt any invasion, insurrection, or publique rebellion against our commonwealth, or shall indeavour to surprize any Towne or Townes, fort or forts therein, or shall treacherously and perfediouslie attempt the alteration and subversion of our frame of politie or Government fundamentallie, he shall be put to death.

95. *A Declaration of the Liberties the Lord Jesus hath given to the Churches*

1.

All the people of god within this Jurisdiction who are not in a church way, and be orthodox in Judgement, and not scandalous in life, shall have full libertie to gather themselves into a Church Estaite. Provided they doe it in a Christian way, with due observation of the rules of Christ revealed in his word.

2.

Every Church hath full libertie to exercise all the ordinances of god, according to the rules of scripture.

[9] Lev. xx. 19, and 18, 20. Deut. xxii. 23, 24. [10] Ex. xxi. 16. [11] Deut. xix. 16, 18, 19.

3.

Every Church hath free libertie of Election and ordination of all their officers from time to time, provided they be able, pious and orthodox.

4.

Every Church hath free libertie of Admission, Recommendation, Dismission, and Expulsion, or deposall of their officers, and members, upon due cause, with free exercise of the Discipline and Censures of Christ according to the rules of his word.

5.

No Injunctions are to be put upon any Church, Church officers or member in point of Doctrine, worship or Discipline, whether for substance or cercumstance besides the Institutions of the lord.

6.

Every Church of Christ hath freedome to celebrate dayes of fasting and prayer, and of thanksgiveing according to the word of god.

7.

The Elders of Churches have free libertie to meete monthly, Quarterly, or otherwise, in convenient numbers and places, for conferences, and consultations about Christian and Church questions and occasions.

8.

All Churches have libertie to deale with any of their members in a church way that are in the hand of Justice. So it be not to retard or hinder the course thereof.

9.

Every Church hath libertie to deale with any magestrate, Deputie of Court or other officer what soe ever that is a member in a church way in case of apparent and just offence given in their places, so it be done with due observance and respect.

10.

Wee allowe private meetings for edification in religion amongst Christians of all sortes of people. So it be without just offence for number, time, place, and other cercumstances.

11.

For the preventing and removeing of errour and offence that may grow and spread in any of the Churches in this Jurisdiction, And for the preserveing of trueith and peace in the severall churches within themselves, and for the maintenance and exercise of brotherly communion, amongst all the churches in the Countrie, It is allowed and ratified, by the Authoritie of this Generall Court as a lawful libertie of the Churches of Christ. That once in every month of the yeare (when the season will beare it) It shall be lawfull for the minesters and Elders, of the Churches neere adjoyneing together, with any other of the breetheren with the consent of the churches to assemble by course in each severall Church one after an other. To the intent after the preaching of the word by such a minister as shall be requested thereto by the Elders of the church where the Assembly is held, The rest of the day may be spent in publique Christian Conference about the discussing and resolveing of any such doubts and cases of conscience concerning matter of doctrine or worship or government of the church as shall be propounded by any of the Breetheren of that church, will leave also to any other Brother to propound his objections or answeres for further satisfaction according to the word of god. Provided that the whole action be guided and moderated by the Elders of the Church where the Assemblie is helde, or by such others as they shall appoint. And that no thing be concluded and imposed by way of Authoritie from one or more churches upon an other, but onely by way of Brotherly conference and consultations. That the trueth may be searched out to the satisfying of every mans conscience in the sight of god according his worde. And because such an Assembly and the worke thereof can not be duly attended to if other lectures be held in the same weeke. It is therefore agreed with the consent of the Churches. That in that weeke when such an Assembly is held, All the lectures in all the neighbouring Churches

for that weeke shall be forborne. That so the publique service of
Christ in this more solemne Assembly may be transacted with greater
deligence and attention.

96. Howsoever these above specified rites, freedomes Immunities,
Authorites and priveledges, both Civill and Ecclesiastical are expressed onely under the name and title of Liberties, and not in the
exact forme of Laws or Statutes, yet we do with one consent fullie
Authorise, and earnestly intreate all that are and shall be in Authoritie to consider them as laws, and not to faile to inflict condigne and
proportionable punishments upon every man impartiallie, that shall
infringe or violate any of them.

97. Wee likewise give full power and libertie to any person that
shall at any time be denyed or deprived of any of them, to commence
and prosecute their suite, Complaint or action against any man that
shall so doe in any Court that hath proper Cognizance or judicature
thereof.

98. Lastly because our dutie and desire is to do nothing suddainlie
which fundamentally concerne us, we decree that these rites and
liberties, shall be Audably read and deliberately weighed at every
Generall Court that shall be held, within three yeares next insueing,
And such of them as shall not be altered or repealed they shall stand
so ratified, That no man shall infringe them without due punishment.

And if any Generall Court within these next thre yeares shall
faile or forget to reade and consider them as abovesaid. The Governor and Deputy Governor for the time being, and every Assistant
present at such Courts, shall forfeite 20sh. a man, and everie Deputie
10sh. a man for each neglect, which shall be paid out of their proper
estate, and not by the Country or the Townes which choose them,
and whensoever there shall arise any question in any Court amonge
the Assistants and Associates thereof about the explanation of these
Rites and liberties, The Generall Court onely shall have power to
interprett them.

ARBITRARY GOVERNMENT DESCRIBED

AND THE

GOVERNMENT of the MASSACHUSETTS VINDICATED FROM THAT ASPERSION

BY JOHN WINTHROP

THEN DEPUTY-GOVERNOR OF THE COMMONWEALTH

(1644)

[In 1644, a dispute arose in Massachusetts between the magistrates and the deputies as to the respective powers of the two branches of the legislature, the deputies claiming judicial authority. Winthrop's opposition to this claim brought upon him and other magistrates the charge of arbitrary government; and in order to clear up the situation he drew up the following document. It is important not only for its presentation of Winthrop's personal views, but for the light it throws upon the origins of the political institutions of the Commonwealth.]

ARBITRARY Government is where a people have men set over them, without their choice or allowance; who have power to govern them, and judge their causes without a rule.

God only hath this prerogative; whose sovereignty is absolute, and whose will is a perfect rule, and reason itself; so as for man to usurp such authority, is tyranny, and impiety.

Where the people have liberty to admit or reject their governors, and to require the rule by which they shall be governed and judged, this is not an arbitrary government.

That the Government of the Massachusetts is such will appear (1) by the foundation of it; (2) by the positive laws thereof; (3) by the constant practice which proves a custom, than which (when it is for common good) there is no law of man more inviolable.

1. The foundation of this Government is the King's Letters Patents: this gave them their form and being, in disposing a certain number of persons into a body politic; whereby they became then (in such a politic respect) as one single person, consisting of several

members, and appoint to each its proper place: it regulates their power and motions as might best conduce to the preservation and good of the whole body.

The parties or members of this body politic are reduced under two kinds, Governor and Company, or Freemen: to the Governor it adds a Deputy, and eighteen Assistants: in these is the power of authority placed, under the name of the Governor (not as a person, but as a State) and in the other (which is named the Company) is placed the power of liberty:—which is not a bare passive capacity of freedom, or immunity, but such a liberty as hath power to act upon the chiefest means of its own welfare (yet in a way of liberty, not of authority) and that under two general heads, election and counsel: (1) they have liberty to elect yearly (or oftener if occasion require) all their Governors and other their general officers, viz., such as should have influence (either judicial or ministerial) into all parts of the jurisdiction; (2) they have liberty of counsel in all the General Assemblies, so as without their counsel and consent no laws, decrees, or orders, of any public nature or concernment, not any taxes, impositions, impresses, or other burdens of what kind soever, can be imposed upon them, their families or estates, by any authority in the Government: which notwithstanding remains still a distinct member, even in those General Assemblies: otherwise our state should be a mere Democratie, if all were Governors or magistrates, and none left to be an object of government, which cannot fall out in any kind of Aristocratie.

To make this clear, we will set down the very words of the Patent.

"(1) The words of Constitution of this body politic are these, A, B, C, and all such others as shall hereafter be admitted and made free of the Company and society hereafter mentioned shall be, etc., one body politic and Corporate, in fact and name, by the name of the Governor and Company of the Massachusetts Bay in New England. And that from henceforth forever there shall be one Governor, one Deputy-Governor, and eighteen Assistants of the same Company, to be from time to time, constituted, elected, and chosen, out of the Freemen of the said Company for the time being; in such manner and form, as hereafter in these presents is expressed, which said officers shall apply themselves to take care for the best disposing and ordering of the great business and affairs of, for, and concerning, the said lands and premises hereby mentioned to be granted, and the plantation thereof, and the government of the people there."

(2) The distribution of power follows, in these words ensuing:— "That the Government of the said Company for the time being or, in his absence by occasion of sickness or otherwise, the Deputy-Governor for the time being, shall have authority from time to time, upon all occasions, to give order, for the assembling of the said Company, and calling them together, to consult and advise of the businesses and affairs of the said Company.

"And that the said Governor, Deputy-Governor, and Assistants of the said Company for the time being shall or may once every month or oftener at their pleasures, assemble and hold and keep a Court, or Assembly of themselves, for the better ordering and directing of their affairs:

"And that any seven, or more persons of the Assistants, together with the Governor or Deputy-Governor so assembled, shall be said, taken, held, and reputed to be, and shall be, a full and sufficient Court or Assembly of the said Company, for the handling, ordering, and dispatching of all such businesses and occurrents, as shall from time to time happen touching or concerning the said Company or plantation."

Then follows a clause, whereby liberty is granted to hold four general Courts in the year, wherein (with the advice and consent of the major part of the freemen) they may admit others to the freedom of the Company, they may make all subordinate officers, and make laws and constitutions, for their welfare and good government.

Then followeth a clause for the annual election of all their officers in these words ensuing:—

"That yearly once in the year forever, namely on the last Wednesday in Easter Term yearly, the Governor, Deputy-Governor, and Assistants of the said Company shall be in the General Court or Assembly, to be held for that day or time, newly chosen for the year ensuing, by such greater part of the said Company, for the time being, then and there present as is aforesaid."

Then follows another branch, whereby, in any of their General

Courts, any insufficient, or delinquent Officer (of what sort soever) may be removed and another forthwith put in place.

The last clause is for the governing of the inhabitants within the plantation. For it being the manner for such as procured patents for Virginia, Bermudas, and the West Indies, to keep the chief government in the hands of the Company residing in England (and so this was intended and with much difficulty we got it abscinded) this clause is inserted in this and all other patents whereby the Company in England might establish a Government and Officers here in any form used in England, as Governor and Council, Justices of the Peace, Mayor, Bailiffs, etc.; and accordingly Mr. Endicott and others with him, were established a Governor and Council here, before the Government was transferred hither: and that clause is expressed in these words:—

"It shall and may be lawful, to and for the Governor, etc., and such of the Freemen of the said Company for the time being, as shall be assembled in any of their General Courts aforesaid, or in any other Courts to be specially summoned and assembled for that purpose, or the greater part of them, whereof the Governor or Deputy-Governor, and six of the Assistants to be always seven; from time to time, to make, ordain, and establish all manner of wholesome and reasonable orders, laws, statutes, and ordinances, directions, and instructions, not contrary to this our Realm of England: as well for settling of the forms and ceremonies of government and magistracy, fit and necessary for the said plantation, and inhabitants there, and for naming and styling of all sorts of officers, both superior and inferior, which they shall find needful for that Government and plantation; and the distinguishing and setting forth of the several duties, powers, and limits of every such office, etc., for disposing and ordering the election of such of the said officers as shall be annual, etc., and for setting down forms of oaths and for ministering of them, etc., and for the directing, ruling, and disposing of all matters and things, whereby our said people inhabitants there, may be so religiously, peaceably, and civilly governed, etc."

Thus it appears that this Government is not arbitrary in the foundation of it, but regulated in all the parts of it.

(2) It will be yet further found by the positive laws thereof:

And first by that of (3) 14—1634; where it is declared, that the General Court only may make freemen; make laws; choose General Officers, as Governor, Deputy, Assistants, Treasurer, etc.; remove such; set out their power and duty; raise moneys; dispose of lands in proprieties; not to be dissolved but by consent of the major part. The freemen of the several towns may send their deputies to every General Court who may do all that the body of freemen might do, except in election of magistrates and officers.

And in the sixty-seventh Liberty it is thus described, viz.—"It is the constant liberty of the freemen, to choose yearly, at the Court of Election, out of the freemen, all the general officers of this jurisdiction. If they please to discharge them at the Court of Elections, by vote, they may do it without showing cause; but if at any other General Court, we hold it due justice, that the reasons thereof be alleged and proved. By general officers, we mean our Governor, Deputy-Governor, Assistants, Treasurer, General of our wars, and our Admiral at sea; and such as are, or may be hereafter, of like general nature."

(3) According to these fundamental rules and positive laws, the course of government hath been carried on in the practice of public administrations to this very day, and where any considerable obliquity hath been discerned, it hath been soon brought to the rule and redressed; for it is not possible in the infancy of a plantation, subject to so many and variable occurrents to hold so exactly to rules, as when a state is once settled.

By what hath been already manifested, this Government is freed from any semblance of arbitrariness either in the form of it, or the general officers in it, which is the first branch in the description of Arbitrary Government.

The other branch, (wherein the main question lies) is concerning the rule so as if it shall appear also, that the Governor and other officers are prescribed such a rule, as may be required of them in all their administrations, then it must needs be granted, that this Government (even in the present state thereof) is, in no respect, arbitrary.

I might show a clear rule out of the Patent itself, but seeing it is more particularly (and as it were *membratim*) delineated in later laws. I will begin there, (3) 25—1636. It was ordered, that until a body of fundamental laws (agreeable to the Word of God) were established, all causes should be heard and determined, according to the laws already in force; and where no law is, there as near the law of God as may be. To omit many particular laws enacted upon occasion, I will set down only the first authority in the Liberties: which is as here followeth:—"No man's life shall be taken away; no man's honor or good name shall be stained; no man's person shall be arrested, restrained, banished, dismembered, or any ways punished; no man shall be deprived of his wife or children; no man's goods or estate shall be taken away from him, or any way damaged, under colour of law or countenance of authority, unless it be by the virtue or equity of some express law of the country, warranting the same, established by a General Court and sufficiently published; or, in case of the defect of a law in any particular case, by the word of God, and in capital cases, or in cases concerning dismembering or banishment, according to that word, to be judged by the General Court."

By these it appears, that the officers of this body politic have a rule to walk by in all their administrations, which rule is the Word of God, and such conclusions and deductions as are, or shall be, regularly drawn from thence.

All commonwealths have had some principles, or fundamentals, from which they have framed deductions to particular cases, as occasion hath required. And though no Commonwealth ever had, or can have, a particular positive rule to dispense power or justice by in every single case, yet where the fundamentals or general rule hold forth such direction as no great damage or injury can befall, either the whole, or any particular part, by any unjust sentence or disorderly proceeding, without manifest breach of such general rule, there the rule may be required, and so the Government is regular and not arbitrary.

The fundamentals which God gave to the Commonwealth of Israel were a sufficient rule to them, to guide all their affairs; we having the same, with all the additions, explanations, and deductions, which have followed; it is not possible we should want a rule in any case, if God give wisdom to discern it.

There are some few cases only (beside the capitals) wherein the penalty is prescribed; and the Lord could have done the like in others, if He had so pleased; but having appointed governments upon earth, to be His vicegerents, He hath given them those few as presidents to direct them and to exercise His gifts in them (Deut. xvii; 9, 10, 11). In the most difficult cases, the judges in supreme authority were to show the sentence of the law; whence three things may be observed: (1) this sentence was to be declared out of the law established, though not obvious to common understanding; (2) this was to be expected in that ordinance; therefore (v. 19,) the King was to have a copy of the law, and to read them all the days of his life; (3) such a sentence was not ordained to be provided before the case fell out, but *pro re nata,* when occasion required, God promised to be present in his own ordinance, to improve such gifts as he should please to confer upon such as he should call to place of government. In the Scripture there are some forms of prayers and of sermons set down; yet no man will infer from thence that ministers should have sermons and prayers prescribed them for every occasion; for that would destroy the ordinance of the ministry, *i. e.,* a reading priest might serve in that office, without any learning or other gifts of the Spirit. So if all penalties were prescribed, the jury should state the case, and the book hold forth the sentence, and any schoolboy might pronounce it; then what need were there of any special wisdom, learning, courage, zeal or faithfulness in a judge?

This being so great a question now on foot, about prescript penalties it will be of use to search as deep into it as we may by the light of Scripture, approved patterns, and other rational arguments; not tying our discourse to method, but laying down things as they come to hand.

England in the right constitution, is not an Arbitrary Government, nor is ours of the Massachusetts; yet juries, both there and here, give damages which (in vulgar sense) are arbitrary, in most cases: as in actions of slander, trespass, battery, breach of covenant, etc.; all which concern the people's liberties no less than fines and other penalties; And if twelve men, who have no calling to office, may (in expectation of God's assistance) be trusted with men's estates in a way of distributive justice without a prescript rule, etc., why may not those whose calling and office hath promise of assistance, have like trust reposed in them, in vindictive justice?

In the Liberties enacted here of purpose to prevent Arbitrary Government, there are near forty Laws, to the violation whereof no penalty is prescribed, nor was ever moved.

God may pronounce sentence against an offender, before the offence be committed, both by his absolute sovereignty, and also because he foreseeth all facts, with all their circumstances; and besides the least degree of the same offence deserves more than that full punishment before his Justice, but man must proceed according to his Commission; by which he cannot sentence another before he hath offended; and the offence examined, proved, laid to the rule, and weighed by all considerable circumstances, and liberty given to the party to answer for himself: nor is there anything more prejudicial to a subject's liberty, than to be sentenced before his cause be heard.

England is a state of long standing, yet we have had more positive and more wholesome laws enacted in our short time than they had in many hundred years. They have indeed some laws with prescribed penalties annexed, but they are for the most part so small as do undervalue the least degree of those offences; they have twelve pence for an Oath: five shillings for drunkenness, etc.; but for all great offences and misdemeanors, as perjury, forgery, conspiracies, cozenages, oppression, riot, batteries, and other breaches of the peace, etc., there is no penalty prescribed; how it is in other states in Europe, I cannot relate (because we know not their laws) otherwise than what appears in their histories, where we find some great offences punished by the discretion of their judges.

Justice ought to render to every man according to his deservings, eye for eye, hand for hand, etc.; and (Luke xii. 47) the servant, who transgressed against knowledge was to be beaten with more stripes than he who transgressed of ignorance. If we had a law, that every lie should be punished forty shillings, and two offenders should be convict at the same time, the one a youth of honest conversation, never known to lie before; and now, suddenly surprised with fear of some discredit, had told a lie wherein was no danger of harm to any other; the other an old notorious liar, and his lie contrived of purpose for a pernicious end: it were not just to punish both these alike. As forty shillings were too little for the one, so it were too much for the other. Besides, penalties (we know) coming of *pæna*, should cause pain or grief to the offenders. It must be an affliction, yet not a destruction except in capital or other heinous crimes: but in prescript penalties, authority shoots at adventure; if the same penalty hits a rich man, it pains him not, it is no affliction to him; but if it lights upon a poor man, it breaks his back.

Every law must be just in every part of it, but if the penalty annexed be unjust, how can it be held forth as a just law? To prescribe a penalty must be by some rule, otherwise it is an usurpation of God's prerogative; but where the law-makers, or declarers, cannot find a rule for prescribing a penalty, if it come before the judges *pro re nata,* there it is determinable by a certain rule, viz., by an ordinance set up of God for that purpose, which hath a sure promise of Divine assistance (Exo. xxi. 22; Deut. xvi. 18). "Judges and Officers shalt thou make, etc., and they shall judge the people with just judgment." (Deut. xxv. 1, 2, and xvii. 9, 10, 11). If a Law were made that if any man were found drunken he should be punished by the judges according to the merit of his offence, this is a just law, because it is warranted by a rule; but if a certain penalty were prescribed, this would not be just, because it wants a rule, but when such a case is brought before the judges, and the quality of the person and other circumstances considered, they shall find a rule to judge by; as if Nabal, and Uriah, and one of the strong drunkards of Ephraim, were all three together accused before the judges for drunkenness, they could so proportion their several sentences, according to the several natures and degrees of their offences, as a just and divine sentence might appear in them all; for a divine sentence is in the lips of the King, his mouth transgresseth not in judgment (Prov. xvi.), but no such promise was ever made to a paper sentence of human authority or invention. He who hath promised His servants to teach them what to answer, even in that hour when they shall be brought before judgment seats, etc., will also teach his ministers, the judges, what sentence to pronounce, if they will also observe His word and trust in Him. "Care not for the morrow, etc." is a rule of general extent, to all cases where our providence may either cross with some rule or ordinance of His, or may occasion us to rely more upon our own strengths and means, than upon His grace and blessing. In the sentence which Solomon gave between the two harlots (1 Kings iii.

28), it is said that all Israel heard of the judgment which the King had judged; and they feared the King, for they saw that the wisdom of God was in him to do judgment. See here, how the wisdom of God was glorified, and the authority of the judge strengthened by this sentence; whereas in men's prescript sentences neither of these can be attained; but if the sentence hit right, all is ascribed to the wisdom of our ancestors; if otherwise, it is endured as a necessary evil, since it may not be altered.

Prescript penalties take away the use of admonition, which is also a divine sentence and an ordinance of God, warranted by Scripture, as appears in Solomon's admonition to Adonijah, and Nehemiah's to those that break the Sabbath (Ecel. xii. 11, 12); "The words of the wise are as goads, and as nails fastened by the masters of assemblies—by these (my son) be admonished." (Prov. xxix. 1; Isa. xi. 4; Prov. xvii. 10). "A reproof entereth more into a wise man, than a hundred stripes into a fool."

Judges are Gods upon earth; therefore, in their administrations, they are to hold forth the wisdom and mercy of God, (which are His attributes) as well as His Justice, as occasion shall require either in respect of the quality of the person, or for a more general good, or evident repentance, in some cases of less public consequence, or avoiding imminent danger to the State, and such like prevalent considerations. (Exo. xxii. 8, 9). For theft and such like trespasses, double restitution was appointed by the Law; but (Lev. vi. 2, 5) in such cases, if the party confessed his sin and brought his offering, he should only restore the principal and add a fifth part thereto. Adultery and incest deserved death, by the Law, in Jacob's time (as appears by Judah his sentence, in the case of Tamar); yet Reuben was punished only with the loss of his birthright, because he was a patriarch. David his life was not taken away for his adultery and murder (but he was otherwise punished) in respect of public interest and advantage; he was valued at ten thousand common men. Bathsheba was not put to death for her adultery, because the King's desire had with her the force of a law. Abiathar was not put to death for his treason, because of his former good service and faithfulness. Shemei was reprieved for a time, and had his pardon in his own power, because of his profession of repentance in such a season.

Those which broke the Sabbath in Nehemiah his time, were not put to death, but first admonished, because the state was not settled, etc. Joab was not put to death for his murders in David's time, for avoiding imminent public danger; the sons of Zeruiah had the advantage of David, by their interest in the men of war; and the commonwealth could not yet spare them. But if judges be tied to a prescript punishment, and no liberty left for dispensation or mitigation in any case, there is no place left for wisdom or mercy; whereas Solomon sayeth (Prov. xx. 28): "Mercy and truth preserve the King, and his throne is upholden by mercy."

I would know by what rule we may take upon us, to prescribe penalties, where God prescribes none. If it be answered, "From God's example," I might reply (1), God prescribes none except capital, but only in such cases as are between party and party, and that is rather in a way of satisfaction to the party wronged, than to justice and intention. (2), God's examples are not warrants for us to go against God's rules; our rule is to give a just sentence, which we cannot do (in most cases) before the offence is committed, etc. Five shillings now may·be more than twenty shillings hereafter, and *e contra*. If examples in Scripture be warrant for us to proceed against rule, then we may pass by murders, adulteries, idolatries, etc., without capital punishments; then we might put the children to death for parents' offences, etc.

If we should inquire also of the end of prescribing penalties, it can be no other but this, to prevent oppression of the people by unjust sentences; then I am again to seek of a rule to weaken the power and justice of an ordinance of God, through distrust of His providence, and promise of assistance in His own ordinance. Who must give the lawmakers wisdom, etc., to prescribe sentences? Must not God? And may we not then trust Him to give as much wisdom, etc., to such judges as He shall set up after us? It is said when they had judges by God's appointment, God was with the judge. So may we still believe that if our posterity all choose judges according to God, He will be with the judges in time to come, as well as with the present.

It may be further demanded, what power we have over the property and estates of the succeeding generations? If we should now prescribe where our posterity should dwell, what quantities of land they should till, what places they should tend unto, what diet they should use, what clothes they should wear, etc., by what rule could we challenge this power? Yet we have example for some of these in Scripture, as of Jonadab, the son of Rechab, etc.; but no man will take these as warrants for us to lay such injunctions upon those which come after us, because they are to have the same interest and freedom in their estates and properties that we have in ours.

And for preventing of oppression, etc., is there no way to help that but by breach of rule? Shall we run into manifest injustice for fear of I know not what future danger of it? Is there not a clear way of help in such cases, by appeal, or petition, to the highest authority? If this will not relieve in a particular case, we shall then be in a very ill case for all our prescript penalties. Besides, there may be such a general law made (as in Magna Charta) that may prevent the over-throwing of men's estates, or lands, etc., by fines, etc., (and I think it is needful, as any law of Liberty we have), whereby the judges may be restrained within certain limits, which, (if occasion should require to exceed,) may be referred to the General Court; and in capital punishments, a liberty in such and such cases, to redeem them at a certain rate. This would sufficiently assure the proper persons and estates from any great oppression, if, withal, our Courts of Judicature were kept but by three or five magistrates at most, which may well be ordered, without any deviation from our Patent. And so the greater number of magistrates should be free from en-gagement in any case which might come to a review upon appeal or petition.

It is an error so to conceit of laws as if they could not be perfect without penalties annexed, for they are as truly distinct as light and darkness. Law was created with and in man, and so is natural to him, but penalty is positive and accidental. Law is *bonum simpliciter,* but *poena* is *simpliciter malum in subiecto;* therefore laws may be declared and given without any penalties annexed.

Isa. x, 1: Woe to them that decree unrighteous decrees: and write grievousness, which they have prescribed; so that where the penalty proves grievous by the unrighteousness of a prescript decree, it will draw a woe after it, as well as unrighteous sentences; (Deut. xxv, 15)

"Thou shall have a perfect and just weight and measure." If God be so strict in commutative justice that every act therein must be by a just and perfect rule, what warrant have we to think that we may dispense distributive or vindictive justice to our brethren by guess, when we prescribe a certain measure to an uncertain merit?

But it will be objected, *volenti non fit injuria;* the people giving us power to make laws to bind them, they do implicitly give their consent to them. To this it may be answered that where they put themselves into our power to bind them to laws and penalties, they can intend no other but such as are just and righteous; and although their implicit consent may bind them to outward obedience, yet it neither ties them to satisfaction, nor frees such law-makers from unrighteousness, nor the law itself from injustice, nor will such a law be a sufficient warrant to the conscience of the judge, to pronounce such a sentence as he knows to be apparently disproportionable to the offence brought before him.

Although my argument conclude against prescript penalties indefinitely, yet I do not deny but they may be lawful in some cases; for an universal affirmative position may be true, though it comprehend not every particular, as when we say, "All the country was rated to such a charge," no man will conceive that every person and every woman, etc., was rated; and when we say such an one was cast out by the whole church, this is a true speech (to common intendment) though every particular member did not consent. Where any penalty may be prescribed by a rule, so as the judge may pronounce a just sentence, I have formerly and shall still join in it.

We will now answer such objections as are made against the liberty required to be left to judges in their sentences.

1, ob. Judges are subject to temptations, if their sentences be not prescribed.

Ans. 1. We may not transgress rules, to avoid temptations; for God will have His servants exercised with temptations, that the power of His grace may be made manifest in man's infirmity. A master will not send his servant about his business in a dark night, to avoid temptations of ill-company or the like which he may possibly meet with in the day time; nor will any Christian man take in his corn or hay before it be ready, for avoiding a temptation of taking it in upon the Sabbath. We do not forbid wine to be brought to us, though we know it is a great occasion of temptation to sin.

2. Those who make laws and prescribe penalties are also men subject to temptations, and may also miscarry through ignorance, heedlessness, or sinister respects; and it is not hard to prove, that the lawmakers, in all states, have committed more, and more pernicious errors than the judges, and there is good reason for it: (1) they, supposing themselves tied to no rule, nor liable to any account, are in the more danger of being mislead; (2) he who prescribes a punishment in a case wherein no person stands before him to be judged, cannot be so wary of shedding innocent blood, or sparing a guilty person, or committing other injustice, as the judge who hath the person and cause before him. When Saul prescribed that capital sentence against such as should taste aught before night, if Jonathan's case had then been before him, he could have judged otherwise. (3) Lawmakers have not so clear a calling in prescribing penalties, as judges have in passing sentences, and therefore there cannot be expected the like blessing of assistance from God. Judges are necessarily tied to give sentence in a cause before them, but lawmakers are not so bound to prescribe sentences.

3. If a judge should sometimes err in his sentence, through misprision or temptation, the error or fault is his own; and the injury or damage extends not far; but an error in the law resteth upon the ordinance itself, and the hurt of it may reach far, even to posterity. There is more righteousness and dishonor in one unjust law than in many unjust sentences.

2, ob. God prescribed some certain penalties, and that in cases where offences do usually vary in their degree and merit.

Ans. 1. We have showed before, how God might do it, in regard to His absolute sovereignty.

2. It is no injustice to Him, because the least degree of the smallest offence (before His judgment seat) deserves the highest degree of punishment.

3. In some of these (as in theft) He varieth the punishment according to the measure and nature of the offence. In others as death, perpetual solitude, etc., being the just reward of such offences in their simple nature, they have not a fit subject, for an increase of punish-

ment to take place upon. He who is put to death for adultery cannot die again for incest concurring therewith, and he who is adjudged to perpetual servitude for stealing a hundred pounds cannot be capable of a further sentence for battery.

4. In all or most of those offences, the penalty was in way of satisfaction to such as were damnified therewith, and in such cases justice will not allow a judge any liberty to alter or remit any thing, nor can any circumstance lead to qualification. A rich man hath the same right of satisfaction for his goods stolen from him as a poor man, and the poorest man's life is the life of man, as well as a prince's.

5. These precedents were given to the judges not with direction to prescribe penalties to other laws that had none, but with command-ment to give judgment in all cases, by the equity of these: (there are some forms of prayer and sermons in Scripture, but this doth not prove *ergo* all, etc.)

3, ob. If the determination of the law were left to the judges, that were Arbitrary Government; and is it not in reason the same, if the punishment of the transgression of the law be committed?

Ans. The reason is not alike in both cases.

1. The determination of law belongs properly to God: He is the only lawgiver; but He hath given power and gifts to man to inter-pret His laws; and this belongs principally to the highest authority in a commonwealth, and subordinately to other magistrates and judges according to their several places.

2. The law is always the same, and not changeable by any circum-stances of aggravation or extenuation, as the penalty is, and there-fore draws a certain guilt upon every transgressor, whether he sin of ignorance, or against knowledge, or presumptuously; and there-fore laws or the interpretations of them, may be prescribed without any danger, because no event can alter the reason, or justice of them, as it may of punishments.

3. The law is more general, and lieth as a burden upon all persons and at all times; but the penalty reaches to none but transgressors, and to such, only when they are brought under sentence, and not before.

4. It is needful that all men should know the laws, and their true

meanings, because they are bound to them, and the safety and welfare of the commonwealth consists in the observation of them; therefore it is needful they should be stated and declared as soon as is possible; but there is not the like necessity or use of declaring their penalties beforehand, for they who are godly and virtuous, will observe them, for conscience and virtue's sake; and for such as must be held in by fear of punishment, it is better they should be kept in fear of a greater punishment than to take liberty to transgress through the contempt of a smaller.

4, ob. It is safe for the commonwealth to have penalties prescribed, because we know not what magistrates or judges we may have hereafter.

Ans. 1. God foresaw that there would be corrupt judges in Israel, yet He left most penalties to their determination.

2. There is no wisdom of any state can so provide but that in many things of greatest concernment they must confide in some men; and so it is in all human affairs: the wisest merchants, and the most wary, are forced to repose great trust in the wisdom and faithfulness of their servants, factors, masters of their ships, etc. All states, in their generals of war, admirals, ambassadors, treasurers, etc., and these are causes of more public consequence than the sentence of a judge in matters of misdemeanor, or other smaller offences.

3. When we have provided against all common and probable events, we may and ought to trust God for safety from such dangers as are only possible, but not likely, to come upon us; especially when our striving to prevent such possible dangers may hazard the deprivation or weakening of a present good, or may draw those or other evils nearer upon us.

This discourse is run out to more length than was intended: the conclusion is this: The Government of the Massachusetts consists of Magistrates and Freemen: in the one is placed the authority, in the other, the liberty of the commonwealth. Either hath power to act, both alone, and both together, yet by a distinct power, the one of liberty, the other of authority. The Freemen act of themselves in electing their magistrates and officers; the magistrates act alone in all occurrences out of court; and both act together in the General Court; yet all limited by certain rules, both in the greater and smaller affairs, so as the Government is regular in a mixed aristocraty, and no ways arbitrary.

The returns of the Committee of the House of Deputies concerning the Book about Arbitrary Government, in the examination thereof; and the votes of the House passed upon each particular, viz.:

In the first part thereof:

1. Concerning the definition therein made, we conceive it is defective.

2. Concerning the distinction therein made of the body politic, and the members thereof, in attributing authority to the one, and only liberty to the other, we find not any such distinction in the Patent.

3. Concerning the clause recited therein (respecting the General Court) which gives only liberty to the freemen to advise and counsel, instead of power and authority (which the Patent allows), we conceive it a taking away of the power and privileges of the freemen.

In the second part of the book, which concerns the rule by which a people should be governed, we find these dangerous positions:

1. That general rules are sufficient to clear a state from Arbitrary Government.

2. That judges ought to have liberty to vary from such general rules when they see cause.

In the following of the first of those two positions there are many dangerous passages, and bitter censuring of all penal laws: as:—

1. That they are paper sentences of human authority and invention.

2. That men's prescript sentences do deny and exclude both the wisdom of God, and the authority of the judge.

3. That to prescribe laws with certain penalties is an usurping of God's authority.

4. That a sentence ought not to be provided before the case fall out, but immediate assistance to be expected.

5. That particular laws including certain penalties are not just, wanting rule.

The introduction of particular instances which are brought to prove this second position, with the reasons and consequences, are pernicious and dangerous.

per Robert Bridges,

By order, etc.

Governor Winthrop's comments on this report, as indorsed by him on the same sheet on which he had carefully copied it, are as follows:—

Answer: the Committee have been mistaken in most of their objections.

1. The Title shows that the author intended not any definition, but a description only, and to make it the more full and clear, he lays it down both affirmatively and negatively; yet a logician may frame it into a definition,—thus Arbitrary Government is a Government exercised without a rule, but the description is false by the cause and by the effects.

2. There is no such distinction as is observed between the body politic and the members thereof, for that were to distinguish between the whole and the parts; but the distinction between the members of that body, giving authority to the one and power and liberty to the other, is warranted by the Patent (as in other places so) particularly in that clause which sayeth that the Governor, etc., shall call the freemen to consult and advise, etc., which is an act of liberty and not of authority; and for the other part of their power, which is matter of election, the late Body of Liberties sayeth it is their constant liberty, not authority.

In the second part:

1. We find not any such position that general rules are sufficient to clear a state of arbitrary government, but we find that the word of God and the laws here established being appointed by order of Court as a rule for the present, are such a rule as may be required by the judges in all their administrations, because a rule may from thence be derived (if God give wisdom to discern it) in any particular case which may fall out; otherwise the Law of God were not perfect, and from what better grounds shall the lawmakers draw all future laws and prescribed penalties.

But if the author had expressed himself in the very words of the position yet it will admit a safe construction, for all laws (not limited to particular parties or occasions) are general rules, and may be so called, though they have a certain penalty annexed.

2. Nor will the book own the second position in the words expressed, but this the judges both from their offices (being God's vicegerents) and from diverse examples in Scripture, which seem to hold forth so much, that some liberty ought to be left to judges in some cases, upon special occasions to hold forth the mercy of God, as well as His justice; nor do we consider that either in the Commonwealth of Israel, or in any other, the judges have been wholly restrained of such liberty.

In the following argument:—

If the Committee had found such dangerous passages as they intimate, they should have done well to have imparted their particular observations therein unto us, that we might have considered of them, for want whereof it cannot be expected we should deliver any opinion about them. The like we may say for such bitter censurings as they mention, only it is usual for men to call such things bitter which themselves disrelish, though they may be harmless and wholesome notwithstanding.

For the five particulars mentioned, they are delivered as arguments or the consectaries thereof, so as the arguments must first be avoided before any judgment can be given about them.

The examples which the author allegeth out of Scripture are only to show how God hath sometimes (in His wisdom and mercy) dispensed with the rigor of His own law; and that princes have sometimes done the like upon public or other prevalent considerations, which cannot be denied to be a truth; and for the warrant they had for it, being (at the most) disputable, it was as free for him to deliver them in his own and some other learned and godly men's apprehensions as it is for others who differ therein; and there can be no more danger in this than in other books and sermons, where the same or other passages of Scripture are truly reported, though not applied to the sense of every godly man, as if one should reason thus: David put the Amorites to torture, therefore, in some cases it is lawful so to do. This will not be judged a pernicious doctrine, though some godly men do question the warrantableness of the example. The like may be said of all such examples in Scripture as are controverted among godly and learned men; but it is otherwise in such places as are not questionable, as if a man should reason thus: David sentenced Mephibosheth before he heard him; therefore it is lawful for judge so to do. This might truly be said to be a pernicious doctrine; or if one should argue thus: Saul made a law with a prescript penalty of death to him that should transgress it; therefore it had been just that Jonathan should have been put to death for transgressing that law; or therefore it is lawful for princes, etc., to prescribe penalties at their own pleasures;—these might be judged to be pernicious doctrines, because the example is unquestionable, etc.

THE AUTHOR'S REVIEW OF HIS WRITING

That which gave me occasion first to inquire after a rule for prescript penalties, was the inequality I saw in some prescribed sentences upon the breach of diverse moral laws; and proceeding in this inquiry, I kept my intention still upon that subject, without respect to such laws as are merely positive, having their authority only and wholly from human institutions: therefore you shall find that all my instances are of that kind, and all my arguments look that way, as in the instances I bring of the laws of England. If I intended the positive and statute laws, it had been a great mistake, for I know well that most of the later Statute Laws have their penalties prescribed, and it must needs be so, for such as are merely positive; for a judge can have no rule for his sentence upon the breach of such a law, except he have it from the law itself: as, for instance, if the law which forbids any man to kill an hare or partridge with a gun, had not also set down the penalty, the judge could not have found out any, which might have been just, because no law of God or nature makes such an act any offence or transgression. But for the Common Laws of England (which are the ancient laws, and of far more esteem for their wisdom and equity than the Statute Laws,) they had no penalties prescribed; and it may be conceived that for such of them as were grounded upon the Word of God, and the light of nature, there must needs be that in the same Word, and in the same light of nature (especially where the image of God in man is in part renewed by Christ) which may lead us to a just punishment for the transgressor of such a law. Nor do I oppose all prescript penalties in moral cases, but only such as do cross some clear rules in the Word of God, as will appear by all my arguments. And for avoiding all danger to the subject for want of prescript penalties in some cases, you may see that to require some such law to be made, as may limit judges within such bounds of moderation as may prevent such dangers, and [it] is one of my express conclusions in the first page, that judges ought to be tied to a rule, and such a rule as may be required of them in all their administrations, and therefore upon what ground I should be charged to assert Arbitrary Government, and that judges should have liberty to do what they may, I leave to your judgment.

As for laws, you shall find also that I conclude the necessity of declaring and stating them, so as all the people may know them, for I ever held it unjust to require of men the obedience of any law which they may not (by common intendment) take notice of. Answerable thereunto hath been my practice. All the useful laws we have had my consent, and such poor help as the Lord enabled me to yield to them; some of which have prescribed penalties, and where I have withheld my consent to any such penalties I have given my reasons for it, which have been such as in some cases have satisfied the Court, and therein I have taken no more liberty than is allowed to every member of the Court. I will not justify every passage in my book: there are two or three words that offence hath been taken at, and although I can give a safe account of them, yet I must confess they do not now please me, but when the matter is good, and the intention of the writer honest, the Lord forbids us to make a man an offender in word.

Whatsoever is erroneous (I say as I did from the first) I shall leave it to its due censure; but for all that is of God, and of the Truth, or the sincerity of my intentions herein to the public weal, or the liberty I had by my place to propound such considerations to the Court, if these be questioned I must stand and fall with them.

JOHN WINTHROP.

THE INSTRUMENT OF GOVERNMENT

(1653)

[The Instrument of Government is important in the history of written constitutions. It was adopted by Cromwell and his Council of Officers on December 16, 1653, and under it Cromwell assumed the office of Lord Protector. When the Parliament for which it provides met in September, 1654, it passed a constitution of which the *Instrument* was the basis.]

THE government of the Commonwealth of England, Scotland, and Ireland, and the dominions thereunto belonging.

I. That the supreme legislative authority of the Commonwealth of England, Scotland, and Ireland, and the dominions thereunto belonging, shall be and reside in one person, and the people assembled in Parliament; the style of which person shall be the Lord Protector of the Commonwealth of England, Scotland, and Ireland.

II. That the exercise of the chief magistracy and the administration of the government over the said countries and dominions, and the people thereof, shall be in the Lord Protector, assisted with a council, the number whereof shall not exceed twenty-one, nor be less than thirteen.

III. That all writs, processes, commissions, patents, grants, and other things, which now run in the name and style of the keepers of the liberty of England by authority of Parliament, shall run in the name and style of the Lord Protector, from whom, for the future, shall be derived all magistracy and honours in these three nations; and have the power of pardons (except in case of murders and treason) and benefit of all forfeitures for the public use; and shall govern the said countries and dominions in all things by the advice of the council, and according to these presents and the laws.

IV. That the Lord Protector, the Parliament sitting, shall dispose and order the militia and forces, both by sea and land, for the peace and good of the three nations, by consent of Parliament; and that the

Lord Protector, with the advice and consent of the major part of the council, shall dispose and order the militia for the ends aforesaid in the intervals of Parliament.

V. That the Lord Protector, by the advice aforesaid, shall direct in all things concerning the keeping and holding of a good correspondency with foreign kings, princes, and states; and also, with the consent of the major part of the council, have the power of war and peace.

VI. That the laws shall not be altered, suspended, abrogated, or repealed, nor any new law made, nor any tax, charge, or imposition laid upon the people, but by common consent in Parliament, save only as is expressed in the thirtieth article.

VII. That there shall be a Parliament summoned to meet at Westminster upon the third day of September, 1654, and that successively a Parliament shall be summoned once in every third year, to be accounted from the dissolution of the present Parliament.

VIII. That neither the Parliament to be next summoned, nor any successive Parliaments, shall, during the time of five months, to be accounted from the day of their first meeting, be adjourned, prorogued, or dissolved, without their own consent.

IX. That as well the next as all other successive Parliaments, shall be summoned and elected in manner hereafter expressed; that is to say, the persons to be chosen within England, Wales, the Isles of Jersey, Guernsey, and the town of Berwick-upon-Tweed, to sit and serve in Parliament, shall be, and not exceed, the number of four hundred. The persons to be chosen within Scotland, to sit and serve in Parliament, shall be, and not exceed, the number of thirty; and the persons to be chosen to sit in Parliament for Ireland shall be, and not exceed, the number of thirty.

X. That the persons to be elected to sit in Parliament from time to time, for the several counties of England, Wales, the Isles of Jersey and Guernsey, and the town of Berwick-upon-Tweed, and all places within the same respectively, shall be according to the proportions and numbers hereafter expressed: that is to say,

Bedfordshire, 5; Bedford Town, 1; Berkshire, 5; Abingdon, 1; Reading, 1; Buckinghamshire, 5; Buckingham Town, 1; Aylesbury, 1; Wycomb,

1; Cambridgeshire, 4; Cambridge Town, 1; Cambridge University, 1; Isle of Ely, 2; Cheshire, 4; Chester, 1; Cornwall, 8; Launceston, 1; Truro, 1; Penryn, 1; East Looe and West Looe, 1; Cumberland, 2; Carlisle, 1; Derbyshire, 4; Derby Town, 1; Devonshire, 11; Exeter, 2; Plymouth, 2; Clifton, Dartmouth, Hardness, 1; Totnes, 1; Barnstable, 1; Tiverton, 1; Honiton, 1; Dorsetshire, 6; Dorchester, 1; Weymouth and Melcomb-Regis, 1; Lyme-Regis, 1; Poole, 1; Durham, 2; City of Durham, 1; Essex, 13; Malden, 1; Colchester, 2; Gloucestershire, 5; Gloucester, 2; Tewkesbury, 1; Cirencester, 1; Herefordshire, 4; Hereford, 1; Leominster, 1; Hertfordshire, 5; St. Alban's, 1; Hertford, 1; Huntingdonshire, 3; Huntingdon, 1; Kent, 11; Canterbury, 2; Rochester, 1; Maidstone, 1; Dover, 1; Sandwich, 1; Queenborough, 1; Lancashire, 4; Preston, 1; Lancaster, 1; Liverpool, 1; Manchester, 1; Leicestershire, 4; Leicester, 2; Lincolnshire, 10; Lincoln, 2; Boston, 1; Grantham, 1; Stamford, 1; Great Grimsby, 1; Middlesex, 4; London, 6; Westminster, 2; Monmouthshire, 3; Norfolk, 10; Norwich, 2; Lynn-Regis, 2; Great Yarmouth, 2; Northamptonshire, 6; Peterborough, 1; Northampton, 1; Nottinghamshire, 4; Nottingham, 2; Northumberland, 3; Newcastle-upon-Tyne, 1; Berwick, 1; Oxfordshire, 5; Oxford City, 1; Oxford University, 1; Woodstock, 1; Rutlandshire, 2; Shropshire, 4; Shrewsbury, 2; Bridgnorth, 1; Ludlow, 1; Staffordshire, 3; Lichfield, 1; Stafford, 1; Newcastle-under-Lyme, 1; Somersetshire, 11; Bristol, 2; Taunton, 2; Bath, 1; Wells, 1; Bridgwater, 1; Southamptonshire, 8; Winchester, 1; Southampton, 1; Portsmouth, 1; Isle of Wight, 2; Andover, 1; Suffolk, 10; Ipswich, 2; Bury St. Edmunds, 2; Dunwich, 1; Sudbury, 1; Surrey, 6; Southwark, 2; Guildford, 1; Reigate, 1; Sussex, 9; Chichester, 1; Lewes, 1; East Grinstead, 1; Arundel, 1; Rye, 1; Westmoreland, 2; Warwickshire, 4; Coventry, 2; Warwick, 1; Wiltshire, 10; New Sarum, 2; Marlborough, 1; Devizes, 1; Worcestershire, 5; Worcester, 2.

YORKSHIRE.—West Riding, 6; East Riding, 4; North Riding, 4; City of York, 2; Kingston-upon-Hull, 1; Beverley, 1; Scarborough, 1; Richmond, 1; Leeds, 1; Halifax, 1.

WALES.—Anglesey, 2; Brecknockshire, 2; Cardiganshire, 2; Carmarthenshire, 2; Carnarvonshire, 2; Denbighshire, 2; Flintshire, 2; Glamorganshire, 2; Cardiff, 1; Merionethshire, 1; Montgomeryshire, 2; Pembrokeshire, 2; Haverfordwest, 1; Radnorshire, 2.

The distribution of the persons to be chosen for Scotland and Ireland, and the several counties, cities, and places therein, shall be according to such proportions and number as shall be agreed upon and declared by the Lord Protector and the major part of the council, before the sending forth writs of summons for the next Parliament.

XI. That the summons to Parliament shall be by writ under the Great Seal of England, directed to the sheriffs of the several and respective counties, with such alteration as may suit with the present government, to be made by the Lord Protector and his council, which the Chancellor, Keeper, or Commissioners of the Great Seal shall seal, issue, and send abroad by warrant from the Lord Protector. If the Lord Protector shall not give warrant for issuing of writs of summons for the next Parliament, before the first of June, 1654, or for the Triennial Parliaments, before the first day of August in every third year, to be accounted as aforesaid; that then the Chancellor, Keeper, or Commissioners of the Great Seal for the time being, shall, without any warrant or direction, within seven days after the said first day of June, 1654, seal, issue, and send abroad writs of summons (changing therein what is to be changed as aforesaid) to the several and respective sheriffs of England, Scotland, and Ireland, for summoning the Parliament to meet at Westminster, the third day of September next; and shall likewise, within seven days after the said first day of August, in every third year, to be accounted from the dissolution of the precedent Parliament, seal, issue, and send forth abroad several writs of summons (changing therein what is to be changed) as aforesaid, for summoning the Parliament to meet at Westminster the sixth of November in that third year. That the said several and respective sheriffs, shall, within ten days after the receipt of such writ as aforesaid, cause the same to be proclaimed and published in every market-town within his county upon the market-days thereof, between twelve and three of the clock; and shall then also publish and declare the certain day of the week and month, for choosing members to serve in Parliament for the body of the said county, according to the tenor of the said writ, which shall be upon Wednesday five weeks after the date of the writ; and shall likewise declare the place where the election shall be made: for which purpose he shall appoint the most convenient place for the whole county to meet in; and shall send precepts for elections to be made in all and every city, town, borough, or place within his county, where elections are to be made by virtue of these presents, to the Mayor, Sheriff, or other head officer of such city, town, borough, or place, within three days after the receipt of such writ and writs; which the said Mayors,

Sheriffs, and officers respectively are to make publication of, and of the certain day for such elections to be made in the said city, town, or place aforesaid, and to cause elections to be made accordingly.

XII. That at the day and place of elections, the Sheriff of each county, and the said Mayors, Sheriffs, Bailiffs, and other head officers within their cities, towns, boroughs, and places respectively, shall take view of the said elections, and shall make return into the chancery within twenty days after the said elections, of the persons elected by the greater number of electors, under their hands and seals, between him on the one part, and the electors on the other part; wherein shall be contained, that the persons elected shall not have power to alter the government as it is hereby settled in one single person and a Parliament.

XIII. That the Sheriff, who shall wittingly and willingly make any false return, or neglect his duty, shall incur the penalty of 2000 marks of lawful English money; the one moiety to the Lord Protector, and the other moiety to such person as will sue for the same.

XIV. That all and every person and persons, who have aided, advised, assisted, or abetted in any war against the Parliament, since the first day of January 1641 (unless they have been since in the service of the Parliament, and given signal testimony of their good affection thereunto) shall be disabled and incapable to be elected, or to give any vote in the election of any members to serve in the next Parliament, or in the three succeeding Triennial Parliaments.

XV. That all such, who have advised, assisted, or abetted the rebellion of Ireland, shall be disabled and incapable for ever to be elected, or give any vote in the election of any member to serve in Parliament; as also all such who do or shall profess the Roman Catholic religion.

XVI. That all votes and elections given or made contrary, or not according to these qualifications, shall be null and void; and if any person, who is hereby made incapable, shall give his vote for election of members to serve in Parliament, such person shall lose and forfeit one full year's value of his real estate, and one full third part of his personal estate; one moiety thereof to the Lord Protector, and the other moiety to him or them who shall sue for the same.

XVII. That the persons who shall be elected to serve in Parliament, shall be such (and no other than such) as are persons of known integrity, fearing God, and of good conversation, and being of the age of twenty-one years.

XVIII. That all and every person and persons seised or possessed to his own use, of any estate, real or personal, to the value of £200, and not within the aforesaid exceptions, shall be capable to elect members to serve in Parliament for counties.

XIX. That the Chancellor, Keeper, or Commissioners of the Great Seal, shall be sworn before they enter into their offices, truly and faithfully to issue forth, and send abroad, writs of summons to Parliament, at the times and in the manner before expressed: and in case of neglect or failure to issue and send abroad writs accordingly, he or they shall for every such offence be guilty of high treason, and suffer the pains and penalties thereof.

XX. That in case writs be not issued out, as is before expressed, but that there be a neglect therein, fifteen days after the time wherein the same ought to be issued out by the Chancellor, Keeper, or Commissioners of the Great Seal; that then the Parliament shall, as often as such failure shall happen, assemble and be held at Westminster, in the usual place, at the times prefixed, in manner and by the means hereafter expressed; that is to say, that the sheriffs of the several and respective counties, sheriffdoms, cities, boroughs, and places aforesaid, within England, Wales, Scotland, and Ireland, the Chancellor, Masters, and Scholars of the Universities of Oxford and Cambridge, and the Mayor and Bailiffs of the borough of Berwick-upon-Tweed and other places aforesaid respectively, shall at the several courts and places to be appointed as aforesaid, within thirty days after the said fifteen days, cause such members to be chosen for their said several and respective counties, sheriffdoms, universities, cities, boroughs, and places aforesaid, by such persons, and in such manner as if several and respective writs of summons to Parliament under the Great Seal had issued and been awarded according to the tenor aforesaid: that if the sheriff, or other persons authorized, shall neglect his or their duty herein, that all and every such sheriff and person authorized as aforesaid, so neglecting his or their duty, shall, for every such offence, be guilty of high treason, and shall suffer the pains and penalties thereof.

XXI. That the clerk, called the clerk of the Commonwealth in Chancery for the time being, and all others, who shall afterwards execute that office, to whom the returns shall be made, shall for the next Parliament, and the two succeeding Triennial Parliaments, the next day after such return, certify the names of the several persons so returned, and of the places for which he and they were chosen respectively, unto the Council; who shall peruse the said returns, and examine whether the persons so elected and returned be such as is agreeable to the qualifications, and not disabled to be elected: and that every person and persons being so duly elected, and being approved of by the major part of the Council to be persons not disabled, but qualified as aforesaid, shall be esteemed a member of Parliament, and be admitted to sit in Parliament, and not otherwise.

XXII. That the persons so chosen and assembled in manner aforesaid, or any sixty of them, shall be, and be deemed the Parliament of England, Scotland, and Ireland; and the supreme legislative power to be and reside in the Lord Protector and such Parliament, in manner herein expressed.

XXIII. That the Lord Protector, with the advice of the major part of the Council, shall at any other time than is before expressed, when the necessities of the State shall require it, summon Parliaments in manner before expressed, which shall not be adjourned, prorogued, or dissolved without their own consent, during the first three months of their sitting. And in case of future war with any foreign State, a Parliament shall be forthwith summoned for their advice concerning the same.

XXIV. That all Bills agreed unto by the Parliament, shall be presented to the Lord Protector for his consent; and in case he shall not give his consent thereto within twenty days after they shall be presented to him, or give satisfaction to the Parliament within the time limited, that then, upon declaration of the Parliament that the Lord Protector hath not consented nor given satisfaction, such Bills shall pass into and become laws, although he shall not give his consent thereunto; provided such Bills contain nothing in them contrary to the matters contained in these presents.

XXV. That Henry Lawrence, Esq., &c.,[1] or any seven of them,

---

[1] The names of fifteen members are given here.

shall be a Council for the purposes expressed in this writing; and
upon the death or other removal of any of them, the Parliament shall
nominate six persons of ability, integrity, and fearing God, for every
one that is dead or removed; out of which the major part of the
Council shall elect two, and present them to the Lord Protector, of
which he shall elect one; and in case the Parliament shall not nominate within twenty days after notice given unto them thereof, the
major part of the Council shall nominate three as aforesaid to
the Lord Protector, who out of them shall supply the vacancy;
and until this choice be made, the remaining part of the Council
shall execute as fully in all things, as if their number were full.
And in case of corruption, or other miscarriage in any of the
Council in their trust, the Parliament shall appoint seven of their
number, and the Council six, who, together with the Lord Chancellor, Lord Keeper, or Commissioners of the Great Seal for
the time being, shall have power to hear and determine such
corruption and miscarriage, and to award and inflict punishment,
as the nature of the offence shall deserve, which punishment
shall not be pardoned or remitted by the Lord Protector; and, in the
interval of Parliaments, the major part of the Council, with the consent of the Lord Protector, may, for corruption or other miscarriage
as aforesaid, suspend any of their number from the exercise of their
trust, if they shall find it just, until the matter shall be heard and
examined as aforesaid.

XXVI. That the Lord Protector and the major part of the Council
aforesaid may, at any time before the meeting of the next Parliament,
add to the Council such persons as they shall think fit, provided the
number of the Council be not made thereby to exceed twenty-one,
and the quorum to be proportioned accordingly by the Lord Protector and the major part of the Council.

XXVII. That a constant yearly revenue shall be raised, settled,
and established for maintaining of 10,000 horse and dragoons, and
20,000 foot, in England, Scotland and Ireland, for the defence and
security thereof, and also for a convenient number of ships for guarding of the seas; besides £200,000 per annum for defraying the other
necessary charges of administration of justice, and other expenses of
the Government, which revenue shall be raised by the customs,

and such other ways and means as shall be agreed upon by the
Lord Protector and the Council, and shall not be taken away
or diminished, nor the way agreed upon for raising the same
altered, but by the consent of the Lord Protector and the Parliament.

XXVIII. That the said yearly revenue shall be paid into the public
treasury, and shall be issued out for the uses aforesaid.

XXIX. That in case there shall not be cause hereafter to keep up
so great a defence both at land or sea, but that there be an abatement
made thereof, the money which will be saved thereby shall remain
in bank for the public service, and not be employed to any other use
but by consent of Parliament, or, in the intervals of Parliament, by
the Lord Protector and major part of the Council.

XXX. That the raising of money for defraying the charge of the
present extraordinary forces, both at sea and land, in respect of the
present wars, shall be by consent of Parliament, and not otherwise:
save only that the Lord Protector, with the consent of the major part
of the Council, for preventing the disorders and dangers which might
otherwise fall out both by sea and land, shall have power, until the
meeting of the first Parliament, to raise money for the purposes
aforesaid; and also to make laws and ordinances for the peace and
welfare of these nations where it shall be necessary, which shall be
binding and in force, until order shall be taken in Parliament concerning the same.

XXXI. That the lands, tenements, rents, royalties, jurisdictions
and hereditaments which remain yet unsold or undisposed of, by
Act or Ordinance of Parliament, belonging to the Commonwealth
(except the forests and chases, and the honours and manors belonging
to the same; the lands of the rebels in Ireland, lying in the four
counties of Dublin, Cork, Kildare, and Carlow; the lands forfeited
by the people of Scotland in the late wars, and also the lands of
Papists and delinquents in England who have not yet compounded),
shall be vested in the Lord Protector, to hold, to him and his successors, Lords Protectors of these nations, and shall not be alienated but
by consent in Parliament. And all debts, fines, issues, amercements,
penalties and profits, certain and casual, due to the Keepers of the
liberties of England by authority of Parliament, shall be due to the

Lord Protector, and be payable into his public receipt, and shall be recovered and prosecuted in his name.

XXXII. That the office of Lord Protector over these nations shall be elective and not hereditary; and upon the death of the Lord Protector, another fit person shall be forthwith elected to succeed him in the Government; which election shall be by the Council, who, immediately upon the death of the Lord Protector, shall assemble in the Chamber where they usually sit in Council; and, having given notice to all their members of the cause of their assembling, shall, being thirteen at least present, proceed to the election; and, before they depart the said Chamber, shall elect a fit person to succeed in the Government, and forthwith cause proclamation thereof to be made in all the three nations as shall be requisite; and the person that they, or the major part of them, shall elect as aforesaid, shall be, and shall be taken to be, Lord Protector over these nations of England, Scotland and Ireland, and the dominions thereto belonging. Provided that none of the children of the late King, nor any of his line or family, be elected to be Lord Protector or other Chief Magistrate over these nations, or any of the dominions thereto belonging. And until the aforesaid election be past, the Council shall take care of the Government, and administer in all things as fully as the Lord Protector, or the Lord Protector and Council are enabled to do.

XXXIII. That Oliver Cromwell, Captain-General of the forces of England, Scotland and Ireland, shall be, and is hereby declared to be, Lord Protector of the Commonwealth of England, Scotland and Ireland, and the dominions thereto belonging, for his life.

XXXIV. That the Chancellor, Keeper or Commissioners of the Great Seal, the Treasurer, Admiral, Chief Governors of Ireland and Scotland, and the Chief Justices of both the Benches, shall be chosen by the approbation of Parliament; and, in the intervals of Parliament, by the approbation of the major part of the Council, to be afterwards approved by the Parliament.

XXXV. That the Christian religion, as contained in the Scriptures, be held forth and recommended as the public profession of these nations; and that, as soon as may be, a provision, less subject to scruple and contention, and more certain than the present, be made for the encouragement and maintenance of able and painful teachers, for the instructing the people, and for discovery and confutation of error, hereby, and whatever is contrary to sound doctrine; and until such provision be made, the present maintenance shall not be taken away or impeached.

XXXVI. That to the public profession held forth none shall be compelled by penalties or otherwise; but that endeavours be used to win them by sound doctrine and the example of a good conversation.

XXXVII. That such as profess faith in God by Jesus Christ (though differing in judgment from the doctrine, worship or discipline publicly held forth) shall not be restrained from, but shall be protected in, the profession of the faith and exercise of their religion; so as they abuse not this liberty to the civil injury of others and to the actual disturbance of the public peace on their parts: provided this liberty be not extended to Popery or Prelacy, nor to such as, under the profession of Christ, hold forth and practice licentiousness.

XXXVIII. That all laws, statutes and ordinances, and clauses in any law, statute or ordinance to the contrary of the aforesaid liberty, shall be esteemed as null and void.

XXXIX. That the Acts and Ordinances of Parliament made for the sale or other disposition of the lands, rents and hereditaments of the late King, Queen, and Prince, of Archbishops and Bishops, &c., Deans and Chapters, the lands of delinquents and forest-lands, or any of them, or of any other lands, tenements, rents and hereditaments belonging to the Commonwealth, shall nowise be impeached or made invalid, but shall remain good and firm; and that the securities given by Act and Ordinance of Parliament for any sum or sums of money, by any of the said lands, the excise, or any other public revenue; and also the securities given by the public faith of the nation, and the engagement of the public faith for satisfaction of debts and damages, shall remain firm and good, and not be made void and invalid upon any pretence whatsoever.

XL. That the Articles given to or made with the enemy, and afterwards confirmed by parliament, shall be performed and made good to the persons concerned therein; and that such appeals as were depending in the last Parliament for relief concerning bills of sale of delinquent's estates, may be heard and determined the next Parliament, any thing in this writing or otherwise to the contrary not-withstanding.

XLI. That every successive Lord Protector over these nations shall take and subscribe a solemn oath, in the presence of the Council, and such others as they shall call to them, that he will seek the peace, quiet and welfare of these nations, cause law and justice to be equally administered; and that he will not violate or infringe the matters and things contained in this writing, and in all other things will, to his power and to the best of his understanding, govern these nations according to the laws, statutes and customs thereof.

XLII. That each person of the Council shall, before they enter upon their trust, take and subscribe an oath, that they will be true and faithful in their trust, according to the best of their knowledge; and that in the election of every successive Lord Protector they shall proceed therein impartially, and do nothing therein for any promise, fear, favour or reward.

A HEALING QUESTION

BY SIR HENRY VANE. (1656)

[In 1656, Cromwell issued a proclamation for a general fast to consider the cause of the continued distracted condition of Britain. In response, Sir Henry Vane, previously Governor of Massachusetts, and one of the most high-minded statesmen of the period of the Commonwealth in England, published the following tract, expounding the principles of civil and religious liberty, and proposing that method of forming a constitution, through a convention called for the purpose, which was actually followed in America after the Revolution.]

A HEALING QUESTION PROPOUNDED AND RESOLVED, UPON OCCASION OF THE LATE PUBLIC AND SEASONABLE CALL TO HUMILIATION, IN ORDER TO LOVE AND UNION AMONG THE HONEST PARTY, AND WITH A DESIRE TO APPLY BALM TO THE WOUND BEFORE IT BECOME INCURABLE.

THE question propounded is, What possibility doth yet remain (all things considered) of reconciling and uniting the dissenting judgments of honest men within the three nations, who still pretend to agree in the spirit, justice, and reason of the same good cause, and what is the means to effect this?

Answ. If it be taken for granted (as, on the magistrate's part, from the ground inviting the people of England and Wales to a solemn day of fasting and humiliation, may not be despaired of) that all the dissenting parties agree still in the spirit and reason of the same righteous cause, the resolution seems very clear in the affirmative; arguing not only for a possibility, but a great probability hereof; nay, a necessity daily approaching nearer and nearer to compel it, if any or all of the dissenting parties intend or desire to be safe from the danger of the common enemy, who is not out of work, though at present much out of sight and observation.

The grounds of this are briefly these: First, the cause hath still the same goodness in it as ever, and is, or ought to be, as much in the hearts of all good people that have adhered to it: it is not less to be valued now, than when neither blood nor treasure were thought too dear to carry it on, and hold it up from sinking; and hath the same omnipotent God, whose great name is concerned in it, as well as his people's outward safety and welfare; who knows, also, how to give a revival to it when secondary instruments and visible means fail or prove deceitful.

Secondly, The persons concerned and engaged in this cause are still the same as before, with the advantage of being more tried, more inured to danger and hardship, and more endeared to one another, by their various and great experiences, as well of their own hearts as their fellow-brethren. These are the same still in heart and desire after the same thing, which is, that, being freed out of the hands of their enemies, they may serve the Lord without fear, in holiness and righteousness all the days of their life.

As they have had this great good finally in their aims (if declarations to men and appeals to God signify anything), so, as a requisite to attain this, they did with great cheerfulness and unanimity draw out themselves to the utmost in the maintenance of a war, when all other means, first essayed, proved ineffectual. In the management of this war, it pleased God, the righteous Judge (who was appealed to in the controversy), so to bless the counsel and forces of the persons concerned and engaged in this cause, as in the end to make them absolute and complete conquerors over their common enemy; and by this means they had added unto the natural right which was in them before (and so declared by their representatives in Parliament assembled), the right of conquest, for the strengthening of their just claim to be governed by national councils, and successive representatives of their own election and setting up. This they once thought they had been in possession of, when it was ratified, as it were, in the blood of the last king. But of late a great interruption having happened unto them in their former expectations, and, instead thereof, something rising up that seems rather accommodated to the private and selfish interest of a particular part (in comparison) than truly adequate to the common good and concern of the whole body engaged in this cause: hence it is that this compacted body is now falling asunder into many dissenting parts (a thing not unforeseen nor unhoped for by the common enemy all along as their last relief); and if these breaches be not timely healed, and the offences (before they take too deep root) removed, they will certainly work more to the advantage of the common enemy than any of their own unwearied endeavours and dangerous contrivances in foreign parts put all together.

A serious discussion and sober enlarging upon these grounds will quickly give an insight into the state of the question, and naturally tend to a plain and familiar resolution thereof.

That which is first to be opened is the nature and goodness of the cause; which, had it not carried in it its own evidence, would scarce have found so many of the people of God adherers to it within the three nations, contributing either their counsels, their purses, their bodily pains, or their affections and prayers, as a combined strength; without which, the military force alone would have been little available to subdue the common enemy, and restore to this whole body their just natural rights in civil things, and true freedom in matters of conscience.

The two last-mentioned particulars, rightly stated, will evidence sufficiently the nature and goodness of this cause.

For the first of these, that is to say, the natural right, which the whole party of honest men adhering to this cause are by success of their arms restored unto, fortified in, and may claim as their undeniable privilege, that righteously cannot be taken from them, nor they debarred from bringing into exercise, it lies in this:

They are to have and enjoy the freedom (by way of dutiful compliance and condescension from all the parts and members of this society) to set up meet persons in the place of supreme judicature and authority among them, whereby they may have the use and benefit of the choicest light and wisdom of the nation that they are capable to call forth, for the rule and government under which they will live; and through the orderly exercise of such measure of wisdom and counsel as the Lord in this way shall please to give unto them, to shape and form all subordinate actings and administrations of rule and government so as shall best answer the public welfare and safety of the whole.

This, in substance, is the right and freedom contained in the nature and goodness of the cause wherein the honest party have been engaged; for in this all the particulars of our civil right and freedom are comprehended, conserved in, and derived from their proper root; in which, while they grow, they will ever thrive, flourish, and increase; whereas, on the contrary, if there be never so many fair branches of liberty planted on the root of a private and selfish interest, they will not long prosper, but must, within a little time, wither and degenerate into the nature of that whereinto they are planted; and hence, indeed, sprung the evil of that government which rose in and with the Norman Conquest.

The root and bottom upon which it stood was not public interest, but the private lust and will of the conqueror, who by force of arms did at first detain the right and freedom which was and is due to the whole body of the people; for whose safety and good, government itself is ordained by God, not for the particular benefit of the rulers, as a distinct and private interest of their own; which yet, for the most part, is not only preferred before the common good, but upheld in opposition thereunto. And as at first the conqueror did, by violence and force, deny this freedom to the people, which was their natural right and privilege, so he and his successors all along lay as bars and impediments to the true national interest and public good, in the very national councils and assemblies themselves, which were constituted in such a manner as most served for the upholding of the private interest of their families; and this being challenged by them as their prerogative, was found by the people assembled in Parliament most unrighteous, burdensome, and destructive to their liberty. And when they once perceived that by this engine all their just rights were like to be destroyed especially (being backed, as it was, with the power of the militia, which the late king, for that purpose, had assumed into his hands, and would not, upon the people's application to him in Parliament, part with into the hands of that great council, who were best to be intrusted with the nation's safety), this was the ground of the quarrel, upon a civil account between the king and his party, and the whole body of adherents to the cause of the people's true liberty; whereof this short touch hath been given, and shall suffice for the opening of the first branch of this clause.

The second branch which remains briefly to be handled is that which also upon the grounds of natural right is to be laid claim unto, but distinguishes itself from the former as it respects a more heavenly and excellent object wherein the freedom is to be exercised and enjoyed, that is to say, matters of religion, or that concern the service and worship of God.

Unto this freedom the nations of the world have right and title by the purchase of Christ's blood, who, by virtue of his death and resurrection, is become the sole Lord and Ruler in and over the conscience; for to this end Christ died, rose, and revived, that he might be Lord both of the dead and of the living, and that every one might give an account of himself, in all matters of God's worship unto God and Christ alone, as their own Master, unto whom they stand or fall in judgment, and are not in these things to be oppressed, or brought before the judgment-seats of men. For why shouldst thou set at naught thy brother in matters of his faith and conscience, and herein intrude into the proper office of Christ, since we are all to stand at the judgment-seat of Christ, whether governors or governed, and by his decision only are capable of being declared with certainty to be in the right or in the wrong?

By virtue, then, of this supreme law, sealed and confirmed in the blood of Christ unto all men (whose souls he challenges a propriety in, to bring under his inward rule in the service and worship of God), it is that all magistrates are to fear and forbear intermeddling with giving rule or imposing in those matters. They are to content themselves with what is plain in their commission, as ordained of God to be his minister unto men for good, while they approve themselves the doers of that which is good in the sight of men, and whereof earthly and worldly judicatures are capable to make a clear and perfect judgment: in which case the magistrate is to be for praise and protection to them. In like manner, he is to be a minister of terror and revenge to those that do evil in matters of outward practice, converse, and dealings in the things of this life between man and man, for the cause whereof the judicatures of men are appointed and set up. But to exceed these limits, as it is not safe or warrantable for the magistrate (in that he who is higher than the highest, regards, and will show himself displeased at it), so neither is it good for the people, who hereby are nourished up in a biting, devouring, wrathful spirit one against another, and are found transgressors of that royal law which forbids us to do that unto another which we would not have them do unto us, were we in their condition.

This freedom, then, is of high concern to be had and enjoyed, as well for the magistrate's sake as for the people's common good; and it consists, as hath been said, in the magistrate forbearing to put forth the power of rule and coercion in things that God hath exempted out of his commission: so that all care requisite for the people's obtaining this may be exercised with great ease, if it be taken in its proper season, and that this restraint be laid upon the supreme power before it be erected, as a fundamental constitution, among others, upon which the free consent of the people is given, to have the persons brought into the exercise of supreme authority over them and on their behalf; and if, besides, as a further confirmation hereunto, it be acknowledged the voluntary act of the ruling power, when once brought into a capacity of acting legislatively, that herein they are bound up, and judge it their duty so to be (both in reference to God, the institutor of magistracy, and in reference to the whole body by whom they are intrusted), this great blessing will hereby be so well provided for that we shall have no cause to fear, as it may be ordered.

By this means a great part of the outward exercise of anti-Christian tyranny and bondage will be plucked up by the very roots, which, till some such course be held in it, will be always apt to renew and sprout out afresh, under some new form or refined appearances, as by late years' experience we have been taught: for, since the fall of the bishops and persecuting presbyteries, the same spirit is apt to arise in the next sort of clergy that can get the ear of the magistrate, and pretend to the keeping and ruling the conscience of the governors, although this spirit and practice hath been all along decried by the faithful adherents to this cause as a most sore oppression and insufferable yoke of bondage, most unrighteously kept up over the consciences of the people, and therefore judged by them most needful to be taken out of the way; and in this matter the present governors have been willing very eminently to give their testimony in their public declarations, however in practice there is much of grievance yet found among us, though more, in probability, from the officiousness of subordinate ministers than any clear purpose or design of the chief in power.

Having thus showed what the true freedom is, in both the branches of it, that shines forth in the righteous cause, wherein the good people of these nations have so deeply engaged, it will not be improper, in the next place, to consider two particulars more that give still farther light into the matter in question, as, first, the qualifications of the persons that have adhered to this cause; secondly, the capacity wherein they have been found from time to time carrying it on.

As to their qualification, they have, in the general, distinguished themselves and been made known by a forwardness to assist and own the public welfare and good of the nation, for the attaining and preserving the just rights and liberties thereof, asserted and witnessed unto in the true stating of this cause, according to the two branches thereof already spoken to. They have showed themselves, upon all occasions, desirers and lovers of true freedom, either in civils or in spirituals, or in both. To express their value thereof, and faithfulness to the same, they have largely contributed, in one kind or other, what was proper to each in his place to do; which actions of theirs proceeding from hearts sincerely affected to the cause, created in them a right to be of an incorporation and society by themselves, under the name of the good party, having been from the beginning unto this day publicly and commonly so acknowledged, by way of distinction from all neuters, close and open enemies, and deceitful friends or apostates. These, in order to the maintaining of this cause, have stood by the army, in defence and support thereof, against all opposition whatever, as those that, by the growing light of these times, have been taught and led forth in their experiences to look above and beyond the letter, form, and outward circumstances of government, into the inward reason and spirit thereof, herein only to fix and terminate, to the leaving behind all empty shadows that would obtrude themselves in the place of true freedom.

Secondly, as to the capacity wherein these persons, thus qualified, have acted, it hath been very variable, and subject to great changes: sometimes in one form, and sometimes in another, and very seldom, if ever at all, so exactly and in all points consonant to the rule of former laws and constitutions of government as to be clearly and fully justified by them any longer than the law of success and conquest did uphold them who had the inward warrant of justice and righteousness to encourage them in such their actings.

The utmost and last reserve, therefore, which they have had, in case all other failed, hath been their military capacity, not only strictly taken for the standing army, but in the largest sense, wherein the whole party may (with the army, and under that military constitu' tion and conduct which, by the providence of God, they shall then be found in) associate themselves in the best order they can for the common defence and safety of the whole; as not ignorant that when once embodied in this their military posture, in such manner as by common consent shall be found requisite for the safety of the body, they are most irresistible, absolute, and comprehensive in their power, having that wherein the substance of all government is contained, and under the protection whereof, and safety that may be maintained thereby, they can contrive and determine in what manner this irresistible, absolute, and boundless power, unto which they are now arrived in this their military capacity, shall have just and due limits set unto it, and be drawn out in a meet and orderly way of exercise for the commonweal and safety of the whole body, under the rule and oversight of a supreme judicature, unto the wisdom of whose laws and orders the sword is to become most entirely subject and subservient; and this without the least cause of jealousy or unsafety, either to the standing army, or any member thereof, or unto the good people adhering to this cause, or any of them, since the interest of both, by this mutual action of either, will be so combined together in one (even in that wherein before they were distinct), that all just cause of difference, fear, animosity, emulation, jealousy, or the like, will be wholly abolished and removed.

For when once the whole body of the good people find that the military interest and capacity is their own, and that into which necessity at the last may bring the whole party (whereof, of right, a place is to be reserved for them), and that herein they are so far from being in subjection or slavery, that in this posture they are most properly sovereign, and possess their right of natural sovereignty, they will presently see a necessity of continuing ever one with their army, raised and maintained by them for the promoting this cause against the common enemy, who in his next attempt will put for all with greater desperateness and rage than ever.

Again, when once the standing army and their governors shall also find that, by setting and keeping up themselves in a divided interest from the rest of the body of honest men, they withhold from themselves those contributions in all voluntary and cheerful assistances, by the affections and prayers, by the persons and purses of the good party, to the weakening themselves thereby, as to any vigorous support from them, in the times of most imminent danger (whereof the late king had an experience, that will not suddenly be out of memory, when he undertook the war, in the beginning of these troubles, against the Scots, and was, in a manner, therein deserted by all the good party in England), they will then find (if they stay not till it be too late) that, by espousing the interest of the people, in submitting themselves with their fellow-adherents to the cause, under the rule and authority of their own supreme judicature, they lose not their power or sovereignty, but, becoming one civil or politic incorporation with the whole party of honest men, they do therein keep the sovereignty, as originally seated in themselves, and part with it only but as by deputation and representation of themselves, when it is brought into an orderly way of exercise, by being put into the hands of persons chosen and intrusted by themselves to that purpose.

By this mutual and happy transition, which may be made between the party of honest men in the three nations virtually in arms, and those actually so now in power at the head of the army; how suddenly would the union of the whole body be consolidated, and made so firm as it will not need to fear all the designs and attempts of the common enemy, especially if herein they unite themselves in the first place to the Lord, as willing to follow his providence, and observe his will in the way and manner of bringing this to pass! in which case we shall not need to fear what all the gates of hell are able to do in opposition thereunto.

It is not, then, the standing and being of the present army and military forces in the three nations that is liable to exception of offence from any dissenting judgments at this time among the honest, well-affected party. In and with them, under God, stand the welfare and outward safety of the whole body; and to be enemies to them, or wish them hurt, were to do it to themselves; and, by trying such conclusions, to play the game of the common enemy, to the utter ruin and destruction, not only of the true freedom aimed at and contended for in the late wars, but of the very persons themselves that have been in any sort active or eminent promoters thereof.

The army, considered as it is in the hands of an honest and wise general, and sober, faithful officers, embodied with the rest of the party of honest men, and espousing still the same cause, and acting in their primitive simplicity, humility, and trust, in reference to the welfare and safety of the whole body, is the only justifiable and most advantageous posture and capacity that the good party at present can find themselves in, in order to the obtaining that true freedom they have fought for, and possessing of it in the establishment thereof upon the true basis and foundation, as hath been showed, of right government.

That wherein the offence lies, and which causes such great thoughts of heart among the honest party (if it may be freely expressed, as sure it may, when the magistrate himself professes he doth but desire and wait for conviction therein), is, in short, this:

That when the right and privilege is returned, nay, is restored by conquest unto the whole body (that forfeited not their interest therein), of freely disposing themselves in such a constitution of righteous government as may best answer the ends held forth in this cause; that, nevertheless, either through delay they should be withheld as they are, or through design they should come at last to be utterly denied the exercise of this their right, upon pretence that they are not in capacity as yet to use it, which, indeed, hath some truth in it, if those that are now in power, and have the command of the arms, do not prepare all things requisite thereunto, as they may, and, like faithful guardians to the Commonwealth, admitted to be in its nonage, they ought.

But if the bringing of true freedom into exercise among men, yea, so refined a party of men, be impossible, why hath this been concealed all this while? and why was it not thought on before so much blood was spilt, and treasure spent? Surely such a thing as this was judged real and practicable, not imaginary and notional.

Besides, why may it not suffice to have been thus long delayed and withheld from the whole body, at least as to its being brought by them into exercise now at last? Surely the longer it is withheld, the stronger jealousies do increase, that it is intended to be assumed and engrossed by a part only, to the leaving the rest of the body (who, in all reason and justice, ought to be equally participants with the other in the right and benefit of the conquest, for as much as the war was managed at the expense and for the safety of the whole) in a condition almost as much exposed, and subject to be imposed upon, as if they had been enemies and conquered, not in any sense conquerors.

If ever such an unrighteous, unkind, and deceitful dealing with brethren should happen, although it might continue above the reach of question from human judicature, yet can we think it possible it should escape and go unpunished by the immediate hand of the righteous Judge of the whole world, when he ariseth out of his place to do right to the oppressed.

Nay, if, instead of favouring and promoting the peopie s common good and welfare, self-interest and private gain should evidently appear to be the things we have aimed at all along; if those very tyrannical principles and anti-Christian relics, which God by us hath punished in our predecessors, should again revive, spring up afresh, and show themselves lodged also and retained in our bosoms, rendering us of the number of those that have forgot they were purged from their old sins, and declaring us to be such as, to please a covetous mind, do withhold from destruction that which God hath designed to the curse of his vengeance: if all those great advantages of serving the Lord's will and design in procuring and advancing his people's true welfare and outward safety, which (as the fruit of his blessing upon our armies) have so miraculously fallen into our hands, shall at last be wrested and misimproved to the enriching and greatening of ourselves—if these things should ever be found among us (which the Lord in mercy forbid!), shall we need to look any farther for the accursed thing? will not our consciences show us, from the light of the Word and Spirit of God, how near a conformity these actions would hold therewith? which sin (Josh., vii.) became a curse to the camp, and withheld the Lord from being any more among them, or going out with their forces. And did the action of Achan import any more than these two things: First, he saved and kept from destruction the goodly Babylonish garment, which was devoted by God thereunto; secondly, he brought not in the fruit and gain of the conquest into the Lord's treasury, but covetously went about to convert it to his own proper use? To do this is to take of the accursed thing, which (Josh., vii.) all Israel was said to do in the sin of Achan, and to have stolen and dissembled likewise, and put it among their own stuff. This caused the anger of the Lord to kindle against Israel, and made them unable to stand before their enemies, but their hearts melted as water. And thus far the Lord is concerned, if such an evil as this shall lie hid in the midst of us. But to return to what we were upon before.

The matter which is in question among the dissenting parts of the whole body of honest men is not so trivial and of such small consequence as some would make it. 'Tis, in effect, the main and whole of the cause; without which all the freedom which the people have or can have is in comparison but shadow and in name only, and therefore can never give that peace and satisfaction to the body which is requisite unto a durable and solid settlement. This is that which makes all sound and safe at the root, and gives the right balance necessary to be held up between sovereignty and subjection in the exercise of all righteous government; applying the use of the sword to the promoting and upholding the public safety and welfare of the whole body, in preference, and, if need be, in opposition unto any of the parts; while yet, by its equal and impartial administration in reference unto each, it doth withal maintain the whole body in a most delightful harmony, welfare, and correspondency. The sword never can, nor is it to be expected ever will do this, while the sovereignty is admitted and placed anywhere else than in the whole bdy of the people that have adhered to the cause, and by them be derived unto their successive representatives, as the most equal and impartial judicature for the effecting hereof.

Where there is, then, a righteous and good constitution of government, there is first, an orderly union of many understandings together, as the public and common supreme judicature or visible sovereignty, set in a way of free and orderly exercise, for the directing and applying the use of the ruling power or the sword, to promote the interest and common welfare of the whole, without any disturbance or annoyance from within or from without; and then, secondly, there is a like union and readiness of will in all the individuals, in their private capacities, to execute and obey (by all the power requisite, and that they are able to put forth) those sovereign laws and orders issued out by their own deputies and trustees.

A supreme judicature, thus made the representative of the whole, is that which, we say, will most naturally care, and most equally provide for the common good and safety. Though by this it is not denied but that the supreme power, when by free consent 'tis placed in a single person or in some few persons, may be capable also to administer righteous government; at least, the body that gives this liberty, when they need not, are to thank themselves if it prove otherwise. But when this free and natural access unto government is interrupted and declined, so as a liberty is taken by any particular member, or number of them, that are to be reputed but a part in comparison of the whole, to assume and engross the office of sovereign rule and power, and to impose themselves as the competent public judge of the safety and good of the whole, without their free and due consent, and to lay claim unto this, as those that find themselves possessed of the sword (and that so advantageously as it cannot be recovered again out of their hands without more apparent danger and damage to the whole body than such attempts are worth), this is that anarchy that is the first rise and step to tyranny, and lays grounds of manifest confusion and disorder, exposing the ruling power to the next hand that on the next opportunity can lay hold on the sword, and so, by a kind of necessity, introduces the highest imposition and bondage upon the whole body, in compelling all the parts, though never so much against the true public interest, to serve and obey, as their sovereign rule and supreme authority, the arbitrary will and judgment of those that bring themselves into rule by the power of the sword, in the right only of a part that sets up itself in preference before, or at least in competition with, the welfare of the whole.

And if this, which is so essential to the wellbeing and right constitution of government, were once obtained, the disputes about the form would not prove so difficult, nor find such opposition, as to keeping the bone of contention and disunion, with much danger to the whole; for if, as the foundation of all, the sovereignty be acknowledged to reside originally in the whole body of adherents to this cause (whose natural and inherent right thereunto is of a far ancienter date than what is obtained by success of their arms, and so cannot be abrogated even by conquest itself, if that were the case), and then if, in consequence hereof, a supreme judicature be set up and orderly constituted, as naturally arising and resulting from the free choice and consent of the whole body taken out from among themselves, as flesh of their flesh and bone of their bone, of the same public spirit and nature with themselves, and the main be by this means secured, what could be propounded afterward as to the form of administration that would much stick?

Would a standing council of state, settled for life, in reference to the safety of the Commonwealth, and for the maintaining intercourse and commerce with foreign states, under the inspection and oversight of the supreme judicature, but of the same fundamental constitution with themselves—would this be disliked? admitting their orders were binding, in the intervals of supreme national assemblies, so far only as consonant to the settled laws of the Commonwealth, the vacancy of any of which, by death or otherwise, might be supplied by the vote of the major part of themselves: nay, would there be any just exception to be taken if (besides both these) it should be agreed (as another part of the fundamental constitution of the government) to place that branch of sovereignty which chiefly respects the execution of laws in a distinct office from that of the legislative power (and yet subordinate to them and to the laws), capable to be intrusted into the hands of one single person, if need require, or in a greater number, as the legislative power should think fit; and, for the greater strength and honour unto this office, that the execution of all laws and orders (that are binding) may go forth in his or their name, and all disobedience thereunto, or contempt thereof, be taken as done to the people's sovereignty, whereof he or they bear the image or representation, subordinate to the legislative power, and at their will to be kept up and continued in the hands of a single person or more, as the experience of the future good or evil of it shall require?

Would such an office as this, thus stated, carry in it any inconsistency with a free state? Nay, if it be well considered, would it not rather be found of excellent use to the wellbeing of magistracy, founded upon this righteous bottom, that such a lieutenancy of the people's sovereignty in these three nations may always reside in some one or more person, in whose administration that which is reward and punishment may shine forth?

And if now it shall be objected that (notwithstanding all these cautions), should once this sovereignty be acknowledged to be in the diffused body of the people (though the adherents to this cause, not only as their natural, but as their acquired right by conquest), they would suddenly put the use and exercise of the legislative power into such hands as would, through their ill qualifiedness to the work, spoil all by mal-administration thereof, and hereby lose the cause instead of upholding and maintaining it.

The answer unto this is, first, that God, by his providence, hath eased our minds much in this solicitude by the course he hath already taken to fit and prepare a choice and selected number of the people unto this work, that are tried and refined by their inward and outward experiences in this great quarrel, and the many changes they have passed through; in respect whereof well qualified persons are to be found, if due care be but taken in the choice of them. And if herein this people of the Lord shall be waiting upon him for his guidance and presence with them, we may have grounds and hope that God (whose name hath all along been called upon in the maintaining of this cause) will pour out so abundantly of his spirit upon his people attending on him in righteous ways, and will also move their hearts to choose persons bearing his image into the magistracy, that a more glorious product may spring up out of this than at first we can expect, to the setting up of the Lord himself as chief judge and lawgiver among us. And unto this the wisdom and honesty of the persons now in power may have an opportunity eminently to come into discovery; for in this case, and upon the grounds already laid, the very persons now in power are they unto whose lot it would fall to set about this preparatory work, and by their orders and directions to dispose the whole body, and bring them into the meetest capacity to effect the same, the most natural way for which would seem to be by a general council, or convention of faithful, honest, and discerning men, chosen for that purpose by the free consent of the whole body of adherents to this cause in the several parts of the nations, and observing the time and place of meeting appointed to them (with other circumstances concerning their election) by order from the present ruling power, but considered as general of the army:

Which convention is not properly to exercise the legislative power, but only to debate freely, and agree upon the particulars that by way of fundamental constitutions shall be laid and inviolably observed as the conditions upon which the whole body so represented doth consent to cast itself into a civil and politic incorporation, and under the visible form and administration of government therein declared, and to be by each individual member of the body subscribed in testimony of his or their particular consent given thereunto: which conditions so agreed (and among them an Act of Oblivion for one) will be without danger of being broken or departed from, considering of what it is they are the conditions, and the nature of the convention wherein they are made, which is of the people represented in their highest state of sovereignty, as they have the sword in their hands unsubjected unto the rules of civil government, but what themselves orderly assembled for that purpose do think fit to make. And the sword, upon these conditions, subjecting itself to the supreme judicature thus to be set up, how suddenly might harmony, righteousness, love, peace, and safety unto the whole body follow hereupon, as the happy fruit of such a settlement, if the Lord have any delight to be among us!

And this once put in a way, and declared for by the general and army (as that which they are clearly convinced, in the sight of God, is their duty to bring about, and which they engage accordingly to see done) how firmly and freely would this oblige the hearts and persons, the counsels and purses, the affections and prayers, with all that is in the power of this whole party to do, in way of assistance and strengthening the hands of those now in power, whatever straits and difficulties they may meet with in the maintenance of the public safety and peace!

This, then, being the state of our present affairs and differences, let it be acknowledged on all hands, and let all be convinced that are concerned, that there is not only a possibility, but a probability, yea, a compelling necessity, of a firm union in this great body, the setting of which in joint and tune again, by a spirit of meekness and fear of the Lord, is the work of the present day, and will prove the only remedy under God to uphold and carry on this blessed cause and work of the Lord in the three nations, that is already come thus far onward in its progress to its desired and expected end of bringing in Christ, the desire of all nations, as the chief Ruler among us.

Now unto this reuniting work let there be a readiness in all the dissenting parts from the highest to the lowest, by cheerfully coming forth to one another in a spirit of self-denial and love instead of war and wrath, and to cast down themselves before the Lord, who is the father of all their spirits, in self-abasement and humiliation, for the mutual offence they have been in, for some time past, one unto another, and great provocation unto God, and reproach unto his most glorious name, who expected to have been served by them with reverence and godly fear; for our God is a consuming fire.

And, as an inducement unto this, let us assure ourselves the means of effecting it will not prove so difficult as other things that have been brought about in the late war, if the minds and spirits of all concerned were once well and duly prepared hereunto by a kindly work of self-denial and self-abasement, set home by the spirit of the Lord upon their consciences, which, if he please, he may do we know not how soon: nay, we shall behold with a discerning eye the inside of that work which God hath been doing among us the three years last past: it would seem chiefly to have been his aim to bring his people into such a frame as this; for in this tract of time there hath been (as we may say) a great silence in heaven, as if God were pleased to stand still and be as a looker on, to see what his people would be in their latter end, and what work they would make of it, if left to their own wisdom and politic contrivances. And as God hath had the silent part, so men, and that good men too, have had the active and busy part, and have, like themselves, made a great sound and noise, like the shout of a king in a mighty host; which, while it hath been a sound only and no more, hath not done much hurt as yet; but the fear and jealousy thereby caused, hath put the whole body out of frame, and made them apt to fall into great confusions and disorder.

And if there be thus arisen a general dissent and disagreement of parts (which is not, nor ought to be, accounted the less considerable because it lies hid and kept in under a patient silence), why should there not be as general a confession and acknowledgment of what each may find themselves overtaken in, and cannot but judge themselves faulty for? this kind of vent being much better than to have it break out in flames of a forward and untimely wrathful spirit, which never works the righteousness of God, especially since what hath been done among us may probably have been more the effect of temptation than the product of any malicious design; and this sort of temptation is very common and incident to men in power (how good soever they may be) to be overtaken in, and thereupon do sudden unadvised actions, which the Lord pardons and overrules for the best, evidently making appear that it is the work of the weak and fleshly part, which his own people carry about with them too much unsubdued; and therefore the Lord thinks fit, by this means, to show them the need of being beholden to their spiritual part to restore them again, and bring them into their right temper and healthful constitution.

And thus, while each dissenting part is aggravating upon it self-faultiness and blame, and none excusing, but all confessing they deserve, in one sort or other, reproof, if not before men, yet in God's sight, who knows how soon it may please God to come into this broken, contrite, and self-denying frame of spirit in the good people within the three nations, and own them, thus truly humbled and abased, for his temple and the place of his habitation and rest, wherein he shall abide forever? of whom it may be said, God is in the midst of her, she shall not be moved; God shall help her, and that right early. or with his morning appearance; at which time he will sit silent no longer, but Heaven will speak again, and become active and powerful in the spirits and hearts of honest men, and in the works of his providences, when either they go out to fight by sea or by land, or remain in council and debates at home for the public weal, and again hear the prayers of his people, and visibly own them as a flock of holy men, as Jerusalem in her solemn feasts: "I will yet for this be inquired of by the house of Israel, saith the Lord, to do it for them: and then they shall know that I the Lord their God am with them, and that they are my people, and that ye my flock, the flock of my pasture, are men that have showed yourselves weak, sinful men, and I am your God, that have declared myself an all-wise and powerful God, saith the Lord God."

POSTSCRIPT

READER,—Upon the perusal of this discourse, thou wilt quickly perceive that these two things are principally aimed at in it by the author: First, to answer in some measure that which is called for by those in power, when they publicly profess they desire nothing more than conviction, and to find out the hidden provocations which either have or yet may bring forth the Lord against these nations, in the way which at present they are in.

Secondly, to remove out of the minds and spirits of the honest party, that still agree in the reason and justice of the good old cause, all things of a private nature and selfish concern (the tendency whereof serves but to foment and strengthen wrath and divisions among them), and in place thereof to set before them that common and public interest, which, if with sincerity embraced, may be the means of not only procuring a firm union among them, but also of conserving them herein.

In order to do this, the author hath not been willing so much to declare his own opinion, or deliver any positive conclusions, as to discuss the business by way of question and answer, and thereby make as near a conjecture as he can of that wherein the several dissenting parts may with better satisfaction meet together, and agree upon a safe and righteous bottom, than to remain at the distance they do, to the apparent advantage of the common enemy, the approaching ruin of themselves, and needless hazard, if not loss, of the cause they have been so deeply engaged in; especially considering that, when once they shall be found beginning to come forth to one another in such a condescending, self-denying spirit, cleansed from the stain of hypocrisy and deceit, they may be well assured that light will spring up among them more and more unto a perfect day; and then those things which at present we have next in view, will prove as shadows ready to flee away before the morning brightness of Christ's heavenly appearance and second coming, through which they will be heightened and improved to their full maturity, to the bringing in that kingdom of his that shall never be moved.

And because an essay hath been already made in a private way to obtain the first thing, that is to say, conviction, which chiefly is in the hand of the Lord to give, the same obligation lies upon the author, with respect to the second, for the exposing of it as now it is unto public view, and therein leaving it also with the Lord for his blessing thereunto.

ELIOT'S BRIEF NARRATIVE[1]

(1670)

[John Eliot (1604–1690), "The Apostle to the Indians," came to New England in 1631, and began his ministrations to the Indians in their own language in 1646. His great work, the translation of the Bible into the tongue of the Massachusetts Indians, was finished in 1658 and published 1661–63. He wrote a number of reports on the progress of Christianity among the Indians, of which the *Brief Narrative* was the last. This pamphlet gives an interesting picture of the conditions of evangelisation among the natives at the end of the first generation of intercourse with the colonists. The movement which was so vigorously started by Eliot was checked before his death by King Philip's war, 1675–6.]

To the Right Worshipful the Commissioners under his Majesties' Great-Seal, for Propagation of the Gospel amongst the poor blind Indians in New-England.

Right Worshipful and Christian Gentlemen:

THAT brief Tract of the present state of the *Indian-Work* in my hand, which I did the last year on the sudden present you with when you call'd for such a thing; That falling short of its end, and you calling for a renewal thereof, with opportunity of more time, I shall begin with our last great motion in that Work done this Summer, because that will lead me to begin with the state of the *Indians* under the hands of my Brethren Mr. *Mahew* and Mr. *Bourn.*

Upon the 17th day of the 6th month, 1670, there was a Meeting at *Maktapog* near *Sandwich* in *Plimouth-Pattent,* to gather a Church among the *Indians:* There were present six of the Magistrates, and many Elders, (all of them Messengers of the Churches within that Jurisdiction) in whose presence, in a day of Fasting and Prayer,

---

[1] The full title of this tract was as follows:

A Brief Narrative of the Progress of the Gospel amongst the *Indians* in *New England,* in the Year 1670, given in by the Reverend Mr. John Eliot, Minister of the Gospel there, in a letter by him directed to the Right Worshipfull the Commissioners under his Majesties Great-Seal for Propagation of the Gospel amongst the poor blind Natives in those United Colonies. *LONDON,* Printed for *John Allen,* formerly living in *Little-Britain* at the Rising-Sun, and now in *Wentworth street* near *Bell-Lane,* 1671.

they making confession of the Truth and Grace of Jesus Christ, did in that solemn Assembly enter into Covenant, to walk together in the Faith and Order of the Gospel; and were accepted and declared to be a Church of Jesus Christ. These *Indians* being of kin to our *Massachuset-Indians* who first prayed unto God, conversed with them, and received amongst them the light and love of the Truth; they desired me to write to Mr. *Leveredge* to teach them: He accepted the Motion: and performed the Work with good success; but afterwards he left that place, and went to *Long-Island,* and there a godly Brother, named *Richard Bourne* (who purposed to remove with Mr. *Leveredge,* but hindered by Divine Providence) undertook the teaching of those *Indians,* and hath continued in the work with good success to this day; him we ordained Pastor: and one of the *Indians,* named *Jude,* should have been ordained Ruling-Elder, but being sick at that time, advice was given that he should be ordained with the first opportunity, as also a Deacon to manage the present Sabbath-day Collections, and other [4] parts of that Office in their season. The same day also were they, and such of their Children as were present, baptized.

From them we passed over to the *Vineyard,* where many were added to the Church both men and women, and were baptized all of them, and their Children also with them; we had the Sacrament of the Lords Supper celebrated in the *Indian-Church,* and many of the *English-Church* gladly joyned with them; for which cause it was celebrated in both languages. On a day of Fasting and Prayer, Elders were ordained, two Teaching-Elders, the one to be a Preacher of the Gospel, to do the Office of a Pastor and Teacher; the other to be a Preacher of the Gospel, to do the Office of a Teacher and Pastor, as the Lord should give them ability and opportunity; Also two Ruling-Elders, with advice to ordain Deacons also, for the Service of Christ in the Church. Things were so ordered by the Lord's guidance, that a Foundation is laid for two Churches more; for first, these of the *Vineyard* dwelling at too great a distance to enjoy with comfort their Sabbath-communion in one place, Advice was given them, that after some experience of walking together in the Order and Ordinances of the Gospel, they should issue forth into another Church; and the Officers are so chosen, that when they shall do so, both Places are furnished with a Teaching and Ruling-Elder.

Also the Teacher of the *Praying Indians* of *Nantuket,* with a Brother of his were received here, who made good Confessions of Jesus Christ; and being asked, did make report unto us that there be about ninety Families who pray unto God in that Island, so effectual is the Light of the Gospel among them. Advice was given, that some of the chief Godly People should joyn to this Church, (for they frequently converse together, though the Islands be seven leagues asunder) and after some experience of walking in the Order of the Gospel, they should issue forth into Church-estate among themselves, and have Officers ordained amongst them.

The Church of the *Vineyard* were desirous to have chosen Mr. *Mahew* to be their Pastor: but he declined it, conceiving that in his present capacity he lieth under greater advantages to stand their Friend, and do them good, to save them from the hands of such as would bereave them of their Lands, &c., but they shall always have his counsel, instruction and management in all their Church-affairs, as hitherto they have had; he will die in this service of Jesus Christ. The *Praying-Indians* of both these islands depend on him, as God's Instrument for their good. [5] Advice also was given for the setling of Schools; every Child capable of learning, equally paying, whether he make use of it or no: Yet if any should sinfully neglect Schooling their Youth, it is a transgression liable to censure under both Orders, Civil and Ecclesiastical, the offence being against both. So we walk at *Natick.*

In as much as now we have ordained *Indian Officers* unto the Ministry of the Gospel, it is needful to add a word or two of Apology: I find it hopeless to expect *English* Officers in our *Indian* Churches; the work is full of hardship, hard labour, and chargeable also, and the *Indians* not yet capable to give considerable support and maintenance; and Men have bodies, and must live of the Gospel: And what comes from England is liable to hazard and uncertainties. On such grounds as these partly, but especially from the secret wise governance of Jesus Christ, the Lord of the Harvest, there is no appearance of hope for their souls feeding in that way: they must be trained up to be able to live of themselves in the ways of the Gospel of Christ; and through the riches of God's Grace and Love, sundry of themselves who are expert in the Scriptures, are able to teach each other: An *English* young man raw in that language, coming to teach among our Christian-*Indians,* would be much to their loss; there be of themselves such as be more able, especially being advantaged that he speaketh his own language, and knoweth their manners. Such *English* as shall hereafter teach them, must begin with a People that begin to pray unto God, (and such opportunities we have many) and then as they grow in knowledge, he will grow (if he be diligent) in ability of speech to communicate the knowledge of Christ unto them. And seeing they must have Teachers amongst themselves, they must also be taught to be Teachers: for which cause I have begun to teach them the Art of Teaching, and I find some of them very capable. And while I live, my purpose is, (by the grace of Christ assisting) to make it one of my chief cares and labours to teach them some of the Liberal Arts and Sciences, and the way how to analize, and lay out into particulars both the Works and Word of God; and how to communicate knowledge to others methodically and skilfully, and especially the method of Divinity. There be sundry Ministers who live in an opportunity of beginning with a People, and for time to come I shall cease my importuning of others, and onely fall to perswade such unto this service of Jesus Christ, it being one part of our Ministerial Charge to preach to the World in the Name of Jesus, and from amongst them to gather Subjects to his holy Kingdom. The Bible, and the Catechism drawn [6] out of the Bible, are general helps to all parts and places about us, and are the ground-work of Community amongst all our *Indian*-Churches and Christians.

I find a blessing, when our Church of *Natick* doth send forth fit Persons unto some remoter places, to teach them the fear of the Lord. But we want maintenance for that Service; it is a chargeable matter to send a Man from his Family: The Labourer is worthy of his Hire: And when they go only to the High-wayes and Hedges, it is not to be expected that they should reward them: If they believe and obey their Message, it is enough. We are determined to send forth some (if the Lord will, and that we live) this Autumn, sundry ways. I see the best way is, *up and be doing:* In all labour there is profit; *Seek and ye shall find*. We have Christ's Example, his Promise, his Presence, his Spirit to assist; and I trust that the Lord will find a way for your encouragement.

Natick is our chief Town, where most and chief of our Rulers, and most of the Church dwells; here most of our chief Courts are kept; and the Sacraments in the Church are for the most part here administred: It is (by the Divine Providence) seated well near in the center of all our praying *Indians,* though Westward the Cords of Christ's Tents are more enlarged. Here we began Civil Government in the year 1650. And here usually are kept the General-Trainings, which seven years ago looked so big that we never had one since till this year, and it was at this time but a small appearance. Here we have two Teachers, *John Speen* and *Anthony;* we have betwixt forty and fifty Communicants at the Lord's Table, when they all appear, but now, some are dead, and some decriped with age; and one under Censure, yet making towards a recovery; one died here the last Winter of the Stone, a temperate, sober, godly man, the first *Indian* that ever was known to have that disease; but now another hath the same disease: Sundry more are proposed, and in way of preparation to joyn unto the Church.

Ponkipog, or *Pakeunit,* is our second Town, where the *Sachems* of the Bloud (as they term their Chief Royal-Line) had their Residence and Rights, which are mostly Alienated to the English Towns: The last Chief Man, of that Line, was last year slain by the *Mauquzogs,* against whom he rashly (without due Attendants and Assistance, and against Counsel) went; yet all, yea, his Enemies say, He died valiantly; they were more afraid to kill him, than he was to die; yet being de- [7] serted by all (some knowingly say through Treason) he stood long, and at last fell alone: Had he had but 10 Men, yea 5 in good order with him, he would have driven all his Enemies before him. His Brother was resident with us in this Town, but he is fallen into sin, and from praying to God. Our Chief Ruler is *Ahauton,* an old stedfast and trusty friend to the *English,* and loveth his Country. He is more loved than feared; the reins of his bridle are too long. *Wakan* is sometimes necessarily called to keep Courts here, to add life and zeal in the punishment of Sinners. Their late Teacher, *William,* is deceased; He was a man of eminent parts, all the *English* acknowledge him, and he was known to many: He was of a ready wit, sound judgment, and affable; he is gone unto the Lord; And *William,* the Son of *Ahauton,* is called to be Teacher in his stead. He is a promising young-man, of a single and upright heart, a good judgment, he Prayeth and Preacheth well, he is studious and industrious, and well accounted of among the *English.*

Hassunnimesut is the next Town in order, dignity, and antiquity; sundry of our chief Friends in the great work of Praying to God, came from them, and there lived their Progenitors, and there lieth their Inheritance, and that is the place of their desires. It lieth upon *Nichmuke* River; the people were well known to the *English* so long as *Connecticot* Road lay that way, and their Religion was judged to be real by all that travelled that journey, and had occasion to lodge, especially to keep a Sabbath among them. The Ruler of the Town is *Anuweekin,* and his brother *Tuppukkoowillin* is Teacher, both sound and godly Men. This Ruler, last Winter, was overtaken with a Passion, which was so observable, that I had occasion to speak with him about it; he was very penitent; I told him, That as to man, I, and all men were ready to forgive him. *Ah!* said he, *I find it the greatest difficulty to forgive myself.* For the encouragement of this place, and for the cherishing of a new Plantation of Praying Indians beyond them, they called *Monatunkanet* to be a Teacher also in that Town, and both of them to take care of the new Praying-Town beyond them. And for the like encouragement, Captain *Gookins* joyned *Petahheg* with *Anuweekin.* The aged Father of this Ruler and Teacher, was last year Baptized, who hath many Children that fear God. In this place we meditate ere long (if the Lord will, and that we live) to gather a Church, that so the Sabbath-Communion of our Christian *Indians* may be the more agree- [8] able to the Divine Institution, which we make too bold with while we live at such distance.

Ogquonikongquamesut is the next Town; where, how we have been afflicted, I may not say. The *English* Town called *Marlborough* doth border upon them, as did the lines of the Tribes of *Judah* and *Benjamin;* the English Meeting-house standeth within the line of the *Indian* Town, although the contiguity and co-inhabitation is not barren in producing matters of interfering; yet our godly *Indians* do obtain a good report of the godly *English,* which is an argument that bringeth light and evidence to my heart, that our *Indians* are really godly. I was very lately among them; they desired me to settle a stated Lecture amongst them, as it is in sundry other Praying Towns, which I did with so much the more gladness and hope of blessing in it, because through Grace the Motion did first spring from themselves. *Solomon* is their Teacher, whom we judge to be a serious and sound Christian; their Ruler is *Owannamug,* whose grave, faithful, and discreet Conversation hath procured him real respect from the *English.* One that was a Teacher in this place, is the man that is now under Censure in the Church; his sin was that adventitious sin which we have brought unto them, Drunkenness, which was never known to them before they knew us *English.* But I account it our duty, and it is much in my desire, as well to teach them Wisdom to Rule such heady Creatures, as skill to get them to be able to bridle their own appetites, when they have means and opportunity of high-spirited enticements. The Wisdom and Power of Grace is not so much seen in the beggarly want of these things, as in the bridling of our selves in the use of them. It is true Dominion, to be able to use them, and not to abuse ourselves by them.

Nashope is our next Praying Town, a place of much Affliction; it was the chief place of Residence, where *Tahattawans* lived, a Sachem of the Blood, a faithful and zealous Christian, a strict yet gentle Ruler; he was a Ruler of 50 in our Civil Order; and when God took him, a chief man in our *Israel* was taken away from us. His only Son was a while vain, but proved good, expert in the Scripture, was Elected to rule in his Father's place, but soon died, insomuch that this place is now destitute of a Ruler. The Teacher of the place is *John Thomas,* a godly understanding Christian, well esteemed of by the *English:* his Father was killed by the *Mauquaogs,* shot to death as he was in [9] the River doing his Eele-wyers. This place lying in the Road-way which the *Mauquaogs* haunted, was much molested by them, and was one year wholly deserted; but this year the People have taken courage and dwell upon it again.

In this place after the great Earthquake, there was some eruption out of the Earth, which left a great *Hiatus* or Cleft a great way together, and out of some Cavities under great Rocks, by a great Pond in that place, there was a great while after often heard an humming noise, as if there were frequent eruptions out of the Ground at that place: yet for Healthfulness the place is much as other places be. For Religion, there be amongst them some Godly Christians, who are received into the Church, and baptized, and others looking that way.

Wamesut is our next Praying-Town; it lyeth at the bottom of the great Falls, on the great River *Merymak,* and at the falling-in of *Concord* River; the Sachem of this Place is named *Nomphon,* said to be a Prince of the Bloud, a Man of a real Noble Spirit: A Brother of his was slain by the *Mauquaogs* as he was upon a Rock fishing in the great River. In revenge whereof he went in the forementioned rash Expedition, but had such about him, and was so circumspect, that he came well off, though he lost one principal Man. This place is very much annoyed by the Mauquaogs, and have much ado to stand their ground.

In this Place Captain *Gookins* ordered a Garrison to be kept the last year, which Order while they attended they were safe; but when the Northern Sachems and Souldiers came, who stirred up ours to go with them on their unsuccessful Expedition, the Town was for the most part scatter'd and their Corn spoyled.

The Teacher of this Place is named *George:* they have not much esteem for Religion, but I am hopefully perswaded of sundry of them; I can go unto them but once in a year.

Panatuket is the upper part of *Merimak*-Falls; so called, because of the noise which the Waters make. Thither the *Penagwog-Indians* are come, and have built a great Fort; Their Sachems refused to pray to God, so signally and sinfully, that Captain *Gookins* and my self were very sensible of it, and were not without some expectation of some interposure of a Divine-Hand, which did eminently come to pass; for in the forenamed expedition they joyned with the Northern Sachems, [10] and were all of them cut off; even all that had so signally refused to pray unto God were now as signally rejected by God, and cut off. I hear not that it was ever known, that so many Sachems and Men of Note were killed in one imprudent Expedition, and that by a few scattered people; for the *Mauquaogs* were not imbodied to receive them, nor prepared, and few at home, which did much greaten the Overthrow of so many great Men, and shews a divine over-ruling hand of God. But now, since the *Penaguog-Sachems* are cut off, the People (sundry of them) dwelling at *Panatuket*-Fort do bow the ear to hear, and submit to pray unto God; to whom *Jethro,* after he had confest Christ and was baptized, was sent to preach Christ to them.

Magunkukquok is another of our Praying-Towns at the remotest Westerly borders of *Natick;* these are gathering together of some *Nipmuk Indians* who left their own places, and sit together in this place, and have given up themselves to pray unto God. They have called *Pomham* to be their Ruler, and *Simon* to be their Teacher. This latter is accounted a good and lively Christian; he is the second man among the *Indians* that doth experience that afflicting disease of the Stone. The Ruler hath made his Preparatory Confession of Christ, and is approved of, and at the next opportunity is to be received and baptized.

I obtained of the General-Court a Grant of a Tract of Land, for the settlement and encouragement of this People; which though as yet it be by some obstructed, yet I hope we shall find some way to accomplish the same.

Quanatusset is the last of our Praying-Towns, whose beginnings have received too much discouragement; but yet the Seed is alive: they are frequently with me; the work is at the birth, there doth only want strength to bring forth. The care of this People is committed joyntly to *Monatunkanit,* and *Tuppunkkoowillin,* the Teachers of *Hassunemesut,* as is abovesaid; and I hope if the Lord continue my life, I shall have a good account to give of that People.

Thus I have briefly touched some of the chiefest of our present Affairs, and commit them to your Prudence, to do [11] with them what you please; committing your Selves, and all your weighty Affairs unto the Guidance and Blessing of the Lord, I rest,

Your Worships to serve you in the Service of our Lord *Jesus.*

JOHN ELLIOT.

Roxbury, this 20th of the 7th month, 1670.

DECLARATION OF RIGHTS

(1765)

[On the passage of the Stamp Act by the British Parliament in March, 1765, requiring that all legal instruments used in the American colonies should bear a government stamp in order to be valid, delegates from nine colonies met in New York on October 7 of the same year, to protest against this and other encroachments upon their rights, and drew up this Declaration. The Stamp Act was repealed in March, 1766.]

THE members of this congress, sincerely devoted, with the warmest sentiments of affection and duty to his majesty's person and government, inviolably attached to the present happy establishment of the protestant succession, and with minds deeply impressed by a sense of the present and impending misfortunes of the British colonies on this continent; having considered as maturely as time will permit, the circumstances of the said colonies, esteem it our indispensable duty to make the following declarations of our humble opinion, respecting the most essential rights and liberties of the colonists, and of the grievances under which they labour, by reason of several late acts of parliament.

1. That his majesty's subjects in these colonies, owe the same allegiance to the crown of Great Britain, that is owing from his subjects born within the realm, and all due subordination to that august body the parliament of Great Britain.

2. That his majesty's liege subjects in these colonies, are entitled to all the inherent rights and liberties of his natural born subjects, within the kingdom of Great Britain.

3. That it is inseparably essential to the freedom of a people, and the undoubted right of Englishmen, that no taxes be imposed on them but with their own consent, given personally, or by their representatives.

4. That the people of these colonies are not, and, from their local circumstances, cannot be, represented in the House of Commons in Great Britain.

5. That the only representatives of the people of these colonies, are persons chosen therein by themselves; and that no taxes ever have been, or can be constitutionally imposed on them, but by their respective legislatures.

6. That all supplies to the crown being free gifts of the people, it is unreasonable and inconsistent with the principles and spirit of the British constitution, for the people of Great Britain to grant to his majesty the property of the colonists.

7. That trial by jury, is the inherent and invaluable right of every British subject in these colonies.

8. That the late act of parliament, entitled, an act for granting and applying certain stamp duties, and other duties, in the British colonies and plantations in America, &c., by imposing taxes on the inhabitants of these colonies, and the said act, and several other acts, by extending the jurisdiction of the courts of admiralty beyond its ancient limits, have a manifest tendency to subvert the rights and liberties of the colonists.

9. That the duties imposed by several late acts of parliament, from the peculiar circumstances of these colonies, will be extremely burdensome and grievous; and from the scarcity of specie, the payment of them absolutely impracticable.

10. That as the profits of the trade of these colonies ultimately center in Great Britain, to pay for the manufactures which they are obliged to take from thence, they eventually contribute very largely to all supplies granted there to the crown.

11. That the restrictions imposed by several late acts of parliament on the trade of these colonies, will render them unable to purchase the manufactures of Great Britain.

12. That the increase, prosperity and happiness of these colonies, depend on the full and free enjoyments of their rights and liberties, and an intercourse with Great Britain mutually affectionate and advantageous.

13. That it is the right of the British subjects in these colonies, to petition the king, or either house of parliament.

Lastly, That it is the indispensable duty of these colonies, to the best of sovereigns, to the mother country, and to themselves, to endeavour by a loyal and dutiful address to his majesty, and humble applications to both houses of parliament, to procure the repeal of the act for granting and applying certain stamp duties, of all clauses of any other acts of parliament, whereby the jurisdiction of the admiralty is extended as aforesaid, and of the other late acts for the restriction of American commerce.

THE DECLARATION OF INDEPENDENCE

(1776)

[In the third session of the second continental congress, Richard Henry Lee of Virginia proposed, and John Adams of Massachusetts seconded, a resolution declaring the United Colonies free and independent states; and Thomas Jefferson, John Adams, Roger Sherman, and Robert Livingstone were appointed a committee to draw up a declaration of independence. This famous document, composed almost entirely by Jefferson, was adopted unanimously on July 4, 1776.]

WHEN in the Course of human events, it becomes necessary for one people to dissolve the political bands which have connected them with another, and to assume among the Powers of the earth, the separate and equal station to which the Laws of Nature and of Nature's God entitle them, a decent respect to the opinions of mankind requires that they should declare the causes which impel them to the separation.

We hold these truths to be self-evident, that all men are created equal, that they are endowed by their Creator with certain unalienable Rights, that among these are Life, Liberty, and the pursuit of Happiness. That to secure these rights, Governments are instituted among Men, deriving their just powers from the consent of the governed, That whenever any Form of Government becomes destructive of these ends, it is the Right of the People to alter or to abolish it, and to institute new Government, laying its foundation on such principles and organizing its powers in such form, as to them shall seem most likely to effect their Safety and Happiness. Prudence, indeed, will dictate that Governments long established should not be changed for light and transient causes; and accordingly all experience hath shown, that mankind are more disposed to suffer, while evils are sufferable, than to right themselves by abolishing the forms to which they are accustomed. But when a long train of abuses and usurpations, pursuing invariably the same Object evinces a design to reduce them under absolute Despotism, it is their right, it is their duty, to throw off such Government, and to provide new Guards for their future security. Such has been the patient sufferance of these Colonies; and such is now the necessity which constrains them to alter their former Systems of Government. The history of the present King of Great Britain is a history of repeated injuries and usurpations, all having in direct object the establishment of an absolute Tyranny over these States. To prove this, let Facts be submitted to a candid world.

He has refused his Assent to Laws, the most wholesome and necessary for the public good.

He has forbidden his Governors to pass Laws of immediate and pressing importance, unless suspended in their operation till his Assent should be obtained; and when so suspended, he has utterly neglected to attend to them.

He has refused to pass other Laws for the accommodation of large districts of people, unless those people would relinquish the right of Representation in the Legislature, a right inestimable to them and formidable to tyrants only.

He has called together legislative bodies at places unusual, uncomfortable, and distant from the depository of their Public Records, for the sole purpose of fatiguing them into compliance with his measures.

He has dissolved Representative Houses repeatedly, for opposing with manly firmness his invasions on the rights of the people.

He has refused for a long time, after such dissolutions, to cause others to be elected; whereby the Legislative Powers, incapable of Annihilation, have returned to the People at large for their exercise; the State remaining in the mean time exposed to all the dangers of invasion from without, and convulsions within.

He has endeavoured to prevent the population of these States; for that purpose obstructing the Laws of Naturalization of Foreigners; refusing to pass others to encourage their migration hither, and raising the conditions of new Appropriations of Lands.

He has obstructed the Administration of Justice, by refusing his Assent to Laws for establishing Judiciary Powers.

He has made Judges dependent on his Will alone, for the tenure of their offices, and the amount and payment of their salaries.

He has erected a multitude of New Offices, and sent hither swarms of Officers to harass our People, and eat out their substance.

He has kept among us, in times of peace, Standing Armies without the Consent of our legislature.

He has affected to render the Military independent of and superior to the Civil Power.

He has combined with others to subject us to a jurisdiction foreign to our constitution, and unacknowledged by our laws; giving his Assent to their acts of pretended legislation:

For quartering large bodies of armed troops among us:

For protecting them, by a mock Trial, from Punishment for any Murders which they should commit on the Inhabitants of these States:

For cutting off our Trade with all parts of the world:

For imposing taxes on us without our Consent:

For depriving us in many cases, of the benefits of Trial by Jury:

For transporting us beyond Seas to be tried for pretended offences:

For abolishing the free System of English Laws in a neighbouring Province, establishing therein an Arbitrary government, and enlarging its Boundaries so as to render it at once an example and fit instrument for introducing the same absolute rule into these Colonies:

For taking away our Charters, abolishing our most valuable Laws, and altering fundamentally the Forms of our Governments:

For suspending our own Legislature, and declaring themselves invested with Power to legislate for us in all cases whatsoever.

He has abdicated Government here, by declaring us out of his Protection and waging War against us.

He has plundered our seas, ravaged our Coasts, burnt our towns, and destroyed the lives of our people.

He is at this time transporting large armies of foreign mercenaries to compleat the works of death, desolation and tyranny, already begun with circumstances of Cruelty & perfidy scarcely paralleled in the most barbarous ages, and totally unworthy the Head of a civilized nation.

He has constrained our fellow Citizens taken Captive on the high Seas to bear Arms against their Country, to become the executioners of their friends and Brethren, or to fall themselves by their Hands.

He has excited domestic insurrections amongst us, and has endeavoured to bring on the inhabitants of our frontiers, the merciless Indian Savages, whose known rule of warfare, is an undistinguished destruction of all ages, sexes and conditions.

In every stage of these Oppressions We have Petitioned for Redress in the most humble terms: Our repeated Petitions have been answered only by repeated injury. A Prince, whose character is thus marked by every act which may define a Tyrant, is unfit to be the ruler of a free People.

Nor have We been wanting in attention to our British brethren. We have warned them from time to time of attempts by their legislature to extend an unwarrantable jurisdiction over us. We have reminded them of the circumstances of our emigration and settlement here. We have appealed to their native justice and magnanimity, and we have conjured them by the ties of our common kindred to disavow these usurpations, which, would inevitably interrupt our connections and correspondence. They too have been deaf to the voice of justice and of consanguinity. We must, therefore, acquiesce in the necessity, which denounces our Separation, and hold them, as we hold the rest of mankind, Enemies in War, in Peace Friends.

We, therefore, the Representatives of the United States of America, in General Congress, Assembled, appealing to the Supreme Judge of the world for the rectitude of our intentions, do, in the Name, and by Authority of the good People of these Colonies, solemnly publish and declare, That these United Colonies are, and of Right ought to be Free and Independent States; that they are Absolved from all Allegiance to the British Crown, and that all political connection between them and the State of Great Britain, is and ought to be totally dissolved; and that as Free and Independent States, they have full Power to levy War, conclude Peace, contract Alliances, establish Commerce, and to do all other Acts and Things which Independent States may of right do. And for the support of this Declaration, with a firm reliance on the Protection of Divine Providence, we mutually pledge to each other our Lives, our Fortunes and our sacred Honor.

JOHN HANCOCK.

New Hampshire

JOSIAH BARTLETT   MATTHEW THORNTON
WM. WHIPPLE

Massachusetts Bay

SAML. ADAMS   ELBRIDGE GERRY
JOHN ADAMS   ROBT. TREAT PAINE

Rhode Island

STEP. HOPKINS   WILLIAM ELLERY

Connecticut

ROGER SHERMAN   WM. WILLIAMS
SAM'EL HUNTINGTON   OLIVER WOLCOTT

New York

WM. FLOYD   FRANS. LEWIS
PHIL. LIVINGSTON   LEWIS MORRIS

New Jersey

RICHD. STOCKTON   JOHN HART
JNO. WITHERSPOON   ABRA. CLARK
FRAS. HOPKINSON

Pennsylvania

ROBT. MORRIS   JAS. SMITH
BENJAMIN RUSH   GEO. TAYLOR
BENJA. FRANKLIN   JAMES WILSON
JOHN MORTON   GEO. ROSS
GEO. CLYMER

Delaware

CÆSAR RODNEY   THO. M'KEAN
GEO. READ

Maryland

SAMUEL CHASE   THOS. STONE
WM. PACA   CHARLES CARROLL of Carrollton

Virginia

GEORGE WYTHE   THOS. NELSON, jr.
RICHARD HENRY LEE   FRANCIS LIGHTFOOT LEE
TH. JEFFERSON   CARTER BRAXTON
BENJA. HARRISON

North Carolina

WM. HOOPER
JOSEPH HEWES

JOHN PENN

South Carolina

EDWARD RUTLEDGE
THOS. HEYWARD, junr

ARTHUR MIDDLETON
THOMAS LYNCH, junr

Georgia

BUTTON GWINNETT
LYMAN HALL

GEO. WALTON

THE MECKLENBURG
DECLARATION OF INDEPENDENCE
(1775)

[On April 30, 1819, the Raleigh (N. C.) *Register* published the following document, said to have been adopted by the Committee of Mecklenburg county, North Carolina, on May 20, 1775, the day after the receipt of the news of the battle of Lexington. The similarity of some of its phrases (here italicized) to phrases in the Declaration of Independence raised questions as to plagiarism on Jefferson's part, or, on the other hand, as to the authenticity of the Mecklenburg document. It is clear that Jefferson never heard of it before 1819; and the explanation most commonly adopted is, that it is a compilation, based in part on general recollections of certain resolutions, still extant, which were drawn up by the committee-men of Mecklenburg on May 31, 1775.]

"1. *R*ESOLVED, That whosoever directly or indirectly abetted, or in any way, form, or manner, countenanced the unchartered and dangerous invasion of our rights, as claimed by Great Britain, is an enemy to this Country—to America—and to the *inherent and inalienable rights* of man.

2. *Resolved,* That we the citizens of Mecklenburg County, do hereby *dissolve the political bands which have connected* us to the Mother Country, and hereby *absolve* ourselves *from all allegiance to the British Crown,* and abjure *all political connection,* contract, or association, with that Nation, who have wantonly trampled on our rights and liberties—and inhumanly shed the innocent blood of American patriots at Lexington.

3. *Resolved,* That we do hereby declare ourselves a *free and independent* people, *are, and of right ought to be,* a sovereign and self-governing Association, under the control of no power other than that of our God and the General Government of the Congress; to the maintenance of which independence, we solemnly *pledge to each other,* our mutual coöperation, *our lives, our fortunes, and our* most *sacred honor.*

4. *Resolved,* That as we now acknowledge the existence and control of no law or legal officer, civil or military, within this County,

we do hereby ordain and adopt, as a rule of life, all, each and every of our former laws—where, nevertheless, the Crown of Great Britain never can be considered as holding rights, privileges, immunities, or authority therein.

5. *Resolved,* That it is also further decreed, that all, each and every military officer in this County, is hereby reinstated to his former command and authority, he acting conformably to these regulations, and that every member present of this delegation shall henceforth be a civil officer, viz. a Justice of the Peace, in the character of a *'Committee-man,'* to issue process, hear and determine all matters of controversy, according to said adopted laws, and to preserve peace, and union, and harmony, in said County, and to use every exertion to spread the love of country and fire of freedom throughout America, until a more general and organized government be established in this province."

ARTICLES
OF CONFEDERATION
(1777)

[The same continental congress which passed the Declaration of Independence, appointed a committee "to prepare and digest the form of confederation to be entered into between these colonies." On July 12, 1776, the committee reported a draft of these articles; and after many changes the congress adopted them on November 15, 1777. They did not, however, become operative till they had been adopted by all the individual states, the last of which, Maryland, finally consented on March 1, 1781. The articles were superseded by the Constitution in 1789.]

To all to whom these Presents shall come, we the undersigned Delegates of the States affixed to our Names send greeting.

WHEREAS, the Delegates of the United States of America in Congress assembled did on the fifteenth day of November in the year of our Lord One Thousand Seven Hundred and Seventy-seven, and in the Second Year of the Independence of America agree to certain articles of Confederation and perpetual Union between the States of Newhampshire, Massachusetts-bay, Rhodeisland and Providence Plantations, Connecticut, New York, New Jersey, Pennsylvania, Delaware, Virginia, North-Carolina, South-Carolina and Georgia in the Words following, viz.

"Articles of Confederation and perpetual Union between the States of Newhampshire, Massachusetts-bay, Rhodeisland and Providence Plantations, Connecticut, New-York, New-Jersey, Pennsylvania, Delaware, Maryland, Virginia, North-Carolina, South-Carolina and Georgia."

Article I. The stile of this confederacy shall be "The United States of America."

Article II. Each State retains its sovereignty, freedom and independence, and every power, jurisdiction and right, which is not by this confederation expressly delegated to the United States, in Congress assembled.

Article III. The said States hereby severally enter into a firm league of friendship with each other, for their common defence, the security of their liberties, and their mutual and general welfare, binding themselves to assist each other, against all force offered to, or attacks made upon them, or any of them, on account of religion, sovereignty, trade, or any other pretence whatever.

ARTICLE IV. The better to secure and perpetuate mutual friendship and intercourse among the people of the different States in this Union, the free inhabitants of each of these States, paupers, vagabonds and fugitives from justice excepted, shall be entitled to all privileges and immunities of free citizens in the several States; and the people of each State shall have free ingress and regress to and from any other State, and shall enjoy therein all the privileges of trade and commerce, subject to the same duties, impositions and restrictions as the inhabitants thereof respectively, provided that such restrictions shall not extend so far as to prevent the removal of property imported into any State, to any other State of which the owner is an inhabitant; provided also that no imposition, duties or restriction shall be laid by any State, on the property of the United States, or either of them.

If any Person guilty of, or charged with treason, felony, or other high misdemeanor in any State, shall flee from justice, and be found in any of the United States, he shall upon demand of the Governor or Executive power, of the State from which he fled, be delivered up and removed to the State having jurisdiction of his offence.

Full faith and credit shall be given in each of these States to the records, acts and judicial proceedings of the courts and magistrates of every other State.

ARTICLE V. For the more convenient management of the general interest of the United States, delegates shall be annually appointed in such manner as the legislature of each State shall direct, to meet in Congress on the first Monday in November, in every year, with a power reserved to each State, to recall its delegates, or any of them, at any time within the year, and to send others in their stead, for the remainder of the year.

No State shall be represented in Congress by less than two, nor by more than seven members; and no person shall be capable of being a delegate for more than three years in any term of six years;

nor shall any person, being a delegate, be capable of holding any office under the United States, for which he, or another for his benefit receives any salary, fees or emolument of any kind.

Each State shall maintain its own delegates in a meeting of the States, and while they act as members of the committee of the States.

In determining questions in the United States, in Congress assembled, each State shall have one vote.

Freedom of speech and debate in Congress shall not be impeached or questioned in any court, or place out of Congress, and the members of Congress shall be protected in their persons from arrests and imprisonments, during the time of their going to and from, and attendance on Congress, except for treason, felony, or breach of the peace.

ARTICLE VI. No State without the consent of the United States in Congress assembled, shall send any embassy to, or receive any embassy from, or enter into any conference, agreement, alliance or treaty with any king, prince or state; nor shall any person holding any office of profit or trust under the United States, or any of them, accept of any present, emolument, office or title of any kind whatever from any king, prince or foreign state; nor shall the United States in Congress assembled, or any of them, grant any title of nobility.

No two or more States shall enter into any treaty, confederation or alliance whatever between them, without the consent of the United States in Congress assembled, specifying accurately the purposes for which the same is to be entered into, and how long it shall continue.

No State shall lay any imposts or duties, which may interfere with any stipulations in treaties, entered into by the United States in Congress assembled, with any king, prince or state, in pursuance of any treaties already proposed by Congress, to the courts of France and Spain.

No vessels of war shall be kept up in time of peace by any State, except such number only, as shall be deemed necessary by the United States in Congress assembled, for the defence of such State, or its trade; nor shall any body of forces be kept up by any State, in time of peace, except such number only, as in the judgment of the United States, in Congress assembled, shall be deemed requisite to garrison the forts necessary for the defence of such State; but every State shall always keep up a well regulated and disciplined militia, sufficiently armed and accoutered, and shall provide and constantly have ready for use, in public stores, a due number of field pieces and tents, and a proper quantity of arms, ammunition and camp equipage.

No State shall engage in any war without the consent of the United States in Congress assembled, unless such State be actually invaded by enemies, or shall have received certain advice of a resolution being formed by some nation of Indians to invade such State, and the danger is so imminent as not to admit of a delay, till the United States in Congress assembled can be consulted: nor shall any State grant commissions to any ships or vessels of war, nor letters of marque or reprisal, except it be after a declaration of war by the United States in Congress assembled, and then only against the kingdom or state and the subjects thereof, against which war has been so declared, and under such regulations as shall be established by the United States in Congress assembled, unless such State be infested by pirates, in which case vessels of war may be fitted out for that occasion, and kept so long as the danger shall continue, or until the United States in Congress assembled shall determine otherwise.

ARTICLE VII. When land-forces are raised by any State for the common defence, all officers of or under the rank of colonel, shall be appointed by the Legislature of each State respectively by whom such forces shall be raised, or in such manner as such State shall direct, and all vacancies shall be filled up by the State which first made the appointment.

ARTICLE VIII. All charges of war, and all other expenses that shall be incurred for the common defence or general welfare, and allowed by the United States in Congress assembled, shall be defrayed out of a common treasury, which shall be supplied by the several States, in proportion to the value of all land within each State, granted to or surveyed for any person, as such land and the buildings and improvements thereon shall be estimated according to such mode as the United States in Congress assembled, shall from time to time direct and appoint.

The taxes for paying that proportion shall be laid and levied by the authority and direction of the Legislatures of the several States within the time agreed upon by the United States in Congress assembled.

ARTICLE IX. The United States in Congress assembled, shall have the sole and exclusive right and power of determining on peace and war, except in the cases mentioned in the sixth article—of sending and receiving ambassadors—entering into treaties and alliances, provided that no treaty of commerce shall be made whereby the legislative power of the respective States shall be restrained from imposing such imposts and duties on foreigners, as their own people are subjected to, or from prohibiting the exportation or importation of any species of goods or commodities whatsoever—of establishing rules for deciding in all cases, what captures on land or water shall be legal, and in what manner prizes taken by land or naval forces in the service of the United States shall be divided or appropriated— of granting letters of marque and reprisal in times of peace—appointing courts for the trial of piracies and felonies committed on the high seas and establishing courts for receiving and determining finally appeals in all cases of captures, provided that no **member** of Congress shall be appointed a judge of any of the said courts.

The United States in Congress assembled shall also be the last resort on appeal in all disputes and differences now subsisting or that hereafter may arise between two or more States concerning boundary, jurisdiction or any other cause whatever; which authority shall always be exercised in the manner following. Whenever the legislative or executive authority or lawful agent of any State in controversy with another shall present a petition to Congress, stating the matter in question and praying for a hearing, notice thereof shall be given by order of Congress to the legislative or executive authority of the other State in controversy, and a day assigned for the appearance of the parties by their lawful agents, who shall then be directed to appoint by joint consent, commissioners or judges to constitute a court for hearing and determining the matter in question: but if they cannot agree, Congress shall name three persons out of each of the United States, and from the list of such persons each party shall alternately strike out one, the petitioners beginning, until the number shall be reduced to thirteen; and from that number not less than seven, nor more than nine names as Congress shall direct, shall in the presence of Congress be drawn out by lot, and the persons whose names shall be so drawn or any five of them, shall be com' missioners or judges, to hear and finally determine the controversy, so always as a major part of the judges who shall hear the cause shall agree in the determination: and if either party shall neglect to attend at the day appointed, without showing reasons, which Congress shall judge sufficient, or being present shall refuse to strike, the Congress shall proceed to nominate three persons out of each State, and the Secretary of Congress shall strike in behalf of such party absent or refusing; and the judgment and sentence of the court to be appointed, in the manner before prescribed, shall be final and conclusive; and if any of the parties shall refuse to submit to the authority of such court, or to appear or defend their claim or cause, the court shall nevertheless proceed to pronounce sentence, or judgment, which shall in like manner be final and decisive, the judgment or sentence and other proceedings being in either case transmitted to Congress, and lodged among the acts of Congress for the security of the parties concerned: provided that every commissioner, before he sits in judgment, shall take an oath to be administered by one of the judges of the supreme or superior court of the State, where the cause shall be tried, "well and truly to hear and determine the matter in question, according to the best of his judgment, without favour, affection or hope of reward:" provided also that no State shall be deprived of territory for the benefit of the United States.

All controversies concerning the private right of soil claimed under different grants of two or more States, whose jurisdiction as they may respect such lands, and the States which passed such grants are adjusted, the said grants or either of them being at the same time claimed to have originated antecedent to such settlement of jurisdiction, shall on the petition of either party to the Congress of the United States, be finally determined as near as may be in the same manner as is before prescribed for deciding disputes respecting territorial jurisdiction between different States.

The United States in Congress assembled shall also have the sole and exclusive right and power of regulating the alloy and value of

coin struck by their own authority, or by that of the respective States
—fixing the standard of weights and measures throughout the United
States—regulating the trade and managing all affairs with the Indians, not members of any of the States, provided that the legislative
right of any State within its own limits be not infringed or violated—
establishing and regulating post-offices from one State to another,
throughout all the United States, and exacting such postage on the
papers passing thro' the same as may be requisite to defray the
expenses of the said office—appointing all officers of the land forces,
in the service of the United States, excepting regimental officers—
appointing all the officers of the naval forces, and commissioning all
officers whatever in the service of the United States—making rules
for the government and regulation of the said land and naval forces,
and directing their operations.

The United States in Congress assembled shall have authority to
appoint a committee, to sit in the recess of Congress, to be denom-
inated "a Committee of the States," and to consist of one delegate
from each State; and to appoint such other committees and civil
officers as may be necessary for managing the general affairs of the
United States under their direction—to appoint one of their number
to preside, provided that no person be allowed to serve in the office
of president more than one year in any term of three years; to ascertain the necessary sums of money to be raised for the service of the
United States, and to appropriate and apply the same for defraying
the public expenses—to borrow money, or emit bills on the credit of
the United States, transmitting every half year to the respective
States an account of the sums of money so borrowed or emitted,
—to build and equip a navy—to agree upon the number of
land forces, and to make requisitions from each State for its quota,
in proportion to the number of white inhabitants in such State;
which requisition shall be binding, and thereupon the Legislature of
each State shall appoint the regimental officers, raise the men and
cloath, arm and equip them in a soldier like manner, at the expense
of the United States; and the officers and men so cloathed, armed
and equipped shall march to the place appointed, and within the
time agreed on by the United States in Congress assembled: but if
the United States in Congress assembled shall, on consideration of

circumstances judge proper that any State should not raise men, or should raise a smaller number than its quota, and that any other State should raise a greater number of men than the quota thereof, such extra number shall be raised, officered, cloathed, armed and equipped in the same as the quota of such State, unless the legislature of such State shall judge that such extra number cannot be safely spared outside of the same, in which case they shall raise, officer, cloath, arm and equip as many of such extra number as they judge can be safely spared. And the officers and men so cloathed, armed and equipped, shall march to the place appointed, and within the time agreed on by the United States in Congress assembled.

The United States in Congress assembled shall never engage in a war, nor grant letters of marque and reprisal in time of peace, nor enter into any treaties or alliances, nor coin money, nor regulate the value thereof, nor ascertain the sums and expenses necessary for the defence and welfare of the United States, or any of them, nor emit bills, nor borrow money on the credit of the United States, nor appropriate money, nor agree upon the number of vessels of war, to be built or purchased, or the number of land or sea forces to be raised, nor appoint a commander in chief of the army or navy, unless nine States assent to the same: nor shall a question on any other point, except for adjourning from day to day be determined, unless by the votes of a majority of the United States in Congress assembled.

The Congress of the United States shall have power to adjourn to any time within the year, and to any place within the United States, so that no period of adjournment be for a longer duration than the space of six months, and shall publish the journal of their proceedings monthly, except such parts thereof relating to treaties, alliances or military operations, as in their judgment require secresy; and the yeas and nays of the delegates of each State on any question shall be entered on the journal, when it is desired by any delegate; and the delegates of a State, or any of them, at his or their request shall be furnished with a transcript of the said journal, except such parts as are above excepted, to lay before the Legislatures of the several States.

ARTICLE X. The committee of the States, or any nine of them, shall be authorized to execute, in the recess of Congress, such of the powers of Congress as the United States in Congress assembled, by the consent of nine States, shall from time to time think expedient to vest them with; provided that no power be delegated to the said committee, for the exercise of which, by the articles of confederation, the voice of nine States in the Congress of the United States assembled is requisite.

ARTICLE XI. Canada acceding to this confederation, and joining in the measures of the United States, shall be admitted into, and entitled to all the advantages of this Union: but no other colony shall be admitted into the same, unless such admission be agreed to by nine States.

ARTICLE XII. All bills of credit emitted, monies borrowed and debts contracted by, or under the authority of Congress, before the assembling of the United States, in pursuance of the present confederation, shall be deemed and considered as a charge against the United States, for payment and satisfaction whereof the said United States, and the public faith are hereby solemnly pledged.

ARTICLE XIII. Every State shall abide by the determinations of the United States in Congress assembled, on all questions which by this confederation are submitted to them. And the articles of this confederation shall be inviolably observed by every State, and the Union shall be perpetual; nor shall any alteration at any time hereafter be made in any of them; unless such alteration be agreed to in a Congress of the United States, and be afterwards confirmed by the Legislatures of every State.

And whereas it hath pleased the Great Governor of the World to incline the hearts of the Legislatures we respectively represent in Congress, to approve of, and to authorize us to ratify the said articles of confederation and perpetual union. Know ye that we, the undersigned delegates, by virtue of the power and authority to us given for that purpose, do by these presents, in the name and in behalf of our respective constituents, fully and entirely ratify and confirm each and every of the said Articles of Confederation and perpetual union, and all and singular the matters and things therein contained: and we do further solemnly plight and engage the faith of our respective constituents, that they shall abide by the determinations of the United States in Congress assembled, on all questions, which by the said confederation are submitted to them. And that the articles thereof shall be inviolably observed by the States we respectively represent, and that the Union shall be perpetual.

In witness whereof we have hereunto set our hands in Congress. Done at Philadelphia in the State of Pennsylvania the ninth day of July in the year of our Lord one thousand seven hundred and seventy-eight, and in the third year of the independence of America.

On the part & behalf of the State of New Hampshire

JOSIAH BARTLETT

JOHN WENTWORTH, Junr
August 8th, 1778

On the part and behalf of the State of Massachusetts Bay

JOHN HANCOCK
SAMUEL ADAMS
ELBRIDGE GERRY

FRANCIS DANA
JAMES LOVELL
SAMUEL HOLTEN

On the part and behalf of the State of Rhode Island and Providence Plantations

WILLIAM ELLERY
HENRY MARCHANT

JOHN COLLINS

On the part and behalf of the State of Connecticut

ROGER SHERMAN
SAMUEL HUNTINGTON
OLIVER WOLCOTT

TITUS HOSMER
ANDREW ADAMS

On the part and behalf of the State of New York

JAS. DUANE
FRA. LEWIS

GOUV. MORRIS
WM. DUER

On the part and in behalf of the State of New Jersey Novr. 26, 1778

JNO. WITHERSPOON

NATHL. SCUDDER

On the part and behalf of the State of Pennsylvania

ROBT. MORRIS
DANIEL ROBERDEAU
JNO. BAYARD SMITH

WILLIAM CLINGAN
JOSEPH REED, 22d July, 1778

On the part & behalf of the State of Delaware

THOS. M'KEAN, Feby. 12, 1779   JOHN DICKINSON, May 5th, 1779
NICHOLAS VAN DYKE

On the part and behalf of the State of Maryland

JOHN HANSON, March 1, 1781   DANIEL CARROLL, Mar. 1, 1781

On the part and behalf of the State of Virginia

RICHARD HENRY LEE   JNO. HARVIE
JOHN BANISTER   FRANCIS LIGHTFOOT LEE
THOMAS ADAMS

On the part and behalf of the State of No. Carolina

JOHN PENN, July 21, 1778   JNO. WILLIAMS
CORNS. HARNETT

On the part & behalf of the State of South Carolina

HENRY LAURENS   RICHD. HUTSON
WILLIAM HENRY DRAYTON   THOS. HEYWARD, Junr
JNO. MATTHEWS

On the part & behalf of the State of Georgia

EDWD. TELFAIR   EDWD. LANGWORTHY
JNO. WALTON, 24th July, 1778

ARTICLES OF CAPITULATION
YORKTOWN
(1781)

[The surrender of Cornwallis, arranged in these articles, virtually brought to a close the hostilities in the war between Great Britain and her American colonies, and assured the independence of the United States.]

Settled between his Excellency General Washington, Commander-in-Chief of the combined Forces of America and France; his Excellency the Count de Rochambeau, Lieutenant-General of the Armies of the King of France, Great Cross of the royal and military Order of St. Louis, commanding the auxiliary Troops of his Most Christian Majesty in America; and his Excellency the Count de Grasse, Lieutenant-General of the Naval Armies of his Most Christian Majesty, Commander of the Order of St. Louis, Commander-in-Chief of the Naval Army of France in the Chesapeake, on the one Part; and the Right Honorable Earl Cornwallis, Lieutenant-General of his Britannic Majesty's Forces, commanding the Garrisons of York and Gloucester; and Thomas Symonds, Esquire, commanding his Britannic Majesty's Naval Forces in York River in Virginia, on the other Part.

ARTICLE I. The garrisons of York and Gloucester, including the officers and seamen of his Britannic Majesty's ships, as well as other mariners, to surrender themselves prisoners of war to the combined forces of America and France. The land troops to remain prisoners to the United States, the navy to the naval army of his Most Christian Majesty.

Granted.

ARTICLE II. The artillery, arms, accoutrements, military chest, and public stores of every denomination, shall be delivered unimpaired to the heads of departments appointed to receive them.

Granted.

ARTICLE III. At twelve o'clock this day the two redoubts on the left flank of York to be delivered, the one to a detachment of American infantry, the other to a detachment of French grenadiers.

Granted.

The garrison of York will march out to a place to be appointed in front of the posts, at two o'clock precisely, with shouldered arms, colors cased, and drums beating a British or German march. They are then to ground their arms, and return to their encampments, where they will remain until they are despatched to the places of their destination. Two works on the Gloucester side will be delivered at one o'clock to a detachment of French and American troops appointed to possess them. The garrison will march out at three o'clock in the afternoon; the cavalry with their swords drawn, trumpets sounding, and the infantry in the manner prescribed for the garrison of York. They are likewise to return to their encampments until they can be finally marched off.

ARTICLE IV. Officers are to retain their side-arms. Both officers and soldiers to keep their private property of every kind; and no part of their baggage or papers to be at any time subject to search or inspection. The baggage and papers of officers and soldiers taken during the siege to be likewise preserved for them.

Granted.

It is understood that any property obviously belonging to the inhabitants of these States, in the possession of the garrison, shall be subject to be reclaimed.

ARTICLE V. The soldiers to be kept in Virginia, Maryland, or Pennsylvania, and as much by regiments as possible, and supplied with the same rations of provisions as are allowed to soldiers in the service of America. A field-officer from each nation, to wit, British, Anspach, and Hessian, and other officers on parole, in the proportion of one to fifty men to be allowed to reside near their respective regi-, ments, to visit them frequently, and be witnesses of their treatment; and that their officers may receive and deliver clothing and other necessaries for them, for which passports are to be granted when applied for.

Granted.

ARTICLE VI. The general, staff, and other officers not employed as mentioned in the above articles, and who choose it, to be permitted to go on parole to Europe, to New York, or to any other American maritime posts at present in the possession of the British forces, at their own option; and proper vessels to be granted by the Count de Grasse to carry them under flags of truce to New York within ten days from this date, if possible, and they to reside in a district to be agreed upon hereafter, until they embark. The officers of the civil department of the army and navy to be included in this article. Passports to go by land to be granted to those to whom vessels cannot be furnished.

Granted.

ARTICLE VII. Officers to be allowed to keep soldiers as servants, according to the common practice of the service. Servants not soldiers are not to be considered as prisoners, and are to be allowed to attend their masters.

Granted.

ARTICLE VIII. The Bonetta sloop-of-war to be equipped, and navigated by its present captain and crew, and left entirely at the disposal of Lord Cornwallis from the hour that the capitulation is signed, to receive an aid-de-camp to carry despatches to Sir Henry Clinton; and such soldiers as he may think proper to send to New York, to be permitted to sail without examination. When his despatches are ready, his Lordship engages on his part, that the ship shall be delivered to the order of the Count de Grasse, if she escapes the dangers of the sea. That she shall not carry off any public stores. Any part of the crew that may be deficient on her return, and the soldiers passengers, to be accounted for on her delivery.

ARTICLE IX. The traders are to preserve their property, and to be allowed three months to dispose of or remove them; and those traders are not to be considered as prisoners of war.

The traders will be allowed to dispose of their effects, the allied army having the right of preëmption. The traders to be considered as prisoners of war upon parole.

ARTICLE X. Natives or inhabitants of different parts of this country, at present in York or Gloucester, are not to be punished on account of having joined the British army.

This article cannot be assented to, being altogether of civil resort.

ARTICLE XI. Proper hospitals to be furnished for the sick and wounded. They are to be attended by their own surgeons on parole; and they are to be furnished with medicines and stores from the American hospitals.

The hospital stores now at York and Gloucester shall be delivered for the use of the British sick and wounded. Passports will be granted for procuring them further supplies from New York, as occasion may require; and proper hospitals will be furnished for the reception of the sick and wounded of the two garrisons.

ARTICLE XII. Wagons to be furnished to carry the baggage of the officers attending the soldiers, and to surgeons when travelling on account of the sick, attending the hospitals at public expense.

They are to be furnished if possible.

ARTICLE XIII. The shipping and boats in the two harbours, with all their stores, guns, tackling, and apparel, shall be delivered up in their present state to an officer of the navy appointed to take possession of them, previously unloading the private property, part of which had been on board for security during the siege.

Granted.

ARTICLE XIV. No article of capitulation to be infringed on pretence of reprisals; and if there be any doubtful expressions in it, they are to be interpreted according to the common meaning and acceptation of the words.

Granted.

Done at Yorktown, in Virginia, October 19th, 1781.

CORNWALLIS,
THOMAS SYMONDS.

Done in the Trenches before Yorktown, in Virginia, October 19th, 1781.

> GEORGE WASHINGTON,
> LE COMTE DE ROCHAMBEAU,
> LE COMTE DE BARRAS,
> *En mon nom & celui du*
> COMTE DE GRASSE.

TREATY WITH GREAT BRITAIN
(1783)

[Less than five months after the surrender of Cornwallis, the British Parliament passed an act to enable the king to make peace till July 1783. In the end of November, 1782, a provisional treaty was signed, the negotiations on behalf of Congress having been conducted by Benjamin Franklin, John Adams, John Jay, and Henry Laurens. On September 3, 1783, this treaty was made definitive in the form here printed, and the complete independence of the American States acknowledged by Great Britain.]

DEFINITIVE TREATY OF PEACE BETWEEN THE UNITED STATES OF AMERICA AND HIS BRITANNIC MAJESTY, CONCLUDED AT PARIS, SEPTEMBER 3, 1783; RATIFIED BY CONGRESS, JANUARY 14, 1784; PROCLAIMED, JANUARY 14, 1784.

IN the name of the Most Holy and Undivided Trinity.

It having pleased the Divine Providence to dispose the hearts of the most serene and most potent Prince George the Third, by the Grace of God King of Great Britain, France, and Ireland, Defender of the Faith, Duke of Brunswick and Luneburg, Arch-Treasurer and Prince Elector of the Holy Roman Empire, &c., and of the United States of America, to forget all past misunderstandings and differences that have unhappily interrupted the good correspondence and friendship which they mutually wish to restore; and to establish such a beneficial and satisfactory intercourse between the two countries, upon the ground of reciprocal advantages and mutual convenience, as may promote and secure to both perpetual peace and harmony: And having for this desirable end already laid the foundation of peace and reconciliation, by the provisional articles, signed at Paris, on the 30th of Nov., 1782, by the commissioners empowered on each part, which articles were agreed to be inserted in and to constitute the treaty of peace proposed to be concluded between the Crown of Great Britain and the said United States, but which treaty was not to be concluded until terms of peace should be agreed upon between Great Britain and France, and His Britannic Majesty should be ready to conclude such treaty accordingly; and the treaty between\ Great Britain and France having since been concluded, His Britannic Majesty and the United States of America, in order to carry into full effect the provisional articles above mentioned, according to the tenor thereof, have constituted and appointed, that is to say, His Britannic Majesty on his part, David Hartley, esqr., member of the Parliament of Great Britain; and the said United States on their part, John Adams, esqr., late a commissioner of the United States of America at the Court of Versailles, late Delegate in Congress from the State of Massachusetts, and chief justice of the said State, and Minister Plenipotentiary of the said United States to their High Mightinesses the States General of the United Netherlands; Benjamin Franklin, esq're, late Delegate in Congress from the State of Pennsylvania, president of the convention of the said State, and Minister Plenipotentiary from the United States of America at the Court of Versailles; John Jay, esq're, late President of Congress, and Chief Justice of the State of New York, and Minister Plenipotentiary from the said United States at the Court of Madrid, to be the Plenipotentiaries for the concluding and signing the present definitive treaty; who, after having reciprocally communicated their respective full powers, have agreed upon and confirmed the following articles:

ARTICLE I

His Britannic Majesty acknowledges the said United States, viz. New Hampshire, Massachusetts Bay, Rhode Island, and Providence Plantations, Connecticut, New York, New Jersey, Pennsylvania, Delaware, Maryland, Virginia, North Carolina, South Carolina, and Georgia, to be free, sovereign and independent States; that he treats with them as such, and for himself, his heirs and successors, relinquishes all claims to the Government, proprietory and territorial rights of the same, and every part thereof.

ARTICLE II

And that all disputes which might arise in future, on the subject of the boundaries of the said United States may be prevented, it is hereby agreed and declared, that the following are, and shall be their boundaries, viz.: From the northwest angle of Nova Scotia, viz. that angle which is formed by a line drawn due north from the source of Saint Croix River to the Highlands; along the said Highlands which divide those rivers that empty themselves into the river St. Lawrence, from those which fall into the Atlantic Ocean, to the northwesternmost head of Connecticut River; thence down along the middle of that river, to the forth-fifth degree of north latitude; from thence, by a line due west on said latitude, until it strikes the river Iroquois or Cataraquy; thence along the middle of said river into Lake Ontario, through the middle of said lake until it strikes the communication by water between that lake and Lake Erie; thence along the middle of said communication into Lake Erie, through the middle of said lake until it arrives at the water communication between that lake and Lake Huron; thence along the middle of said water communication into the Lake Huron; thence through the middle of said lake to the water communication between that Lake and Lake Superior; thence through Lake Superior northward of the Isles Royal and Phelipeaux, to the Long Lake; thence through the middle of said Long Lake, and the water communication between it and the Lake of the Woods, to the said Lake of the Woods; thence through the said lake to the most northwestern point thereof, and from thence on a due west course to the river Mississippi; thence by a line to be drawn along the middle of the said river Mississippi until it shall intersect the northernmost part of the thirty-first degree of north latitude. South, by a line to be drawn due east from the determination of the line last mentioned, in the latitude of thirty-one degrees north of the Equator, to the middle of the river Apalachicola or Catahouche; thence along the middle thereof to its junction with the Flint River; thence, straight to the head of St. Mary's River; and thence down along the middle of St. Mary's River to the Atlantic Ocean. East, by a line to be drawn along the middle of the river St. Croix, from its mouth in the Bay of Fundy to its source, and from its source directly north to the aforesaid Highlands, which divide the rivers that fall into the Atlantic Ocean from those which fall into the river St. Lawrence; comprehending all islands within twenty leagues of any part of the shores of the United States, and lying between lines to be drawn due east from the points where the aforesaid boundaries between Nova Scotia on the one part, and East Florida on the other, shall respectively touch the Bay of Fundy and the Atlantic Ocean; excepting such islands as now are, or heretofore have been, within the limits of the said province of Nova Scotia.

ARTICLE III

It is agreed that the people of the United States shall continue to enjoy unmolested the right to take fish of every kind on the Grand Bank, and on all the other banks of Newfoundland; also in the Gulph of Saint Lawrence, and at all other places in the sea where the inhabitants of both countries used at any time heretofore to fish. And also that the inhabitants of the United States shall have liberty to take fish of every kind on such part of the coast of Newfoundland as British fishermen shall use (but not to dry or cure the same on that island) and also on the coasts, bays, and creeks of all other of His Britannic Majesty's dominions in America; and that the American fishermen shall have liberty to dry and cure fish in any of the unsettled bays, harbours, and creeks of Nova Scotia, Magdalen Islands, and Labrador, so long as the same shall remain unsettled; but so soon as the same or either of them shall be settled, it shall not be lawful for the said fishermen to dry or cure fish at such settlement, without a previous agreement for that purpose with the inhabitants, proprietors, or possessors of the ground.

ARTICLE IV

It is agreed that creditors on either side shall meet with no lawful impediment to the recovery of the full value in sterling money, of all bona fide debts heretofore contracted.

ARTICLE V

It is agreed that the Congress shall earnestly recommend it to the legislatures of the respective States, to provide for the restitution of all estates, rights, and properties which have been confiscated, belonging to real British subjects, and also of the estates, rights and properties of persons resident in districts in the possession of His Majesty's arms, and who have not borne arms against the said United States. And that persons of any other description shall have free liberty to go to any part or parts of any of the thirteen United States, and therein to remain twelve months, unmolested in their endeavours to obtain the restitution of such of their estates, rights, and properties as may have been confiscated; and that Congress shall also earnestly recommend to the several States a reconsideration and revision of all acts or laws regarding the premises, so as to render the said laws or acts perfectly consistent, not only with justice and equity, but with that spirit of conciliation which, on the return of the blessings of peace, should universally prevail. And that Congress shall also earnestly recommend to the several States, that the estates, rights, and properties of such last mentioned persons, shall be restored to them, they refunding to any persons who may be now in possession, the bona fide price (where any has been given) which such persons may have paid on purchasing any of the said lands, rights, or properties, since the confiscation. And it is agreed, that all persons who have any interest in confiscated lands, either by debts, marriage settlements, or otherwise, shall meet with no lawful impediment in the prosecution of their just rights.

Article VI

That there shall be no future confiscations made, nor any prosecutions commenc'd against any person or persons for, or by reason of the part which he or they may have taken in the present war; and that no person shall, on that account, suffer any future loss or damage, either in his person, liberty, or property; and that those who may be in confinement on such charges, at the time of the ratification of the treaty in America, shall be immediately set at liberty, and the prosecutions so commenced be discontinued.

Article VII

There shall be a firm and perpetual peace between His Britannic Majesty and the said States, and between the subjects of the one and the citizens of the other, wherefore all hostilities, both by sea and land, shall from henceforth cease: All prisoners on both sides shall be set at liberty, and His Britannic Majesty shall, with all convenient speed, and without causing any destruction, or carrying away any negroes or other property of the American inhabitants, withdraw all his armies, garrisons, and fleets from the said United States, and from every port, place, and harbour within the same; leaving in all fortifications the American artillery that may be therein: And shall also order and cause all archives, records, deeds, and papers, belonging to any of the said States, or their citizens, which, in the course of the war, may have fallen into the hands of his officers, to be forthwith restored and deliver'd to the proper States and persons to whom they belong.

Article VIII

The navigation of the river Mississippi, from its source to the ocean, shall forever remain free and open to the subjects of Great Britain, and the citizens of the United States.

Article IX

In case it should so happen that any place or territory belonging to Great Britain or to the United States, should have been conquer'd by the arms of either from the other, before the arrival of the said provisional articles in America, it is agreed, that the same shall be restored without difficulty, and without requiring any compensation.

Article X

The solemn ratifications of the present treaty, expedited in good and due form, shall be exchanged between the contracting parties, in the space of six months, or sooner if possible, to be computed from the day of the signature of the present treaty. In witness whereof, we the undersigned, their Ministers Plenipotentiary, have in their name and in virtue of our full powers, signed with our hands the present definitive treaty, and caused the seals of our arms to be affix'd thereto.

Done at Paris, this third day of September, in the year of our Lord one thousand seven hundred and eighty-three.

D. Hartley	[l. s.]
John Adams	[l. s.]
B. Franklin	[l. s.]
John Jay	[l. s.]

CONSTITUTION
OF THE UNITED STATES

(1787)

[On May 25, 1787, fifty-five delegates from the various States met in Philadelphia, to discuss the drawing up of a Constitution to take the place of the Articles of Confederation. Washington presided; and, after a long struggle and many compromises, the resultant document was referred to the several States on September 28 of the same year. By June 21, 1789, the required nine out of the thirteen States had ratified it, and the new federal government was established at New York on April 30, 1789. The dates of the amendments are as follows: I–X, Nov. 3, 1791; XI, Jan 8, 1798; XII, Sept. 25, 1804; XIII, Feb. 1, 1865; XIV, July 28, 1868; XV, March 30, 1870; XVI, Feb. 25, 1913; XVII, May 31, 1913; XVIII, Jan. 29, 1919; XIX, Aug. 26, 1920.]

We, the People of the United States, in Order to form a more perfect Union, establish Justice, insure domestic Tranquility, provide for the common defence, promote the general Welfare, and secure the Blessings of Liberty to ourselves and our Posterity, do ordain and establish this CONSTITUTION for the United States of America.

ARTICLE I

SECTION 1 All legislative Powers herein granted shall be vested in a Congress of the United States, which shall consist of a Senate and House of Representatives.

SECTION 2 (1) The House of Representatives shall be composed of Members chosen every second Year by the People of the several States, and the Electors in each State shall have the Qualifications requisite for Electors of the most numerous Branch of the State Legislature.

(2) No person shall be a Representative who shall not have attained to the Age of Twenty-five years, and been seven Years a Citizen of the United States, and who shall not, when elected, be an inhabitant of that State in which he shall be chosen.

(3) Representatives and direct Taxes shall be apportioned among the several States which may be included within this Union, accord-

ing to their respective Numbers, which shall be determined by adding to the whole Number of free Persons, including those bound to Service for a Term of Years, and excluding Indians not taxed, three fifths of all other Persons. The actual Enumeration shall be made within three Years after the first Meeting of the Congress of the United States, and within every subsequent Term of ten Years, in such Manner as they shall by Law direct. The Number of Representatives shall not exceed one for every thirty Thousand, but each State shall have at Least one Representative; and until such enumeration shall be made, the State of New Hampshire shall be entitled to chuse three, Massachusetts eight, Rhode Island and Providence Plantations one, Connecticut five, New York six, New Jersey four, Pennsylvania eight, Delaware one, Maryland six, Virginia ten, North Carolina five, South Carolina five, and Georgia three.

(4) When vacancies happen in the Representation from any State, the Executive Authority thereof shall issue Writs of Election to fill such Vacancies.

(5) The House of Representatives shall chuse their Speaker and other Officers; and shall have the sole Power of Impeachment.

SECTION 3 (1) The Senate of the United States shall be composed of two Senators from each State, chosen by the Legislature thereof, for six Years; and each Senator shall have one Vote.

(2) Immediately after they shall be assembled in Consequence of the first Election, they shall be divided as equally as may be into three Classes. The Seats of the Senators of the first Class shall be vacated at the Expiration of the second Year, of the second Class at the Expiration of the fourth Year, and of the third Class at the Expiration of the sixth Year, so that one third may be chosen every second Year; and if Vacancies happen by Resignation, or otherwise, during the Recess of the Legislature of any State, the Executive thereof may make temporary Appointments until the next meeting of the Legislature, which shall then fill such Vacancies.

(3) No Person shall be a Senator who shall not have attained to the Age of thirty Years, and been nine Years a Citizen of the United States, and who shall not, when elected, be an Inhabitant of that State for which he shall be chosen.

(4) The Vice President of the United States shall be President of the Senate, but shall have no Vote, unless they be equally divided.

(5) The Senate shall chuse their other Officers, and also a President pro tempore, in the Absence of the Vice President, or when he shall exercise the Office of President of the United States.

(6) The Senate shall have the sole Power to try all Impeachments. When sitting for that Purpose, they shall be on Oath or Affirmation. When the President of the United States is tried, the Chief Justice shall preside: And no Person shall be convicted without the Concurrence of two thirds of the Members present.

(7) Judgment in Cases of Impeachment shall not extend further than to removal from Office, and disqualification to hold and enjoy any Office of honor, Trust or Profit under the United States: but the Party convicted shall nevertheless be liable and subject to Indictment, Trial, Judgment and Punishment, according to Law.

SECTION 4 (1) The Times, Places and Manner of holding Elections for Senators and Representatives, shall be prescribed in each State by the Legislature thereof; but the Congress may at any time by Law make or alter such Regulations, except as to the Places of chusing Senators.

(2) The Congress shall assemble at least once in every Year, and such Meeting shall be on the first Monday in December, unless they shall by Law appoint a different Day.

SECTION 5 (1) Each House shall be the Judge of the Elections, Returns and Qualifications of its own Members, and a Majority of each shall constitute a Quorum to do Business; but a smaller Number may adjourn from day to day, and may be authorized to compel the Attendance of absent Members, in such Manner, and under such Penalties as each House may provide.

(2) Each House may determine the Rules of its Proceedings, punish its Members for disorderly Behavior, and, with the Concurrence of two thirds, expel a Member.

(3) Each House shall keep a Journal of its Proceedings, and from time to time publish the same, excepting such Parts as may in their Judgment require Secrecy; and the Yeas and Nays of the Members of either House on any question shall, at the Desire of one fifth of those present, be entered on the Journal.

(4) Neither House, during the Session of Congress, shall, without the Consent of the other, adjourn for more than three days, nor to any other Place than that in which the two Houses shall be sitting.

SECTION 6 (1) The Senators and Representatives shall receive a Compensation for their Services, to be ascertained by Law, and paid out of the Treasury of the United States. They shall in all Cases, except Treason, Felony and Breach of the Peace, be privileged from Arrest during their Attendance at the Session of their respective Houses, and in going to and returning from the same; and for any Speech or Debate in either House, they shall not be questioned in any other Place.

(2) No Senator or Representative shall, during the Time for which he was elected, be appointed to any civil Office under the Authority of the United States, which shall have been created, or the Emoluments whereof shall have been encreased during such time; and no Person holding any Office under the United States, shall be a Member of either House during his Continuance in Office.

SECTION 7 (1) All Bills for raising Revenue shall originate in the House of Representatives; but the Senate may propose or concur with Amendments as on other Bills.

(2) Every Bill which shall have passed the House of Representatives and the Senate, shall, before it become a Law, be presented to the President of the United States; If he approve he shall sign it, but if not he shall return it, with his Objections to that House in which it shall have originated, who shall enter the Objections at large on their Journal, and proceed to reconsider it. If after such Reconsideration two thirds of that House shall agree to pass the Bill, it shall be sent, together with the Objections, to the other House, by which it shall likewise be reconsidered, and if approved by two thirds of that House, it shall become a Law. But in all such Cases the Votes of both Houses shall be determined by Yeas and Nays, and the Names of the Persons voting for and against the Bill shall be entered on the Journal of each House respectively. If any Bill shall not be returned by the President within ten Days (Sundays excepted) after it shall have been presented to him, the Same shall be a law, in like Manner as if he had signed it, unless the Congress

by their Adjournment prevent its Return, in which Case it shall not be a Law.

(3) Every Order, Resolution, or Vote to which the Concurrence of the Senate and House of Representatives may be necessary (except on a question of Adjournment) shall be presented to the President of the United States; and before the Same shall take Effect, shall be approved by him, or being disapproved by him, shall be repassed by two thirds of the Senate and House of Representatives, according to the Rules and Limitations prescribed in the Case of a Bill.

SECTION 8 (1) The Congress shall have Power To lay and collect Taxes, Duties, Imposts and Excises, to pay the Debts and provide for the common Defence and general Welfare of the United States; but all Duties, Imposts and Excises shall be uniform throughout the United States;

(2) To borrow money on the Credit of the United States;

(3) To regulate Commerce with foreign Nations, and among the several States, and with the Indian Tribes;

(4) To establish an uniform Rule of Naturalization, and uniform Laws on the subject of Bankruptcies throughout the United States;

(5) To coin Money, regulate the Value thereof, and of foreign Coin, and to fix the Standard of Weights and Measures;

(6) To provide for the Punishment of counterfeiting the Securities and current Coin of the United States;

(7) To establish Post Offices and post Roads;

(8) To promote the Progress of Science and useful Arts, by securing for limited Times to Authors and Inventors the exclusive Right to their respective Writings and Discoveries;

(9) To constitute Tribunals inferior to the Supreme Court;

(10) To define and Punish Piracies and Felonies committed on the high Seas, and Offences against the Law of Nations;

(11) To declare War, grant Letters of Marque and Reprisal, and make Rules concerning Captures on Land and Water;

(12) To raise and support Armies, but no Appropriation of Money to that Use shall be for a longer Term than two Years;

(13) To provide and maintain a Navy;

(14) To make Rules for the Government and Regulation of the land and naval Forces;

(15) To provide for calling forth the Militia to execute the Laws of the Union, suppress Insurrections and repel Invasions;

(16) To provide for organizing, arming, and disciplining, the Militia, and for governing such Part of them as may be employed in the Service of the United States, reserving to the States respectively, the Appointment of the Officers, and the Authority of training the Militia according to the discipline prescribed by Congress;

(17) To exercise exclusive Legislation in all Cases whatsoever, over such District (not exceeding ten Miles square) as may, by Cession of particular States, and the Acceptance of Congress, become the Seat of the Government of the United States, and to exercise like Authority over all Places purchased by the Consent of the Legislature of the State in which the Same shall be, for the Erection of Forts, Magazines, Arsenals, dock-Yards, and other needful Buildings;—And

(18) To make all Laws which shall be necessary and proper for carrying into Execution the foregoing Powers, and all other Powers vested by this Constitution in the Government of the United States, or in any Department or Officer thereof.

SECTION 9 (1) The Migration or Importation of such Persons as any of the States now existing shall think proper to admit, shall not be prohibited by the Congress prior to the Year one thousand eight hundred and eight, but a Tax or Duty may be imposed on such Importation, not exceeding ten dollars for each Person.

(2) The Privilege of the Writ of Habeas Corpus shall not be suspended unless when in Cases of Rebellion or Invasion the public Safety may require it.

(3) No Bill of Attainder or ex post facto Law shall be passed.

(4) No Capitation, or other direct, tax shall be laid, unless in Proportion to the Census or Enumeration herein before directed to be taken.

(5) No Tax or Duty shall be laid on Articles exported from any State.

(6) No preference shall be given by any Regulation of Commerce or Revenue to the Ports of one State over those of another: nor shall

Vessels bound to, or from, one State, be obliged to enter, clear, or pay Duties in another.

(7) No Money shall be drawn from the Treasury, but in Consequence of Appropriations made by Law; and a regular Statement and Account of the Receipts and Expenditures of all public Money shall be published from time to time.

(8) No Title of Nobility shall be granted by the United States: And no Person holding any Office of Profit or Trust under them, shall, without the Consent of the Congress, accept of any present, Emolument, Office, or Title, of any kind whatever, from any King, Prince, or foreign State.

Section 10 (1) No State shall enter into any Treaty, Alliance, or Confederation; grant Letters of Marque and Reprisal; coin Money; emit Bills of Credit; make any Thing but gold and silver Coin a Tender in Payment of Debts; pass any Bill of Attainder, ex post facto Law, or Law impairing the Obligation of Contracts, or grant any Title of Nobility.

(2) No State shall, without the Consent of the Congress, lay any Imposts or Duties on Imports or Exports, except what may be absolutely necessary for executing it's inspection Laws: and the net Produce of all Duties and Imposts, laid by any State on Imports or Exports, shall be for the Use of the Treasury of the United States; and all such Laws shall be subject to the Revision and controul of the Congress.

(3) No State shall, without the Consent of Congress, lay any Duty of Tonnage, keep Troops, or Ships of War in time of Peace, enter into any Agreement or Compact with another State, or with a foreign Power, or engage in War, unless actually invaded, or in such imminent Danger as will not admit of Delay.

Article II

Section 1 (1) The executive Power shall be vested in a President of the United States of America. He shall hold his Office during the Term of four Years, and, together with the Vice President, chosen for the same Term, be elected, as follows:

(2) Each State shall appoint, in such Manner as the Legislature thereof may direct, a Number of Electors, equal to the whole Number of Senators and Representatives to which the State may be entitled in the Congress: but no Senator or Representative, or Person holding an Office of Trust or Profit under the United States, shall be appointed an Elector.

The electors shall meet in their respective States, and vote by ballot for two Persons, of whom one at least shall not be an Inhabitant of the same State with themselves. And they shall make a List of all the Persons voted for, and of the Number of Votes for each; which List they shall sign and certify, and transmit sealed to the Seat of Government of the United States, directed to the President of the Senate. The President of the Senate shall, in the Presence of the Senate and House of Representatives, open all the Certificates, and the Votes shall then be counted. The Person having the greatest Number of Votes shall be the President, if such Number be a Majority of the whole Number of Electors appointed; and if there be more than one who have such Majority and have an equal Number of Votes, then the House of Representatives shall immediately chuse by Ballot one of them for President; and if no person have a Majority, then from the five highest on the List the said House shall in like Manner chuse the President. But in chusing the President, the Votes shall be taken by States, the Representation from each State having one Vote; A quorum for this Purpose shall consist of a Member or Members from two-thirds of the States, and a Majority of all the States shall be necessary to a Choice. In every Case, after the Choice of the President, the person having the greatest Number of Votes of the Electors shall be the Vice President. But if there should remain two or more who have equal votes, the Senate shall chuse from them by Ballot the Vice-President.

(3) The Congress may determine the Time of chusing the Electors, and the Day on which they shall give their Votes; which Day shall be the same throughout the United States.

(4) No Person except a natural born Citizen, or a Citizen of the United States, at the time of the Adoption of this Constitution,

shall be eligible to the Office of President; neither shall any Person be eligible to that Office who shall not have attained to the Age of thirty five Years, and been fourteen Years a Resident within the United States.

(5) In Case of the Removal of the President from Office, or of his Death, Resignation, or Inability to discharge the Powers and Duties of the said Office, the same shall devolve on the Vice President, and the Congress may by Law provide for the Case of Removal, Death, Resignation, or Inability, both of the President and Vice President, declaring what Officer shall then act as President, and such Officer shall act accordingly, until the Disability be removed, or a President shall be elected.

(6) The President shall, at stated Times, receive for his Services, a Compensation, which shall neither be encreased nor diminished during the Period for which he shall have been elected, and he shall not receive within that Period any other Emolument from the United States, or any of them.

(7) Before he enter on the Execution of his Office, he shall take the following Oath or Affirmation:—"I do solemnly swear (or affirm) that I will faithfully execute the Office of President of the United States, and will to the best of my Ability, preserve, protect and defend the Constitution of the United States."

Section 2 (1) The President shall be Commander in Chief of the Army and Navy of the United States, and of the Militia of the several States, when called into actual Service of the United States; he may require the Opinion, in writing, of the principal Officer in each of the executive Departments, upon any subject relating to the Duties of their respective Offices, and he shall have Power to grant Reprieves and Pardons for Offences against the United States, except in Cases of Impeachment.

(2) He shall have Power, by and with the Advice and Consent of the Senate, to make Treaties, provided two-thirds of the Senators present concur; and he shall nominate, and by and with the Advice and Consent of the Senate, shall appoint Ambassadors, other public Ministers and Councils, Judges of the supreme Court, and all other Officers of the United States, whose Appointments are not herein

otherwise provided for, and which shall be established by Law: but the Congress may by Law vest the Appointment of such inferior Officers as they think proper, in the President alone, in the Courts of Law, or in the Heads of Departments.

(3) The President shall have power to fill up all Vacancies that may happen during the Recess of the Senate, by granting Commissions which shall expire at the End of their next Session.

SECTION 3 He shall from time to time give to the Congress Information of the State of the Union, and recommend to their Consideration such Measures as he shall judge necessary and expedient; he may, on extraordinary Occasions, convene both Houses, or either of them, and in Case of Disagreement between them, with Respect to the Time of Adjournment, he may adjourn them to such Time as he shall think proper; he shall receive Ambassadors and other public Ministers; he shall take Care that the Laws be faithfully executed, and shall Commission all the Officers of the United States.

SECTION 4 The President, Vice President and all civil Officers of the United States, shall be removed from Office on Impeachment for, and Conviction of, Treason, Bribery, or other high Crimes and Misdemeanors.

ARTICLE III

SECTION 1 The judicial Power of the United States, shall be vested in one supreme Court, and in such inferior Courts as the Congress may from time to time ordain and establish. The Judges, both of the supreme and inferior Courts, shall hold their Offices during good Behavior, and shall, at stated Times, receive for their Services, a Compensation, which shall not be diminished during their Continuance in Office.

SECTION 2 (1) The judicial Power shall extend to all Cases, in Law and Equity, arising under this Constitution, the Laws of the United States, and Treaties made, or which shall be made, under their Authority;—to all Cases affecting Ambassadors, other public Ministers and Consuls;—to all Cases of admiralty and maritime Jurisdiction;—to Controversies to which the United States shall be a party;—to Controversies between two or more States;—

between a State and Citizens of another State;—between Citizens of different States,—between Citizens of the same State claiming Lands under Grants of different States, and between a State, or the Citizens thereof, and foreign States, Citizens or subjects.

(2) In all Cases affecting Ambassadors, other public Ministers and Consuls, and those in which a State shall be a Party, the Supreme Court shall have original Jurisdiction. In all the other Cases before mentioned, the Supreme Court shall have appellate Jurisdiction, both as to Law and Fact, with such Exceptions, and under such Regulations as the Congress shall make.

(3) The Trial of all Crimes, except in Cases of Impeachment, shall be by Jury; and such Trial shall be held in the State where the said Crimes shall have been committed; but when not committed within any State, the Trial shall be at such Place or Places as the Congress may by Law have directed.

SECTION 3   (1) Treason against the United States, shall consist only in levying War against them, or in adhering to their Enemies, giving them Aid and Comfort. No person shall be convicted of Treason unless on the Testimony of two Witnesses to the same overt Act, or on Confession in open Court.

(2) The Congress shall have Power to declare the Punishment of Treason, but no Attainder of Treason shall work Corruption of Blood, or Forfeiture except during the Life of the Person attainted.

ARTICLE IV

SECTION 1   Full Faith and Credit shall be given in each State to the public Acts, Records, and judicial Proceedings of every other State. And the Congress may by general Laws prescribe the Manner in which such Acts, Records and Proceedings shall be proved, and the Effect thereof.

SECTION 2   (1) The Citizens of each State shall be entitled to all Privileges and Immunities of Citizens in the several States.

(2) A person charged in any State with Treason, Felony, or other Crime, who shall flee from Justice, and be found in another State, shall on Demand of the executive Authority of the State from which he fled, be delivered up to be removed to the State having Jurisdiction of the Crime.

(3) No person held to Service or Labour in one State, under the Laws thereof, escaping into another, shall, in Consequence of any Law or Regulation therein, be discharged from such Service or Labour, but shall be delivered up on Claim of the Party to whom such service or Labour may be due.

SECTION 3 (1) New States may be admitted by the Congress into this Union; but no new State shall be formed or erected within the Jurisdiction of any other State; nor any State be formed by the Junction of two or more States, or Parts of States, without the Consent of the Legislatures of the States concerned as well as of the Congress.

(2) The Congress shall have Power to dispose of and make all needful Rules and Regulations respecting the Territory or other Property belonging to the United States; and nothing in this Constitution shall be so construed as to Prejudice any Claims of the United States, or of any particular State.

SECTION 4 The United States shall guarantee to every State in this Union a Republican Form of Government, and shall protect each of them against Invasion; and on Application of the Legislature, or of the Executive (when the Legislature cannot be convened) against domestic Violence.

ARTICLE V

The Congress, whenever two thirds of both Houses shall deem it necessary, shall propose Amendments to this Constitution, or, on the Application of the Legislatures of two thirds of the several States, shall call a Convention for proposing Amendments, which, in either Case, shall be valid to all Intents and Purposes, as Part of this Constitution, when ratified by the Legislatures of three fourths of the several States, or by Conventions in three fourths thereof, as the one or the other Mode of Ratification may be proposed by the Congress; Provided that no Amendment which may be made prior to the Year One thousand eight hundred and eight shall in any Manner affect the first and fourth Clauses in the Ninth Section of the first Article; and that no State, without its Consent, shall be deprived of its equal Suffrage in the Senate.

Article VI

(1) All Debts contracted and Engagements entered into, before the Adoption of this Constitution, shall be as valid against the United States under this Constitution, as under the Confederation.

(2) This Constitution, and the Laws of the United States which shall be made in pursuance thereof; and all Treaties made, or which shall be made, under the Authority of the United States, shall be the supreme Law of the Land; and the Judges in every State shall be bound thereby, any Thing in the Constitution or Laws of any State to the Contrary notwithstanding.

(3) The Senators and Representatives before mentioned, and the Members of the several State Legislatures, and all executive and judicial Officers, both of the United States and of the several States, shall be bound by Oath or Affirmation, to support this Constitution; but no religious Test shall ever be required as a Qualification to any Office or public Trust under the United States.

Article VII

The Ratification of the Conventions of nine States, shall be sufficient for the Establishment of this Constitution between the States so ratifying the Same.

Done in Convention by the Unanimous Consent of the States present, the Seventeenth Day of September in the Year of our Lord one thousand seven hundred and Eighty seven and of the Independence of the United States of America the Twelfth. In Witness whereof We have hereunto subscribed our Names,

Go. Washington
Presidt. and Deputy from Virginia.

New Hampshire

John Langdon   Nicholas Gilman

Massachusetts

Nathaniel Gorham   Rufus King

Connecticut

Wm. Saml. Johnson   Roger Sherman

New York

ALEXANDER HAMILTON

New Jersey

WIL: LIVINGSTON
DAVID BREARLEY

WM. PATTERSON
JONA: DAYTON

Pennsylvania

B. FRANKLIN
THOMAS MIFFLIN
ROBT. MORRIS
GEO. CLYMER

THOS. FITZSIMONS
JARED INGERSOLL
JAMES WILSON
GOUV. MORRIS

Delaware

GEO. READ
GUNNING BEDFORD, JUN
JOHN DICKINSON

RICHARD BASSETT
JACO: BROOM

Maryland

JAMES McHENRY
DAN OF ST. THOS. JENIFER

DANL. CARROLL

Virginia

JOHN BLAIR

JAMES MADISON, JR

North Carolina

WM. BLOUNT
RICHD DOBBS SPAIGHT

HU. WILLIAMSON

South Carolina

J. RUTLEDGE
CHARLES COTESWORTH
    PINCKNEY.

CHARLES PINCKNEY
PIERCE BUTLER

Georgia

WILLIAM FEW
    Attest

ABR. BALDWIN
WILLIAM JACKSON *Secretary*

AMENDMENTS

Articles in Addition to, and Amendment of, the Constitution of the United States of America, Proposed by Congress, and Ratified by the Legislatures of the Several States Pursuant to the Fifth Article of the Original Constitution.

ARTICLE I

Congress shall make no law respecting an establishment of religion, or prohibiting the free exercise thereof; or abridging the freedom of speech, or of the press; or the right of the people peaceably to assemble, and to petition the Government for a redress of grievances.

ARTICLE II

A well regulated Militia, being necessary to the security of a free State, the right of the people to keep and bear Arms, shall not be infringed.

ARTICLE III

No soldier shall, in time of peace be quartered in any house, without the consent of the Owner, nor in time of war, but in a manner to be prescribed by law.

ARTICLE IV

The right of the people to be secure in their persons, houses, papers, and effects, against unreasonable searches and seizures, shall not be violated, and no Warrants shall issue, but upon probable cause, supported by Oath or affirmation, and particularly describing the place to be searched, and the persons or things to be seized.

ARTICLE V

No person shall be held to answer for a capital, or otherwise infamous crime, unless on a presentment or indictment of a Grand Jury, except in cases arising in the land or naval forces, or in the Militia, when in actual service in time of War or in public danger; nor shall any person be subject for the same offence to be twice put in jeopardy of life or limb; nor shall be compelled in any Criminal Case to be a witness against himself, nor be deprived of life, liberty, or property, without due process of law; nor shall private property be taken for public use, without just compensation.

ARTICLE VI

In all criminal prosecutions, the accused shall enjoy the right to a speedy and public trial, by an impartial jury of the State and district wherein the crime shall have been committed, which district shall have been previously ascertained by law, and to be informed of the nature and cause of the accusation; to be confronted with the witnesses against him; to have compulsory process for obtaining Witnesses in his favor, and to have the Assistance of Counsel for his defence.

ARTICLE VII

In suits at common law, where the value in controversy shall exceed twenty dollars, the right of trial by jury shall be preserved, and no fact tried by a jury shall be otherwise re-examined in any Court of the United States, than according to the rules of the common law.

ARTICLE VIII

Excessive bail shall not be required, nor excessive fines imposed, nor cruel and unusual punishments inflicted.

ARTICLE IX

The enumeration in the Constitution, of certain rights, shall not be construed to deny or disparage others retained by the people.

ARTICLE X

The powers not delegated to the United States by the Constitution, nor prohibited by it to the States, are reserved to the States respectively, or to the people.

ARTICLE XI

The Judicial power of the United States shall not be construed to extend to any suit in law or equity, commenced or prosecuted against one of the United States by Citizens of another State, or by Citizens or Subjects of any Foreign State.

ARTICLE XII

The Electors shall meet in their respective States, and vote by ballot for President and Vice-President, one of whom, at least, shall not be an inhabitant of the same State with themselves; they shall name in their ballots the person voted for as President, and in distinct ballots the person voted for as Vice-President, and they shall make distinct lists of all persons voted for as President, and of all persons voted for as Vice-President, and of the number of votes for each, which lists they shall sign and certify, and transmit sealed to the seat of the government of the United States, directed to the President of the Senate;—The President of the Senate shall, in presence of the Senate and House of Representatives open all the certificates and the votes shall then be counted;

—The person having the greatest number of votes for President, shall be the President, if such number be a majority of the whole number of Electors appointed; and if no person have such majority, then from the persons having the highest numbers not exceeding three on the list of those voted for as President, the House of Representatives shall choose immediately, by ballot, the President. But in choosing the President, the votes shall be taken by States, the representation from each State having one vote; a quorum for this purpose shall consist of a member or members from two-thirds of the States, and a majority of all the States shall be necessary to a choice. And if the House of Representatives shall not choose a President whenever the right of choice shall devolve upon them, before the fourth day of March next following, then the Vice-President shall act as President, as in the case of the death or other constitutional disability of the President. The person having the greatest number of votes as Vice-President, shall be the Vice-President, if such number be a majority of the whole number of Electors appointed, and if no person have a majority, then from the two highest numbers on the list, the Senate shall choose the Vice-President; a quorum for the purpose shall consist of two-thirds of the whole number of Senators, and a majority of the whole number shall be necessary to a choice. But no person constitutionally ineligible to the office of President shall be eligible to that of Vice-President of the United States.

ARTICLE XIII

SECTION 1 Neither slavery nor involuntary servitude, except as a punishment for crime whereof the party shall have been duly convicted, shall exist within the United States, or any place subject to their jurisdiction.

SECTION 2 Congress shall have power to enforce this article by appropriate legislation.

ARTICLE XIV

SECTION 1 All persons born or naturalized in the United States, and subject to the jurisdiction thereof, are citizens of the United States and of the State wherein they reside. No State shall make or enforce any law which shall abridge the privilege or immunities of citizens of the United States; nor shall any State deprive any person of life, liberty, or property, without due process of law; nor deny to any person within its jurisdiction the equal protection of the laws.

SECTION 2 Representatives shall be apportioned among the several States according to their respective numbers, counting the whole number of persons in each State, excluding Indians not taxed. But when the right to vote at any election for the choice of electors for President and Vice-President of the United States, Representatives in Congress, the

Executive and Judicial officers of a State, or the members of the Legis lature thereof, is denied to any of the male inhabitants of such States, being twenty-one years of age, and citizens of the United States, or in any way abridged, except for participation in rebellion, or other crime, the basis of representation therein shall be reduced in the proportion which the number of such male citizens shall bear to the whole number of male citizens twenty-one years of age in such State.

SECTION 3 No person shall be a Senator or Representative in Congress, or elector of President and Vice-President, or hold any office, civil or military, under the United States, or under any State, who, having previously taken an oath, as a member of Congress, or as an officer of the United States, or as a member of any State legislature, or as an executive or judicial officer of any State, to support the Constitution of the United States, shall have engaged in insurrection or rebellion against the same, or given aid or comfort to the enemies thereof. But Congress may by a vote of two-thirds of each House, remove such disability.

SECTION 4 The validity of the public debt of the United States, authorized by law, including debts incurred for payment of pensions and bounties for services in suppressing insurrection or rebellion, shall not be questioned. But neither the United States nor any State shall assume or pay any debt or obligation incurred in aid of insurrection or rebellion against the United States, or any claim for the loss or emancipation of any slave; but all such debts, obligations and claims shall be held illegal and void.

SECTION 5 The Congress shall have power to enforce, by appropriate legislation, the provisions of this article.

ARTICLE XV

SECTION 1 The right of citizens of the United States to vote shall not be denied or abridged by the United States or by any State on account of race, color, or previous condition of servitude.

SECTION 2 The Congress shall have power to enforce this article by appropriate legislation.

ARTICLE XVI

The Congress shall have power to lay and collect taxes on incomes, from whatever source derived, without apportionment among the several States, and without regard to any census or enumeration.

ARTICLE XVII

SECTION 1 The Senate of the United States shall be composed of two Senators from each State, elected by the people thereof, for six years; and each Senator shall have one vote. The electors in each State shall have the qualifications requisite for electors of the most numerous branch of the State Legislatures.

SECTION 2   When vacancies happen in the representation of any State in the Senate, the executive authority of such State shall issue writs of election to fill such vacancies:. Provided, That the Legislature of any State may empower the Executive thereof to make temporary appointment until the people fill the vacancies by election as the Legislature may direct.

SECTION 3   This amendment shall not be so construed as to affect the election or term of any Senator chosen before it becomes valid as part of the Constitution.

ARTICLE XVIII

SECTION 1   After one year from the ratification of this article the manufacture, sale, or transportation of intoxicating liquors within, the importation thereof into, or the exportation thereof from the United States and all territory subject to the jurisdiction thereof for beverage purposes is hereby prohibited.

SECTION 2   The Congress and the several States shall have concurrent power to enforce this article by appropriate legislation.

SECTION 3   This article shall be inoperative unless it shall have been ratified as an amendment to the Constitution by the legislatures of the several States, as provided in the Constitution, within seven years from the date of the submission hereof to the States by the Congress.

ARTICLE XIX

SECTION 1   The right of citizens of the United States to vote shall not be denied or abridged by the United States or by any State on account of sex.

SECTION 2   Congress shall have power, by appropriate legislation, to enforce the provisions of this article.

THE FEDERALIST

NOS. I AND II

(1787)

[In the interval between the drawing up of the Constitution and its ratification, there appeared in *The Independent Journal* and other New York newspapers a series of eighty-five articles under the general heading of *The Federalist,* devoted to expounding and defending the new instrument of government. Most of the articles were written by Hamilton, some twenty-nine by Madison (whose work the Constitution largely was), and five by Jay. Together they form one of the great classics on government; and they exercised a highly important influence in favor of the adoption of the Constitution.]

FOR THE INDEPENDENT JOURNAL

THE FŒDERALIST, NO. I

BY ALEXANDER HAMILTON

TO THE PEOPLE OF THE STATE OF NEW YORK:

AFTER an unequivocal experience of the inefficacy of the subsisting Fœderal Government, you are called upon to deliberate on a new Constitution for the United States of America. The subject speaks its own importance; comprehending in its consequences, nothing less than the existence of the UNION, the safety and welfare of the parts of which it is composed, the fate of an empire, in many respects, the most interesting in the world. It has been frequently remarked, that it seems to have been reserved to the people of this country, by their conduct and example, to decide the important question, whether societies of men are really capable or not, of establishing good government from reflection and choice, or whether they are forever destined to depend, for their political constitutions, on accident and force. If there be any truth in the remark, the crisis, at which we are arrived, may with propriety be regarded as the æra in which that decision is to be made; and a wrong election of the part we shall act, may, in this view, deserve to be considered as the general misfortune of mankind

This idea will add the inducements of philanthropy to those of patriotism to heighten the solicitude, which all considerate and good men must feel for the event. Happy will it be if our choice should be directed by a judicious estimate of our true interests, unperplexed and unbiased by considerations not connected with the public good. But this is a thing more ardently to be wished, than seriously to be expected. The plan offered to our deliberations, affects too many particular interests, innovates upon too many local institutions, not to involve in its discussion a variety of objects foreign to its merits, and of views, passions and prejudices little favorable to the discovery of truth.

Among the most formidable of the obstacles which the new Constitution will have to encounter, may readily be distinguished the obvious interest of a certain class of men in every State to resist all changes which may hazard a diminution of the power, emolument and consequence of the offices they hold under the State-establishments—and the perverted ambition of another class of men, who will either hope to aggrandize themselves by the confusion of their country, or will flatter themselves with fairer prospects of elevation from the subdivision of the empire into several partial confederacies, than from its union under one Government.

It is not, however, my design to dwell upon observations of this nature. I am well aware that it would be disingenuous to resolve indiscriminately the opposition of any set of men (merely because their situations might subject them to suspicion) into interested or ambitious views: Candor will oblige us to admit, that even such men may be actuated by upright intentions; and it cannot be doubted, that much of the opposition which has made its appearance, or may hereafter make its appearance, will spring from sources, blameless at least, if not respectable; the honest errors of minds led astray by preconceived jealousies and fears. So numerous indeed and so powerful are the causes, which serve to give a false bias to the judgment, that we, upon many occasions, see wise and good men on the wrong as well as on the right side of questions, of the first magnitude to society. This circumstance, if duly attended to, would furnish a lesson of moderation to those, who are ever so much persuaded of their being in the right, in any controversy.

And a further reason for caution, in this respect, might be drawn from the reflection, that we are not always sure, that those who advocate the truth are influenced by purer principles than their antagonists. Ambition, avarice, personal animosity, party opposition, and many other motives, not more laudable than these, are apt to operate as well upon those who support, as upon those who oppose, the right side of a question. Were there not even these inducements to moderation, nothing could be more ill-judged than that intolerant spirit, which has, at all times, characterized political parties. For, in politics as in religion, it is equally absurd to aim at making proselytes by fire and sword. Heresies in either can rarely be cured by persecution.

And yet however just these sentiments will be allowed to be, we have already sufficient indications, that it will happen in this as in all former cases of great national discussion. A torrent of angry and malignant passions will be let loose. To judge from the conduct of the opposite parties, we shall be led to conclude, that they will mutually hope to evince the justness of their opinions, and to increase the number of their converts by the loudness of their declamations, and the bitterness of their invectives. An enlightened zeal for the energy and efficiency of government will be stigmatized, as the offspring of a temper fond of despotic power, and hostile to the principles of liberty. An over scrupulous jealousy of danger to the rights of the people, which is more commonly the fault of the head than of the heart, will be represented as mere pretence and artifice; the stale bait for popularity at the expense of public good. It will be forgotten, on the one hand, that jealousy is the usual concomitant of violent love, and that the noble enthusiasm of liberty is too apt to be infected with a spirit of narrow and illiberal distrust. On the other hand, it will be equally forgotten, that the vigor of Government is essential to the security of liberty; that, in the contemplation of a sound and well-informed judgment, their interest can never be separated; and that a dangerous ambition more often lurks behind the specious mask of zeal for the rights of the people, than under the forbidding appearance of zeal for the firmness and efficiency of Government. History will teach us, that the former has been found a much more certain road to the introduction of

despotism, than the latter; and that of those men who have overturned the liberties of republics the greatest number have begun
their career, by paying an obsequious court to the people; commencing Demagogues, and ending Tyrants.

In the course of the preceding observations I have had an eye, my
Fellow-Citizens, to putting you upon your guard against all attempts, from whatever quarter, to influence your decision in a
matter of the utmost moment to your welfare by any impressions
other than those which may result from the evidence of truth. You
will, no doubt, at the same time, have collected from the general
scope of them that they proceed from a source not unfriendly to the
new Constitution. Yes, my Countrymen, I owe to you, that, after
having given it an attentive consideration, I am clearly of opinion,
it is your interest to adopt it. I am convinced, that this is the safest
course for your liberty, your dignity, and your happiness. I affect
not reserves, which I do not feel. I will not amuse you with an
appearance of deliberation, when I have decided. I frankly acknowledge to you my convictions, and I will freely lay before you the
reasons on which they are founded. The consciousness of good intentions disdains ambiguity. I shall not however multiply professions on this head. My motives must remain in the depository
of my own breast: My arguments will be open to all, and may be
judged of by all. They shall at least be offered in a spirit which will
not disgrace the cause of truth.

I propose, in a series of papers, to discuss the following interesting
particulars.—*The utility of the UNION to your political prosperity
—The insufficiency of the present Confederation to preserve that
Union—The necessity of a Government at least equally energetic
with the one proposed, to the attainment of this object—The conformity of the proposed Constitution to the true principles of republican Government—Its analogy to your own State Constitution
—and lastly, The additional security which its adoption will afford
to the preservation of that species of Government, to liberty, and to
property.*

In the progress of this discussion, I shall endeavor to give a satisfactory answer to all the objections which shall have made their
appearance, that may seem to have any claim to your attention.

It may perhaps be thought superfluous to offer arguments to prove the utility of the UNION, a point, no doubt, deeply engraved on the hearts of the great body of the people in every State, and one, which it may be imagined, has no adversaries. But the fact is, that we already hear it whispered in the private circles of those who oppose the new Constitution, that the Thirteen States are of too great extent for any general system, and that we must of necessity, resort to separate confederacies of distinct portions of the whole.[1] This doctrine will, in all probability, be gradually propagated, till it has votaries enough to countenance an open avowal of it. For nothing can be more evident, to those who are able to take an enlarged view of the subject, than the alternative of an adoption of the new Constitution or a dismemberment of the Union. It will, therefore, be of use to begin by examining the advantages of that Union, the certain evils, and the probable dangers, to which every State will be exposed from its dissolution. This shall accordingly constitute the subject of my next address.   PUBLIUS.

FOR THE INDEPENDENT JOURNAL
THE FŒDERALIST, NO. II
BY JOHN JAY

To the People of the State of New York:

When the people of America reflect that they are now called upon to decide a question, which, in its consequences, must prove one of the most important, that ever engaged their attention, the propriety of their taking a very comprehensive, as well as a very serious, view of it, will be evident.

Nothing is more certain than the indispensable necessity of Government, and it is equally undeniable, that whenever and however it is instituted, the people must cede to it some of their natural rights, in order to vest it with requisite powers. It is well worthy of consideration, therefore, whether it would conduce more to the interest of the people of America, that they should, to all general purposes, be one nation, under one Fœderal Government, or that they should divide themselves into separate confederacies, and give to the head

---

[1] The same idea, tracing the arguments to their consequences, is held out in several of the late publications against the new Constitution.—*Publius.*

of each, the same kind of powers which they are advised to place in one national Government.

It has until lately been a received and uncontradicted opinion, that the prosperity of the people of America depended on their continuing firmly united, and the wishes, prayers, and efforts of our best and wisest Citizens have been constantly directed to that object. But Politicians now appear, who insist that this opinion is erroneous, and that instead of looking for safety and happiness in union, we ought to seek it in a division of the States into distinct confederacies or sovereignties. However extraordinary this new doctrine may appear, it nevertheless has its advocates; and certain characters who were much opposed to it formerly, are at present of the number. Whatever may be the arguments or inducements which have wrought this change in the sentiments and declarations of these Gentlemen, it certainly would not be wise in the people at large to adopt these new political tenets without being fully convinced that they are founded in truth and sound Policy.

It has often given me pleasure to observe, that Independent America was not composed of detached and distant territories, but that one connected, fertile, wide-spreading country was the portion of our western sons of liberty. Providence has in a particular manner blessed it with a variety of soils and productions and watered it with innumerable streams, for the delight and accommodation of its inhabitants. A succession of navigable waters forms a kind of chain round its borders, as if to bind it together; while the most noble rivers in the world, running at convenient distances, present them with highways for the easy communication of friendly aids, and the mutual transportation and exchange of their various commodities.

With equal pleasure I have as often taken notice, that Providence has been pleased to give this one connected country, to one united people; a people descended from the same ancestors, speaking the same language, professing the same religion, attached to the same principles of government, very similar in their manners and customs, and who, by their joint counsels, arms and efforts, fighting side by side throughout a long and bloody war, have nobly established their general Liberty and Independence.

This country and this people seem to have been made for each other, and it appears as if it was the design of Providence, that an inheritance so proper and convenient for a band of brethren, united to each other by the strongest ties, should never be split into a number of unsocial, jealous, and alien sovereignties.

Similar sentiments have hitherto prevailed among all orders and denominations of men among us. To all general purposes we have uniformly been one people; each individual citizen everywhere enjoying the same national rights, privileges, and protection. As a nation we have made peace and war: as a nation we have vanquished our common enemies: as a nation we have formed alliances and made treaties, and entered into various compacts and conventions with foreign States.

A strong sense of the value and blessings of Union induced the people, at a very early period, to institute a Fœderal Government to preserve and perpetuate it. They formed it almost as soon as they had a political existence; nay, at a time, when their habitations were in flames, when many of their Citizens were bleeding, and when the progress of hostility and desolation left little room for those calm and mature inquiries and reflections, which must ever precede the formation of a wise and well-balanced government for a free people. It is not to be wondered at, that a Government instituted in times so inauspicious, should on experiment be found greatly deficient and inadequate to the purpose it was intended to answer.

This intelligent people perceived and regretted these defects. Still continuing no less attached to Union, than enamored of Liberty, they observed the danger, which immediately threatened the former and more remotely the latter; and being persuaded that ample security for both, could only be found in a national Government more wisely framed, they, as with one voice, convened the late Convention at Philadelphia, to take that important subject under consideration.

This Convention, composed of men who possessed the confidence of the people, and many of whom had become highly distinguished by their patriotism, virtue, and wisdom, in times which tried the minds and hearts of men, undertook the arduous task. In the mild season of peace, with minds unoccupied by other subjects, they passed many months in cool, uninterrupted, and daily consultations; and finally, without having been awed by power, or influenced by any passions except love for their Country, they presented and recommended to the people the plan produced by their joint and very unanimous councils.

Admit, for so is the fact, that this plan is only *recommended,* not imposed, yet let it be remembered, that it is neither recommended to *blind* approbation, nor to blind reprobation; but to that sedate and candid consideration, which the magnitude and importance of the subject demand, and which it certainly ought to receive. But this, (as was remarked in the foregoing number of this Paper,) is more to be wished than expected, that it may be so considered and examined. Experience on a former occasion teaches us not to be too sanguine in such hopes. It is not yet forgotten, that well grounded apprehensions of imminent danger induced the people of America to form the Memorable Congress of 1774. That Body recommended certain measures to their Constituents, and the event proved their wisdom; yet it is fresh in our memories how soon the Press began to teem with Pamphlets and weekly Papers against those very measures. Not only many of the Officers of Government, who obeyed the dictates of personal interest, but others, from a mistaken estimate of consequences, or the undue influence of former attachments, or whose ambition aimed at objects which did not correspond with the public good, were indefatigable in their endeavors to persuade the people to reject the advice of that Patriotic Congress. Many indeed were deceived and deluded, but the great majority of the people reasoned and decided judiciously; and happy they are in reflecting that they did so.

They considered that the Congress was composed of many wise and experienced men. That being convened from different parts of the country they brought with them and communicated to each other a variety of useful information. That in the course of the time they passed together in inquiring into and discussing the true interests of their country, they must have acquired very accurate knowledge on that head. That they were individually interested in the public liberty and prosperity, and therefore that it was not less their inclination than their duty, to recommend only such measures as after the most mature deliberation they really thought prudent and advisable.

These and similar considerations then induced the people to rely greatly on the judgment and integrity of the Congress; and they took their advice, notwithstanding the various arts and endeavors used to deter and dissuade them from it. But if the people at large had reason to confide in the men of that Congress, few of whom had then been fully tried or generally known, still greater reason have they now to respect the judgment and advice of the Convention, for it is well known that some of the most distinguished members of that Congress, who have been since tried and justly approved for patriotism and abilities, and who have grown old in acquiring political information, were also members of this Convention, and carried into it their accumulated knowledge and experience.

It is worthy of remark, that not only the first, but every succeeding Congress, as well as the late Convention, have invariably joined with the people in thinking that the prosperity of America depended on its Union. To preserve and perpetuate it, was the great object of the people in forming that Convention, and it is also the great object of the plan which the Convention has advised them to adopt. With what propriety, therefore, or for what good purposes, are attempts at this particular period, made by some men, to depreciate the importance of the Union? Or why is it suggested that three or four confederacies would be better than one? I am persuaded in my own mind, that the people have always thought right on this subject, and that their universal and uniform attachment to the cause of the Union rests on great and weighty reasons, which I shall endeavor to develop and explain in some ensuing papers. They who promote the idea of substituting a number of distinct confederacies in the room of the plan of the Convention, seem clearly to foresee that the rejection of it would put the continuance of the Union in the utmost jeopardy: that certainly would be the case, and I sincerely wish that it may be as clearly foreseen by every good Citizen, that whenever the dissolution of the Union arrives, America will have reason to exclaim in the words of the Poet, "FAREWELL! A LONG FAREWELL, TO ALL MY GREATNESS."   PUBLIUS.

OPINION OF
CHIEF JUSTICE MARSHALL

IN THE CASE OF McCULLOCH VS.
THE STATE OF MARYLAND
(1819)

[John Marshall (1755–1835), third Chief Justice of the Supreme Court of the United States, and the greatest of American judges, laid down in the following opinion certain principles which have come to be accepted as fundamental in all questions touching the respective powers of the Federal government and the State legislatures. In 1816, Congress had incorporated the Bank of the United States; and in 1818, the legislature of Maryland had passed a law taxing "all Banks, or branches thereof, in the State of Maryland, not chartered by the legislature." The purpose of this law was to prevent the United States Bank from doing business in the State. McCulloch, the Cashier of the Baltimore branch, refused to pay the tax, was sued in the State courts, and lost. The case was appealed to the United States Supreme Court, where the Maryland decision was unanimously reversed. Chief Justice Marshall, in writing the opinion of the court, is regarded as having established certain principles on which depend "the stability of our peculiar dual system of national and local governments."]

MR. Chief Justice Marshall delivered the opinion of the Court.

In the case now to be determined, the defendant, a sovereign State, denies the obligation of a law enacted by the legislature of the Union, and the plaintiff, on his part, contests the validity of an act which has been passed by the legislature of that State. The constitution of our country, in its most interesting and vital parts, is to be considered; the conflicting powers of the government of the Union and of its members, as marked in that constitution, are to be discussed; and an opinion given, which may essentially influence the great operations of the government. No tribunal can approach such a question without a deep sense of its importance, and of the awful responsibility involved in its decision. But it must be decided peacefully, or remain a source of hostile legislation, perhaps of hostility of a still more serious nature; and if it is to be so decided, by this tribunal alone can the decision be made. On the

Supreme Court of the United States has the Constitution of our country devolved this important duty.

The first question made in the cause is, has Congress power to incorporate a bank?

It has been truly said, that this can scarcely be considered as an open question, entirely unprejudiced by the former proceedings of the nation respecting it. The principle now contested was introduced at a very early period of our history, has been recognised by many successive legislatures, and has been acted upon by the judicial department, in cases of peculiar delicacy, as a law of undoubted obligation.

It will not be denied that a bold and daring usurpation might be resisted, after an acquiescence still longer and more complete than this. But it is conceived that a doubtful question, one on which human reason may pause, and the human judgment be suspended, in the decision of which the great principles of liberty are not concerned, but the respective powers of those who are equally the representatives of the people, are to be adjusted; if not put at rest by the practice of the government, ought to receive a considerable impression from that practice. An exposition of the Constitution, deliberately established by legislative acts, on the faith of which an immense property has been advanced, ought not to be lightly disregarded.

The power now contested was exercised by the first Congress elected under the present Constitution. The bill for incorporating the bank of the United States did not steal upon an unsuspecting legislature, and pass unobserved. Its principle was completely understood, and was opposed with equal zeal and ability. After being resisted, first in the fair and open field of debate, and afterwards in the executive cabinet, with as much persevering talent as any measure has ever experienced, and being supported by arguments which convinced minds as pure and as intelligent as this country can boast, it became a law. The original act was permitted to expire; but a short experience of the embarrassments to which the refusal to revive it exposed the government, convinced those who were most prejudiced against the measure of its necessity, and induced the passage of the present law. It would require no ordinary share of intrepidity to assert that a measure adopted under these circumstances was a bold and plain usurpation, to which the Constitution gave no countenance.

These observations belong to the cause; but they are not made under the impression that, were the question entirely new, the law would be found irreconcilable with the Constitution.

In discussing this question, the counsel for the State of Maryland have deemed it of some importance, in the construction of the Constitution, to consider that instrument not as emanating from the people, but as the act of sovereign and independent States. The powers of the general government, it has been said, are delegated by the States, who alone are truly sovereign; and must be exercised in subordination to the States, who alone possess supreme dominion.

It would be difficult to sustain this proposition. The Convention which framed the Constitution was indeed elected by the State legislatures. But the instrument, when it came from their hands, was a mere proposal, without obligation, or pretensions to it. It was reported to the then existing Congress of the United States, with a request that it might "be submitted to a Convention of Delegates, chosen in each State by the People thereof, under the recommendation of its Legislature, for their assent and ratification." This mode of proceeding was adopted; and by the Convention, by Congress, and by the State Legislatures, the instrument was submitted to the people. They acted upon it in the only manner in which they can act safely, effectively, and wisely, on such a subject, by assembling in Convention. It is true, they assembled in their several States—and where else should they have assembled? No political dreamer was ever wild enough to think of breaking down the lines which separate the States, and of compounding the American people into one common mass. Of consequence, when they act, they act in their States. But the measures they adopt do not, on that account, cease to be the measures of the people themselves, or become the measures of the State governments.

From these Conventions the Constitution derives its whole authority. The government proceeds directly from the people; is "ordained and established" in the name of the people; and is declared to be ordained, "in order to form a more perfect union, establish justice, ensure domestic tranquillity, and secure the blessings of liberty to themselves and to their posterity." The assent of the States, in their sovereign capacity, is implied in calling a Convention, and thus submitting that instrument to the people. But the people were at perfect liberty to accept or reject it; and their act was final. It required not the affirmance, and could not be negatived, by the State governments. The Constitution, when thus adopted, was of complete obligation, and bound the State sovereignties.

It has been said, that the people had already surrendered all their powers to the State sovereignties, and had nothing more to give. But, surely, the question whether they may resume and modify the powers granted to government does not remain to be settled in this country. Much more might the legitimacy of the general government be doubted, had it been created by the States. The powers delegated to the State sovereignties were to be exercised by themselves, not by a distinct and independent sovereignty, created by themselves. To the formation of a league, such as was the confederation, the State sovereignties were certainly competent. But when, "in order to form a more perfect union," it was deemed necessary to change this alliance into an effective government, possessing great and sovereign powers, and acting directly on the people, the necessity of referring it to the people, and of deriving its powers directly from them, was felt and acknowledged by all.

The government of the Union, then, (whatever may be the influence of this fact on the case,) is, emphatically, and truly, a government of the people. In form and in substance it emanates from them. Its powers are granted by them, and are to be exercised directly on them, and for their benefit.

This government is acknowledged by all to be one of enumerated powers. The principle, that it can exercise only the powers granted to it, would seem too apparent to have required to be enforced by all those arguments which its enlightened friends, while it was depending before the people, found it necessary to urge. That principle is now universally admitted. But the question respecting the extent of the powers actually granted, is perpetually arising, and will probably continue to arise, as long as our system shall exist.

In discussing these questions, the conflicting powers of the general and State governments must be brought into view, and the supremacy of their respective laws, when they are in opposition, must be settled.

If any one proposition could command the universal assent of mankind, we might expect it would be this—that the government of the Union, though limited in its powers, is supreme within its sphere of action. This would seem to result necessarily from its nature. It is the government of all; its powers are delegated by all; it represents all, and acts for all. Though any one State may be willing to control its operations, no State is willing to allow others to control them. The nation, on those subjects on which it can act, must necessarily bind its component parts. But this question is not left to mere reason: the people have, in express terms, decided it, by saying, "this constitution, and the laws of the United States, which shall be made in pursuance thereof," "shall be the supreme law of the land," and by requiring that the members of the State legislatures, and the officers of the executive and judicial departments of the States, shall take the oath of fidelity to it.

The government of the United States, then, though limited in its powers, is supreme; and its laws, when made in pursuance of the Constitution, form the supreme law of the land, "any thing in the Constitution or laws of any State to the contrary notwithstanding."

Among the enumerated powers, we do not find that of establishing a bank or creating a corporation. But there is no phrase in the instrument which, like the Articles of Confederation, excludes incidental or implied powers; and which requires that every thing granted shall be expressly and minutely described. Even the 10th amendment, which was framed for the purpose of quieting the excessive jealousies which had been excited, omits the word "expressly," and declares only that the powers "not delegated to the United States, nor prohibited to the States, are reserved to the States or to the people;" thus leaving the question, whether the particular power which may become the subject of contest has been delegated to the one government, or prohibited to the other, to depend on a fair construction of the whole instrument. The men who drew and adopted this amendment had experienced the embarrassments resulting from the insertion of this word in the Articles of Confederation, and probably omitted it to avoid those embarrassments. A constitution, to contain an accurate detail of all the subdivisions of which its great powers will admit, and of all the means by which they may be carried into execution, would partake of the prolixity of the legal code, and could scarcely be embraced by the human mind. It would probably never be understood by the public. Its nature, therefore, requires, that only its great outlines should be marked, its important objects designated, and the minor ingredients which compose those objects be deduced from the nature of the objects themselves. That this idea was entertained by the framers of the American Constitution, is not only to be inferred from the nature of the instrument, but from the language. Why else were some of the limitations, found in the ninth section of the 1st article, introduced? It is also, in some degree, warranted by their having omitted to use any restrictive term which might prevent its receiving a fair and just interpretation. In considering this question, then, we must never forget, that it is *a constitution* we are expounding.

Although, among the enumerated powers of government, we do not find the word "bank" or "incorporation," we find the great powers to lay and collect taxes; to borrow money; to regulate commerce; to declare and conduct a war; and to raise and support armies and navies. The sword and the purse, all the external relations, and no inconsiderable portion of the industry of the nation, are entrusted to its government. It can never be pretended that these vast powers draw after them others of inferior importance, merely because they are inferior. Such an idea can never be advanced. But it may with great reason be contended, that a government, entrusted with such ample powers, on the due execution of which the happiness and prosperity of the nation so vitally depends, must also be entrusted with ample means for their execution. The power being given, it is the interest of the nation to facilitate its execution. It can never be their interest, and cannot be presumed to have been their intention, to clog and embarrass its execution by withholding the most appropriate means. Throughout this vast republic, from the St. Croix to the Gulf of Mexico, from the Atlantic to the Pacific, revenue is to be collected and expended, armies are to be marched and supported. The exigencies of the nation may require that the treasure raised in the north should be transported to the south, *that* raised in the east conveyed to the west, or that this order should be reversed. Is that construction of the Constitution to be preferred which would render these operations difficult, hazardous, and expensive? Can we adopt that construction, (unless the words imperiously require it,) which would impute to the framers of that instrument, when granting these powers for the public good, the intention of impeding their exercise by withholding a choice of means? If, indeed, such be the mandate of the Constitution, we have only to obey; but that instrument does not profess to enumerate the means by which the powers it confers may be executed; nor does it prohibit the creation of a corporation, if the existence of such a being be essential to the beneficial exercise of those powers. It is then, the subject of fair inquiry, how far such means may be employed.

It is not denied that the powers given to the government imply the ordinary means of execution. That, for example, of raising revenue, and applying it to national purposes, is admitted to imply the power of conveying money from place to place, as the exigencies of the nation may require, and of employing the usual means of conveyance. But it is denied that the government has its choice of means; or, that it may employ the most convenient means; if, to employ them, it be necessary to erect a corporation.

On what foundation does this argument rest? On this alone: The power of creating a corporation, is one appertaining to sovereignty, and is not expressly conferred on Congress. This is true. But all legislative powers appertain to sovereignty. The original power of giving the law on any subject whatsoever, is a sovereign power; and if the government of the Union is restrained from creating a corporation, as a means for performing its functions, on the single reason that the creation of a corporation is an act of sovereignty; if the sufficiency of this reason be acknowledged, there would be some difficulty in sustaining the authority of Congress to pass other laws for the accomplishment of the same objects.

The government which has a right to do an act, and has imposed on it the duty of performing that act, must, according to the dictates of reason, be allowed to select the means; and those who contend that it may not select any appropriate means, that one particular mode of effecting the object is excepted, take upon themselves the burden of establishing that exception.

The creation of a corporation, it is said, appertains to sovereignty. This is admitted. But to what portion of sovereignty does it appertain? Does it belong to one more than to another? In America, the powers of sovereignty are divided between the government of the Union, and those of the States. They are each sovereign, with respect to the objects committed to it, and neither sovereign with respect to the objects committed to the other. We cannot comprehend that train of reasoning which would maintain, that the extent of power granted by the people is to be ascertained, not by the nature and terms of the grant, but by its date. Some State constitutions were formed *before,* some *since* that of the United States. We cannot believe that their relation to each other is in any degree dependent upon this circumstance. Their respective powers must, we think, be precisely the same as if they had been formed at the same time. Had they been formed at the same time, and had the people conferred on the general government the power contained in the Constitution, and on the States the whole residuum of power, would it have been asserted that the government of the Union was not sovereign with respect to those objects which were entrusted to it, in relation to which its laws were declared to be supreme? If this could not have been asserted, we cannot well comprehend the process of reasoning which maintains, that a power appertaining to sovereignty cannot be connected with the vast portion of it which is granted to the general government, so far as it is calculated to subserve the legitimate objects of that government. The power of creating a corporation, though appertaining to sovereignty, is not, like the power of making war, or levying taxes, or of regulating commerce, a great substantive and independent power, which cannot be implied as incidental to other powers, or used as a means of executing them. It is never the end for which other powers are exercised, but a means by which other objects are accomplished. No contributions are made to charity for the sake of an incorporation, but a corporation is created to administer the charity; no seminary of learning is instituted in order to be incorporated, but the corporate character is conferred to subserve the purposes of education. No city was ever built with the sole object of being incorporated, but is incorporated as affording the best means of being well governed. The power of creating a corporation is never used for its own sake, but for the purpose of effecting something else. No sufficient reason is, therefore, perceived, why it may not pass as incidental to those powers which are expressly given, if it be a direct mode of executing them.

But the Constitution of the United States has not left the right of Congress to employ the necessary means, for the execution of the powers conferred on the government, to general reasoning. To its enumeration of powers is added that of making "all laws which shall be necessary and proper, for carrying into execution the foregoing powers, and all other powers vested by this Constitution, in the government of the United States, or in any department thereof."

The counsel for the State of Maryland have urged various arguments, to prove that this clause, though in terms a grant of power, is not so in effect; but is really restrictive of the general right, which might otherwise be implied, of selecting means for executing the enumerated powers.

In support of this proposition, they have found it necessary to contend, that this clause was inserted for the purpose of conferring on Congress the power of making laws. That, without it, doubts might be entertained, whether Congress could exercise its powers in the form of legislation.

But could this be the object for which it was inserted? A government is created by the people, having legislative, executive, and judicial powers. Its legislative powers are vested in a Congress, which is to consist of a Senate and House of Representatives. Each house may determine the rule of its proceedings; and it is declared that every bill which shall have passed both houses, shall, before it becomes a law, be presented to the President of the United States. The 7th section describes the course of proceedings, by which a bill shall become a law; and, then, the 8th section enumerates the powers of Congress. Could it be necessary to say, that a legislature should exercise legislative powers, in the shape of legislation? After allowing each house to prescribe its own course of proceeding, after describing the manner in which a bill should become a law, would it have entered into the mind of a single member of the Convention, that an express power to make laws was necessary to enable the legislature to make them? That a legislature, endowed with legislative powers, can legislate, is a proposition too self-evident to have been questioned.

But the argument on which most reliance is placed, is drawn from the peculiar language of this clause. Congress is not empowered by it to make all laws, which may have relation to the powers conferred on the government, but such only as may be *"necessary and proper"* for carrying them into execution. The word *"necessary"* is considered as controlling the whole sentence, and as limiting the right to pass laws for the execution of the granted powers, to such as are indispensable, and without which the power would be nugatory. That it excludes the choice of means, and leaves to Congress in each case, that only which is most direct and simple.

Is it true, that this is the sense in which the word "necessary" is always used? Does it always import an absolute physical necessity, so strong, that one thing, to which another may be termed necessary, cannot exist without that other? We think it does not. If reference be had to its use, in the common affairs of the world, or in approved authors, we find that it frequently imports no more than that one thing is convenient, or useful, or essential to another. To employ the means necessary to an end, is generally understood as employing any means calculated to produce the end, and not as being confined to those single means, without which the end would be entirely unattainable. Such is the character of human language, that no word conveys to the mind, in all situations, one single definite idea; and nothing is more common than to use words in a figurative sense. Almost all compositions contain words, which, taken in their rigorous sense, would convey a meaning different from that which is obviously intended. It is essential to just construction, that many words which import something excessive, should be understood in a more mitigated sense—in that sense which common usage justifies. The word "necessary" is of this description. It has not a fixed character peculiar to itself. It admits of all degrees of comparison; and is often connected with other words, which increase or diminish the impression the mind receives of the urgency it imports. A thing may be necessary, very necessary, absolutely or indispensably necessary. To no mind would the same idea be conveyed, by these several phrases. This comment on the word is well illustrated, by the passage cited at the bar, from the 10th section of the 1st article of the Constitution. It is, we think, impossible to compare the sentence which prohibits a State from laying "imposts, or duties on imports or exports, except what may be *absolutely* necessary for executing its inspection laws," with that which authorizes Congress "to make all laws which shall be necessary and proper for carrying into execution" the powers of the general government, without feeling a conviction that the convention understood itself to change materially the meaning of the word "necessary," by prefixing the word "absolutely." This word, then, like others, is used in various senses; and, in its construction, the subject, the context, the intention of the person using them, are all to be taken into view.

Let this be done in the case under consideration. The subject is the execution of those great powers on which the welfare of a nation essentially depends. It must have been the intention of those who gave these powers, to insure, as far as human prudence could insure, their beneficial execution. This could not be done by confiding the choice of means to such narrow limits as not to leave it in the power of Congress to adopt any which might be appropriate, and which were conducive to the end. This provision is made in a constitution intended to endure for ages to come, and consequently, to be adapted to the various *crises* of human affairs. To have prescribed the means by which government should, in all future time, execute its powers, would have been to change, entirely, the character of the instrument, and give it the properties of a legal code. It would have been an unwise attempt to provide, by immutable rules, for exigencies which, if foreseen at all, must have been seen dimly, and which can be best provided for as they occur. To have declared that the best means shall not be used, but those alone without which the power given would be nugatory, would have been to deprive the legislature of the capacity to avail itself of experience, to exercise its reason, and to accommodate its legislation to circumstances. If we apply this principle of construction to any of the powers of the government, we shall find it so pernicious in its operation that we shall be compelled to discard it. The powers vested in Congress may certainly be carried into execution, without prescribing an oath of office. The power to exact this security for the faithful performance of duty, is not given, nor is it indispensably necessary. The different departments may be established; taxes may be imposed and collected; armies and navies may be raised and maintained; and money may be borrowed, without requiring an oath of office. It might be argued, with as much plausibility as other incidental powers have been assailed, that the Convention was not unmindful of this subject. The oath which might be exacted—that of fidelity to the Constitution—is prescribed, and no other can be required. Yet, he would be charged with insanity who should contend, that the legislature might not superadd, to the oath directed by the Constitution such other oath of office as its wisdom might suggest.

So, with respect to the whole penal code of the United States: whence arises the power to punish in cases not prescribed by the Constitution? All admit that the government may, legitimately, punish any violation of its laws; and yet, this is not among the enumerated powers of Congress. The right to enforce the observance of law, by punishing its infraction, might be denied with the more plausibility, because it is expressly given in some cases. Congress is empowered "to provide for the punishment of counterfeiting the securities and current coin of the United States," and "define and punish piracies and felonies committed on the high seas, and offences against the law of nations." The several powers of Congress may exist, in a very imperfect state to be sure, but they may exist and be carried into execution, although no punishment should be inflicted in cases where the right to punish is not expressly given.

Take, for example, the power "to establish post offices and post roads." This power is executed by the single act of making the establishment. But, from this has been inferred the power and duty of carrying the mail along the post road, from one post office to another. And, from this implied power, has again been inferred the right to punish those who steal letters from the post office, or rob the mail. It may be said, with some plausibility, that the right to carry the mail, and to punish those who rob it, is not indispensably necessary to the establishment of a post office and post road. This right is indeed essential to the beneficial exercise of the power, but not indispensably necessary to its existence. So, of the punishment of the crimes of stealing or falsifying a record or process of a Court of the United States, or of perjury in such Court. To punish these offences is certainly conducive to the due administration of justice. But courts may exist, and may decide the causes brought before them, though such crimes escape punishment.

The baneful influence of this narrow construction on all the operations of the government, and the absolute impracticability of maintaining it without rendering the government incompetent to its great objects, might be illustrated by numerous examples drawn from the Constitution, and from our laws. The good sense of the public has pronounced, without hesitation, that the power of punishment appertains to sovereignty, and may be exercised whenever the sovereign has a right to act, as incidental to his constitutional powers. It is a means for carrying into execution all sovereign powers, and may be used, although not indispensably necessary. It is a right incidental to the power, and conducive to its beneficial exercise.

If this limited construction of the word "necessary" must be abandoned in order to punish, whence is derived the rule which would reinstate it, when the government would carry its powers into execution by means not vindictive to their nature? If the word "necessary" means "needful," "requisite," "essential," "conducive to," in order to let in the power of punishment for the infraction of law; why is it not equally comprehensive when required to authorize the use of means which facilitate the execution of the powers of government without the infliction of punishment?

In ascertaining the sense in which the word "necessary" is used in this clause of the Constitution, we may derive some aid from that with which it is associated. Congress shall have power "to make all laws which shall be necessary and *proper* to carry into execution" the powers of the government. If the word "necessary" was used in that strict and rigorous sense for which the counsel for the State of Maryland contend, it would be an extraordinary departure from the usual course of the human mind, as exhibited in composition, to add a word, the only possible effect of which is to qualify that strict and rigorous meaning; to present to the mind the idea of some choice of means of legislation not straitened and compressed within the narrow limits for which gentlemen contend.

But the argument which most conclusively demonstrates the error of the construction contended for by the counsel for the State of Maryland, is founded on the intention of the Convention, as manifested in the whole clause. To waste time and argument in proving that, without it, Congress might carry its powers into execution, would be not much less idle than to hold a lighted taper to the sun. As little can it be required to prove, that in the absence of this clause, Congress would have some choice of means. That it might employ those which, in its judgment, would most advantageously effect the object to be accomplished. That any means adapted to the end, any means which tended directly to the execution of the constitutional powers of the government, were in themselves constitutional. This clause, as construed by the State of Maryland, would abridge, and almost annihilate this useful and necessary right of the legislature to select its means. That this could not be intended, is, we should think, had it not been already controverted, too apparent for controversy. We think so for the following reasons:

1st. The clause is placed among the powers of Congress, not among the limitations on those powers.

2nd. Its terms purport to enlarge, not to diminish the powers vested in the government. It purports to be an additional power, not a restriction on those already granted. No reason has been, or can be assigned for thus concealing an intention to narrow the discretion of the national legislature under words which purport to enlarge it. The framers of the Constitution wished its adoption, and well know that it would be endangered by its strength, not by its weakness. Had they been capable of using language which would convey to the eye one idea, and after deep reflection, impress on the mind another, they would rather have disguised the grant of power, than its limitation. If, then, their intention had been, by this clause, to restrain the free use of means which might otherwise have been implied, that intention would have been inserted in another place, and would have been expressed in terms resembling these. "In carrying into execution the foregoing powers, and all others," &c. "no laws shall be passed but, such as are necessary and proper." Had the intention been to make this clause restrictive, it would unquestionably have been so in form as well as in effect.

The result of the most careful and attentive consideration bestowed upon this clause is, that if it does not enlarge, it cannot be construed to restrain the powers of Congress, or to impair the right of the legislature to exercise its best judgment in the selection of measures to carry into execution the constitutional powers of the government. If no other motive for its insertion can be suggested, a sufficient one is found in the desire to remove all doubts respecting the right to legislate on that vast mass of incidental powers which must be involved in the Constitution, if that instrument be not a splendid bauble.

We admit, as all must admit, that the powers of the government are limited, and that its limits are not to be transcended. But we think the sound construction of the Constitution must allow to the national legislature that discretion, with respect to the means by which the powers it confers are to be carried into execution, which will enable that body to perform the high duties assigned to it, in the manner most beneficial to the people. Let the end be legitimate, let it be within the scope of the Constitution, and all means which are appropriate, which are plainly adapted to that end, which are not prohibited, but consist with the letter and spirit of the Constitution, are constitutional.

That a corporation must be considered as a means not less usual, not of higher dignity, not more requiring a particular specification than other means, has been sufficiently proved. If we look to the origin of corporations, to the manner in which they have been framed in that government from which we have derived most of our legal principles and ideas, or to the uses to which they have been applied, we find no reason to suppose that a constitution, omitting, and wisely omitting, to enumerate all the means for carrying into execution the great powers vested in government, ought to have specified this. Had it been intended to grant this power as one which should be distinct and independent, to be exercised in any case whatever, it would have found a place among the enumerated powers of the government. But being considered merely as a means, to be employed only for the purpose of carrying into execution the given powers, there could be no motive for particularly mentioning it.

The propriety of this remark would seem to be generally acknowledged by the universal acquiescence in the construction which has been uniformly put on the 3rd section of the 4th article of the Constitution. The power to "make all needful rules and regulations respecting the territory or other property belonging to the United States," is not more comprehensive, than the power "to make all laws which shall be necessary and proper for carrying into execution" the powers of the government. Yet all admit the constitutionality of a territorial government, which is a corporate body. If a corporation may be employed indiscriminately with other means to carry into execution the powers of the government, no particular reason can be assigned for excluding the use of a bank, if required for its fiscal operations. To use one, must be within the discretion of Congress, if it be an appropriate mode of executing the powers of government. That it is a convenient, a useful, and essential instrument in the prosecution of its fiscal operations, is not now a subject of controversy. All those who have been concerned in the administration of our finances, have concurred in representing its importance and necessity; and so strongly have they been felt, that statesmen of the first class, whose previous opinions against it had been confirmed by every circumstance which can fix the human judgment, have yielded those opinions to the exigencies of the nation. Under the confederation, Congress, justifying the measure by its necessity, transcended perhaps its powers to obtain the advantage of a bank; and our own legislation attests the universal conviction of the utility of this measure. The time has passed away when it can be necessary to enter into any discussion in order to prove the importance of this instrument, as a means to effect the legitimate objects of the government.

But, were its necessity less apparent, none can deny its being an appropriate measure; and if it is, the degree of its necessity, as has been very justly observed, is to be discussed in another place. Should Congress, in the execution of its powers, adopt measures which are prohibited by the Constitution; or should Congress, under the pretext of executing its powers, pass laws for the accomplishment of objects not entrusted to the government; it would become the painful duty of this tribunal, should a case requiring such a decision come before it, to say that such an act was not the law of the land. But where the law is not prohibited, and is really calculated to effect any of the objects entrusted to the government, to undertake here to inquire into the degree of its necessity, would be to pass the line which circumscribes the judicial department, and to tread on legislative ground. This court disclaims all pretensions to such a power.

After this declaration, it can scarcely be necessary to say, that the existence of State banks can have no possible influence on the question. No trace is to be found in the Constitution of an intention to create a dependence of the government of the Union on those of the States, for the execution of the great powers assigned to it. Its means are adequate to its ends; and on those means alone was it expected to rely for the accomplishment of its ends. To impose on it the necessity of resorting to means which it cannot control, which another government may furnish or withhold, would render its course precarious, the result of its measures uncertain, and create a dependence on other governments, which might disappoint its most important designs, and is incompatible with the language of the Constitution. But were it otherwise, the choice of means implies a right to choose a national bank in preference to State banks, and Congress alone can make the election.

After the most deliberate consideration, it is the unanimous and decided opinion of this Court, that the act to incorporate the Bank of the United States is a law made in pursuance of the Constitution, and is a part of the supreme law of the land.

The branches, proceeding from the same stock, and being conducive to the complete accomplishment of the object, are equally constitutional. It would have been unwise to locate them in the charter, and it would be unnecessarily inconvenient to employ the legislative power in making those subordinate arrangements. The great duties of the bank are prescribed, those duties require branches; and the bank itself may, we think, be safely trusted with the selection of places where those branches shall be fixed; reserving always to the government the right to require that a branch shall be located where it may be deemed necessary.

WASHINGTON'S
FIRST INAUGURAL ADDRESS
(1789)

[At the first election held under the Constitution, George Washington, who had been chairman of the convention which framed the Constitution, was unanimously chosen President. The inaugural address was delivered in Federal Hall, at Wall and Nassau Streets, New York, April 30, 1789.]

Fellow-Citizens:

AMONG the vicissitudes incident to life, no event could have filled me with greater anxieties, than that of which the notification was transmitted by your order, and received on the 14th day of the present month. On the one hand, I was summoned by my country, whose voice I can never hear but with veneration and love, from a retreat which I had chosen with the fondest predilection, and, in my flattering hopes, with an immutable decision, as the asylum of my declining years; a retreat which was rendered every day more necessary as well as more dear to me, by the addition of habit to inclination, and of frequent interruptions in my health to the gradual waste committed on it by time. On the other hand, the magnitude and difficulty of the trust, to which the voice of my country called me, being sufficient to awaken in the wisest and most experienced of her citizens a distrustful scrutiny into his qualifications, could not but overwhelm with despondence one, who, inheriting inferior endowments from nature, and unpracticed in the duties of civil administration, ought to be peculiarly conscious of his own deficiencies. In this conflict of emotions, all I dare aver, is, that it has been my faithful study to collect my duty from a just appreciation of every circumstance by which it might be affected. All I dare hope is, that, if in executing this task, I have been too much swayed by a grateful remembrance of former instances, or by an affectionate sensibility to this transcendent proof of the confidence of my fellow-citizens; and have thence too little consulted my incapacity as well as disinclination for the weighty and untried cares before me; my error will be palliated by the motives which misled me, and its consequences be judged by my country with some share of the partiality in which they originated.

Such being the impressions under which I have, in obedience to the public summons, repaired to the present station, it would be peculiarly improper to omit, in this first official act, my fervent supplications to that Almighty Being, who rules over the universe, who presides in the councils of nations, and whose providential aids can supply every human defect, that his benediction may consecrate to the liberties and happiness of the people of the United States a government instituted by themselves for these essential purposes, and may enable every instrument employed in its administration to execute with success the functions allotted to his charge. In tendering this homage to the great Author of every public and private good, I assure myself that it expresses your sentiments not less than my own; nor those of my fellow-citizens at large, less than either. No people can be bound to acknowledge and adore the invisible hand, which conducts the affairs of men, more than the people of the United States. Every step, by which they have advanced to the character of an independent nation, seems to have been distinguished by some token of providential agency. And, in the important revolution just accomplished in the system of their united government, the tranquil deliberations and voluntary consent of so many distinct communities, from which the event has resulted, cannot be compared with the means by which most governments have been established, without some return of pious gratitude along with an humble anticipation of the future blessings which the past seems to presage. These reflections, arising out of the present crisis, have forced themselves too strongly on my mind to be suppressed. You will join with me, I trust, in thinking that there are none, under the influence of which the proceedings of a new and free government can more auspiciously commence.

By the article establishing the executive department, it is made the duty of the President "to recommend to your consideration such measures as he shall judge necessary and expedient." The circumstances, under which I now meet you, will acquit me from entering into that subject farther than to refer you to the great constitutional charter under which we are assembled; and which, in defining your powers, designates the objects to which your attention is to be given. It will be more consistent with those circumstances, and far more congenial with the feelings which actuate me, to substitute, in place of a recommendation of particular measures, the tribute that is due to the talents, the rectitude, and the patriotism, which adorn the characters selected to devise and adopt them. In these honorable qualifications I behold the surest pledges, that as, on one side, no local prejudices or attachments, no separate views or party animosities, will misdirect the comprehensive and equal eye, which ought to watch over this great assemblage of communities and interests; so, on another, that the foundations of our national policy will be laid in the pure and immutable principles of private morality, and the preëminence of a free government be exemplified by all the attributes, which can win the affections of its citizens, and command the respect of the world.

I dwell on this prospect with every satisfaction, which an ardent love for my country can inspire; since there is no truth more thoroughly established, than that there exists in the economy and course of nature an indissoluble union between virtue and happiness, between duty and advantage, between the genuine maxims of an honest and magnanimous policy, and the solid rewards of public prosperity and felicity; since we ought to be no less persuaded that the propitious smiles of Heaven can never be expected on a nation that disregards the eternal rules of order and right, which Heaven itself has ordained; and since the preservation of the sacred fire of liberty, and the destiny of the republican model of government, are justly considered as *deeply,* perhaps as *finally* staked on the experiment intrusted to the hands of the American people.

Besides the ordinary objects submitted to your care, it will remain with your judgment to decide, how far an exercise of the occasional power delegated by the fifth article of the Constitution is rendered expedient at the present juncture by the nature of objections which have been urged against the system, or by the degree of inquietude which has given birth to them. Instead of undertaking particular recommendations on this subject, in which I could be guided by no lights derived from official opportunities, I shall again give way to my entire confidence in your discernment and pursuit of the public good; for I assure myself, that, whilst you carefully avoid every alteration, which might endanger the benefits of a united and effective government, or which ought to await the future lessons of experience, a reverence for the characteristic rights of freemen, and a regard for the public harmony, will sufficiently influence your deliberations on the question, how far the former can be more impregnably fortified, or the latter be safely and advantageously promoted.

To the preceding observations I have one to add, which will be most properly addressed to the House of Representatives. It concerns myself, and will therefore be as brief as possible. When I was first honored with a call into the service of my country, then on the eve of an arduous struggle for its liberties, the light in which I contemplated my duty required, that I should renounce every pecuniary compensation. From this resolution I have in no instance departed. And being still under the impressions which produced it, I must decline as inapplicable to myself, any share in the personal emoluments, which may be indispensably included in a permanent provision for the executive department; and must accordingly pray, that the pecuniary estimates for the station in which I am placed, may, during my continuance in it, be limited to such actual expenditures as the public good may be thought to require.

Having thus imparted to you my sentiments, as they have been awakened by the occasion which brings us together, I shall take my present leave; but not without resorting once more to the benign Parent of the human race, in humble supplication, that, since he has been pleased to favor the American people with opportunities for deliberating in perfect tranquillity, and dispositions for deciding with unparalleled unanimity on a form of government for the security of their union and the advancement of their happiness; so his divine blessing may be equally *conspicuous* in the enlarged views, the temperate consultations, and the wise measures, on which the success of this government must depend.

TREATY
WITH THE SIX NATIONS
(1794)

[The confederation of Indian tribes known as the Iroquois, or Six Nations, included the Mohawks, the Oneidas, the Onondagas, the Cayugas, the Senecas, and the Tuscaroras. This treaty, concluded November 11, 1794, fixed the limits of the territory to be left in the possession of these tribes, who had fought against the colonies in the War of Independence.]

THE President of the United States having determined to hold a conference with the Six Nations of Indians, for the purpose of removing from their minds all causes of complaint, and establishing a firm and permanent friendship with them; and Timothy Pickering being appointed sole agent for that purpose; and the agent having met and conferred with the Sachems, Chiefs and Warriors of the Six Nations, in a general council: Now in order to accomplish the good design of this conference, the parties have agreed on the following articles, which, when ratified by the President, with the advice and consent of the Senate of the United States, shall be binding on them and the Six Nations.

ARTICLE I

Peace and friendship are hereby firmly established, and shall be perpetual, between the United States and the Six Nations.

ARTICLE II

The United States acknowledge the lands reserved to the Oneida, Onondaga and Cayuga Nations, in their respective treaties with the state of New York, and called their reservations, to be their property; and the United States will never claim the same, nor disturb them or either of the Six Nations, nor their Indian friends residing thereon and united with them, in the free use and enjoyment thereof: but the said reservations shall remain theirs, until they choose to sell the same to the people of the United States who have right to purchase.

Article III

The land of the Seneka nation is bounded as follows: Beginning on Lake Ontario, at the north-west corner of the land they sold to Oliver Phelps, the line run westerly along the lake, as far as O-yōng-wong-yeh Creek at Johnson's Landing-place, about four miles eastward from the fort of Niagara; then southerly up that creek to its main fork, then straight to the main fork of Stedman's Creek, which empties into the river Niagara, above Fort Schlosser, and then onward, from that fork, continuing the same straight course, to that river; (this line, from the mouth of O-yōng-wong-yeh Creek to the river Niagara, above Fort Schlosser, being the eastern boundary of a strip of land, extending from the same line to Niagara River, which the Seneka nation ceded to the King of Great Britain, at a treaty held about thirty years ago, with Sir William Johnson;) then the line runs along the river Niagara to Lake Erie; then along Lake Erie to the north-east corner of a triangular piece of land which the United States conveyed to the state of Pennsylvania, as by the President's patent, dated the third day of March, 1792; then due south to the northern boundary of that state; then due east to the south-west corner of the land sold by the Seneka nation to Oliver Phelps; and then north and northerly, along Phelps's line, to the place beginning on Lake Ontario. Now, the United States acknowledge all the land within the aforementioned boundaries, to be the property of the Seneka nation; and the United States will never claim the same, nor disturb the Seneka nation, nor any of the Six Nations, or their Indian friends residing thereon and united with them, in the free use and enjoyment thereof: but it shall remain theirs, until they choose to sell the same to the people of the United States, who have the right to purchase.

Article IV

The United States having thus described and acknowledged what lands belong to the Oneidas, Onondagas, Cayugas, and Senekas, and engaged never to claim the same, nor to disturb them, or any of the Six Nations, or their Indian friends residing thereon and united with them, in the free use and enjoyment thereof: Now the Six Nations, and each of them, hereby engage that they will never claim any other lands within the boundaries of the United States; nor ever disturb the people of the United States in the free use and enjoyment thereof.

ARTICLE V

The Seneka nation, all others of the Six Nations concurring, cede to the United States the right of making a wagon road from Fort Schlosser to Lake Erie, as far south as Buffaloe Creek; and the people of the United States shall have the free and undisturbed use of this road, for the purposes of travelling and transportation. And the Six Nations, and each of them, will forever allow to the people of the United States, a free passage through their lands, and the free use of their harbors and rivers adjoining and within their respective tracts of land, for the passing and securing of vessels and boats, and liberty to land their cargoes when necessary for their safety.

ARTICLE VI

In consideration of the peace and friendship hereby established, and of the engagements entered into by the Six Nations; and because the United States desire, with humanity and kindness, to contribute to their comfortable support; and to render the peace and friendship hereby established strong and perpetual; the United States now deliver to the Six Nations, and the Indians of the other nations residing among and united with them, a quantity of goods of the value of ten thousand dollars. And for the same considerations, and with a view to promote the future welfare of the Six Nations, and of their Indian friends aforesaid, the United States will add the sum of three thousand dollars to the one thousand five hundred dollars, heretofore allowed them by an article ratified by the President, on the twenty-third day of April 1792; making in the whole, four thousand five hundred dollars; which shall be expended yearly forever, in purchasing clothing, domestic animals, implements of husbandry and other utensils suited to their circumstances, and in compensating useful artificers, who shall reside with them or near them, and be employed for their benefit. The immediate application of the whole annual allowance now stipulated, to be made by the superintendent appointed by the President for the affairs of the Six Nations, and their Indian friends aforesaid.

Article VII

Lest the firm peace and friendship now established should be interrupted by the misconduct of individuals, the United States and Six Nations agree, that for injuries done by individuals on either side, no private revenge or retaliation shall take place; but, instead thereof, complaint shall be made by the party injured, to the other: By the Six Nations or any of them, to the President of the United States, or the Superintendent by him appointed: and by the Superintendent, or other person appointed by the President, to the principal chiefs of the Six Nations, or of the nation to which the offender belongs: and such prudent measures shall then be pursued as shall be necessary to preserve our peace and friendship unbroken; until the legislature (or great council) of the United States shall make the equitable provision for the purpose.

Note: It is clearly understood by the parties to this treaty, that the annuity stipulated in the sixth article, is to be applied to the benefit of such of the Six Nations and of their Indian friends united with them as aforesaid, as do or shall reside within the boundaries of the United States: for the United States do not interfere with nations, tribes or families, of Indians elsewhere resident.

WASHINGTON'S FAREWELL ADDRESS

(1796)

[Washington refused to be a candidate for a third term of the Presidency; and in May, 1796, he sent to Hamilton a rough draft of his farewell address, asking for his criticism. After much revision by both the document was published on Sept. 19, and was read to the House of Representatives. The advice contained in it has ever since exercised a profound influence on the policy of the nation.]

Friends and Fellow-Citizens:

THE period for a new election of a Citizen, to administer the Executive Government of the United States, being not far distant, and the time actually arrived, when your thoughts must be employed in designating the person, who is to be clothed with that important trust, it appears to me proper, especially as it may conduce to a more distinct expression of the public voice, that I should now apprize you of the resolution I have formed, to decline being considered among the number of those, out of whom a choice is to be made.

I beg you, at the same time, to do me the justice to be assured, that this resolution has not been taken, without a strict regard to all the considerations appertaining to the relation, which binds a dutiful citizen to his country—and that, in withdrawing the tender of service which silence in my situation might imply, I am influenced by no diminution of zeal for your future interest, no deficiency of grateful respect for your past kindness; but am supported by a full conviction that the step is compatible with both.

The acceptance of, and continuance hitherto in, the office to which your suffrages have twice called me, have been a uniform sacrifice of inclination to the opinion of duty, and to a deference for what appeared to be your desire.—I constantly hoped that it would have been much earlier in my power, consistently with motives, which I was not at liberty to disregard, to return to that retirement, from which I had been reluctantly drawn.—The strength of my inclination to do this, previous to the last election, had even led to the preparation of an address to declare it to you; but mature reflection on the then perplexed and critical posture of our affairs with foreign Nations, and the unanimous advice of persons entitled to my confidence, impelled me to abandon the idea.—

I rejoice, that the state of your concerns, external as well as internal, no longer renders the pursuit of inclination incompatible with the sentiment of duty, or propriety; and am persuaded, whatever partiality may be retained for my services, that, in the present circumstances of our country, you will not disapprove my determination to retire.

The impressions, with which I first undertook the arduous trust, were explained on the proper occasion. In the discharge of this trust, I will only say, that I have, with good intentions, contributed towards the organization and administration of the government, the best exertions of which a very fallible judgment was capable.—Not unconscious, in the outset, of the inferiority of my qualifications, experience in my own eyes, perhaps still more in the eyes of others, has strengthened the motives to diffidence of myself; and every day the increasing weight of years admonishes me more and more, that the shade of retirement is as necessary to me as it will be welcome.—Satisfied, that, if any circumstances have given peculiar value to my services, they were temporary, I have the consolation to believe, that, while choice and prudence invite me to quit the political scene, patriotism does not forbid it.

In looking forward to the moment, which is intended to terminate the career of my public life, my feelings do not permit me to suspend the deep acknowledgment of that debt of gratitude, which I owe to my beloved country,—for the many honors it has conferred upon me; still more for the stedfast confidence with which it has supported me; and for the opportunities I have thence enjoyed of manifesting my inviolable attachment, by services faithful and persevering, though in usefulness unequal to my zeal.—If benefits have resulted to our country from these services, let it always be remembered to your praise, and as an instructive example in our annals, that under circumstances in which the Passions, agitated in every direction, were liable to mislead, amidst appearances sometimes dubious, vicissitudes of fortune often discouraging, in situations in which not unfrequently want of success has countenanced the spirit of criticism, the constancy of your support was the essential prop of the efforts, and a guarantee of the plans by which they were effected.—Profoundly penetrated with this idea, I shall carry it with me to my grave, as a strong incitement to unceasing vows that Heaven may continue to you the choicest tokens of its beneficence—that your union and brotherly affection may be perpetual—that the free Constitution, which is the work of your hands, may be sacredly maintained—that its administration in every department may be stamped with wisdom and virtue—that, in fine, the happiness of the people of these States, under the auspices of liberty, may be made complete, by so careful a preservation and so prudent a use of this blessing, as will acquire to them the glory of recommending it to the applause, the affection, and adoption of every nation, which is yet a stranger to it.

Here, perhaps, I ought to stop.—But a solicitude for your welfare, which cannot end but with my life, and the apprehension of danger, natural to that solicitude, urge me on an occasion like the present, to offer to your solemn contemplation, and to recommend to your frequent review, some sentiments; which are the result of much reflection, of no inconsiderable observation and which appear to me all important to the permanency of your felicity as a People. These will be offered to you with the more freedom, as you can only see in them the disinterested warnings of a parting friend, who can possibly have no personal motive to bias his counsel.—Nor can I forget, as an encouragement to it, your indulgent reception of my sentiments on a former and not dissimilar occasion.

Interwoven as is the love of liberty with every ligament of your hearts, no recommendation of mine is necessary to fortify or confirm the attachment.—

The Unity of Government, which constitutes you ore people, is also now dear to you.—It is justly so; for it is a main Pillar in the Edifice of your real independence; the support of your tranquillity at home; your peace abroad; of your safety; of your prosperity in every shape; of that very Liberty, which you so highly prize.—But as it is easy to foresee, that, from different causes, and from different quarters, much pains will be taken, many artifices employed, to weaken in your minds the conviction of this truth;—as this is the point in your political fortress against which the batteries of internal and external enemies will be most constantly and actively (though often covertly and insidiously) directed it is of infinite moment, that you should properly estimate the immense value of your national Union to your collective and individual happiness;—that you should cherish a cordial, habitual, and immoveable attachment to it; accustoming yourselves to think and speak of it as of the Palladium of your political safety and prosperity; watching for its preservation with jealous anxiety; discountenancing whatever may suggest even a suspicion, that it can in any event be abandoned, and indignantly frowning upon the first dawning of every attempt to alienate any portion of our Country from the rest, or to enfeeble the sacred ties which now link together the various parts.

For this you have every inducement of sympathy and interest.—Citizens by birth or choice of a common country, that country has a right to concentrate your affections.—The name of AMERICAN, which belongs to you, in your national capacity, must always exalt the just pride of Patriotism, more than any appellation derived from local discriminations. With slight shades of difference, you have the same Religion, Manners, Habits, and Political Principles. You have in a common cause fought and triumphed together; the Independence and Liberty you possess are the work of joint counsels, and joint efforts—of common dangers, sufferings, and successes.—

But these considerations, however powerfully they address themselves to your sensibility, are greatly outweighed by those which apply more immediately to your Interest. Here every portion of our country finds the most commanding motives for carefully guarding and preserving the Union of the whole.

The *North,* in an unrestrained intercourse with the *South,* protected by the equal Laws of a common government, finds, in the productions of the latter, great additional resources of maritime and commercial enterprise—and precious materials of manufacturing industry.—The *South,* in the same intercourse, benefiting by the agency of the *North,* sees its agriculture grow and its commerce expand. Turning partly into its own channels the seamen of the *North,* it finds its particular navigation envigorated;—and, while it contributes, in different ways, to nourish and increase the general mass of the national navigation, it looks forward to the protection of a maritime strength to which itself is unequally adapted. The *East,* in a like intercourse with the *West,* already finds, and in the progressive improvement of interior communications, by land and water, will more and more find, a valuable vent for the commodities which it brings from abroad, or manufactures at home.—The *West* derives from the *East* supplies requisite to its growth and comfort, and—what is perhaps of still greater consequence, it must of necessity owe the *secure* enjoyment of indispensable *outlets* for its own productions to the weight, influence, and the future maritime strength of the Atlantic side of the Union, directed by an indissoluble community of interest as *one Nation.*—Any other tenure by which the *West* can hold this essential advantage, whether derived from its own separate strength, or from an apostate and unnatural connection with any foreign power, must be intrinsically precarious.

While then every part of our Country thus feels an immediate and particular interest in Union, all the parts combined in the united mass of means and efforts cannot fail to find greater strength, greater resource, proportionably greater security from external danger, a less frequent interruption of their Peace by foreign Nations; and, what is of inestimable value! they must derive from Union an exemption from those broils and wars between themselves, which so frequently afflict neighbouring countries, not tied together by the same governments; which their own rivalships alone would be sufficient to produce; but which opposite foreign alliances, attachments, and intrigues would stimulate and embitter.—Hence likewise they will avoid the necessity of those overgrown Military establishments, which, under any form of government, are inauspicious to liberty, and which are to be regarded as particularly hostile to Republican Liberty. In this sense it is, that your Union ought to be considered as a main prop to your liberty, and that the love of the one ought to endear to you the preservation of the other.

These considerations speak a persuasive language to every reflecting and virtuous mind, and exhibit the continuance of the UNION as a primary object of Patriotic desire. Is there a doubt, whether a common government can embrace so large a sphere?—Let experience solve it. To listen to mere speculation in such a case were criminal.— We are authorized to hope that a proper organization of the whole, with the auxiliary agency of governments for the respective sub-divisions, will afford a happy issue to the experiment. It is well worth a fair and full experiment. With such powerful and obvious motives to Union, affecting all parts of our country, while experience shall not have demonstrated its impracticability, there will always be reason to distrust the patriotism of those, who in any quarter may endeavour to weaken its bands.—

In contemplating the causes which may disturb our Union, it occurs as matter of serious concern, that any ground should have been furnished for characterizing parties by *geographical* discrimina-tions—*Northern* and *Southern, Atlantic* and *Western;* whence de-signing men may endeavour to excite a belief, that there is a real difference of local interests and views. One of the expedients of Party to acquire influence, within particular districts, is to misrepre-sent the opinions and aims of other districts.—You cannot shield yourselves too much against the jealousies and heart burnings, which spring from these misrepresentations;—they tend to render alien to each other those, who ought to be bound together by fraternal affec-tion.—The inhabitants of our Western country have lately had a useful lesson on this head—they have seen, in the negotiation by the Executive, and in the unanimous ratification by the Senate, of the treaty with Spain, and in the universal satisfaction at that event, throughout the United States, a decisive proof how unfounded were the suspicions propagated among them of a policy in the General Government and in the Atlantic States unfriendly to their interests in regard to the MISSISSIPPI—they have been witnesses to the forma-tion of two Treaties, that with Great Britain, and that with Spain, which secure to them every thing they could desire, in respect to our Foreign Relations, towards confirming their prosperity.—Will it not be their wisdom to rely for the preservation of these advantages on the UNION by which they were procured?—Will they not henceforth be deaf to those advisers, if such there are, who would sever them from their Brethren, and connect them with Aliens?—

To the efficacy and permanency of your Union, a Government for the whole is indispensable.—No alliances, however strict between the parts can be an adequate substitute.—They must inevitably experience the infractions and interruptions which all alliances in all times have experienced. Sensible of this momentous truth, you have improved upon your first essay, by the adoption of a Constitution of Government, better calculated than your former for an intimate Union, and for the efficacious management of your common concerns.—This government, the offspring of our own choice uninfluenced and unawed, adopted upon full investigation and mature deliberation, completely free in its principles, in the distribution of its powers, uniting security with energy, and containing within itself a provision for its own amendment, has a just claim to your confidence and your support.—Respect for its authority, compliance with its Laws, acquiescence in its measures, are duties enjoined by the fundamental maxims of true Liberty.—The basis of our political systems is the right of the people to make and to alter their Constitutions of Government.—But the Constitution which at any time exists, 'till changed by an explicit and authentic act of the whole People, is sacredly obligatory upon all.—The very idea of the power and the right of the People to establish Government presupposes the duty of every individual to obey the established Government.

All obstructions to the execution of the Laws, all combinations and associations, under whatever plausible character, with the real design to direct, controul, counteract, or awe the regular deliberation and action of the constituted authorities, are destructive of this fundamental principle, and of fatal tendency.—They serve to organize faction, to give it an artificial and extraordinary force—to put in the place of the delegated will of the nation, the will of a party;—often a small but artful and enterprising minority of the community;—and, according to the alternate triumphs of different parties, to make the public administration the mirror of the ill-concerted and incongruous projects of faction, rather than the organ of consistent and wholesome plans digested by common councils, and modified by mutual interests.—However combinations or associations of the above descriptions may now and then answer popular ends, they are likely, in the course of time and things, to become potent engines, by which cunning, ambitious, and unprincipled men will be enabled to subvert the Power of the People, and to usurp for themselves the reins of Government; destroying afterwards the very engines, which have lifted them to unjust dominion.—

Towards the preservation of your Government, and the permanency of your present happy state, it is requisite, not only that you steadily discountenance irregular oppositions to its acknowledged authority, but also that you resist with care the spirit of innovation upon its principles, however specious the pretexts.—One method of assault may be to effect, in the forms of the Constitution, alterations which will impair the energy of the system, and thus to undermine what cannot be directly overthrown.—In all the changes to which you may be invited, remember that time and habit are at least as necessary to fix the true character of Governments, as of other human institutions—that experience is the surest standard, by which to test the real tendency of the existing Constitution of a Country—that facility in changes upon the credit of mere hypothesis and opinion exposes to perpetual change, from the endless variety of hypothesis and opinion:—and remember, especially, that, for the efficient management of your common interests, in a country so extensive as ours, a Government of as much vigor as is consistent with the perfect security of Liberty is indispensible.—Liberty itself will find in such a government, with powers properly distributed and adjusted, its surest Guardian.—It is, indeed, little else than a name, where the Government is too feeble to withstand the enterprise of faction, to confine each member of the society within the limits prescribed by the laws, and to maintain all in the secure and tranquil enjoyment of the rights of person and property.

I have already intimated to you the danger of parties in the State, with particular reference to the founding of them on Geographical discriminations.—Let me now take a more comprehensive view, and warn you in the most solemn manner against the baneful effects of the Spirit of Party, generally.

This Spirit, unfortunately, is inseparable from our nature, having its root in the strongest passions of the human mind.—It exists under different shapes in all Governments, more or less stifled, controuled, or repressed; but, in those of the popular form, it is seen in its greatest rankness, and is truly their worst enemy.—

The alternate domination of one faction over another, sharpened by the spirit of revenge, natural to party dissension, which in different ages and countries has perpetrated the most horrid enormities, is itself a frightful despotism.—But this leads at length to a more formal and permanent despotism.—The disorders and miseries, which result, gradually incline the minds of men to seek security and repose in the absolute power of an Individual; and sooner or later the chief of some prevailing faction, more able or more fortunate than his competitors, turns this disposition to the purposes of his own elevation, on the ruins of Public Liberty.

Without looking forward to an extremity of this kind, (which nevertheless ought not to be entirely out of sight), the common and continual mischiefs of the spirit of Party are sufficient to make it the interest and duty of a wise people to discourage and restrain it.—

It serves always to distract the Public Councils, and enfeeble the Public administration. It agitates the community with ill-founded jealousies and false alarms, kindles the animosity of one part against another, foments occasionally riot and insurrection.—It opens the door to foreign influence and corruption, which find a facilitated access to the Government itself through the channels of party passions. Thus the policy and the will of one country, are subjected to the policy and will of another.

There is an opinion, that parties in free countries are useful checks upon the Administration of the Government, and serve to keep alive the spirit of Liberty.—This within certain limits is probably true—and in Governments of a Monarchical cast, Patriotism may look with indulgence, if not with favor, upon the spirit of party.— But in those of the popular character, in Governments purely elective, it is a spirit not to be encouraged.—From their natural tendency, it is certain there will always be enough of that spirit for every salutary purpose,—and there being constant danger of excess, the effort ought to be, by force of public opinion, to mitigate and assuage it.—A fire not to be quenched; it demands a uniform vigilance to prevent its bursting into a flame, lest, instead of warming, it should consume.

It is important, likewise, that the habits of thinking in a free country should inspire caution in those intrusted with its administration, to confine themselves within their respective constitutional spheres; avoiding in the exercise of the powers of one department to encroach upon another. The spirit of encroachment tends to consolidate the powers of all the departments in one, and thus to create, whatever the form of government, a real despotism.—A just estimate of that love of power, and proneness to abuse it, which predominates in the human heart, is sufficient to satisfy us of the truth of this position.—The necessity of reciprocal checks in the exercise of political power, by dividing and distributing it into different depositories, and constituting each the Guardian of the Public Weal against invasions by the others, has been evinced by experiments ancient and modern; some of them in our country and under our own eyes.— To preserve them must be as necessary as to institute them. If, in the opinion of the People, the distribution or modification of the Constitutional powers be in any particular wrong, let it be corrected by an amendment in the way which the Constitution designates.—But let there be no change by usurpation; for though this, in one instance, may be the instrument of good, it is the customary weapon by which free governments are destroyed.—The precedent must always greatly overbalance in permanent evil any partial or transient benefit which the use can at any time yield.—

Of all the dispositions and habits, which lead to political prosperity, Religion, and Morality are indispensable supports.—In vain would that man claim the tribute of Patriotism, who should labor to subvert these great pillars of human happiness, these firmest props of the duties of Men and Citizens.—The mere Politician, equally with the pious man, ought to respect and to cherish them.—A volume could not trace all their connexions with private and public felicity.— Let it simply be asked where is the security for property, for reputation, for life, if the sense of religious obligation *desert* the oaths, which are the instruments of investigation in Courts of Justice? And let us with caution indulge the supposition, that morality can be maintained without religion.—Whatever may be conceded to the influence of refined education on minds of peculiar structure—reason and experience both forbid us to expect, that national morality can prevail in exclusion of religious principle.—

'Tis substantially true, that virtue or morality is a necessary spring of popular government.—The rule indeed extends with more or less force to every species of Free Government.—Who that is a sincere friend to it can look with indifference upon attempts to shake the foundation of the fabric?—

Promote, then, as an object of primary importance, institutions for the general diffusion of knowledge. In proportion as the structure of a government gives force to public opinion, it is essential that public opinion should be enlightened.

As a very important source of strength and security, cherish public credit.—One method of preserving it is, to use it as sparingly as possible:—avoiding occasions of expense by cultivating peace, but remembering also that timely disbursements to prepare for danger frequently prevent much greater disbursements to repel it—avoiding likewise the accumulation of debt, not only by shunning occasions of expense, but by vigorous exertions in time of Peace to discharge the debts which unavoidable wars may have occasioned, not ungenerously throwing upon posterity the burthen which we ourselves ought to bear. The execution of these maxims belongs to your Representatives, but it is necessary that public opinion should coöperate.— To facilitate to them the performance of their duty, it is essential that you should practically bear in mind, that towards the payment of debts there must be Revenue—that to have Revenue there must be taxes—that no taxes can be devised, which are not more or less inconvenient and unpleasant—that the intrinsic embarrassment, inseparable from the selection of the proper objects (which is always a choice of difficulties) ought to be a decisive motive for a candid construction of the conduct of the Government in making it, and for a spirit of acquiescence in the measures for obtaining Revenue, which the public exigencies may at any time dictate.—

Observe good faith and justice towards all Nations. Cultivate peace and harmony with all.—Religion and Morality enjoin this conduct; and can it be, that good policy does not equally enjoin it?— It will be worthy of a free, enlightened, and, at no distant period, a great nation, to give to mankind the magnanimous and too novel example of a People always guided by an exalted justice and benevolence.—Who can doubt that in the course of time and things, the fruits of such a plan would richly repay any temporary advantages, which might be lost by a steady adherence to it? Can it be that Providence has not connected the permanent felicity of a Nation with its virtue? The experiment, at least, is recommended by every sentiment which ennobles human nature.—Alas! is it rendered impossible by its vices?

In the execution of such a plan nothing is more essential than that permanent, inveterate antipathies against particular nations and passionate attachments for others, should be excluded; and that, in place of them, just and amicable feelings towards all should be cultivated.—The Nation, which indulges towards another an habitual hatred or an habitual fondness, is in some degree a slave. It is a slave to its animosity or to its affection, either of which is sufficient to lead it astray from its duty and its interest.—Antipathy in one nation against another disposes each more readily to offer insult and injury, to lay hold of slight causes of umbrage, and to be haughty and intractable, when accidental or trifling occasions of dispute occur.—Hence frequent collisions, obstinate, envenomed and bloody contests.—The Nation prompted by ill-will and resentment, sometimes impels to War the Government, contrary to the best calculations of policy.—The Government sometimes participates in the national propensity, and adopts through passion what reason would reject;—at other times, it makes the animosity of the Nation subservient to projects of hostility instigated by pride, ambition, and other sinister and pernicious motives.—The peace often, sometimes perhaps the Liberty, of Nations has been the victim.—

So likewise a passionate attachment of one Nation for another produces a variety of evils.—Sympathy for the favorite nation, facilitating the illusion of an imaginary common interest in cases where no real common interest exists, and infusing into one the enmities of the other, betrays the former into a participation in the quarrels and wars of the latter, without adequate inducement or justification. It leads also to concessions to the favorite Nation of privileges denied to others, which is apt doubly to injure the Nation making the concessions; by unnecessarily parting with what ought to have been retained; and by exciting jealousy, ill-will, and a disposition to retaliate, in the parties from whom equal privileges are withheld; and it gives to ambitious, corrupted, or deluded citizens, (who devote themselves to the favorite Nation) facility to betray or sacrifice the interests of their own country, without odium, sometimes even with popularity:—gilding, with the appearances of a virtuous sense of obligation, a commendable deference for public opinion, or a laudable zeal for public good, the base or foolish compliances of ambition, corruption, or infatuation.—

As avenues to foreign influence in innumerable ways, such attachments are particularly alarming to the truly enlightened and independent Patriot.—How many opportunities do they afford to tamper with domestic factions, to practise the arts of seduction, to mislead public opinion, to influence or awe the public councils! Such an attachment of a small or weak, towards a great and powerful nation, dooms the former to be the satellite of the latter.

Against the insidious wiles of foreign influence, I conjure you to believe me, fellow-citizens, the jealousy of a free people ought to be *constantly* awake; since history and experience prove that foreign influence is one of the most baneful foes of republican Government.—But that jealousy, to be useful, must be impartial; else it becomes the instrument of the very influence to be avoided, instead of a defense against it.—Excessive partiality for one foreign nation, and excessive dislike of another, cause those whom they actuate to see danger only on one side, and serve to veil and even second the arts of influence on the other. Real Patriots, who may resist the intrigues of the favourite, are liable to become suspected and odious; while its tools and dupes usurp the applause and confidence of the people, to surrender their interests.

The great rule of conduct for us, in regard to foreign Nations, is, in extending our commercial relations, to have with them as little *Political* connection as possible.—So far as we have already formed engagements, let them be fulfilled with perfect good faith.—Here let us stop.—

Europe has a set of primary interests, which to us have none, or a very remote relation.—Hence she must be engaged in frequent controversies, the causes of which are essentially foreign to our concerns.—Hence, therefore, it must be unwise in us to implicate ourselves, by artificial ties in the ordinary vicissitudes of her politics, or the ordinary combinations and collisions of her friendships, or enmities.

Our detached and distant situation invites and enables us to pursue a different course.—If we remain one People, under an efficient government, the period is not far off, when we may defy material injury from external annoyance; when we may take such an attitude as will cause the neutrality we may at any time resolve upon to be scrupulously respected. When belligerent nations, under the impossibility of making acquisitions upon us, will not lightly hazard the giving us provocation when we may choose peace or war, as our interest, guided by our justice, shall counsel.

Why forego the advantages of so peculiar a situation?—Why quit our own to stand upon foreign ground?—Why, by interweaving our destiny with that of any part of Europe, entangle our peace and prosperity in the toils of European ambition, rivalship, interest, humor, or caprice?—

'Tis our true policy to steer clear of permanent alliances, with any portion of the foreign world;—so far, I mean, as we are now at liberty to do it;—for let me not be understood as capable of patronizing infidelity to existing engagements. (I hold the maxim no less applicable to public than to private affairs, that honesty is always the best policy.)—I repeat it therefore let those engagements be observed in their genuine sense.—But in my opinion it is unnecessary and would be unwise to extend them.—

Taking care always to keep ourselves, by suitable establishments, on a respectable defensive posture, we may safely trust to temporary alliances for extraordinary emergencies.—

Harmony, liberal intercourse with all nations, are recommended by policy, humanity, and interest. But even our commercial policy should hold an equal and impartial hand:—neither seeking nor granting exclusive favors or preferences;—consulting the natural course of things;—diffusing and diversifying by gentle means the streams of commerce, but forcing nothing;—establishing with Powers so disposed—in order to give trade a stable course, to define the rights of our Merchants, and to enable the Government to support them—conventional rules of intercourse, the best that present circumstances and mutual opinion will permit; but temporary, and liable to be from time to time abandoned or varied, as experience and circumstances shall dictate; constantly keeping in view, that 'tis folly in one nation to look for disinterested favors from another;—that it must pay with a portion of its independence for whatever it may accept under that character—that by such acceptance, it may place itself in the condition of having given equivalents for nominal favors, and yet of being reproached with ingratitude for not giving more. There can be no greater error than to expect or calculate upon real favors from Nation to Nation. 'T is an illusion, which experience must cure, which a just pride ought to discard.

In offering to you, my Countrymen, these counsels of an old and affectionate friend, I dare not hope they will make the strong and lasting impression, I could wish,—that they will controul the usual current of the passions, or prevent our Nation from running the course which has hitherto marked the destiny of Nations. But if I may even flatter myself, that they may be productive of some partial benefit; some occasional good; that they may now and then recur to moderate the fury of party spirit, to warn against the mischiefs of foreign intrigue, to guard against the impostures of pretended patriotism, this hope will be a full recompense for the solicitude for your welfare, by which they have been dictated.—

How far in the discharge of my official duties, I have been guided by the principles which have been delineated, the public Records and other evidences of my conduct must witness to You and to the world.—To myself the assurance of my own conscience is, that I have at least believed myself to be guided by them.

In relation to the still subsisting War in Europe, my Proclamation of the 22d of April 1793, is the index to my plan.—Sanctioned by your approving voice and by that of your Representatives in both Houses of Congress, the spirit of that measure has continually governed me:—uninfluenced by any attempts to deter or divert me from it.

After deliberate examination with the aid of the best lights I could obtain, I was well satisfied that our country, under all the circumstances of the case, had a right to take, and was bound in duty and interest to take, a Neutral position.—Having taken it, I determined, as far as should depend upon me, to maintain it, with moderation, perseverance, and firmness.—

The considerations which respect the right to hold this conduct, it is not necessary on this occasion to detail. I will only observe, that, according to my understanding of the matter, that right, so far from being denied by any of the Belligerent Powers, has been virtually admitted by all.—

The duty of holding a neutral conduct may be inferred, without any thing more, from the obligation which justice and humanity impose on every Nation, in cases in which it is free to act, to maintain inviolate the relations of Peace and Amity towards other Nations.—

The inducements of interest for observing that conduct will best be referred to your own reflections and experience.—With me, a predominant motive has been to endeavour to gain time to our country to settle and mature its yet recent institutions, and to progress without interruption to that degree of strength and consistency, which is necessary to give it, humanly speaking, the command of its own fortunes.

Though, in reviewing the incidents of my Administration, I am unconscious of intentional error—I am nevertheless too sensible of my defects not to think it probable that I may have committed many errors.—Whatever they may be, I fervently beseech the Almighty to avert or mitigate the evils to which they may tend.—I shall also carry with me the hope that my country will never cease to view them with indulgence; and that, after forty-five years of my life dedicated to its service with an upright zeal, the faults of incompetent abilities will be consigned to oblivion, as myself must soon be to the mansions of rest.

Relying on its kindness in this as in other things, and actuated by that fervent love towards it, which is so natural to a man, who views in it the native soil of himself and his progenitors for several generations;—I anticipate with pleasing expectation that retreat. in which I promise myself to realize, without alloy, the sweet enjoyment of partaking, in the midst of my fellow-citizens, the benign influence of good Laws under a free Government, the ever favorite object of my heart, and the happy reward, as I trust, of our mutual cares, labors, and dangers.

TREATY WITH FRANCE

(1803)

[By a treaty concluded in 1795, Spain had agreed to allow to the United States the use of New Orleans or an equivalent port on the Mississippi; but in 1802 she violated this agreement by closing the Mississippi, and ceding all Louisiana to France. The United States, realizing the danger of having such a power as France holding the natural outlet for a large proportion of the produce of the country, appropriated $2,000,000 to purchase New Orleans. Livingston and Monroe concluded with Napoleon the purchase of the whole Louisiana territory for $15,000,000; their action was ratified; and the United States took possession on Dec. 20, 1805.]

TREATY WITH FRANCE FOR THE CESSION OF LOUISIANA, CONCLUDED AT PARIS, APRIL 30, 1803; RATIFICATION ADVISED BY SENATE, OCTOBER 20, 1803; RATIFIED BY PRESIDENT OCTOBER 21, 1803; RATIFICATIONS EXCHANGED AT WASHINGTON OCTOBER 21, 1803; PROCLAIMED OCTOBER 21, 1803.

THE President of the United States of America, and the First Consul of the French Republic, in the name of the French people, desiring to remove all source of misunderstanding relative to objects of discussion mentioned in the second and fifth articles of the convention of the 8th Vendemiaire, an 9 (30th September, 1800) relative to the rights claimed by the United States, in virtue of the treaty concluded at Madrid, the 27th of October, 1795, between His Catholic Majesty and the said United States, and willing to strengthen the union and friendship which at the time of the said convention was happily re-established between the two nations, have respectively named their Plenipotentiaries, to wit: the President of the United States, [of America,] by and with the advice and consent of the Senate of the said States, Robert R. Livingston, Minister Plenipotentiary of the United States, and James Monroe, Minister Plenipotentiary and Envoy Extraordinary of the said States, near the Government of the French Republic; and the First Consul, in the name of the French people, Citizen Francis Barbé Marbois, Minister of the Public Treasury;

who, after having respectively exchanged their full powers, have agreed to the following articles:

ARTICLE I

Whereas by the article of the third of the treaty concluded at St. Idelfonso, the 9th Vendémiaire, an 9 (1st October, 1800,) between the First Consul of the French Republic and His Catholic Majesty, it was agreed as follows: "His Catholic Majesty promises and engages on his part, to cede to the French Republic, six months after the full and entire execution of the conditions and stipulations herein relative to His Royal Highness the Duke of Parma, the colony or province of Louisiana, with the same extent that it now has in the hands of Spain, and that it had when France possessed it, and such as it should be after the treaties subsequently entered into between Spain and other States." And whereas, in pursuance of the treaty, and particularly of the third article, the French Republic has an incontestable title to the domain and to the possession of the said territory: The First Consul of the French Republic desiring to give to the United States a strong proof of his friendship, doth hereby cede to the said United States, in the name of the French Republic, forever and in full sovereignty, the said territory, with all its rights and appurtenances, as fully and in the same manner as they have been acquired by the French Republic, in virtue of the above-mentioned treaty, concluded with His Catholic Majesty.

ARTICLE II

In the cession made by the preceding article are included the adjacent islands belonging to Louisiana, all public lots and squares, vacant lands, and all public buildings, fortifications, barracks and other edifices which are not private property. The archives, papers, and documents, relative to the domain and sovereignty of Louisiana and its dependences, will be left in the possession of the commissaries of the United States, and copies will be afterwards given in due form to the magistrates and municipal officers of such of the said papers and documents as may be necessary to them.

ARTICLE III

The inhabitants of the ceded territory shall be incorporated in the Union of the United States, and admitted as soon as possible, according to the principles of the Federal Constitution, to the enjoyment of all the rights, advantages, and immunities of citizens of the United States; and in the meantime they shall be maintained and protected in the free enjoyment of their liberty, property, and the religion which they profess.

ARTICLE IV

There shall be sent by the Government of France a commissary to Louisiana, to the end that he do every act necessary, as well to receive from the officers of His Catholic Majesty the said country and its dependences, in the name of the French Republic, if it has not been already done, as to transmit it in the name of the French Republic to the commissary or agent of the United States.

ARTICLE V

Immediately after the ratification of the present treaty by the President of the United States, and in case that of the First Consul shall have been previously obtained, the commissary of the French Republic shall remit all military posts of New Orleans, and other parts of the ceded territory, to the commissary or commissaries named by the President to take possession; the troops, whether of France or Spain, who may be there shall cease to occupy any military post from the time of taking possession, and shall be embarked as soon as possible, in the course of three months after the ratification of this treaty.

ARTICLE VI

The United States promise to execute such treaties and articles as may have been agreed between Spain and the tribes and nations of Indians, until, by mutual consent of the United States and the said tribes or nations, other suitable articles shall have been agreed upon.

Article VII

As it is reciprocally advantageous to the commerce of France and the United States to encourage the communication of both nations for a limited time in the country ceded by the present treaty, until general arrangements relative to the commerce of both nations may be agreed on; it has been agreed between the contracting parties, that the French ships coming directly from France or any of her colonies, loaded only with the produce and manufactures of France or her said colonies; and the ships of Spain coming directly from Spain or any of her colonies, loaded only with the produce or manufactures of Spain or her colonies, shall be admitted during the space of twelve years in the port of New Orleans, and in all other legal ports of entry within the ceded territory, in the same manner as the ships of the United States coming directly from France or Spain, or any of their colonies, without being subject to any other or greater duty on merchandize, or other or greater tonnage than that paid by the citizens of the United States.

During the space of time above mentioned, no other nation shall have a right to the same privileges in the ports of the ceded territory; the twelve years shall commence three months after the exchange of ratifications, if it shall take place in France, or three months after it shall have been notified at Paris to the French Government, if it shall take place in the United States; it is however well understood that the object of the above article is to favor the manufactures, commerce, freight, and navigation of France and of Spain, so far as relates to the importations that the French and Spanish shall make into the said ports of the United States, without in any sort affecting the regulations that the United States may make concerning the exportation of the produce and merchandize of the United States, or any right they may have to make such regulations.

Article VIII

In future and forever after the expiration of the twelve years, the ships of France shall be treated upon the footing of the most favoured nations in the ports above mentioned.

Article IX

The particular convention signed this day by the respective ministers, having for its object to provide for the payment of debts due to the citizens of the United States by the French Republic prior to the 30th Septr., 1800, (8th Vendémiaire, an 9,) is approved, and to have its execution in the same manner as if it had been inserted in this present treaty; and it shall be ratified in the same form and in the same time, so that the one shall not be ratified distinct from the other.

Another particular convention signed at the same date as the present treaty relative to a definitive rule between the contracting parties is in the like manner approved, and will be ratified in the same form, and in the same time, and jointly.

Article X

The present treaty shall be ratified in good and due form, and the ratifications shall be exchanged in the space of six months after the date of the signature by the Ministers Plenipotentiary, or sooner if possible.

In faith whereof, the respective Plenipotentiaries have signed these articles in the French and English languages; declaring nevertheless that the present treaty was originally agreed to in the French language; and have thereunto affixed their seals.

Done at Paris the tenth day of Floréal, in the eleventh year of the French Republic, and the 30th of April, 1803.

Robt. R. Livingston [L. S.]

Jas. Monroe [L. S.]

F. Barbé Marbois [L. S.]

TREATY
WITH GREAT BRITAIN

(1814)

[This treaty brought to a close the "War of 1812."]

TREATY OF PEACE AND AMITY BETWEEN HIS BRITANNIC MAJESTY
AND THE UNITED STATES OF AMERICA, CONCLUDED AT GHENT,
DECEMBER 24, 1814; RATIFICATION ADVISED BY SENATE, FEBRUARY
16, 1815; RATIFIED BY PRESIDENT, FEBRUARY 17, 1815; RATIFICA-
TIONS EXCHANGED AT WASHINGTON, FEBRUARY 17, 1815; PRO-
CLAIMED, FEBRUARY 18, 1815.

HIS Britannic Majesty and the United States of America,
desirous of terminating the war which has unhappily sub-
sisted between the two countries, and of restoring, upon
principles of perfect reciprocity, peace, friendship, and good understanding between them, have, for that purpose, appointed their
respective Plenipotentiaries, that is to say:

His Britannic Majesty, on his part, has appointed the Right Hon-
ourable James Lord Gambier, late Admiral of the White, now
Admiral of the Red Squadron of His Majesty's fleet, Henry Goul-
burn, Esquire, a member of the Imperial Parliament, and Under
Secretary of State, and William Adams, Esquire, Doctor of Civil
Laws; and the President of the United States, by and with the ad-
vice and consent of the Senate thereof, has appointed John Quincy
Adams, James A. Bayard, Henry Clay, Jonathan Russell, and Albert
Gallatin, citizens of the United States;

Who, after a reciprocal communication of their respective full
powers, have agreed upon the following articles:

ARTICLE I

There shall be a firm and universal peace between His Britannic
Majesty and the United States, and between their respective coun-

tries, territories, cities, towns, and people, of every degree, without exception of places or persons. All hostilities, both by sea and land, shall cease as soon as this treaty shall have been ratified by both parties, as hereinafter mentioned. All territory, places, and possessions whatsoever, taken by either party from the other during the war, or which may be taken after the signing of this treaty, excepting only the islands hereinafter mentioned, shall be restored without delay, and without causing any destruction or carrying away any of the artillery or other public property originally captured in the said forts or places, and which shall remain therein upon the exchange of the ratifications of this treaty, or any slaves or other private property. And all archives, records, deeds, and papers, either of a public nature or belonging to private persons, which, in the course of the war, may have fallen into the hands of the officers of either party, shall be, as far as may be practicable, forthwith restored and delivered to the proper authorities and persons to whom they respectively belong. Such of the islands in the Bay of Passamaquoddy as are claimed by both parties, shall remain in the possession of the party in whose occupation they may be at the time of the exchange of the ratifications of this treaty, until the decision respecting the title to the said islands shall have been made in conformity with the fourth article of this treaty. No disposition made by this treaty as to such possession of the islands and territories claimed by both parties shall, in any manner whatever, be construed to affect the right of either.

Article II

Immediately after the ratifications of this treaty by both parties, as hereinafter mentioned, orders shall be sent to the armies, squadrons, officers, subjects and citizens of the two Powers to cease from all hostilities. And to prevent all causes of complaint which might arise on account of the prizes which may be taken at sea after the said ratifications of this treaty, it is reciprocally agreed that all vessels and effects which may be taken after the space of twelve days from the said ratifications, upon all parts of the coast of North America, from the latitude of twenty-three degrees north to the latitude of fifty degrees north, and as far eastward in the Atlantic

Ocean as the thirty-sixth degree of west longitude from the meridian of Greenwich, shall be restored on each side: that the time shall be thirty days in all other parts of the Atlantic Ocean north of the equinoctial line or equator, and the same time for the British and Irish Channels, for the Gulf of Mexico, and all parts of the West Indies; forty days for the North Seas, for the Baltic, and for all parts of the Mediterranean; sixty days for the Atlantic Ocean south of the equator, as far as the latitude of the Cape of Good Hope; ninety days for every other part of the world south of the equator; and one hundred and twenty days for all other parts of the world, without exception.

ARTICLE III

All prisoners of war taken on either side, as well by land as by sea, shall be restored as soon as practicable after the ratifications of this treaty, as hereinafter mentioned, on their paying the debts which they may have contracted during their captivity. The two contracting parties respectively engage to discharge, in specie, the advances which may have been made by the other for the sustenance and maintenance of such prisoners.

ARTICLE IV

Whereas it was stipulated by the second article in the treaty of peace of one thousand seven hundred and eighty-three, between His Britannic Majesty and the United States of America, that the boundary of the United States should comprehend all islands within twenty leagues of any part of the shores of the United States, and lying between lines to be drawn due east from the points where the aforesaid boundaries, between Nova Scotia on the one part, and East Florida on the other, shall respectively touch the Bay of Fundy and the Atlantic Ocean, excepting such islands as now are, or heretofore have been, within the limits of Nova Scotia; and whereas the several islands in the Bay of Passamaquoddy, which is part of the Bay of Fundy, and the Island of Grand Menan, in the said Bay of Fundy, are claimed by the United States as being comprehended within their aforesaid boundaries, which said islands are claimed as belonging to His Britannic Majesty, as having been, at the time of and previous to the aforesaid treaty of one thousand seven hundred and eighty-three, within the limits of the Province of Nova Scotia. In order, therefore, finally to decide upon these claims, it is agreed that they shall be referred to two Commissioners to be appointed in the following manner, viz: One Commissioner shall be appointed by His Britannic Majesty, and one by the President of the United States, by and with the advice and consent of the Senate thereof; and the said two Commissioners so appointed shall be sworn impartially to examine and decide upon the said claims according to such evidence as shall be laid before them on the part of His Britannic Majesty and of the United States respectively. The said Commissioners shall meet at St. Andrews, in the Province of New Brunswick, and shall have power to adjourn to such other place or places as they shall think fit. The said Commissioners shall, by a declaration or report under their hands and seals, decide to which of the two contracting parties the several islands aforesaid do respectively belong, in conformity with the true intent of the said treaty of peace of one thousand seven hundred and eighty-three. And if the said Commissioners shall agree in their decision, both parties shall consider such decision as final and conclusive. It is further agreed that, in the event of the two Commissioners differing upon all or any of the matters so referred to them, or in the event of both or either of the said Commissioners refusing, or declining, or wilfully omitting to act as such, they shall make, jointly or separately, a report or reports, as well to the Government of His Britannic Majesty as to that of the United States, stating in detail the points on which they differ, and the grounds upon which their respective opinions have been formed, or the grounds upon which they, or either of them, have so refused, declined, or omitted to act. And His Britannic Majesty and the Government of the United States hereby agree to refer the report or reports of the said Commissioners to some friendly sovereign or State, to be then named for that purpose, and who shall be requested to decide on the differences which may be stated in the said report or reports, or upon the report of one Commissioner, together with the grounds upon which the other Commissioner shall have refused, declined, or omitted to act, as the case may be. And if the Commissioner so refusing, declining, or omitting to act, shall also wilfully omit to state the grounds upon which he has so done, in such manner that the said statement may be referred to such friendly sovereign or State, together with the report of such other Commissioner, then such sovereign or State shall decide ex parte upon the said report alone. And His Britannic Majesty and the Government of the United States engage to consider the decision of such friendly sovereign or State to be final and conclusive on all the matters so referred.

Article V

Whereas neither that point of the highlands lying due north from the source of the river St. Croix, and designated in the former treaty of peace between the two Powers as the northwest angle of Nova Scotia, nor the northwesternmost head of Connecticut River, has yet been ascertained; and whereas that part of the boundary line between the dominions of the two Powers which extends from the source of the river St. Croix directly north to the above mentioned north west angle of Nova Scotia, thence along the said highlands which divide those rivers that empty themselves into the river St. Lawrence from those which fall into the Atlantic Ocean to the northwesternmost head of Connecticut River, thence down along the middle of that river to the forty-fifth degree of north latitude; thence by a line due west on said latitude until it strikes the river Iroquois or Cataraquy, has not yet been surveyed: it is agreed that for these several purposes two Commissioners shall be appointed, sworn, and authorized to act exactly in the manner directed with respect to those mentioned in the next preceding article, unless otherwise specified in the present article. The said Commissioners shall meet at St. Andrews, in the Province of New Brunswick, and shall have power to adjourn to such other place or places as they shall think fit. The said Commissioners shall have power to ascertain and determine the points above mentioned, in conformity with the provisions of the said treaty of peace of one thousand seven hundred and eighty-three, and shall cause the boundary aforesaid, from the source of the river St. Croix to the river Iroquois or Cataraquy, to be surveyed and marked according to the said provisions. The said Commissioners shall make a map of the said boundary, and

annex to it a declaration under their hands and seals, certifying it
to be the true map of the said boundary, and particularizing the
latitude and longitude of the northwest angle of Nova Scotia, of
the northwesternmost head of Connecticut River, and of such other
points of the said boundary as they may deem proper. And both
parties agree to consider such map and declaration as finally and
conclusively fixing the said boundary. And in the event of the said
two Commissioners differing, or both or either of them refusing,
declining, or wilfully omitting to act, such reports, declarations, or
statements shall be made by them, or either of them, and such reference to a friendly sovereign or State shall be made in all respects
as in the latter part of the fourth article is contained, and in as full
a manner as if the same was herein repeated.

Article VI

Whereas by the former treaty of peace that portion of the boundary
of the United States from the point where the forty-fifth degree of
north latitude strikes the river Iroquois or Cataraquy to the Lake
Superior, was declared to be "along the middle of said river into
Lake Ontario, through the middle of said lake, until it strikes the
communication by water between that lake and Lake Erie, thence
along the middle of said communication into Lake Erie, through
the middle of said lake until it arrives at the water communication
into Lake Huron, thence through the middle of said lake to the
water communication between that lake and Lake Superior;" and
whereas doubts have arisen what was the middle of the said river,
lakes, and water communications, and whether certain islands lying
in the same were within the dominions of His Britannic Majesty or
of the United States: In order, therefore, finally to decide these
doubts, they shall be referred to two Commissioners, to be appointed,
sworn, and authorized to act exactly in the manner directed with
respect to those mentioned in the next preceding article, unless
otherwise specified in this present article. The said Commissioners
shall meet, in the first instance, at Albany, in the State of New
York, and shall have power to adjourn to such other place or places
as they shall think fit. The said Commissioners shall, by a report
or declaration, under their hands and seals, designate the boundary

through the said river, lakes, and water communications, and decide to which of the two contracting parties the several islands lying within the said rivers, lakes, and water communications, do respectively belong, in conformity with the true intent of the said treaty of one thousand seven hundred and eighty-three. And both parties agree to consider such designation and decision as final and conclusive. And in the event of the said two Commissioners differing, or both or either of them refusing, declining, or wilfully omitting to act, such reports, declarations, or statements shall be made by them, or either of them, and such reference to a friendly sovereign or State shall be made in all respects as in the latter part of the fourth article is contained and in as full a manner as if the same was herein repeated.

ARTICLE VII

It is further agreed that the said two last-mentioned Commissioners, after they shall have executed the duties assigned to them in the preceding article, shall be, and they are hereby, authorized upon their oaths impartially to fix and determine, according to the true intent of the said treaty of peace of one thousand seven hundred and eighty-three, that part of the boundary between the dominions of the two Powers which extends from the water communication between Lake Huron and Lake Superior, to the most northwestern point of the Lake of the Woods, to decide to which of the two parties the several islands lying in the lakes, water communications, and rivers, forming the said boundary, do respectively belong, in conformity with the true intent of the said treaty of peace of one thousand seven hundred and eighty-three; and to cause such parts of the said boundary as require it to be surveyed and marked. The said Commissioners shall, by a report or declaration under their hands and seals, designate the boundary aforesaid, state their decision on the points thus referred to them, and particularize the latitude and longitude of the most northwestern point of the Lake of the Woods, and of such other parts of the said boundary as they may deem proper. And both parties agree to consider such designation and decision as final and conclusive. And in the event of the said two Commissioners differing, or both or either of them refusing, declining, or wilfully omitting to act, such reports, declarations, or statements shall be made by them, or either of them, and such reference to a friendly sovereign or state shall be made in all respects as in the latter part of the fourth article is contained, and in as full a manner as if the same was herein repeated.

Article VIII

The several boards of two Commissioners mentioned in the four preceding articles shall respectively have power to appoint a secretary, and to employ such surveyors or other persons as they shall judge necessary. Duplicates of all their respective reports, declarations, statements, and decisions, and of their accounts, and of the journal of their proceedings, shall be delivered by them to the agents of His Britannic Majesty and to the agents of the United States, who may be respectively appointed and authorized to manage the business on behalf of their respective Governments. The said Commissioners shall be respectively paid in such manner as shall be agreed between the two contracting parties, such agreement being to be settled at the time of the exchange of the ratifications of this treaty. And all other expenses attending the said commissions shall be defrayed equally by the two parties. And in the case of death, sickness, resignation, or necessary absence, the place of every such Commissioner, respectively, shall be supplied in the same manner as such Commissioner was first appointed, and the new Commissioner shall take the same oath or affirmation, and do the same duties. It is further agreed between the two contracting parties, that in case any of the islands mentioned in any of the preceding articles, which were in the possession of one of the parties prior to the commencement of the present war between the two countries, should, by the decision of any of the boards of commissioners aforesaid, or of the sovereign or State so referred to, as in the four next preceding articles contained, fall within the dominions of the other party, all grants of land made previous to the commencement of the war, by the party having had such possession, shall be as valid as if such island or islands had, by such decision or decisions, been adjudged to be within the dominions of the party having had such possession.

Article IX

The United States of America engage to put an end, immediately after the ratification of the present treaty, to hostilities with all the tribes or nations of Indians with whom they may be at war at the time of such ratification; and forthwith to restore to such tribes or nations, respectively, all the possessions, rights, and privileges which they may have enjoyed or been entitled to in one thousand eight hundred and eleven, previous to such hostilities. Provided always that such tribes or nations shall agree to desist from all hostilities against the United States of America, their citizens and subjects, upon the ratification of the present treaty being notified to such tribes or nations, and shall so desist accordingly. And his Britannic Majesty engages, on his part, to put an end immediately after the ratification of the present treaty, to hostilities with all the tribes or nations of Indians with whom he may be at war at the time of such ratification, and forthwith to restore to such tribes or nations respectively all the possessions, rights, and privileges which they may have enjoyed or been entitled to in one thousand eight hundred and eleven, previous to such hostilities. Provided always that such tribes or nations shall agree to desist from all hostilities against His Britannic Majesty, and his subjects, upon ratification of the present treaty being notified to such tribes or nations, and shall so desist accordingly.

Article X

Whereas the traffic in slaves is irreconcilable with the principles of humanity and justice, and whereas both His Majesty and the United States are desirous of continuing their efforts to promote its entire abolition, it is hereby agreed that both the contracting parties shall use their best endeavours to accomplish so desirable an object.

Article XI

This treaty, when the same shall have been ratified on both sides, without alteration by either of the contracting parties, and the ratifications mutually exchanged, shall be binding on both parties, and the ratifications shall be exchanged at Washington, in the space of four months from this day, or sooner if practicable.

In faith whereof we, the respective Plenipotentiaries, have signed this treaty, and have thereunto affixed our seals.

Done, in triplicate, at Ghent, the twenty-fourth day of December, one thousand eight hundred and fourteen.

GAMBIER	[L. S.]
HENRY GOULBURN	[L. S.]
WILLIAM ADAMS	[L. S.]
JOHN QUINCY ADAMS	[L. S.]
J. A. BAYARD	[L. S.]
H. CLAY	[L. S.]
JONA. RUSSELL	[L. S.]
ALBERT GALLATIN	[L. S.]

ARRANGEMENT AS TO THE NAVAL FORCE

TO BE RESPECTIVELY MAINTAINED ON THE AMERICAN LAKES

(1817)

[The following letters contain the standing agreement between Great Britain and the United States as to the naval force to be maintained by either country in the Great Lakes.]

Mr. Bagot to Mr. Rush.

WASHINGTON, April 28th, 1817.

THE undersigned, His Britannic Majesty's Envoy Extraordinary and Minister Plenipotentiary, has the honour to acquaint Mr. Rush, that having laid before His Majesty's Government the correspondence which passed last year between the Secretary of the Department of State and the undersigned upon the subject of a proposal to reduce the Naval Force of the respective countries upon the American Lakes, he has received commands of His Royal Highness, the Prince Regent, to acquaint the Government of the United States, that His Royal Highness is willing to accede to the proposition made to the undersigned by the Secretary of the Department of State in his note of the 2d of August last.

His Royal Highness acting in the name and on the behalf of His Majesty, agrees, that the Naval force to be maintained upon the American Lakes by His Majesty and the Government of the United States shall henceforth be confined to the following vessels on each side. That is: —

On Lake Ontario to one vessel not exceeding one hundred Tons burthen and armed with one eighteen pound cannon.

On the upper lakes to two vessels not exceeding like burthen each and armed with like force.

On the waters of Lake Champlain to one vessel not exceeding like burthen and armed with like force.

And His Royal Highness agrees that all other armed vessels on these Lakes shall be forthwith dismantled, and that no other vessels of war shall be there built or armed.

His Royal Highness further agrees that if either Party should hereafter be desirous of annulling this stipulation and should give notice to that effect to the other Party, it shall cease to be binding after the expiration of six months from the date of such notice.

The undersigned has it in command from His Royal Highness, the Prince Regent, to acquaint the American Government, that His Royal Highness has issued orders to His Majesty's officers on the lakes directing that the Naval force so to be limited shall be restricted to such services as will in no respect interfere with the proper duties of the armed vessels of the other Party.

The undersigned has the honour to renew to Mr. Rush the assurances of his highest consideration.   CHARLES BAGOT.

Mr. Rush to Mr. Bagot.

DEPARTMENT OF STATE,
April 29th, 1817.

The undersigned, acting Secretary of State, has the honor to acknowledge the receipt of Mr. Bagot's note of the 28th of this month informing him that, having laid before the Government of His Britannic Majesty, the correspondence which passed last year between the Secretary of State and himself upon the subject of a proposal to reduce the naval force of the two countries upon the American Lakes, he had received the commands of His Royal Highness, The Prince Regent, to inform this Government that His Royal Highness was willing to accede to the proposition made by the Secretary of State in his note of the second of August last.

The undersigned has the honor to express to Mr. Bagot the satisfaction which the President feels at His Royal Highness, The Prince Regent's having acceded to the proposition of this Government as contained in the note alluded to. And in further answer to Mr. Bagot's note, the undersigned, by direction of the President, has the honor to state, that this Government, cherishing the same sentiments expressed in the note of the second of August, agrees, that the naval force to be maintained upon the Lakes of the United States and Great Britain shall henceforth, be confined to the following vessels on each side—that is:

On Lake Ontario to one vessel not exceeding One Hundred Tons burden and armed with an eighteen pound cannon. On the Upper Lakes to two vessels not exceeding the like burden each, and armed with like force, and on the waters of Lake Champlain to one vessel not exceeding like burden and armed with like force.

And it agrees that all other armed vessels on these Lakes, shall be forthwith dismantled, and that no other vessels of war shall be there built or armed. And it further agrees, that if either party should hereafter be desirous of annulling this stipulation and should give notice to that effect to the other party, it shall cease to be binding after the expiration of six months from the date of such notice.

The undersigned, is also directed by The President to state, that proper orders will be forthwith issued by this Government to restrict the naval force thus limited to such services as will in no respect interfere with the proper duties of the armed vessels of the other party.

The undersigned, eagerly avails himself of this opportunity to tender to Mr. Bagot the assurances of his distinguished consideration and respect.

RICHARD RUSH.

TREATY WITH SPAIN

(1819)

[While in the hands of Spain, Florida was the source of much annoyance to the Southern States. Fugitive slaves took refuge there; the white population was largely of a lawless character; and the Seminole Indians often made incursions into Georgia. After the United States had been forced to invade the territory and take possession of part of it, Spain ceded it by the treaty of 1819.]

TREATY OF AMITY, SETTLEMENT, AND LIMITS BETWEEN THE UNITED STATES OF AMERICA AND HIS CATHOLIC MAJESTY, CONCLUDED AT WASHINGTON, FEBRUARY 22, 1819; RATIFICATION ADVISED BY SENATE, FEBRUARY 24, 1819; RATIFIED BY PRESIDENT; RATIFIED BY THE KING OF SPAIN, OCTOBER 24, 1820; RATIFICATION AGAIN ADVISED BY SENATE, FEBRUARY 19, 1821; RATIFIED BY PRESIDENT, FEBRUARY 22, 1821; RATIFICATIONS EXCHANGED AT WASHINGTON, FEBRUARY 22, 1821; PROCLAIMED, FEBRUARY 22, 1821.

THE United States of America and His Catholic Majesty, desiring to consolidate, on a permanent basis, the friendship and good correspondence which happily prevails between the two parties have determined to settle and terminate all their differences and pretensions, by a treaty, which shall designate, with precision, the limits of their respective bordering territories in North America.

With this intention, the President of the United States, has furnished with their full powers, John Quincy Adams, Secretary of State of the said United States; and His Catholic Majesty has appointed the Most Excellent Lord Don Luis De Onis, Gonzales, Lopez y Vara, Lord of the town of Rayaces, Perpetual Regidor of the Corporation of the city of Salamanca, Knight Grand Cross of the Royal American Order of Isabella the Catholic, decorated with the Lys of La Vendée, Knight Pensioner of the Royal and Distinguished Spanish Order of Charles the Third, Member of the Supreme Assembly of the said Royal Order; of the Council of His

Majesty; His Secretary, with Exercise of Decrees, and His Envoy Extraordinary and Minister Plenipotentiary near the United States of America;

And the said Plenipotentiaries, after having exchanged their powers, have agreed upon and concluded the following articles:

ARTICLE I

There shall be a firm and inviolable peace and sincere friendship between the United States and their citizens and His Catholic Majesty, his successors and subjects, without exception of persons or places.

ARTICLE II

His Catholic Majesty cedes to the United States, in full property and sovereignty, all the territories which belong to him, situated to the eastward of the Mississippi, known by the name of East and West Florida. The adjacent islands dependent on said provinces, all public lots and squares, vacant lands, public edifices, fortifications, barracks, and other buildings, which are not private property, archives and documents, which relate directly to the property and sovereignty of said provinces, are included in this article. The said archives and documents shall be left in possession of the commissaries or officers of the United States, duly authorized to receive them.

ARTICLE III

The boundary line between the two countries, west of the Mississippi, shall begin on the Gulph of Mexico, at the mouth of the river Sabine, in the sea, continuing north, along the western bank of that river, to the 32d degree of latitude; thence, by a line due north, to the degree of latitude where it strikes the Rio Roxo of Nachitoches, or Red River; then following the course of the Rio Roxo westward, to the degree of longitude 100 west from London and 23 from Washington; then, crossing the said Red River, and running thence by a line due north, to the river Arkansas; thence, following the course of the southern bank of the Arkansas, to its source, in latitude 42 north; and thence, by that parallel of latitude, to the South Sea. The whole being as laid down in Melish's map of the United States, published at Philadelphia, improved to the first of January, 1818. But if the source of the Arkansas River shall be found to fall north or south of latitude 42, then the line shall run from the said source due south or north, as the case may be, till it meets the said parallel of latitude 42, and thence, along the said parallel, to the South Sea: All the islands in the Sabine, and the said Red and Arkansas Rivers, throughout the course thus described, to belong to the United States; but the use of the waters, and the navigation of the Sabine to the sea, and of the said rivers Roxo and Arkansas, throughout the extent of the said boundary, on their respective banks, shall be common to the respective inhabitants of both nations.

The two high contracting parties agree to cede and renounce all their rights, claims, and pretensions, to the territories described by the said line, that is to say: The United States hereby to His Catholic Majesty, and renounce forever, all their rights, claims and pretensions, to the territories lying west and south of the above-described line; and, in like manner, His Catholic Majesty cedes to the said United States all his rights, claims, and pretensions to any territories east and north of the said line, and for himself, his heirs, and successors, renounces all claim to the said territories forever.

Article IV

To fix this line with more precision, and to place the landmarks which shall designate exactly the limits of both nations, each of the contracting parties shall appoint a Commissioner and a surveyor, who shall meet before the termination of one year from the date of the ratification of this treaty at Nachitoches, on the Red River, and proceed to run and mark the said line, from the mouth of the Sabine to the Red River, and from the Red River to the river Arkansas, and to ascertain the latitude of the source of the said river Arkansas, in conformity to what is above agreed upon and stipulated, and the line of latitude 42, to the South Sea: they shall make out plans, and keep journals of their proceedings, and the result agreed upon by them shall be considered as part of this treaty, and shall have the same force as if it were inserted therein. The two Governments will amicably agree respecting the necessary articles to be furnished to those persons, and also as to their respective escorts, should such be deemed necessary.

ARTICLE V

The inhabitants of the ceded territories shall be secured in the free exercise of their religion, without any restriction; and all those who may desire to remove to the Spanish dominions shall be permitted to sell or export their effects, at any time whatever, without being subject, in either case, to duties.

ARTICLE VI

The inhabitants of the territories which His Catholic Majesty cedes to the United States, by this treaty, shall be incorporated in the Union of the United States, as soon as may be consistent with the principles of the Federal Constitution, and admitted to the enjoyment of all the privileges, rights, and immunities of the citizens of the United States.

ARTICLE VII

The officers and troops of His Catholic Majesty, in the territories hereby ceded by him to the United States, shall be withdrawn, and possession of the places occupied by them shall be given within six months after the exchange of the ratifications of this treaty, or sooner if possible, by the officers of His Catholic Majesty to the commissioners or officers of the United States duly appointed to receive them; and the United States shall furnish the transports and escorts necessary to convey the Spanish officers and troops and their baggage to the Havana.

ARTICLE VIII

All the grants of land made before the 24th of January, 1818, by His Catholic Majesty, or by his lawful authorities, in the said territories ceded by His Majesty to the United States, shall be ratified and confirmed to the persons in possession of the lands, to the same extent that the same grants would be valid if the territories had remained under the dominion of His Catholic Majesty. But the owners in possession of such lands, who, by reason of the recent circumstances of the Spanish nation, and the revolutions in Europe, have been prevented from fulfilling all the conditions of their grants, shall complete them within the terms limited in the same, respectively, from the date of this treaty; in default of which the said grants shall be null and void. All grants made since the said 24th of January, 1818, when the first proposal, on the part of His Catholic Majesty, for the cession of the Floridas was made, are hereby declared and agreed to be null and void.

Article IX

The two high contracting parties, animated with the most earnest desire of conciliation, and with the object of putting an end to all the differences which have existed between them, and of confirming the good understanding which they wish to be forever maintained between them, reciprocally renounce all claims for damages or injuries which they, themselves, as well as their respective citizens and subjects, may have suffered until the time of signing this treaty.

The renunciation of the United States will extend to all the injuries mentioned in the convention of the 11th of August, 1802.

(2) To all claims on account of prizes made by French privateers, and condemned by French Consuls, within the territory and jurisdiction of Spain.

(3) To all claims of indemnities on account of the suspension of the right of deposit at New Orleans in 1802.

(4) To all claims of citizens of the United States upon the Government of Spain, arising from the unlawful seizures at sea, and in the ports and territories of Spain, or the Spanish colonies.

(5) To all claims of citizens of the United States upon the Spanish Government, statements of which, soliciting the interposition of the Government of the United States, have been presented to the Department of State, or to the Minister of the United States in Spain, since the date of the convention of 1802, and until the signature of this treaty.

The renunciation of His Catholic Majesty extends—

(1) To all the injuries mentioned in the convention of the 11th of August, 1802.

(2) To the sums which His Catholic Majesty advanced for the return of Captain Pike from the Provincias Internas.

(3) To all injuries caused by the expedition of Miranda, that was fitted out and equipped at New York.

(4) To all claims of Spanish subjects upon the Government of the United States arizing from unlawful seizures at sea, or within the ports and territorial jurisdiction of the United States.

Finally, to all the claims of subjects of His Catholic Majesty upon the Government of the United States in which the interposition of his Catholic Majesty's Government has been solicited, before the date of this treaty and since the date of the convention of 1802, or which may have been made to the department of foreign affairs of His Majesty, or to His Minister in the United States.

And the high contracting parties, respectively, renounce all claim to indemnities for any of the recent events or transactions of their respective commanders and officers in the Floridas.

The United States will cause satisfaction to be made for the injuries, if any, which, by process of law, shall be established to have been suffered by the Spanish officers, and individual Spanish inhabitants, by the late operations of the American Army in Florida.

Article X

The convention entered into between the two Governments, on the 11th of August, 1802, the ratifications of which were exchanged the 21st December, 1818, is annulled.

Article XI

The United States, exonerating Spain from all demands in future, on account of the claims of their citizens to which the renunciations herein contained extend, and considering them entirely cancelled, undertake to make satisfaction for the same, to an amount not exceeding five millions of dollars. To ascertain the full amount and validity of those claims, a commission, to consist of three Commissioners, citizens of the United States, shall be appointed by the President, by and with the advice and consent of the Senate, which commission shall meet at the city of Washington, and, within the space of three years from the time of their first meeting, shall receive, examine, and decide upon the amount and validity of all the claims included within the descriptions above mentioned. The said Commissioners shall take an oath or affirmation, to be entered on the record of their proceedings, for the faithful and diligent discharge of their duties; and, in case of the death, sickness, or necessary absence of any such Commissioner, his place may be supplied by the appointment, as aforesaid, or by the President of the United States, during the recess of the Senate, of another Commissioner in his stead. The said Commissioners shall be authorized to hear and examine, on oath, every question relative to the said claims, and to receive all suitable authentic testimony concerning the same. And the Spanish Government shall furnish all such documents and elucidations as may be in their possession, for the adjustment of the said claims, according to the principles of justice, the laws of nations, and the stipulations of the treaty between the two parties of 27th October, 1795; the said documents to be specified, when demanded, at the instance of the said Commissioners.

The payment of such claims as may be admitted and adjusted by the said Commissioners, or the major part of them, to an amount not exceeding five millions of dollars, shall be made by the United States, either immediately at their Treasury, or by the creation of stock, bearing an interest of six per cent. per annum, payable from the proceeds of sales of public lands within the territories hereby ceded to the United States, or in such other manner as the Congress of the United States may prescribe by law.

The records of the proceedings of the said Commissioners, together with the vouchers and documents produced before them, relative to the claims to be adjusted and decided upon by them, shall, after the close of their transactions, be deposited in the Department of State of the United States; and copies of them, or any part of them, shall be furnished to the Spanish Government, if required, at the demand of the Spanish Minister in the United States.

ARTICLE XII

The treaty of limits and navigation, of 1795, remains confirmed in all and each one of its articles excepting the 2, 3, 4, 21, and the second clause of the 22d article, which having been altered by this treaty, or having received their entire execution, are no longer valid.

With respect to the 15th article of the same treaty of friendship, limits, and navigation of 1795, in which it is stipulated that the flag shall cover the property, the two high contracting parties agree that this shall be so understood with respect to those Powers who recognize this principle; but if either of the two contracting parties shall be at war with a third party, and the other neutral, the flag of the neutral shall cover the property of enemies whose Government acknowledge this principle, and not of others.

Article XIII

Both contracting parties, wishing to favour their mutual commerce, by affording in their ports every necessary assistance to their respective merchant-vessels, have agreed that the sailors who shall desert from their vessels in the ports of the other, shall be arrested and delivered up, at the instance of the Consul, who shall prove, nevertheless, that the deserters belonged to the vessels that claimed them, exhibiting the document that is customary in their nation: that is to say, the American Consul in a Spanish port shall exhibit the document known by the name of articles, and the Spanish Consul in American ports the roll of the vessel; and if the name of the deserter or deserters who are claimed shall appear in the one or the other, they shall be arrested, held in custody, and delivered to the vessel to which they shall belong.

Article XIV

The United States hereby certify that they have not received any compensation from France for the injuries they suffered from her privateers, Consuls, and tribunals on the coasts and in the ports of Spain, for the satisfaction of which provision is made by this treaty; and they will present an authentic statement of the prizes made, and of their true value, that Spain may avail herself of the same in such manner as she may deem just and proper.

Article XV

The United States, to give to His Catholic Majesty, a proof of their desire to cement the relations of amity subsisting between the two nations, and to favour the commerce of the subjects of His Catholic Majesty, agree that Spanish vessels, coming laden only with productions of Spanish growth or manufactures, directly from the ports of Spain, or of her colonies, shall be admitted, for the term of twelve years, to the ports of Pensacola and St. Augustine, in the Floridas, without paying other or higher duties on their cargoes, or of tonnage, than will be paid by the vessels of the United States. During the said term no other nation shall enjoy the same privileges within the ceded territories. The twelve years shall commence three months after the exchange of the ratifications of this treaty.

Article XVI

The present treaty shall be ratified in due form, by the contracting parties, and the ratifications shall be exchanged in six months from this time, or sooner if possible.

In witness whereof we, the underwritten Plenipotentiaries of the United States of America and of His Catholic Majesty, have signed, by virtue of our powers, the present treaty of amity, settlement, and limits, and have thereunto affixed our seals, respectively.

Done at Washington this twenty-second day of February, one thousand eight hundred and nineteen.

John Quincy Adams [L. S.]
Luis de Onis [L. S.]

THE MONROE DOCTRINE

(1823)

[The reaction in favor of monarchical government which followed the fall of Napoleon had among its consequences the proposal of Spain to regain her South American colonies, which had won their independence. Russia also began to extend her claims on the Pacific coast. It was with reference to such tendencies that President Monroe included in his message of 1823, this statement of the policy of the United States toward foreign powers attempting "to extend their system to this portion of the hemisphere." This doctrine was not ratified by Congress, and its validity depends, not on international law, but merely on the power of the United States to enforce it.]

AT THE proposal of the Russian imperial government made through the minister of the Emperor residing here, a full power and instructions have been transmitted to the Minister of the United States at St. Petersburgh, to arrange, by amicable negotiation, the respective rights and interests of the two nations on the northwest coast of this continent. A similar proposal has been made by his Imperial Majesty to the government of Great Britain, which has likewise been acceded to. The government of the United States has been desirous, by this friendly proceeding, of manifesting the great value which they have invariably attached to the friendship of the emperor, and their solicitude to cultivate the best understanding with his government. In the discussions to which this interest has given rise, and in the arrangements by which they may terminate, the occasion has been judged proper for asserting, as a principle in which the rights and interests of the United States are involved, that the American continents, by the free and independent condition which they have assumed and maintain, are henceforth not to be considered as subjects for future colonization by any European powers.

*   *   *   *   *   *   *   *   *   *   *

It was stated at the commencement of the last session, that a great effort was then making in Spain and Portugal, to improve the condition of the people of those countries, and that it appeared to be conducted with extraordinary moderation. It need scarcely be remarked, that the result has been, so far, very different from what was then anticipated. Of events in that quarter of the globe, with which we have so much intercourse, and from which we derive our origin, we have always been anxious and interested spectators. The citizens of the United States cherish sentiments the most friendly, in favor of the liberty and happiness of their fellow men on that side of the Atlantic. In the wars of the European powers, in matters relating to themselves, we have never taken any part, nor does it comport with our policy, so to do. It is only when our rights are invaded, or seriously menaced, that we resent injuries, or make preparation for our defence. With the movements in this hemisphere, we are, of necessity, more immediately connected, and by causes which must be obvious to all enlightened and impartial observers. The political system of the allied powers is essentially different, in this respect, from that of America. This difference proceeds from that which exists in their respective governments. And to the defence of our own, which has been achieved by the loss of so much blood and treasure, and matured by the wisdom of their most enlightened citizens, and under which we have enjoyed unexampled felicity, this whole nation is devoted. We owe it, therefore, to candor, and to the amicable relations existing between the United States and those powers, to declare, that we should consider any attempt on their part to extend their system to any portion of this hemisphere, as dangerous to our peace and safety. With the existing colonies or dependencies of any European power, we have not interfered, and shall not interfere. But with the governments who have declared their independence, and maintained it, and whose independence we have, on great consideration, and on just principles, acknowledged, we could not view any interposition for the purpose of oppressing them, or controlling, in any other manner, their destiny, by any European power, in any other light than as the manifestation of an unfriendly disposition towards the United States. In the war between those new governments and Spain, we declared our neutrality at the time of their recognition, and to this we have adhered, and shall continue to adhere, provided no change shall occur, which, in the judgment of the competent authorities of this government, shall make a corresponding change, on the part of the United States, indispensable to their security.

The late events in Spain and Portugal, shew that Europe is still unsettled. Of this important fact, no stronger proof can be adduced than that the allied powers should have thought it proper, on any principle satisfactory to themselves, to have interposed, by force, in the internal concerns of Spain. To what extent such interposition may be carried, on the same principle, is a question, to which all independent powers, whose governments differ from theirs, are interested; even those most remote, and surely none more so than the United States. Our policy, in regard to Europe, which was adopted at an early stage of the wars which have so long agitated that quarter of the globe, nevertheless remains the same, which is, not to interfere in the internal concerns of any of its powers; to consider the government *de facto* as the legitimate government for us; to cultivate friendly relations with it, and to preserve those relations by a frank, firm, and manly policy; meeting, in all instances, the just claims of every power; submitting to injuries from none. But, in regard to these continents, circumstances are eminently and conspicuously different. It is impossible that the allied powers should extend their political system to any portion of either continent, without endangering our peace and happiness: nor can any one believe that our Southern Brethren, if left to themselves, would adopt it of their own accord. It is equally impossible, therefore, that we should behold such interposition, in any form, with indifference. If we look to the comparative strength and resources of Spain and those new governments, and their distance from each other, it must be obvious that she can never subdue them. It is still the true policy of the United States to leave the parties to themselves, in the hope that other powers will pursue the same course.

TREATY
WITH GREAT BRITAIN
(1842)

[The purpose of the Webster-Ashburton Treaty was to settle various outstanding questions between Great Britain and the United States, mainly concerned with boundary-lines. With the exception of the Oregon line, most of the frontier between Canada and the United States was defined by this agreement. The boundary west of the Rocky Mountains was decided in 1846.]

TREATY BETWEEN THE UNITED STATES OF AMERICA AND HER BRITANNIC MAJESTY RELATIVE TO BOUNDARIES, SUPPRESSION OF THE SLAVE TRADE, AND EXTRADITION OF CRIMINALS, CONCLUDED AT WASHINGTON, AUGUST 9, 1842; RATIFICATION ADVISED BY SENATE, AUGUST 20, 1842; RATIFIED BY PRESIDENT, AUGUST 22, 1842; RATIFICATIONS EXCHANGED AT LONDON, OCTOBER 13, 1842; PROCLAIMED NOVEMBER 10, 1842.

WHEREAS certain portions of the line of boundary between the United States of America and the British dominions in North America, described in the second article of the treaty of peace of 1783, have not yet been ascertained and determined, notwithstanding the repeated attempts which have been heretofore made for that purpose; and whereas it is now thought to be for the interest of both parties, that, avoiding further discussion of their respective rights, arising in this respect under the said treaty, they should agree on a conventional line in said portions of the said boundary, such as may be convenient to both parties, with such equivalents and compensations as are deemed just and reasonable; and whereas, by the treaty concluded at Ghent on the 24th day of December, 1814, between the United States and His Britannic Majesty, an article was agreed to and inserted of the following tenor, viz.: "Art. 10. Whereas the traffic in slaves is irreconcilable with the principles of humanity and justice; and whereas both His Majesty and the United States are desirous of continuing their efforts to promote its entire abolition, it is hereby agreed that both the contracting parties shall use their best endeavors to accomplish so desirable an object;" and whereas, notwithstanding the laws which have at various times been passed by the two Governments, and the efforts made to suppress it, that criminal traffic is still prosecuted and carried on; and whereas the United States of America and Her Majesty the Queen of the United Kingdom of Great Britain and Ireland are determined that, so far as may be in their power, it shall be effectually abolished; and whereas it is found expedient, for the better administration of justice and the prevention of crime within the territories and jurisdiction of the two parties respectively, that persons committing the crimes hereinafter enumerated, and being fugitives from justice, should, under certain circumstances, be reciprocally delivered up: The United States of America and Her Britannic Majesty, having resolved to treat on these several subjects, have for that purpose appointed their respective Plenipotentiaries to negotiate and conclude a treaty, that is to say:

The President of the United States has, on his part, furnished with full powers Daniel Webster, Secretary of State of the United States, and Her Majesty the Queen of the United Kingdom of Great Britain and Ireland has, on her part, appointed the Right Honorable Alexander Lord Ashburton, a peer of the said United Kingdom, a member of Her Majesty's Most Honorable Privy Council, and Her Majesty's Minister Plenipotentiary on a special mission to the United States;

Who, after a reciprocal communication of their respective full powers, have agreed to and signed the following articles:

ARTICLE I

It is hereby agreed and declared that the line of boundary shall be as follows: Beginning at the monument at the source of the river St. Croix as designated and agreed to by the Commissioners under the fifth article of the treaty of 1794, between the Governments of the United States and Great Britain; thence, north, following the exploring line run and marked by the surveyors of the two Governments in the years 1817 and 1818, under the fifth article of the treaty of Ghent, to its intersection with the river St. John, and to the middle of the channel thereof; thence, up the middle of the main channel of the said river St. John, to the mouth of the river St. Francis; thence, up the middle of the channel of the said river St. Francis, and of the lakes through which it flows, to the outlet of the Lake Pohenagamook; thence, southwesterly, in a straight line, to a point on the northwest branch of the river St. John, which point shall be ten miles distant from the main branch of the St. John, in a straight line, and in the nearest direction; but if the said point shall be found to be less than seven miles from the nearest point of the summit or crest of the highlands that divide those rivers which empty themselves into the river Saint Lawrence from those which fall into the river Saint John, then the said point shall be made to recede down the said northwest branch of the river St. John, to a point seven miles in a straight line from the said summit or crest; thence, in a straight line, in a course about south, eight degrees west, to the point where the parallel of latitude of 46° 25′ north intersects the southwest branch of the St. John's; thence, southerly, by the said branch, to the source thereof in the highlands at the Metjarmette portage; thence, down along the said highlands which divide the waters which empty themselves into the river Saint Lawrence from those which fall into the Atlantic Ocean, to the head of Hall's Stream; thence, down the middle of said stream, till the line thus run intersects the old line of boundary surveyed and marked by Valentine and Collins, previously to the year 1774, as the 45th degree of north latitude, and which has been known and understood to be the line of actual division between the States of New York and Vermont on one side, and the British province of Canada on the other; and from said point of intersection, west, along the said dividing line, as heretofore known and understood, to the Iroquois or St. Lawrence River.

Article II

It is moreover agreed, that from the place where the joint Commissioners terminated their labors under the sixth article of the treaty of Ghent, to wit, at a point in the Neebish Channel, near Muddy Lake, the line shall run into and along the ship-channel between Saint Joseph and St. Tammany Islands, to the division of the channel at or near the head of St. Joseph's Island; thence, turning eastwardly and northwardly around the lower end of St. George's or Sugar Island, and following the middle of the channel which divides St. George's from St. Joseph's Island; thence up the east Neebish Channel, nearest to St. George's Island, through the middle of Lake George; thence, west of Jonas' Island, into St. Mary's River, to a point in the middle of that river, about one mile above St. George's or Sugar Island, so as to appropriate and assign the said island to the United States; thence, adopting the line traced on the maps by the Commissioners, thro' the river St. Mary and Lake Superior, to a point north of Ile Royale, in said lake, one hundred yards to the north and east of Ile Chapeau, which last-mentioned island lies near the northeastern point of Ile Royale, where the line marked by the Commissioners terminates; and from the last-mentioned point, southwesterly, through the middle of the sound between Ile Royale and the northwestern main land, to the mouth of Pigeon River, and up the said river, to and through the north and south Fowl Lakes, to the lakes of the height of land between Lake Superior and the Lake of the Woods; thence, along the water communication to Lake Saisaginaga, and through that lake; thence, to and through Cypress Lake, Lac du Bois Blanc, Lac la Croix, Little Vermilion Lake, and Lake Namecan and through the several smaller lakes, straits, or streams, connecting the lakes here mentioned, to that point in Lac la Pluie, or Rainy Lake, at the Chaudière Falls, from which the Commissioners traced the line to the most northwestern point of the Lake of the Woods; thence, along the said line, to the said most northwestern point, being in latitude 49° 23' 55" north and in longitude 95° 14' 38" west from the observatory at Greenwich; thence, according to existing treaties, due south to its intersection with the 49th parallel of north latitude, and along that parallel to the Rocky Mountains. It being understood that all the water communications and all the usual portages along the line from Lake Superior to the Lake of the Woods, and also Grand Portage, from the shore of Lake Superior to the Pigeon River, as now actually used, shall be free and open to the use of the citizens and subjects of both countries.

ARTICLE III

In order to promote the interests and encourage the industry of all the inhabitants of the countries watered by the river St. John and its tributaries, whether living within the State of Maine or the province of New Brunswick, it is agreed that, where, by the provisions of the present treaty, the river St. John is declared to be the line of boundary, the navigation of the said river shall be free and open to both parties, and shall in no way be obstructed by either; that all the produce of the forest, in logs, lumber, timber, boards, staves, or shingles, or of agriculture, not being manufactured, grown on any of those parts of the State of Maine watered by the river St. John, or by its tributaries, of which fact reasonable evidence shall, if required, be produced, shall have free access into and through the said river and its said tributaries, having their source within the State of Maine, to and from the sea-port at the mouth of the said river St. John's, and to and round the falls of the said river, either by boats, rafts, or other conveyance; that when within the province of New Brunswick, the said produce shall be dealt with as if it were the produce of the said province; that, in like manner, the inhabitants of the territory of the upper St. John, determined by this treaty to belong to Her Britannic Majesty, shall have free access to and through the river, for their produce, in those parts where the said river runs wholly through the State of Maine; Provided, always, that this agreement shall give no right to either party to interfere with any regulations not inconsistent with the terms of this treaty which the governments, respectively, of Maine or of New Brunswick may make respecting the navigation of the said river, where both banks thereof shall belong to the same party.

ARTICLE IV

All grants of land heretofore made by either party, within the limits of the territory which by this treaty falls within the dominions of the other party, shall be held valid, ratified, and confirmed to the persons in possession under such grants, to the same extent as if such territory had by this treaty fallen within the dominions of the party by whom such grants were made; and all equitable possessory claims, arising from a possession and improvement of any lot or parcel of land by the person actually in possession, or by those under whom such person claims, for more than six years before the date of this treaty, shall, in like manner, be deemed valid, and be confirmed and quieted by a release to the persons entitled thereto, of the title to such lot or parcel of land, so described as best to include the improvements made thereon; and in all other respects the two contracting parties agree to deal upon the most liberal principles of equity with the settlers actually dwelling upon the territory falling to them, respectively, which has heretofore been in dispute between them.

Article V

Whereas in the course of the controversy respecting the disputed territory on the northeastern boundary, some moneys have been received by the authorities of Her Britannic Majesty's province of New Brunswick, with the intention of preventing depredations, on the forests of the said territory, which moneys were to be carried to a fund called the "disputed territory fund," the proceeds whereof it was agreed should be hereafter paid over to the parties interested, in the proportions to be determined by a final settlement of boundaries, it is hereby agreed that a correct account of all receipts and payments on the said fund shall be delivered to the Government of the United States within six months after the ratification of this treaty; and the proportion of the amount due thereon to the States of Maine and Massachusetts, and any bonds or securities appertaining thereto shall be paid and delivered over to the Government of the United States; and the Government of the United States agrees to receive for the use of, and pay over to, the States of Maine and Massachusetts, their respective portions of said fund, and further, to pay and satisfy said States, respectively, for all claims for expenses incurred by them in protecting the said heretofore disputed territory and making a survey thereof in 1838; the Government of the United States agreeing with the States of Maine and Massachusetts to pay them the further sum of three hundred thousand dollars, in equal moieties, on account of their assent to the line of boundary described in this treaty, and in consideration of the conditions and equivalents received therefor from the Government of Her Britannic Majesty.

ARTICLE VI

It is furthermore understood and agreed that, for the purpose of running and tracing those parts of the line between the source of the St. Croix and the St. Lawrence River which will require to be run and ascertained, and for marking the residue of said line by proper monuments on the land, two Commissioners shall be appointed, one by the President of the United States, by and with the advice and consent of the Senate thereof, and one by Her Britannic Majesty; and the said Commissioners shall meet at Bangor, in the State of Maine, on the first day of May next, or as soon thereafter as may be, and shall proceed to mark the line above described, from the source of St. Croix to the river St. John; and shall trace on proper maps the dividing-line along said river and along the river St. Francis to the outlet of the Lake Pohenagamook; and from the outlet of the said lake they shall ascertain, fix, and mark, by proper and durable monuments on the land, the line described in the first article of this treaty; and the said Commissioners shall make to each of their respective Governments a joint report or declaration, under their hands and seals, designating such line of boundary, and shall accompany such report or declaration with maps, certified by them to be true maps of the new boundary.

ARTICLE VII

It is further agreed that the channels in the river St. Lawrence on both sides of the Long Sault Islands and of Barnhart Island, the channels in the river Detroit on both sides of the island Bois Blanc, and between that Island and both the American and Canadian shores, and all the several channels and passages between the various islands lying near the junction of the river St. Clair with the lake of that name, shall be equally free and open to the ships, vessels, and boats of both parties.

Article VIII

The parties mutually stipulate that each shall prepare, equip, and maintain in service on the coast of Africa a sufficient and adequate squadron or naval force of vessels of suitable numbers and descriptions, to carry in all not less than eighty guns, to enforce, separately and respectively, the laws, rights and obligations of each of the two countries for the suppression of the slave-trade, the said squadrons to be independent of each other, but the two Governments stipulating, nevertheless, to give such orders to the officers commanding their respective forces as shall enable them most effectually to act in concert and co-operation, upon mutual consultation, as exigencies may arise, for the attainment of the true object of this article, copies of all such orders to be communicated by each Government to the other, respectively.

Article IX

Whereas, notwithstanding all efforts which may be made on the coast of Africa for suppressing the slave-trade, the facilities for carrying on that traffic and avoiding the vigilance of cruisers, by the fraudulent use of flags and other means, are so great, and the temptations for pursuing it, while a market can be found for slaves, so strong, as that the desired result may be long delayed unless all markets be shut against the purchase of African negroes, the parties to this treaty agree that they will unite in all becoming representations and remonstrances with any and all Powers within whose dominions such markets are allowed to exist, and that they will urge upon all such Powers the propriety and duty of closing such markets effectually, at once and forever.

Article X

It is agreed that the United States and Her Britannic Majesty shall, upon mutual requisitions by them, or their Ministers, officers, or authorities, respectively made, deliver up to justice all persons who, being charged with the crime of murder, or assault with intent to commit murder, or piracy, or arson, or robbery, or forgery, or the utterance of forged paper, committed within the jurisdiction of either shall seek an asylum or shall be found within the territories of the other: Provided, that this shall only be done upon such evidence of criminality as, according to the laws of the place where the fugitive or person so charged shall be found, would justify his apprehension and commitment for trial if the crime or offence had there been committed; and the respective judges and other magistrates of the two Governments shall have power, jurisdiction, and authority, upon complaint made under oath, to issue a warrant for the apprehension of the fugitive or person so charged, that he may be brought before such judges or other magistrates, respectively, to the end that the evidence of criminality may be heard and considered; and if, on such hearing, the evidence be deemed sufficient to sustain the charge, it shall be the duty of the examining judge or magistrate to certify the same to the proper executive authority, that a warrant may issue for the surrender of such fugitive. The expense of such apprehension and delivery shall be borne and defrayed by the party who makes the requisition and receives the fugitive.

Article XI

The eighth article of this treaty shall be in force for five years from the date of the exchange of the ratification, and afterwards until one or the other party shall signify a wish to terminate it. The tenth article shall continue in force until one or the other of the parties shall signify its wish to terminate it, and no longer.

Article XII

The present treaty shall be duly ratified, and the mutual exchange of ratification shall take place in London, within six months from the date hereof, or earlier if possible.

In faith whereof we, the respective Plenipotentiaries, have signed this treaty and have hereunto affixed our seals.

Done, in duplicate, at Washington, the ninth day of August, anno Domini one thousand eight hundred and forty-two.

DANL. WEBSTER [L. S.]
ASHBURTON [L. S.]

TREATY WITH MEXICO

(1848)

[By the Louisiana Purchase, Texas had become a part of the United States; but in 1819 it had been ceded to Spain in the negotiations for Florida. Two years later Mexico, including Texas, had become independent, and the United States made two unsuccessful attempts to purchase Texas from Mexico. The settlement of Texas by immigrants from the United States finally led to the secession of Texas and its annexation by the United States, with the result that the Mexican War broke out in May, 1846. It was closed by this treaty, by which the United States gained not only Texas but New Mexico and Upper California.]

TREATY OF PEACE, FRIENDSHIP, LIMITS, AND SETTLEMENT BETWEEN THE UNITED STATES OF AMERICA AND THE UNITED MEXICAN STATES, CONCLUDED AT GUADALUPE HIDALGO, FEBRUARY 2, 1848; RATIFICATION ADVISED BY SENATE, WITH AMENDMENTS, MARCH 10, 1848; RATIFIED BY PRESIDENT, MARCH 16, 1848; RATIFICATIONS EXCHANGED AT QUERETARO, MAY 30, 1848; PROCLAIMED, JULY 4, 1848.

IN THE name of Almighty God:

The United States of America and the United Mexican States animated by a sincere desire to put an end to the calamities of the war which unhappily exists between the two Republics, and to establish upon a solid basis relations of peace and friendship, which shall confer reciprocal benefits upon the citizens of both, and assure the concord, harmony, and mutual confidence wherein the two people should live, as good neighbours, have for that purpose appointed their respective plenipotentiaries, that is to say:

The President of the United States has appointed Nicholas P. Trist, a citizen of the United States, and the President of the Mexican Republic has appointed Don Luis Gonzaga Cuevas, Don Bernardo Couto, and Don Miguel Atristain, citizens of the said Republic;

Who, after a reciprocal communication of their respective full powers, have, under the protection of Almighty God, the author of peace, arranged, agreed upon, and signed the following:

Treaty of Peace, Friendship, Limits, and Settlement between the United States of America and the Mexican Republic.

ARTICLE I

There shall be firm and universal peace between the United States of America and the Mexican Republic, and between their respective countries, territories, cities, towns, and people, without exception of places or persons.

ARTICLE II

Immediately upon the signature of this treaty, a convention shall be entered into between a commissioner or commissioners appointed by the General-in-chief of the forces of the United States, and such as may be appointed by the Mexican Government, to the end that a provisional suspension of hostilities shall take place, and that, in the places occupied by the said forces, constitutional order may be re-established, as regards the political, administrative, and judicial branches, so far as this shall be permitted by the circumstances of military occupation.

ARTICLE III

Immediately upon the ratification of the present treaty by the Government of the United States, orders shall be transmitted to the commanders of their land and naval forces, requiring the latter (provided this treaty shall then have been ratified by the Government of the Mexican Republic, and the ratifications exchanged) immediately to desist from blockading any Mexican ports and requiring the former (under the same condition) to commence, at the earliest moment practicable, withdrawing all troops of the United States then in the interior of the Mexican Republic, to points that shall be selected by common agreement, at a distance from the seaports not exceeding thirty leagues; and such evacuation of the interior of the Republic shall be completed with the least possible delay; the Mexican Government hereby binding itself to afford every facility in its power for rendering the same convenient to the troops, on their march and in their new positions, and for promoting a good understanding between them and the inhabitants. In like manner orders shall be despatched to the persons in charge of the custom-houses at all ports occupied by the forces of the United States, requiring them (under the same condition) immediately to deliver possession of the same to the persons authorized by the Mexican Government to receive it, together with all bonds and evidences of debt for duties on importations and on exportations, not yet fallen due. Moreover, a faithful and exact account shall be made out, showing the entire amount of all duties on imports and on exports, collected at such custom-houses, or elsewhere in Mexico, by authority of the United States, from and after the day of ratification of this treaty by the Government of the Mexican Republic; and also an account of the cost of collection; and such entire amount, deducting only the cost of collection, shall be delivered to the Mexican Government, at the city of Mexico, within three months after the exchange of ratifications.

The evacuation of the capital of the Mexican Republic by the troops of the United States, in virtue of the above stipulation, shall be completed in one month after the orders there stipulated for shall have been received by the commander of said troops, or sooner if possible.

Article IV

Immediately after the exchange of ratifications of the present treaty all castles, forts, territories, places, and possessions, which have been taken or occupied by the forces of the United States during the present war, within the limits of the Mexican Republic, as about to be established by the following article, shall be definitely restored to the said Republic, together with all the artillery, arms, apparatus of war, munitions, and other public property, which were in the said castles and forts when captured, and which shall remain there at the time when this treaty shall be duly ratified by the Government of the Mexican Republic. To this end, immediately upon the signature of this treaty, orders shall be despatched to the American officers commanding such castles and forts, securing against the removal or destruction of any such artillery, arms, apparatus of war, munitions, or other public property. The city of Mexico, within the inner line of intrenchments surrounding the said city, is comprehended in the above stipulation, as regards the restoration of artillery, apparatus of war, &c.

The final evacuation of the territory of the Mexican Republic, by the forces of the United States, shall be completed in three months from the said exchange of ratifications, or sooner if possible; the Mexican Government hereby engaging, as in the foregoing article, to use all means in its power for facilitating such evacuation, and rendering it convenient to the troops, and for promoting a good understanding between them and the inhabitants.

If, however, the ratification of this treaty by both parties should not take place in time to allow the embarcation of the troops of the United States to be completed before the commencement of the sickly season, at the Mexican ports on the Gulf of Mexico, in such case a friendly arrangement shall be entered into between the General-in-chief of the said troops and the Mexican Government, whereby healthy and otherwise suitable places, at a distance from the ports not exceeding thirty leagues, shall be designated for the residence of such troops as may not yet have embarked, until the return of the healthy season. And the space of time here referred to as comprehending the sickly season shall be understood to extend from the first day of May to the first day of November.

All prisoners of war taken on either side, on land or on sea, shall be restored as soon as practicable after the exchange of ratifications of this treaty. It is also agreed that if any Mexicans should now be held as captives by any savage tribe within the limits of the United States, as about to be established by the following article, the Government of the said United States will exact the release of such captives, and cause them to be restored to their country.

Article V

The boundary line between the two Republics shall commence in the Gulf of Mexico, three leagues from land, opposite the mouth of the Rio Grande, otherwise called Rio Bravo del Norte, or opposite the mouth of its deepest branch, if it should have more than one branch emptying directly into the sea; from thence up the middle of that river, following the deepest channel, where it has more than one, to the point where it strikes the southern boundary of New Mexico; thence, westwardly, along the whole southern boundary of New Mexico (which runs north of the town called Paso) to its western termination; thence, northward, along the western line of New Mexico, until it intersects the first branch of the river Gila; (or if it should not intersect any branch of that river, then to the point on the said line nearest to such branch, and thence in a direct line to the same); thence down the middle of the said branch and of the said river, until it empties into the Rio Colorado; thence across the Rio Colorado, following the division line between Upper and Lower California, to the Pacific Ocean.

The southern and western limits of New Mexico, mentioned in this article, are those laid down in the map entitled *"Map of the United Mexican States, as organized and defined by various acts of the Congress of said republic, and constructed according to the best authorities. Revised edition. Published at New York, in 1847, by J. Disturnell;"* of which map a copy is added to this treaty, bearing the signatures and seals of the undersigned Plenipotentiaries. And, in order to preclude all difficulty in tracing upon the ground the limit separating Upper from Lower California, it is agreed that the said limit shall consist of a straight line drawn from the middle of the Rio Gila, where it unites with the Colorado, to a point on the coast of the Pacific Ocean, distant one marine league due south of the southernmost point of the port of San Diego, according to the plan of said port made in the year 1782 by Don Juan Pantoja, second sailing-master of the Spanish fleet, and published at Madrid in the year 1802, in the atlas to the voyage of the schooners Sutil and Mexicana; of which plan a copy is hereunto added, signed and sealed by the respective Plenipotentiaries.

In order to designate the boundary line with due precision, upon authoritative maps, and to establish upon the ground land-marks which shall show the limits of both republics, as described in the present article, the two Governments shall each appoint a commissioner and a surveyor, who, before the expiration of one year from the date of the exchange of ratifications of this treaty, shall meet at the port of San Diego, and proceed to run and mark the said boundary in its whole course to the mouth of the Rio Bravo del Norte. They shall keep journals and make out plans of their operations; and the result agreed upon by them shall be deemed a part of this treaty, and shall have the same force as if it were inserted therein.

The two Governments will amicably agree regarding what may be necessary to these persons, and also as to their respective escorts, should such be necessary.

The boundary line established by this article shall be religiously respected by each of the two republics, and no change shall ever be made therein, except by the express and free consent of both nations, lawfully given by the General Government of each, in conformity with its own constitution.

Article VI

The vessels and citizens of the United States shall, in all time, have a free and uninterrupted passage by the Gulf of California, and by the river Colorado below its confluence with the Gila, to and from their possessions situated north of the boundary line defined in the preceding article; it being understood that this passage is to be by navigating the Gulf of California and the river Colorado, and not by land, without the express consent of the Mexican Government.

If, by the examinations which may be made, it should be ascertained to be practicable and advantageous to construct a road, canal, or railway, which should in whole or in part run upon the river Gila, or upon its right or its left bank, within the space of one marine league from either margin of the river, the Governments of both republics will form an agreement regarding its construction, in order that it may serve equally for the use and advantage of both countries.

Article VII

The river Gila, and the part of the Rio Bravo del Norte lying below the southern boundary of New Mexico, being, agreeably to the fifth article, divided in the middle between the two republics, the navigation of the Gila and of the Bravo below said boundary shall be free and common to the vessels and citizens of both countries; and neither shall, without the consent of the other, construct any work that may impede or interrupt, in whole or in part, the exercise of this right; not even for the purpose of favoring new methods of navigation. Nor shall any tax or contribution, under any denomination or title, be levied upon vessels or persons navigating the same, or upon merchandise or effects transported thereon, except in the case of landing upon one of their shores. If, for the purpose of making the said rivers navigable, or for maintaining them in such state, it should be necessary or advantageous to establish any tax or contribution, this shall not be done without the consent of both Governments.

The stipulations contained in the present article shall not impair the territorial rights of either republic within its established limits.

ARTICLE VIII

Mexicans now established in territories previously belonging to Mexico, and which remain for the future within the limits of the United States, as defined by the present treaty, shall be free to continue where they now reside, or to remove at any time to the Mexican Republic, retaining the property which they possess in the said territories, or disposing thereof, and removing the proceeds wherever they please, without their being subjected, on this account, to any contribution, tax, or charge whatever.

Those who shall prefer to remain in the said territories may either retain the title and rights of Mexican citizens, or acquire those of citizens of the United States. But they shall be under the obligation to make their election within one year from the date of the exchange of ratifications of this treaty; and those who shall remain in the said territories after the expiration of that year, without having declared their intention to retain the character of Mexicans, shall be considered to have elected to become citizens of the United States.

In the said territories, property of every kind, now belonging to Mexicans not established there, shall be inviolably respected. The present owners, the heirs of these, and all Mexicans who may hereafter acquire said property by contract, shall enjoy with respect to it guarantees equally ample as if the same belonged to citizens of the United States.

ARTICLE IX

The Mexicans who, in the territories aforesaid, shall not preserve the character of citizens of the Mexican Republic, conformably with what is stipulated in the preceding article, shall be incorporated into the Union of the United States, and be admitted at the proper time (to be judged of by the Congress of the United States) to the enjoyment of all the rights of citizens of the United States, according to the principles of the Constitution; and in the mean time, shall be maintained and protected in the free enjoyment of their liberty and property, and secured in the free exercise of their religion without restriction.

ARTICLE X

[Stricken out.]

ARTICLE XI

Considering that a great part of the territories, which, by the present treaty, are to be comprehended for the future within the limits of the United States, is now occupied by savage tribes, who will hereafter be under the exclusive control of the Government of the United States, and whose incursions within the territory of Mexico would be prejudicial in the extreme, it is solemnly agreed that all such incursions shall be forcibly restrained by the Government of the United States whensoever this may be necessary; and that when they cannot be prevented, they shall be punished by the said Government, and satisfaction for the same shall be exacted—all in the same way, and with equal diligence and energy, as if the same incursions were meditated or committed within its own territory, against its own citizens.

It shall not be lawful, under any pretext whatever, for any inhabitant of the United States to purchase or acquire any Mexican, or any foreigner residing in Mexico, who may have been captured by Indians inhabiting the territory of either of the two republics; nor to purchase or acquire horses, mules, cattle, or property of any kind, stolen within Mexican territory by such Indians.

And in the event of any person or persons, captured within Mexican territory by Indians, being carried into the territory of the United States, the Government of the latter engages and binds itself, in the most solemn manner, so soon as it shall know of such captives being within its territory, and shall be able so to do, through the faithful exercise of its influence and power, to rescue them and return them to their country, or deliver them to the agent or representative of the

Mexican Government. The Mexican authorities will, as far as practicable, give to the Government of the United States notice of such captures; and its agents shall pay the expenses incurred in the maintenance and transmission of the rescued captives; who, in the mean time, shall be treated with the utmost hospitality by the American authorities at the place where they may be. But if the Government of the United States, before receiving such notice from Mexico, should obtain intelligence, through any other channel, of the existence of Mexican captives within its territory, it will proceed forthwith to effect their release and delivery to the Mexican agent, as above stipulated.

For the purpose of giving to these stipulations the fullest possible efficacy, thereby affording the security and redress demanded by their true spirit and intent, the Government of the United States will now and hereafter pass, without unnecessary delay, and always vigilantly enforce, such laws as the nature of the subject may require. And, finally, the sacredness of this obligation shall never be lost sight of by the said Government, when providing for the removal of the Indians from any portion of the said territories, or for its being settled by citizens of the United States; but, on the contrary, special care shall then be taken not to place its Indian occupants under the necessity of seeking new homes, by committing those invasions which the United States have solemnly obliged themselves to restrain.

Article XII

In consideration of the extension acquired by the boundaries of the United States, as defined in the fifth article of the present treaty, the Government of the United States engages to pay to that of the Mexican Republic the sum of fifteen millions of dollars.

Immediately after the treaty shall have been duly ratified by the Government of the Mexican Republic, the sum of three millions of dollars shall be paid to the said Government by that of the United States, at the city of Mexico, in the gold or silver coin of Mexico. The remaining twelve millions of dollars shall be paid at the same place, and in the same coin, in annual instalments of three millions of dollars each, together with interest on the same at the rate of six per centum per annum. This interest shall begin to run upon the whole sum of twelve millions from the day of the ratification of the present treaty by the Mexican Government, and the first of the instalments shall be paid at the expiration of one year from the same day. Together with each annual instalment, as it falls due, the whole interest accruing on such instalment from the beginning shall also be paid.

Article XIII

The United States engage, moreover, to assume and pay to the claimants all the amounts now due them, and those hereafter to become due, by reason of the claims already liquidated and decided against the Mexican Republic, under the conventions between the two republics severally concluded on the eleventh day of April, eighteen hundred and thirty-nine, and on the thirtieth day of January, eighteen hundred and forty-three; so that the Mexican Republic shall be absolutely exempt, for the future, from all expense whatever on account of the said claims.

Article XIV

The United States do furthermore discharge the Mexican Republic from all claims of citizens of the United States, not heretofore decided against the Mexican Government, which may have arisen previously to the date of the signature of this treaty; which discharge shall be final and perpetual, whether the said claims be rejected or be allowed by the board of commissioners provided for in the following article, and whatever shall be the total amount of those allowed.

Article XV

The United States, exonerating Mexico from all demands on account of the claims of their citizens mentioned in the preceding article, and considering them entirely and forever cancelled, whatever their amount may be, undertake to make satisfaction for the same, to an amount not exceeding three and one-quarter millions of dollars. To ascertain the validity and amount of those claims, a board of commissioners shall be established by the Government of the United States, whose awards shall be final and conclusive; provided that, in deciding upon the validity of each claim, the board shall be guided and governed by the principles and rules of decision prescribed by the first and fifth articles of the unratified convention, concluded at the city of Mexico on the twentieth day of November, one thousand eight hundred and forty-three; and in no case shall an award be made in favour of any claim not embraced by these principles and rules.

If, in the opinion of the said board of commissioners or of the claimants, any books, records, or documents, in the possession or power of the Government of the Mexican Republic, shall be deemed necessary to the just decision of any claim, the commissioners, or the claimants through them, shall, within such period as Congress may designate, make an application in writing for the same, addressed to the Mexican Minister of Foreign Affairs, to be transmitted by the Secretary of State of the United States; and the Mexican Government engages, at the earliest possible moment after the receipt of such demand, to cause any of the books, records, or documents so specified, which shall be in their possession or power (or authenticated copies or extracts of the same), to be transmitted to the said Secretary of State, who shall immediately deliver them over to the said board of commissioners; provided that no such application shall be made by or at the instance of any claimant, until the facts which it is expected to prove by such books, records, or documents, shall have been stated under oath or affirmation.

Article XVI

Each of the contracting parties reserves to itself the entire right to fortify whatever point within its territory it may judge proper so to fortify for its security.

Article XVII

The treaty of amity, commerce, and navigation, concluded at the city of Mexico, on the fifth day of April, A. D. 1831, between the United States of America and the United Mexican States, except the additional article, and except so far as the stipulations of the said treaty may be incompatible with any stipulation contained in the present treaty, is hereby revived for the period of eight years from the day of the exchange of ratifications of this treaty, with the same force and virtue as if incorporated therein; it being understood that each of the contracting parties reserves to itself the right, at any time after the said period of eight years shall have expired, to terminate the same by giving one year's notice of such intention to the other party.

Article XVIII

All supplies whatever for troops of the United States in Mexico, arriving at ports in the occupation of such troops previous to the final evacuation thereof, although subsequently to the restoration of the custom-houses at such ports, shall be entirely exempt from duties and charges of any kind; the Government of the United States hereby engaging and pledging its faith to establish and vigilantly to enforce, all possible guards for securing the revenue of Mexico, by preventing the importation, under cover of this stipulation, of any articles other than such, both in kind and in quantity, as shall really be wanted for the use and consumption of the forces of the United States during the time they may remain in Mexico. To this end it shall be the duty of all officers and agents of the United States to denounce to the Mexican authorities at the respective ports any attempts at a fraudulent abuse of this stipulation, which they may know of, or may have reason to suspect, and to give to such authorities all the aid in their power with regard thereto; and every such attempt, when duly proved and established by sentence of a competent tribunal, shall be punished by the confiscation of the property so attempted to be fraudulently introduced.

Article XIX

With respect to all merchandise, effects, and property whatsoever, imported into ports of Mexico, whilst in the occupation of the forces of the United States, whether by citizens of either republic, or by citizens or subjects of any neutral nation, the following rules shall be observed:

(1) All such merchandise, effects, and property, if imported previously to the restoration of the custom-houses to the Mexican authorities, as stipulated for in the third article of this treaty, shall be exempt from confiscation, although the importation of the same be prohibited by the Mexican tariff.

(2) The same perfect exemption shall be enjoyed by all sucn merchandise, effects, and property, imported subsequently to the restoration of the custom-houses, and previously to the sixty days fixed in the following article for the coming into force of the Mexican tariff at such ports respectively; the said merchandise, effects, and property being, however, at the time of their importation, subject to the payment of duties, as provided for in the said following article.

(3) All merchandise, effects, and property described in the two rules foregoing shall, during their continuance at the place of importation, and upon their leaving such place for the interior, be exempt from all duty, tax, or imposts of every kind, under whatsoever title or denomination. Nor shall they be there subject to any charge whatsoever upon the sale thereof.

(4) All merchandise, effects, and property, described in the first and second rules, which shall have been removed to any place in the interior, whilst such place was in the occupation of the forces of the United States, shall, during their continuance therein, be exempt from all tax upon the sale or consumption thereof, and from every kind of impost or contribution, under whatsoever title or denomination.

(5) But if any merchandise, effects, or property, described in the first and second rules, shall be removed to any place not occupied at the time by the forces of the United States, they shall, upon their introduction into such place, or upon their sale or consumption there, be subject to the same duties which, under the Mexican laws, they would be required to pay in such cases if they had been imported in time of peace, through the maritime custom-houses, and had there paid the duties conformably with the Mexican tariff.

(6) The owners of all merchandise, effects, or property, described in the first and second rules, and existing in any port of Mexico, shall have the right to reship the same, exempt from all tax, impost, or contribution whatever.

With respect to the metals, or other property, exported from any Mexican port whilst in the occupation of the forces of the United States, and previously to the restoration of the custom-house at such port, no person shall be required by the Mexican authorities, whether general or state, to pay any tax, duty, or contribution upon any such exportation, or in any manner to account for the same to the said authorities.

ARTICLE XX

Through consideration for the interests of commerce generally, it is agreed, that if less than sixty days should elapse between the date of the signature of this treaty and the restoration of the custom-houses, conformably with the stipulation in the third article, in such case all merchandise, effects and property whatsoever, arriving at the Mexican ports after the restoration of the said custom-houses, and previously to the expiration of sixty days after the day of signature of this treaty, shall be admitted to entry; and no other duties shall be levied thereon than the duties established by the tariff found in force at such custom-houses at the time of the restoration of the same. And to all such merchandise, effects, and property, the rules established by the preceding article shall apply.

ARTICLE XXI

If unhappily any disagreement should hereafter arise between the Governments of the two republics, whether with respect to the interpretation of any stipulation in this treaty, or with respect to any other particular concerning the political or commercial relations of the two nations, the said Governments, in the name of those nations, do promise to each other that they will endeavour, in the most sincere and earnest manner, to settle the differences so arising, and to preserve the state of peace and friendship in which the two countries are now placing themselves, using, for this end, mutual representations and pacific negotiations. And if, by these means, they should not be enabled to come to an agreement, a resort shall not, on this account, be had to reprisals, aggression, or hostility of any kind, by the one republic against the other, until the Government of that which deems itself aggrieved shall have maturely considered, in the spirit of peace and good neighbourship, whether it would not be better that such difference should be settled by the arbitration of commissioners appointed on each side, or by that of a friendly nation. And should such course be proposed by either party, it shall be acceded to by the other, unless deemed by it altogether incompatible with the nature of the difference, or the circumstances of the case.

Article XXII

If (which is not to be expected, and which God forbid) war should unhappily break out between the two republics, they do now, with a view to such calamity, solemnly pledge themselves to each other and to the world to observe the following rules; absolutely where the nature of the subject permits, and as closely as possible in all cases where such absolute observance shall be impossible:

(1) The merchants of either republic then residing in the other shall be allowed to remain twelve months (for those dwelling in the interior), and six months (for those dwelling at the seaports) to collect their debts and settle their affairs; during which periods they shall enjoy the same protection, and be on the same footing, in all respects, as the citizens or subjects of the most friendly nations; and, at the expiration thereof, or at any time before, they shall have full liberty to depart, carrying off all their effects without molestation or hindrance, conforming therein to the same laws which the citizens or subjects of the most friendly nations are required to conform to. Upon the entrance of the armies of either nation into the territories of the other, women and children, ecclesiastics, scholars of every faculty, cultivators of the earth, merchants, artisans, manufacturers, and fishermen, unarmed and inhabiting unfortified towns, villages, or places, and in general all persons whose occupations are for the common subsistence and benefit of mankind, shall be allowed to continue their respective employments, unmolested in their persons. Nor shall their houses or goods be burnt or otherwise destroyed, nor their cattle taken, nor their fields wasted, by the armed force into whose power, by the events of war, they may happen to fall; but if the necessity arise to take anything from them for the use of such armed force, the same shall be paid for at an equitable price. All churches, hospitals, schools, colleges, libraries, and other establishments for charitable and beneficent purposes, shall be respected, and all persons connected with the same protected in the discharge of their duties, and the pursuit of their vocations.

(2) In order that the fate of prisoners of war may be alleviated, all such practices as those of sending them into distant, inclement, or unwholesome districts, or crowding them into close and noxious places, shall be studiously avoided. They shall not be confined in dungeons, prisonships, or prisons; nor be put in irons, or bound, or otherwise restrained in the use of their limbs. The officers shall enjoy liberty on their paroles, within convenient districts, and have comfortable quarters; and the common soldiers shall be disposed in cantonments, open and extensive enough for air and exercise, and lodged in barracks as roomy and good as are provided by the party in whose power they are for its own troops. But if any officer shall break his parole by leaving the district so assigned him, or any other prisoner shall escape from the limits of his cantonment, after they shall have been designated to him, such individual, officer, or other prisoner, shall forfeit so much of the benefit of this article as provides for his liberty on parole or in cantonment. And if any officer so breaking his parole, or any common soldier so escaping from the limits assigned him, shall afterwards be found in arms, previously to his being regularly exchanged, the person so offending shall be dealt with according to the established laws of war. The officers shall be daily furnished, by the party in whose power they are, with as many rations, and of the same articles, as are allowed, either in kind or by commutation, to officers of equal rank in its own army; and all others shall be daily furnished with such ration as is allowed to a common soldier in its own service; the value of all which supplies shall, at the close of the war, or at periods to be agreed upon between the respective commanders, be paid by the other party, on a mutual adjustment of accounts for the subsistence of prisoners; and such accounts shall not be mingled with or set off against any others, nor the balance due on them withheld, as a compensation or reprisal for any cause whatever, real or pretended. Each party shall be allowed to keep a commissary of prisoners, appointed by itself, with every cantonment of prisoners, in possession of the other; which commissary shall see the prisoners as often as he pleases; shall be allowed to receive, exempt from all duties or taxes, and to distribute, whatever comforts may be sent to them by

their friends; and shall be free to transmit his reports in open letters to the party by whom he is employed.

And it is declared that neither the pretence that war dissolves all treaties, nor any other whatever, shall be considered as annulling or suspending the solemn covenant contained in this article. On the contrary, the state of war is precisely that for which it is provided; and, during which, its stipulations are to be as sacredly observed as the most acknowledged obligations under the law of nature or nations.

Article XXIII

This treaty shall be ratified by the President of the United States of America, by and with the advice and consent of the Senate thereof; and by the President of the Mexican Republic, with the previous approbation of its general Congress; and the ratifications shall be exchanged in the City of Washington, or at the seat of Government of Mexico, in four months from the date of the signature hereof, or sooner if practicable.

In faith whereof we, the respective Plenipotentiaries, have signed this treaty of peace, friendship, limits, and settlement, and have hereunto affixed our seals respectively. Done in quintuplicate, at the city of Guadalupe Hidalgo, on the second day of February, in the year of our Lord one thousand eight hundred and forty-eight.

N. P. Trist	[L. S.]
Luis P. Cuevas	[L S.]
Bernado Couto	[L S.]
Migl. Atristain	[L. S.]

FUGITIVE SLAVE ACT

(1850)

[The Fugitive Slave Act was part of the group of measures known collectively as the "Compromise of 1850." By this compromise, the anti-slavery party gained the admission of California as a free state, and the prohibition of slave-trading in the District of Columbia. The slavery party, on the other hand, besides concessions with regard to Texas, gained this act, which, however, by its stringency did much to rouse abolitionist sentiment in the North.]

*B*E IT *enacted by the Senate and House of Representatives of the United States of America in Congress assembled,* That the persons who have been, or may hereafter be, appointed commissioners, in virtue of any act of Congress, by the Circuit Courts of the United States, and Who, in consequence of such appointment, are authorized to exercise the powers that any justice of the peace, or other magistrate of any of the United States, may exercise in respect to offenders for any crime or offense against the United States, by arresting, imprisoning, or bailing the same under and by the virtue of the thirty-third section of the act of the twenty-fourth of September seventeen hundred and eighty-nine, entitled "An Act to establish the judicial courts of the United States" shall be, and are hereby, authorized and required to exercise and discharge all the powers and duties conferred by this act.

SEC. 2. *And be it further enacted,* That the Superior Court of each organized Territory of the United States shall have the same power to appoint commissioners to take acknowledgments of bail and affidavits, and to take depositions of witnesses in civil causes, which is now possessed by the Circuit Court of the United States; and all commissioners who shall hereafter be appointed for such purposes by the Superior Court of any organized Territory of the United States, shall possess all the powers, and exercise all the duties, conferred by law upon the commissioners appointed by the Circuit Courts of the United States for similar purposes, and shall moreover exercise and discharge all the powers and duties conferred by this act.

SEC. 3. *And be it further enacted,* That the Circuit Courts of the United States shall from time to time enlarge the number of the commissioners, with a view to afford reasonable facilities to reclaim fugitives from labor, and to the prompt discharge of the duties imposed by this act.

SEC. 4. *And be it further enacted,* That the commissioners above named shall have concurrent jurisdiction with the judges of the Circuit and District Courts of the United States, in their respective circuits and districts within the several States, and the judges of the Superior Courts of the Territories, severally and collectively, in term-time and vacation; shall grant certificates to such claimants, upon satisfactory proof being made, with authority to take and remove such fugitives from service or labor, under the restrictions herein contained, to the State or Territory from which such persons may have escaped or fled.

SEC. 5. *And be it further enacted,* That it shall be the duty of all marshals and deputy marshals to obey and execute all warrants and precepts issued under the provisions of this act, when to them directed; and should any marshal or deputy marshal refuse to receive such warrant, or other process, when tendered, or to use all proper means diligently to execute the same, he shall, on conviction thereof, be fined in the sum of one thousand dollars, to the use of such claimant, on the motion of such claimant, by the Circuit or District Court for the district of such marshal; and after arrest of such fugitive, by such marshal or his deputy, or whilst at any time in his custody under the provisions of this act, should such fugitive escape, whether with or without the assent of such marshal or his deputy, such marshal shall be liable, on his official bond, to be prosecuted for the benefit of such claimant, for the full value of the service or labor of said fugitive in the State, Territory, or District whence he escaped: and the better to enable the said commissioners, when thus appointed, to execute their duties faithfully and efficiently, in conformity with the requirements of the Constitution of the United States and of this act, they are hereby authorized and empowered, within their counties respectively, to appoint, in writing under their hands, any one or more suitable persons, from time to time, to execute all such warrants and other process as may be issued by them in the lawful performance of their respective duties; with authority to such commissioners, or the persons to be appointed by them, to execute process as aforesaid, to summon and call to their aid the bystanders, or *posse comitatus* of the proper county, when necessary to ensure a faithful observance of the clause of the Constitution referred to, in conformity with the provisions of this act; and all good citizens are hereby commanded to aid and assist in the prompt and efficient execution of this law, whenever their services may be required, as aforesaid, for that purpose; and said warrants shall run, and be executed by said officers, any where in the State within which they are issued.

SEC. 6. *And be it further enacted,* That when a person held to service or labor in any State or Territory of the United States, ha' heretofore or shall hereafter escape into another State or Territory of the United States, the person or persons to whom such service or labor may be due, or his, her, or their agent or attorney, duly authorized, by power of attorney, in writing, acknowledged and certified under the seal of some legal officer or court of the State or Territory in which the same may be executed, may pursue and reclaim such fugitive person, either by procuring a warrant from some one of the courts, judges, or commissioners aforesaid, of the proper circuit, district, or county, for the apprehension of such fugitive from service or labor, or by seizing and arresting such fugitive, where the same can be done without process, and by taking, or causing such person to be taken, forthwith before such court, judge, or commissioner, whose duty it shall be to hear and determine the case of such claimant in a summary manner; and upon satisfactory proof being made, by deposition or affidavit, in writing, to be taken and certified by such court, judge, or commissioner, or by other satisfactory testimony, duly taken and certified by some court, magistrate, justice of the peace, or other legal officer authorized to administer an oath and take depositions under the laws of the State or Territory from which such person owing service or labor may have escaped, with a certificate of such magistracy or other authority, as aforesaid, with the seal of the proper court or officer thereto attached, which seal shall be sufficient to establish the competency of the proof, and with proof, also by affidavit, of the identity of the person whose service

or labor is claimed to be due as aforesaid, that the person so arrested
does in fact owe service or labor to the person or persons claiming
him or her, in the State or Territory from which such fugitive may
have escaped as aforesaid, and that said person escaped, to make
out and deliver to such claimant, his or her agent or attorney, a
certificate setting forth the substantial facts as to the service or labor
due from such fugitive to the claimant, and of his or her escape
from the State or Territory in which he or she was arrested, with
authority to such claimant, or his or her agent or attorney, to use
such reasonable force and restraint as may be necessary, under the
circumstances of the case, to take and remove such fugitive person
back to the State or Territory whence he or she may have escaped
as aforesaid. In no trial or hearing under this act shall the testimony
of such alleged fugitive be admitted in evidence; and the certificates
in this and the first [fourth] section mentioned, shall be conclusive
of the right of the person or persons in whose favor granted, to remove such fugitive to the State or Territory from which he escaped,
and shall prevent all molestation of such person or persons by any
process issued by any court, judge, magistrate, or other person whom-
soever.

SEC. 7. *And be it further enacted,* That any person who shall
knowingly and willingly obstruct, hinder, or prevent such claimant,
his agent or attorney, or any person or persons lawfully assisting
him, her, or them, from arresting such a fugitive from service or
labor, either with or without process as aforesaid, or shall rescue, or
attempt to rescue, such fugitive from service or labor, from the
custody of such claimant, his or her agent or attorney, or other
person or persons lawfully assisting as aforesaid, when so arrested,
pursuant to the authority herein given and declared; or shall aid,
abet, or assist such person so owing service or labor as aforesaid,
directly or indirectly, to escape from such claimant, his agent or attorney, or other person or persons legally authorized as aforesaid;
or shall harbor or conceal such fugitive, so as to prevent the discovery and arrest of such person, after notice or knowledge of the
fact that such person was a fugitive from service or labor as aforesaid,
shall, for either of said offences, be subject to a fine not exceeding
one thousand dollars, and imprisonment not exceeding six months,

by indictment and conviction before the District Court of the United States for the district in which such offence may have been committed, or before the proper court of criminal jurisdiction, if committed within any one of the organized Territories of the United States; and shall moreover forfeit and pay, by way of civil damages to the party injured by such illegal conduct, the sum of one thousand dollars for each fugitive so lost as aforesaid, to be recovered by action of debt, in any of the District or Territorial Courts aforesaid, within whose jurisdiction the said offence may have been committed.

Sec. 8. *And be it further enacted,* That the marshals, their deputies, and the clerks of the said District and Territorial Courts, shall be paid, for their services, the like fees as may be allowed for similar services in other cases; and where such services are rendered exclusively in the arrest, custody, and delivery of the fugitive to the claimant, his or her agent or attorney, or where such supposed fugitive may be discharged out of custody for the want of sufficient proof as aforesaid, then such fees are to be paid in whole by such claimant, his or her agent or attorney; and in all cases where the proceedings are before a commissioner, he shall be entitled to a fee of ten dollars in full for his services in each case, upon the delivery of the said certificate to the claimant, his agent or attorney; or a fee of five dollars in cases where the proof shall not, in the opinion of such commissioner, warrant such certificate and delivery, inclusive of all services incident to such arrest and examination, to be paid, in either case, by the claimant, his or her agent or attorney. The person or persons authorized to execute the process to be issued by such commissioner for the arrest and detention of fugitives from service or labor as aforesaid, shall also be entitled to a fee of five dollars each for each person he or they may arrest, and take before any commissioner as aforesaid, at the instance and request of such claimant, with such other fees as may be deemed reasonable by such commissioner for such other additional services as may be necessarily performed by him or them; such as attending at the examination, keeping the fugitive in custody, and providing him with food and lodging during his detention, and until the final determination of such commissioners; and, in general, for performing such other duties as may be required by such claimant, his or her attorney or agent, or commissioner in the premises, such fees to be made up in conformity with the fees usually charged by the officers of the courts of justice within the proper district or county, as near as may be practicable, and paid by such claimants, their agents or attorneys, whether such supposed fugitives from service or labor be ordered to be delivered to such claimant by the final determination of such commissioner or not.

SEC. 9. *And be it further enacted,* That, upon affidavit made by the claimant of such fugitive, his agent or attorney, after such certificate has been issued, that he has reason to apprehend that such fugitive will be rescued by force from his or their possession before he can be taken beyond the limits of the State in which the arrest is made, it shall be the duty of the officer making the arrest to retain such fugitive in his custody, and to remove him to the State whence he fled, and there to deliver him to said claimant, his agent, or attorney. And to this end, the officer aforesaid is hereby authorized and required to employ so many persons as he may deem necessary to overcome such force, and to retain them in his service so long as circumstances may require. The said officer and his assistants, while so employed, to receive the same compensation, and to be allowed the same expenses, as are now allowed by law for transportation of criminals, to be certified by the judge of the district within which the arrest is made, and paid out of the treasury of the United States.

SEC. 10. *And be it further enacted,* That when any person held to service or labor in any State or Territory, or in the District of Columbia, shall escape therefrom, the party to whom such service or labor shall be due, his, her, or their agent or attorney, may apply to any court of record therein, or judge thereof in vacation, and make satisfactory proof to such court, or judge in vacation, of the escape aforesaid, and that the person escaping owed service or labor to such party. Whereupon the court shall cause a record to be made of the matters so proved, and also a general description of the person so escaping, with such convenient certainty as may be; and a transcript of such record, authenticated by the attestation of the clerk and of the seal of the said court, being produced in any other State, Territory, or district in which the person so escaping may be found, and being exhibited to any judge, commissioner, or other officei authorized by the law of the United States to cause persons escaping from service or labor to be delivered up, shall be held and taken to be full and conclusive evidence of the fact of escape, and that the service or labor of the person escaping is due to the party in such record mentioned. And upon the production by the said party of other and further evidence if necessary, either oral or by affidavit, in addition to what is contained in the said record of the identity of the person escaping, he or she shall be delivered up to the claimant. And the said court, commissioner, judge, or other person authorized by this act to grant certificates to claimants or fugitives, shall, upon the production of the record and other evidences aforesaid, grant to such claimant a certificate of his right to take any such person identified and proved to be owing service or labor as aforesaid, which certificate shall authorize such claimant to seize or arrest and transport such person to the State or Territory from which he escaped: *Provided,* That nothing herein contained shall be construed as requiring the production of a transcript of such record as evidence as aforesaid. But in its absence the claim shall be heard and determined upon other satisfactory proofs, competent in law.

Approved, September 18, 1850.

LINCOLN'S
FIRST INAUGURAL ADDRESS
(1861)

[The platform on which Abraham Lincoln was elected President is sufficiently indicated in his inaugural address. But between the date of his election on that platform and his inauguration, seven Southern States had seceded from the Union, formed a provisional government, and seized most of the forts, etc., belonging to the United States within the seceding territory. It was this situation that Lincoln faced as he took up the task of government.]

FELLOW-CITIZENS of the United States: In compliance with a custom as old is the Government itself, I appear before you to address you briefly, and to take in your presence the oath prescribed by the Constitution of the United States to be taken by the President "before he enters on the execution of his office."

I do not consider it necessary at present for me to discuss those matters of administration about which there is no special anxiety or excitement.

Apprehension seems to exist among the people of the Southern States that by the accession of a Republican Administration their property and their peace and personal security are to be endangered. There has never been any reasonable cause for such apprehension. Indeed, the most ample evidence to the contrary has all the while existed and been open to their inspection. It is found in nearly all the published speeches of him who now addresses you. I do but quote from one of those speeches when I declare that "I have no purpose, directly or indirectly, to interfere with the institution of slavery in the States where it exists. I believe I have no lawful right to do so, and I have no inclination to do so." Those who nominated and elected me did so with full knowledge that I had made this and many similar declarations, and had never recanted them. And, more than this, they placed in the platform for my acceptance, and as a law to themselves and to me, the clear and emphatic resolution which I now read:

"*Resolved,* That the maintenance inviolate of the rights of the States, and especially the right of each State to order and control its own domestic institutions according to its own judgment exclusively, is essential to that balance of power on which the perfection and endurance of our political fabric depend, and we denounce the lawless invasion by armed force of the soil of any State or Territory, no matter under what pretext, as among the gravest of crimes."

I now reiterate these sentiments; and, in doing so, I only press upon the public attention the most conclusive evidence of which the case is susceptible, that the property, peace, and security of no section are to be in any wise endangered by the now incoming Administration. I add, too, that all the protection which, consistently with the Constitution and the laws, can be given, will be cheerfully given to all the States when lawfully demanded, for whatever cause—as cheerfully to one section, as to another.

There is much controversy about the delivering up of fugitives from service or labor. The clause I now read is as plainly written in the Constitution as any other of its provisions:

"No person held to service or labor in one State, under the laws thereof, escaping into another, shall in consequence of any law or regulation therein be discharged from such service or labor, but shall be delivered up on claim of the party to whom such service or labor may be due."

It is scarcely questioned that this provision was intended by those who made it for the reclaiming of what we call fugitive slaves; and the intention of the lawgiver is the law. All Members of Congress swear their support to the whole Constitution—to this provision as much as to any other. To the proposition, then, that slaves whose cases come within the terms of this clause, "shall be delivered up," their oaths are unanimous. Now, if they would make the effort in good temper, could they not with nearly equal unanimity frame and pass a law by means of which to keep good that unanimous oath?

There is some difference of opinion whether this clause should be enforced by national or by State authority; but surely that difference is not a very material one. If the slave is to be surrendered, it can be of but little consequence to him, or to others, by which authority it is done. And should any one, in any case, be content that his oath shall go unkept, on a merely unsubstantial controversy as to *how* it shall be kept?

Again, in any law upon this subject, ought not all the safeguards of liberty known in civilized and humane jurisprudence to be introduced so that a free man be not, in any case, surrendered as a slave? And might it not be well at the same time to provide by law for the enforcement of that clause in the Constitution which guarantees that "the citizen of each State shall be entitled to all privileges and immunities of citizens in the several States"?

I take the official oath to-day with no mental reservations and with no purpose to construe the Constitution or laws by any hypercritical rules. And while I do not choose now to specify particular acts of Congress as proper to be enforced, I do suggest that it will be much safer for all, both in official and private stations, to conform to and abide by all those acts which stand unrepealed, than to violate any of them trusting to find impunity in having them held to be unconstitutional.

It is seventy-two years since the first inauguration of a President under our National Constitution. During that period fifteen different and greatly distinguished citizens have, in succession, administered the Executive branch of the Government. They have conducted it through many perils, and generally with great success. Yet, with all this scope of precedent, I now enter upon the same task for the brief constitutional term of four years under great and peculiar difficulty. A disruption of the Federal Union, heretofore only menaced, is now formidably attempted.

I hold that, in contemplation of universal law and of the Constitution, the Union of these States is perpetual. Perpetuity is implied, if not expressed, in the fundamental law of all national governments. It is safe to assert that no government proper ever had a provision in its organic law for its own termination. Continue to execute all the express provisions of our National Constitution, and the Union will endure forever—it being impossible to destroy it except by some action not provided for in the instrument itself.

Again, if the United States be not a Government proper, but an association of States in the nature of contract merely, can it, as a contract, be peaceably unmade by less than all the parties who made it? One party to a contract may violate it—break it, so to speak, but does it not require all to lawfully rescind it?

Descending from these general principles, we find the proposition that, in legal contemplation, the Union is perpetual, confirmed by the history of the Union itself. The Union is much older than the Constitution. It was formed, in fact, by the Articles of Association in 1774. It was matured and continued by the Declaration of Independence in 1776. It was further matured, and the faith of all the then thirteen States expressly plighted and engaged that it should be perpetual, by the Articles of Confederation in 1778. And, finally, in 1787, one of the declared objects for ordaining and establishing the Constitution was, *"to form a more perfect Union."*

But if the destruction of the Union by one, or by a part only, of the States be lawfully possible, the Union is *less* perfect than before the Constitution, having lost the vital element of perpetuity.

It follows from these views that no State, upon its own mere motion, can lawfully get out of the Union; that *resolves* and *ordinances* to that effect are legally void; and that acts of violence, within any State or States, against the authority of the United States, are insurrectionary or revolutionary, according to circumstances.

I therefore consider that, in view of the Constitution and the laws, the Union is unbroken; and to the extent of my ability I shall take care, as the Constitution itself expressly enjoins upon me, that the laws of the Union be faithfully executed in all of the States. Doing this I deem to be only a simple duty on my part; and I shall perform it, so far as practicable, unless my rightful masters, the American people, shall withhold the requisite means, or in some authoritative manner direct the contrary. I trust this will not be regarded as a menace, but only as the declared purpose of the Union that it will constitutionally defend and maintain itself.

In doing this there needs to be no bloodshed or violence; and there shall be none, unless it be forced upon the national authority. The power confided to me will be used to hold, occupy, and possess the property and places belonging to the Government, and to collect the duties and imposts; but beyond what may be necessary for these objects, there will be no invasion, no using of force against or among the people anywhere. Where hostility to the United States, in any interior locality, shall be so great and universal as to prevent competent resident citizens from holding the Federal offices, there will be no attempt to force obnoxious strangers among the people for that object. While the strict legal right may exist in the Government to enforce the exercise of these offices, the attempt to do so would be so irritating, and so nearly impracticable withal, that I deem it better to forego for the time the uses of such offices.

The mails, unless repelled, will continue to be furnished in all parts of the Union. So far as possible, the people everywhere shall have that sense of perfect security which is most favorable to calm thought and reflection. The course here indicated will be followed unless current events and experience shall show a modification or change to be proper, and in every case and exigency my best discretion will be exercised according to circumstances actually existing, and with a view and a hope of a peaceful solution of the national troubles, and the restoration of fraternal sympathies and affections.

That there are persons in one section or another who seek to destroy the Union at all events, and are glad of any pretext to do it, I will neither affirm nor deny; but if there be such, I need address no word to them. To those, however, who really love the Union may I not speak?

Before entering upon so grave a matter as the destruction of our national fabric, with all its benefits, its memories, and its hopes, would it not be wise to ascertain precisely why we do it? Will you hazard so desperate a step while there is any possibility that any portion of the ills you fly from have no real existence? Will you, while the certain ills you fly to are greater than all the real ones you fly from—will you risk the commission of so fearful a mistake?

All profess to be content in the Union, if all constitutional rights can be maintained. Is it true, then, that any right, plainly written in the Constitution, has been denied? I think not. Happily the human mind is so constituted, that no party can reach to the audacity of doing this. Think, if you can, of a single instance in which a plainly written provision of the Constitution has ever been denied. If by the mere force of numbers a majority should deprive a minority in any clearly written constitutional right, it might, in a moral point of view, justify revolution—certainly would if such a right were a vital one. But such is not our case. All the vital rights of minorities and of individuals are so plainly assured to them by affirmations and negations, guaranties and prohibitions, in the Constitution, that controversies never arise concerning them. But no organic law can ever be framed with a provision specifically applicable to every question which may occur in practical administration. No foresight can anticipate, nor any document of reasonable length contain, express provisions for all possible questions. Shall fugitives from labor be surrendered by national or by State authority? The Constitution does not expressly say. *May* Congress prohibit slavery in the Territories? The Constitution does not expressly say. *Must* Congress protect slavery in the Territories? The Constitution does not expressly say.

From questions of this class spring all our constitutional controversies, and we divide upon them into majorities and minorities. If the minority will not acquiesce, the majority must, or the Government must cease. There is no other alternative; for continuing the Government is acquiescence on one side or the other.

If a minority in such case will secede rather than acquiesce, they make a precedent which in turn will divide and ruin them; for a minority of their own will secede from them whenever a majority refuses to be controlled by such minority. For instance, why may not any portion of a new confederacy a year or two hence arbitrarily secede again, precisely as portions of the present Union now claim to secede from it? All who cherish disunion sentiments are now being educated to the exact temper of doing this.

Is there such perfect identity of interests among the States to compose a new Union as to produce harmony only, and prevent renewed secession?

Plainly, the central idea of secession is the essence of anarchy. A majority held in restraint by constitutional checks and limitations, and always changing easily with deliberate changes of popular opinions and sentiments, is the only true sovereign of a free people. Whoever rejects it does, of necessity, fly to anarchy or to despotism. Unanimity is impossible; the rule of a minority, as a permanent arrangement, is wholly inadmissible; so that, rejecting the majority principle, anarchy or despotism in some form is all that is left.

I do not forget the position, assumed by some, that constitutional questions are to be decided by the Supreme Court; nor do I deny that such decisions must be binding, in any case, upon the parties to a suit, as to the object of that suit, while they are also entitled to very high respect and consideration in all parallel cases by all other departments of the Government. And while it is obviously possible that such decision may be erroneous in any given case, still the evil effect following it, being limited to that particular case, with the chance that it may be overruled and never become a precedent for other cases, can better be borne than could the evils of a different practice. At the same time, the candid citizen must confess that if the policy of the Government, upon vital questions affecting the whole people, is to be irrevocably fixed by decisions of the Supreme Court, the instant they are made, in ordinary litigation between parties in personal actions, the people will have ceased to be their own rulers, having to that extent practically resigned their government into the hands of that eminent tribunal. Nor is there in this view any assault upon the court or the judges. It is a duty from which they may not shrink to decide cases properly brought before them, and it is no fault of theirs if others seek to turn their decisions to political purposes.

One section of our country believes slavery is *right,* and ought to be extended, while the other believes it is *wrong,* and ought not to be extended. This is the only substantial dispute. The fugitive-slave clause of the Constitution, and the law for the suppression of the foreign slave trade, are each as well enforced, perhaps, as any law can ever be in a community where the moral sense of the people imperfectly supports the law itself. The great body of the people abide by the dry legal obligation in both cases, and a few break over in each. This, I think, cannot be perfectly cured; and it would be worse in both cases *after* the separation of the sections, than before. The foreign slave trade, now imperfectly suppressed, would be ultimately revived without restriction, in one section; while fugitive slaves, now only partially surrendered, would not be surrendered at all by the other.

Physically speaking, we cannot separate. We cannot remove our respective sections from each other, nor build an impassable wall between them. A husband and wife may be divorced, and go out of the presence and beyond the reach of each other; but the different parts of our country cannot do this. They cannot but remain face to face, and intercourse, either amicable or hostile, must continue between them. Is it possible, then, to make that intercourse more advantageous or more satisfactory *after* separation than *before?* Can aliens make treaties easier than friends can make laws? Can treaties be more faithfully enforced between aliens than laws can among friends? Suppose you go to war, you cannot fight always; and when, after much loss on both sides, and no gain on either, you cease fighting, the identical old questions as to terms of intercourse are again upon you.

This country, with its institutions, belongs to the people who inhabit it. Whenever they shall grow weary of the existing Government, they can exercise their *constitutional* right of amending it, or their *revolutionary* right to dismember or overthrow it. I cannot be ignorant of the fact that many worthy and patriotic citizens are desirous of having the National Constitution amended. While I make no recommendation of amendments, I fully recognize the rightful authority of the people over the whole subject, to be exercised in either of the modes prescribed in the instrument itself; and I should, under existing circumstances, favor rather than oppose, a fair opportunity being afforded the people to act upon it. I will venture to add that to me the convention mode seems preferable, in that it allows amendments to originate with the people themselves, instead of only permitting them to take or reject propositions originated by others, not especially chosen for the purpose, and which might not be precisely such as they would wish to either accept or refuse. I understand a proposed amendment to the Constitution—which amendment, however, I have not seen—has passed Congress, to the effect that the Federal Government shall never interfere with the domestic institutions of the States, including that of persons held to service. To avoid misconstruction of what I have said, I depart from my purpose, not to speak of particular amendments, so far as to say that, holding such a provision to now be implied constitutional law, I have no objection to its being made express and irrevocable.

The Chief Magistrate derives all his authority from the people, and they have conferred none upon him to fix terms for the separation of the States. The people themselves can do this also if they choose; but the Executive, as such, has nothing to do with it. His duty is to administer the present Government, as it came to his hands, and to transmit it, unimpaired by him, to his successor.

Why should there not be a patient confidence in the ultimate justice of the people? Is there any better or equal hope in the world? In our present differences is either party without faith of being in the right? If the Almighty Ruler of Nations, with his eternal truth and justice, be on your side of the North, or on yours of the South, that truth and that justice will surely prevail by the judgment of this great tribunal of the American people.

By the frame of the Government under which we live, this same people have wisely given their public servants but little power for mischief; and have, with equal wisdom, provided for the return of that little, to their own hands at very short intervals. While the people retain their virtue and vigilance, no administration, by any extreme of wickedness or folly, can very seriously injure the government in the short space of four years.

My countrymen, one and all, think calmly and *well* upon this whole subject. Nothing valuable can be lost by taking time. If there be an object to *hurry* any of you in hot haste to a step which you would never take *deliberately,* that object will be frustrated by taking time; but no good object can be frustrated by it. Such of you as are now dissatisfied, still have the old Constitution unimpaired, and, on the sensitive point, the laws of your own framing under it; while the new Administration will have no immediate power, if it would, to change either. If it were admitted that you who are dissatisfied hold the right side in the dispute, there still is no single good reason for precipitate action. Intelligence, patriotism, Christianity, and a firm reliance on Him who has never yet forsaken this favored land are still competent to adjust, in the best way, all our present difficulty.

In *your* hands, my dissatisfied fellow-countrymen, and not in *mine,* is the momentous issue of civil war. The Government will not assail *you*. You can have no conflict without being yourselves the aggressors. *You* have no oath registered in Heaven to destroy the Government, while I shall have the most solemn one to "preserve, protect, and defend it."

I am loth to close. We are not enemies, but friends. We must not be enemies. Though passion may have strained, it must not break our bonds of affection. The mystic chords of memory, stretching from every battle-field and patriot grave to every living heart and hearthstone all over this broad land, will yet swell the chorus of the Union, when again touched, as surely they will be, by the better angels of our nature.

EMANCIPATION
PROCLAMATION

(1863)

[The war for the maintenance of the Union had been going on for a year and a half before Lincoln issued the preliminary proclamation quoted in the beginning of the present document. The emancipation proclamation of January 1, 1863, enlarged the basis of the conflict, and from the point of view of foreign nations gave the North the advantage of a moral as well as a political issue.]

WHEREAS, on the twenty-second day of September, in the year of our Lord one thousand eight hundred and sixty-two, a proclamation was issued by the President of the United States, containing, among other things, the following, to wit:

"That on the first day of January, in the year of our Lord one thousand eight hundred and sixty-three, all persons held as slaves within any State, or designated part of a State, the people whereof shall then be in rebellion against the United States, shall be then, thenceforward, and forever free; and the Executive Government of the United States, including the military and naval authority thereof, will recognize and maintain the freedom of such persons, and will do no act or acts to repress such persons, or any of them, in any efforts they may make for their actual freedom.

"That the Executive will, on the first day of January aforesaid, by proclamation, designate the States and parts of States, if any, in which the people thereof respectively, shall then be in rebellion against the United States; and the fact that any State, or the people thereof, shall on that day be in good faith represented in the Congress of the United States by members chosen thereto at elections wherein a majority of the qualified voters of such State shall have participated, shall in the absence of strong countervailing testimony, be deemed conclusive evidence that such State, and the people thereof, are not then in rebellion against the United States."

Now, therefore, I, Abraham Lincoln, President of the United

States, by virtue of the power in me vested as commander-in-chief of the Army and Navy of the United States, in time of actual armed rebellion against authority and government of the United States, and as a fit and necessary war measure for suppressing said rebellion, do, on this first day of January, in the year of our Lord one thousand eight hundred and sixty-three, and in accordance with my purpose so to do, publicly proclaimed for the full period of one hundred days from the day first above mentioned, order and designate as the States and parts of States wherein the people thereof, respectively, are this day in rebellion against the United States, the following, to wit:

Arkansas, Texas, Louisiana (except the parishes of St. Bernard, Plaquemines, Jefferson, St. John, St. Charles, St. James, Ascension, Assumption, Terrebonne, Lafourche, St. Mary, St. Martin, and Orleans, including the city of New Orleans), Mississippi, Alabama, Florida, Georgia, South Carolina, North Carolina, and Virginia (except the forty-eight counties designated as West Virginia, and also the counties of Berkley, Accomac, Northampton, Elizabeth City, York, Princess Ann, and Norfolk, including the cities of Norfolk and Portsmouth), and which excepted parts are, for the present, left precisely as if this proclamation were not issued.

And by virtue of the power and for the purpose aforesaid, I do order and declare that all persons held as slaves within said designated States and parts of States are, and henceforward shall be, free; and that the Executive government of the United States, including the military and naval authorities thereof, will recognize and maintain the freedom of said persons.

And I hereby enjoin upon the people so declared to be free to abstain from all violence, unless in necessary self-defence; and I recommend to them that, in all cases when allowed, they labor faithfully for reasonable wages.

And I further declare and make known, that such persons of suitable condition, will be received into the armed service of the United States to garrison forts, positions, stations, and other places, and to man vessels of all sorts in said service.

And upon this act, sincerely believed to be an act of justice, warranted by the Constitution, upon military necessity, I invoke the considerate judgment of mankind and the gracious favor of Almighty God.

In witness whereof, I have hereunto set my hand, and caused the seal of the United States to be affixed.

Done at the city of Washington, this first day of January, in the year of our Lord one thousand eight hundred and sixty-three, and of the Independence of the United States of America the eighty-seventh.

ABRAHAM LINCOLN.

L. S.

By the President:

WILLIAM H. SEWARD,
Secretary of State.

THE
BATTLE OF GETTYSBURG
BY FRANK ARETAS HASKELL

[Frank Aretas Haskell was born at Tunbridge, Vermont, on July 13, 1828. He graduated at Dartmouth College in 1854, and went to Madison, Wisconsin, to practice law. On the outbreak of the War, he received a commission as First Lieutenant of Company I, of the Sixth Wisconsin Volunteer Infantry, and served as Adjutant of his regiment until April 14, 1862, when he became aide-de-camp to General John Gibbon, commander of the Iron Brigade. This was his rank in the battle of Gettysburg. On Feb. 9, 1864, Haskell was appointed Colonel of the Thirty-sixth Wisconsin; and on June 3, of the same year, he fell when leading a charge at the battle of Cold Harbor, one of the most distinguished soldiers of the Army of the Potomac.

This account of Gettysburg was written by Haskell to his brother, shortly after the battle, and was not intended for publication. This fact ought to be borne in mind in connection with some severe reflections cast by the author upon certain officers and soldiers of the Union army. The present text follows the unabridged reprint of the Wisconsin Historical Commission; and the notes on Haskell's estimates of numbers and losses have been supplied by Colonel Thomas L. Livermore, the well-known authority on this subject.]

THE great battle of Gettysburg is now an event of the past. The composition and strength of the armies, their leaders, the strategy, the tactics, the result, of that field are to-day by the side of those of Waterloo—matters of history. A few days ago these things were otherwise. This great event did not so "cast its shadow before," as to moderate the hot sunshine that streamed upon our preceding march, or to relieve our minds of all apprehension of the result of the second great Rebel invasion of the soil North of the Potomac.

No, not many days since, at times we were filled with fears and forebodings. The people of the country, I suppose, shared the anxieties of the army, somewhat in common with us, but they could not have felt them as keenly as we did. We were upon the immediate theatre of events, as they occurred from day to day, and were of them. We were the army whose province it should be to meet this invasion and repel it; on us was the immediate responsibility for results, most momentous for good or ill, as yet in the future. And so in addition to the solicitude of all good patriots, we felt that our own honor as men and as an army, as well as the safety of the Capitol and the country, were at stake.

And what if that invasion should be successful, and in the coming battle, the Army of the Potomac should be overpowered? Would it not be? When our army was much larger than at present—had rested all winter—and, nearly perfect in all its departments and arrangements, was the most splendid army this continent ever saw, only a part of the Rebel force, which it now had to contend with, had defeated it—its leader, rather—at Chancellorsville! Now the Rebel had his whole force assembled, he was flushed with recent victory, was arrogant in his career of unopposed invasion, at a favorable season of the year. His daring plans, made by no unskilled head, to transfer the war from his own to his enemies' ground, were being successful. He had gone a day's march from his front before Hooker moved, or was aware of his departure. Then, I believe, the army in general, both officers and men, had no confidence in Hooker, in either his honesty or ability.

Did they not charge him, personally, with the defeat at Chancellorsville? Were they not still burning with indignation against him for that disgrace? And now, again under his leadership, they were marching against the enemy! And they knew of nothing, short of the providence of God, that could, or would, remove him. For many reasons, during the marches prior to the battle, we were anxious, and at times heavy at heart.

But the Army of the Potomac was no band of school girls. They were not the men likely to be crushed or utterly discouraged by any new circumstances in which they might find themselves placed. They had lost some battles, they had gained some. They knew what defeat was, and what was victory. But here is the greatest praise that I can bestow upon them, or upon any army: With the elation of victory, or the depression of defeat, amidst the hardest toils of the campaign, under unwelcome leadership, at all times, and under all circumstances, they were a reliable army still. The Army of the Potomac would do as it was told, always.

Well clothed, and well fed—there never could be any ground for complaint on these heads—but a mighty work was before them. Onward they moved—night and day were blended—over many a weary mile, through dust, and through mud, in the broiling sunshine, in the flooding rain, over steeps, through defiles, across rivers, over last year's battle fields, where the skeletons of our dead brethren, by hundreds, lay bare and bleaching, weary, without sleep for days, tormented with the newspapers, and their rumors, that the enemy was in Philadelphia, in Baltimore, in all places where he was not, yet these men could still be relied upon, I believe, when the day of conflict should come. *"Haec olim meminisse juvabit."* We did not then know this. I mention them now, that you may see that in those times we had several matters to think about, and to do, that were not as pleasant as sleeping upon a bank of violets in the shade.

In moving from near Falmouth, Va., the army was formed in several columns, and took several roads. The Second Corps, the rear of the whole, was the last to move, and left Falmouth at daybreak, on the 15th of June, and pursued its march through Aquia, Dumfries, Wolf Run Shoales, Centerville, Gainesville, Thoroughfare Gap—this last we left on the 25th, marching back to Haymarket, where we had a skirmish with the cavalry and horse artillery of the enemy—Gum Spring, crossing the Potomac at Edward's Ferry, thence through Poolesville, Frederick, Liberty, and Union Town. We marched from near Frederick to Union Town, a distance of thirty-two miles, from eight o'clock A. M. to nine P. M., on the 28th, and I think this is the longest march, accomplished in so short a time, by a corps during the war. On the 28th, while we were near this latter place, we breathed a full breath of joy, and of hope. The Providence of God had been with us—we ought not to have doubted it— General Meade commanded the Army of the Potomac.

Not a favorable time, one would be apt to suppose, to change the General of a large army, on the eve of battle, the result of which might be to destroy the Government and country! But it should have been done long before. At all events, any change could not have been for the worse, and the Administration, therefore, hazarded little, in making it now. From this moment my own mind was easy concerning results. I now felt that we had a clear-headed, honest soldier, to command the army, who would do his best always—that there would be no repetition of Chancellorsville. Meade was not as much known in the Army as many of the other corps commanders, but the officers who knew, all thought highly of him, a man of great modesty, with none of those qualities which are noisy and assuming, and hankering for cheap newspaper fame, not at all of the *"gallant"* Sickles stamp. I happened to know much of General Meade—he and General Gibbon had always been very intimate, and I had seen much of him—I think my own notions concerning General Meade at this time, were shared quite generally by the army; at all events, all who knew him shared them.

By this time, by reports that were not mere rumors, we began to hear frequently of the enemy, and of his proximity. His cavalry was all about us, making little raids here and there, capturing now and then a few of our wagons, and stealing a good many horses, but doing us really the least amount possible of harm, for we were not by these means impeded at all, and his cavalry gave no information at all to Lee, that he could rely upon, of the movements of the Army of the Potomac. The Infantry of the enemy was at this time in the neighborhood of Hagerstown, Chambersburg, and some had been at Gettysburg, possibly were there now. Gettysburg was a point of strategic importance, a great many roads, some ten or twelve at least concentrating there, so the army could easily converge to, or, should a further march be necessary, diverge from this point. General Meade, therefore, resolved to try to seize Gettysburg, and accordingly gave the necessary orders for the concentration of his different columns there. Under the new auspices the army brightened, and moved on with a more elastic step towards the yet undefined field of conflict.

The 1st Corps, General Reynolds, already having the advance, was ordered to push forward rapidly, and take and hold the town, if he could. The rest of the Army would assemble to his support. Buford's Cavalry co-operated with this corps, and on the morning of the 1st of July found the enemy near Gettysburg and to the West, and promptly engaged him. The First Corps having bivouacked the night before, South of the town, came up rapidly to Buford's support, and immediately a sharp battle was opened with the advance of the enemy. The First Division (Gen. Wadsworth) was the first of the infantry to become engaged, but the other two, commanded respectively by Generals Robinson and Doubleday, were close at hand,

and forming the line of battle to the West and North-west of the town, at a mean distance of about a mile away, the battle continued for some hours, with various success, which was on the whole with us until near noon. At this time a lull occurred, which was occupied, by both sides, in supervising and re-establishing the hastily formed lines of the morning. New Divisions of the enemy were constantly arriving and taking up positions, for this purpose marching in upon the various roads that terminate at the town, from the West and North. The position of the First Corps was then becoming perilous in the extreme, but it was improved a little before noon by the arrival upon the field of two Divisions of the Eleventh Corps (Gen. Howard), these Divisions commanded respectively by Generals Schurz and Barlow, who by order posted their commands to the right of the First Corps, with their right retired, forming an angle with the line of the First Corps. Between three and four o'clock in the afternoon the enemy, now in overwhelming force, resumed the battle, with spirit. The portion of the Eleventh Corps making but feeble opposition to the advancing enemy, soon began to fall back.

Back in disorganized masses they fled into the town, hotly pursued, and in lanes, in barns, in yards and cellars, throwing away their arms, they sought to hide like rabbits, and were there captured, unresisting, by hundreds.

The First Corps, deprived of this support, if support it could be called, outflanked upon either hand, and engaged in front, was compelled to yield the field. Making its last stand upon what is called "Seminary Ridge," not far from the town, it fell back in considerable confusion, through the South-west part of the town, making brave resistance, however, but with considerable loss. The enemy did not see fit to follow, or to attempt to, further than the town, and so the fight of the 1st of July closed here. I suppose our losses during the day would exceed four thousand, of whom a large number were prisoners. Such usually is the kind of loss sustained by the Eleventh Corps. You will remember that the old "Iron Brigade" is in the First Corps, and consequently shared this fight, and I hear their conduct praised on all hands.

In the 2nd Wis., Col. Fairchild lost his left arm; Lieut. Col. Stevens was mortally wounded, and Major Mansfield was wounded; Lieut.

Col. Callis, of the 7th Wis., and Lieut. Col. Dudley, of the 19th Ind., were badly, dangerously, wounded, the latter by the loss of his right leg above the knee.

I saw *"John Burns,"* the only citizen of Gettysburg who fought in the battle, and I asked him what troops he fought with. He said: "O, I pitched in with them Wisconsin fellers." I asked what sort of men they were, and he answered: "They fit terribly. The Rebs couldn't make anything of them fellers."

And so the brave 'compliment the brave. This man was touched by three bullets from the enemy, but not seriously wounded.

But the loss of the enemy to-day was severe also, probably in killed and wounded, as heavy as our own, but not so great in prisoners.

Of these latter, the "Iron Brigade" captured almost an entire Mississippi Brigade, however.

Of the events so far, of the 1st of July, I do not speak from personal knowledge. I shall now tell my introduction to these events.

At eleven o'clock A. M., on that day, the Second Corps was halted at Taneytown, which is thirteen miles from Gettysburg, South, and there awaiting orders, the men were allowed to make coffee and rest. At between one and two o'clock in the afternoon, a message was brought to Gen. Gibbon, requiring his immediate presence at the headquarters of Gen. Hancock, who commanded the Corps. I went with Gen. Gibbon, and we rode at a rapid gallop, to Gen. Hancock.

At Gen. Hancock's headquarters the following was learned: The First Corps had met the enemy at Gettysburg, and had possession of the town. Gen. Reynolds was badly, it was feared mortally, wounded; the fight of the First Corps still continued. By Gen. Meade's order, Gen. Hancock was to hurry forward and take command upon the field, of all troops there, or which should arrive there. The Eleventh Corps was near Gettysburg when the messenger who told of the fight left there, and the Third Corps was marching up, by order, on the Emmetsburg Road—Gen. Gibbon—he was not the ranking officer of the Second Corps after Hancock—was ordered to assume the command of the Second Corps.

All this was sudden, and for that reason at least, exciting; but there were other elements in this information, that aroused our profoundest interest. The great battle that we had so anxiously looked for during so many days, had at length opened, and it was a relief, in some sense, to have these accidents of time and place established. What would be the result? Might not the enemy fall upon and destroy the First Corps before succor could arrive?

Gen. Hancock, with his personal staff, at about two o'clock P. M., galloped off towards Gettysburg; Gen. Gibbon took his place in command of the Corps, appointing me his acting Assistant Adjutant General. The Second Corps took arms at once, and moved rapidly towards the field. It was not long before we began to hear the dull booming of the guns, and as we advanced, from many an eminence or opening among the trees, we could look out upon the white battery smoke, puffing up from the distant field of blood, and drifting up to the clouds. At these sights and sounds, the men looked more serious than before and were more silent, but they marched faster, and straggled less. At about five o'clock P. M., as we were riding along at the head of the column, we met an ambulance, accompanied by two or three mounted officers—we knew them to be staff officers of Gen. Reynolds—their faces told plainly enough what load the vehicle carried—it was the dead body of Gen. Reynolds. Very early in the action, while seeing personally to the formation of his lines under fire, he was shot through the head by a musket or rifle bullet, and killed almost instantly. His death at this time affected us much, for he was one of the *soldier* Generals of the army, a man whose soul was in his country's work, which he did with a soldier's high honor and fidelity.

I remember seeing him often at the first battle of Fredericksburg—he then commanded the First Corps—and while Meade's and Gibbon's Divisions were assaulting the enemy's works, he was the very beau ideal of the gallant general. Mounted upon a superb black horse, with his head thrown back and his great black eyes flashing fire, he was every where upon the field, seeing all things and giving commands in person. He died as many a friend, and many a foe to the country have died in this war.

Just as the dusk of evening fell, from Gen. Meade, the Second Corps had orders to halt, where the head of the column then was, and to go into position for the night. The Second Division (Gibbon's) was accordingly put in position, upon the left of the (Taneytown) road, its left near the South-eastern base of "Round Top"—of which mountain more anon—and the right near the road; the Third Division was posted upon the right of the road, abreast of the Second, and the first Division in the rear of these two—all facing towards Gettysburg.

Arms were stacked, and the men lay down to sleep, alas! many of them their last but the great final sleep upon the earth.

Late in the afternoon as we came near the field, from some slightly wounded men we met, and occasional stragglers from the scene of operations in front, we got many rumors, and much disjointed information of battle, of lakes of blood, of rout and panic and undescribable disaster, from all of which the narrators were just fortunate enough to have barely escaped, the sole survivors. These stragglers are always terrible liars!

About nine o'clock in the evening, while I was yet engaged in showing the troops their positions, I met Gen. Hancock, then on his way from the front, to Gen. Meade, who was back toward Taneytown; and he, for the purpose of having me advise Gen. Gibbon, for his information, gave me quite a detailed account of the situation of matters at Gettysburg, and of what had transpired subsequently to his arrival.

He had arrived and assumed command there, just when the troops of the First and Eleventh Corps, after their repulse, were coming in confusion through the town. Hancock is just the man for such an emergency as this. Upon horseback I think he was the most magnificent looking General in the whole Army of the Potomac at that time. With a large, well shaped person, always dressed with elegance, even upon that field of confusion, he would look as if he was "monarch of all he surveyed," and few of his subjects would dare to question his right to command, or do aught else but to obey. His quick eye, in a flash, saw what was to be done, and his voice and his royal right hand at once commenced to do it. Gen. Howard had put one of his Divisions—Steinwehr—with some batteries, in position, upon a commanding eminence, at the "Cemetery," which, as a reserve, had not participated in the fight of the day, and this Division was now of course steady. Around this Division the fugitives were stopped. and the shattered Brigades and Regiments, as they returned, were formed upon either flank, and faced toward the enemy again. A show of order at least, speedily came from chaos—the rout was at an end—the First and Eleventh Corps were in line of battle again—not very systematically formed perhaps—in a splendid position, and in a condition to offer resistance, should the enemy be willing to try them. These formations were all accomplished long before night. Then some considerable portion of the Third Corps—Gen. Sickles—came up by the Emmetsburg road, and was formed to the left of the Taneytown road, on an extension of the line that I have mentioned; and all the Twelfth Corps—Gen. Slocum—arriving before night, the Divisions were put in position, to the right of the troops already there, to the East of the Baltimore Pike. The enemy was in town, and behind it, and to the East and West, and appeared to be in strong force, and was jubilant over his day's success. Such was the posture of affairs as evening came on of the first of July. Gen. Hancock was hopeful, and in the best of spirits; and from him I also learned that the reason for halting the Second Corps in its present position, was that it was not then known where, in the coming fight, the line of battle would be formed, up near the town, where the troops then were, or further back towards Taneytown. He would give his views upon this subject to Gen. Meade, which were in favor of the line near the town—the one that was subsequently adopted—and Gen. Meade would determine.

The night before a great pitched battle would not ordinarily, I suppose, be a time for much sleep for Generals and their staff officers. We needed it enough, but there was work to be done. This war makes strange confusion of night and day! I did not sleep at all that night. It would, perhaps, be expected, on the eve of such great events, that one should have some peculiar sort of feeling, something extraordinary, some great arousing and excitement of the sensibilities and faculties, commensurate with the event itself; this certainly would be very poetical and pretty, but so far as I was concerned, and I think I can speak for the army in this matter, there was nothing of the kind. Men who had volunteered to fight the battles of the country, had met the enemy in many battles, and had been constantly before them, as had the Army of the Potomac, were too old soldiers and long ago too well had weighed chances and probabilities, to be so disturbed now. No, I believe, the army slept soundly that night, and well, and I am glad the men did, for they needed it.

At midnight Gen. Meade and staff rode by Gen. Gibbon's Head Quarters, on their way to the field; and in conversation with Gen. Gibbon, Gen. Meade announced that he had decided to assemble the whole army before Gettysburg, and offer the enemy battle there. The Second Corps would move at the earliest daylight, to take up its position.

At three o'clock, A. M., of the second of July, the sleepy soldiers of the Corps were aroused; before six the Corps was up to the field, and halted temporarily by the side of the Taneytown road, upon which it had marched, while some movements of the other troops were being made, to enable it to take position in the order of battle. The morning was thick and sultry, the sky overcast with low, vapory clouds. As we approached all was astir upon the crests near the Cemetery, and the work of preparation was speedily going on. Men looked like giants there in the mist, and the guns of the frowning batteries so big, that it was a relief to know that they were our friends.

Without a topographical map, some description of the ground and location is necessary to a clear understanding of the battle. With the sketch I have rudely drawn, without scale or compass, I hope you may understand my description. The line of battle as it was established, on the evening of the first, and morning of the second of July was in the form of the letter "U," the troops facing outwards. And the "Cemetery," which is at the point of the sharpest curvature of the line, being due South of the town of Gettysburg. "Round Top," the extreme left of the line, is a small, woody, rocky elevation, a very little West of South of the town, and nearly two miles from it.

The sides of this are in places very steep, and its rocky summit is almost inaccessible. A short distance North of this is a smaller elevation called "Little Round Top." On the very top of "Little Round Top," we had heavy rifled guns in position during the battle. Near the right of the line is a small, woody eminence, named "Culp's Hill." Three roads come up to the town from the South, which near the town are quite straight, and at the town the external ones unite, forming an angle of about sixty, or more degrees. Of these, the farthest to the East is the "Baltimore Pike," which passes by the East entrance to the Cemetery; the farthest to the West is the "Emmetsburg road," which is wholly outside of our line of battle, but near the Cemetery, is within a hundred yards of it; the "Taneytown road" is between these, running nearly due North and South, by the Eastern base of "Round Top," by the Western side of the Cemetery, and uniting with the Emmetsburg road between the Cemetery and the town. High ground near the Cemetery, is named "Cemetery Ridge."

The Eleventh Corps—Gen. Howard—was posted at the Cemetery, some of its batteries and troops, actually among the graves and monuments, which they used for shelter from the enemy's fire, its left resting upon the Taneytown road, extending thence to the East, crossing the Baltimore Pike, and thence bending backwards towards the South-east; on the right of the Eleventh came the First Corps, now, since the death of Gen. Reynolds, commanded by Gen. Newton, formed in a line curving still more towards the South. The troops of these two Corps, were re-formed on the morning of the second, in order that each might be by itself, and to correct some things not done well during the hasty formations here the day before.

To the right of the First Corps, and on an extension of the same line, along the crest and down the South-eastern slope of Culp's Hill, was posted the Twelfth Corps—Gen. Slocum—its right, which was the extreme right of the line of the army, resting near a small stream called "Rock Run." No changes, that I am aware of, occurred in the formation of this Corps, on the morning of the Second. The Second Corps, after the brief halt that I have mentioned, moved up and took position, its right resting upon the Taneytown road, at the left of the Eleventh Corps, and extending the line thence, nearly a half mile, almost due South, towards Round Top, with its Divisions in the following order, from right to left: The Third, Gen. Alex Hays; the Second (Gibbon's), Gen. Harrow, (temporarily); the First, Gen. Caldwell. The formation was in line by brigade in column, the brigade being in column by regiment, with forty paces interval between regimental lines, the Second and Third Divisions having each one, and the First Division, two brigades—there were four brigades in the First—similarly formed, in reserve, one hundred and fifty paces in the rear of the line of their respective Divisions. That is, the line of the Corps, exclusive of its reserves, was the length of six regiments, deployed,[1] and the intervals between them, some of which were left wide for the posting of the batteries, and consisted of four common deployed lines, each of two ranks of men, and a little more than one-third over in reserve.

The five batteries, in all twenty-eight guns, were posted as follows: Woodruff's regular, six twelve-pound Napoleon's, brass, between the two brigades, in line of the Third Division; Arnold's "A" first R. I., six three-inch Parrotts, rifled, and Cushing's Regular, four three-inch Ordnance, rifled, between the Third and Second Division; Hazard's, (commanded during the battle by Lieut. Brown,) "B" first R. I., and Rhorty's N. G. each, six twelve-pound Napoleon's, brass, between the Second and First Division.

I have been thus specific in the description of the posting and formation of the Second Corps, because they were works that I assisted to perform; and also that the other Corps were similarly posted, with reference to the strength of the lines, and the intermixing of infantry and artillery. From this, you may get a notion of the whole.

The Third Corps—Gen. Sickles—the remainder of it arriving upon the field this morning, was posted upon the left of the Second extending the line still in the direction of Round Top, with its left resting near "Little Round Top." The left of the Third Corps was the extreme left of the line of battle, until changes occurred, which will be mentioned in the proper place. The Fifth Corps—Gen. Sykes —coming on the Baltimore Pike about this time, was massed there, near the line of battle, and held in reserve until some time in the afternoon, when it changed position, as I shall describe.

I cannot give a detailed account of the cavalry, for I saw but little of it. It was posted near the wings, and watched the roads and the movements of the enemy upon the flanks of the enemy, but further than this participated but little in the battle. Some of it was also used for guarding the trains, which were far to the rear. The artillery reserve, which consisted of a good many batteries, were posted between the Baltimore Pike and the Taneytown road, on very nearly

---

[1] As the Second and Third Divisions had three brigades each, it follows that two brigades from each of the three divisions were in the front line.—T. L. L.

the center of a direct line passing through the extremities of the wings. Thus it could be readily sent to any part of the line. The Sixth Corps—Gen. Sedgwick—did not arrive upon the field until some time in the afternoon, but it was now not very far away, and was coming up rapidly on the Baltimore Pike. No fears were entertained that "Uncle John," as his men call Gen. Sedgwick, would not be in the right place at the right time.

These dispositions were all made early, I think before eight o'clock in the morning. Skirmishers were posted well out all around the line, and all put in readiness for battle. The enemy did not yet demonstrate himself. With a look at the ground now, I think you may understand the movements of the battle. From Round Top, by the line of battle, round to the extreme right, I suppose is about three miles. From this same eminence to the Cemetery, extends a long ridge or hill—more resembling a great wave than a hill, however—with its crest, which was the line of battle, quite direct, between the points mentioned. To the West of this, that is towards the enemy, the ground falls away by a very gradual descent, across the Emmetsburg road, and then rises again, forming another ridge, nearly parallel to the first, but inferior in altitude, and something over a thousand yards away. A belt of woods extends partly along this second ridge, and partly farther to the West, at distances of from one thousand to thirteen hundred yards away from our line. Between these ridges, and along their slopes, that is, in front of the Second and Third Corps, the ground is cultivated, and is covered with fields of wheat, now nearly ripe, with grass and pastures, with some peach orchards, with fields of waving corn, and some farm houses, and their out buildings along the Emmetsburg road. There are very few places within the limits mentioned where troops and guns could move concealed. There are some oaks of considerable growth, along the position of the right of the Second Corps, a group of small trees, sassafras and oak, in front of the right of the Second Division of this Corps also; and considerable woods immediately in front of the left of the Third Corps, and also to the West of, and near Round Top. At the Cemetery, where is Cemetery Ridge, to which the line of the Eleventh Corps conforms, is the highest point in our line, except Round Top. From this the ground falls quite abruptly to the town, the nearest point of which is some five hundred yards away from the line, and is cultivated, and checkered with stone fences.

The same is the character of the ground occupied by, and in front of the left of the First Corps, which is also on a part of Cemetery Ridge. The right of this Corps, and the whole of the Twelfth, are along Culp's Hill, and in woods, and the ground is very rocky, and in places in front precipitous—a most admirable position for defense from an attack in front, where, on account of the woods, no artillery could be used with effect by the enemy. Then these last three mentioned Corps, had, by taking rails, by appropriating stone fences, by felling trees, and digging the earth, during the night of the first of July, made for themselves excellent breast works, which were a very good thing indeed. The position of the First and Twelfth Corps was admirably strong, therefore. Within the line of battle is an irregular basin, somewhat woody and rocky in places, but presenting few obstacles to the moving of troops and guns, from place to place along the lines, and also affording the advantage that all such movements, by reason of the surrounding crests, were out of view of the enemy. On the whole this was an admirable position to fight a defensive battle, good enough, I thought, when I saw it first, and better I believe than could be found elsewhere in a circle of many miles. Evils, sometimes at least, are blessings in disguise, for the repulse of our forces, and the death of Reynolds, on the first of July, with the opportune arrival of Hancock to arrest the tide of fugitives and fix it on these heights, gave us this position—perhaps the position gave us the victory. On arriving upon the field, Gen. Meade established his headquarters at a shabby little farm house on the left of the Taneytown road, the house nearest the line, and a little more than five hundred yards in the rear of what became the center of the position of the Second Corps, a point where he could communicate readily and rapidly with all parts of the army. The advantages of the position, briefly, were these: the flanks were quite well protected by the natural defences there, Round Top up the left, and a rocky, steep, untraversable ground up the right. Our line was more elevated than that of the enemy, consequently our artillery had a greater range and power than theirs. On account of the convexity of our line, every part of the line could be reinforced by troops having to move a shorter distance than if the line were straight; further, for the same reason, the line of the enemy must be concave, and, consequently, longer, and with an equal force, thinner, and so weaker than ours. Upon those parts of our line which were wooded, neither we nor the enemy could use artillery; but they were so strong by nature, aided by art, as to be readily defended by a small, against a very large, body of infantry. When the line was open, it had the advantage of having open country in front, consequently, the enemy here could not surprise, as we were on a crest, which besides the other advantages that I have mentioned, had this: the enemy must advance to the attack up an ascent, and must therefore move slower, and be, before coming upon us, longer under our fire, as well as more exhausted. These, and some other things, rendered our position admirable—for a defensive battle.

So, before a great battle, was ranged the Army of the Potomac. The day wore on, the weather still sultry, and the sky overcast, with a mizzling effort at rain. When the audience has all assembled, time seems long until the curtain rises; so to-day. "Will there be a battle to-day?" "Shall we attack the Rebel?" "Will he attack us?" These and similar questions, later in the morning, were thought or asked a million times.

Meanwhile, on our part, all was put in the last state of readiness for battle. Surgeons were busy riding about selecting eligible places for Hospitals, and hunting streams, and springs, and wells. Ambulances, and ambulance men, were brought up near the lines, and stretchers gotten ready for use. Who of us could tell but that he would be the first to need them? The Provost Guards were busy driving up all stragglers, and causing them to join their regiments. Ammunition wagons were driven to suitable places, and pack mules bearing boxes of cartridges; and the commands were informed where they might be found. Officers were sent to see that the men had each his hundred rounds of ammunition. Generals and their Staffs were riding here and there among their commands to see that all was right. A staff officer, or an orderly might be seen galloping furiously in the transmission of some order or message.—All, all was ready—and yet the sound of no gun had disturbed the air or ear to-day.

And so the men stacked their arms—in long bristling rows they stood along the crests—and were at ease. Some men of the Second and Third Corps pulled down the rail fences near and piled them up for breastworks in their front. Some loitered, some went to sleep upon the ground, some, a single man, carrying twenty canteens slung over his shoulder, went for water. Some made them a fire and boiled a dipper of coffee. Some with knees cocked up, enjoyed the soldier's peculiar solace, a pipe of tobacco. Some were mirthful and chatty, and some were serious and silent. Leaving them thus—I suppose of all arms and grades there were about a hundred thousand of them somewhere about that field—each to pass the hour according to his duty or his humor, let us look to the enemy.

Here let me state, that according to the best information that I could get, I think a fair estimate of the Rebel force engaged in this battle would be a little upwards of a hundred thousand men of all arms. Of course we can't now know, but there are reasonable data for this estimate. At all events there was no great disparity of numbers in the two opposing armies. We thought the enemy to be somewhat more numerous than we, and he probably was.[2] But if ninety-five men should fight with a hundred and five, the latter would not always be victors—and slight numerical differences are of much less consequence in great bodies of men.

Skillful generalship and good fighting are the jewels of war. These concurring are difficult to overcome; and these, not numbers, must determine this battle.

During all the morning—and of the night, too—the skirmishers of the enemy had been confronting those of the Eleventh, First and Twelfth Corps. At the time of the fight of the First, he was seen in heavy force North of the town—he was believed to be now in the same neighborhood, in full force. But from the woody character of the country, and thereby the careful concealment of troops, which

[2] The returns of the Union army for June 30 gave 89,238 infantry and artillery, and 14,973 cavalry "present for duty." If there is deducted 5,520 in three brigades of the Sixth Corps and 2,337 in detachments, which, although available, were not opposed to the enemy, and the usual per cent of non-combatants, 88,289 remains for the number engaged.

The number engaged on the Confederate side in the same manner, is estimated at 75,000, from the returns of May 31, July 20 and 31. See Livermore's "Numbers and Losses," pp. 69, 102, 103.—T. L. L.

the Rebel is always sure to effect, during the early part of the morning almost nothing was actually seen by us of the invaders of the North. About nine o'clock in the morning, I should think, our glasses began to reveal them at the West and North-west of the town, a mile and a half away from our lines. They were moving towards our left, but the woods of Seminary Ridge so concealed them that we could not make out much of their movements. About this time some rifled guns in the Cemetery, at the left of the Eleventh Corps, opened fire—almost the first shots of any kind this morning—and when it was found they were firing at a Rebel line of skirmishers merely, that were advancing upon the left of that, and the right of the Second Corps, the officer in charge of the guns was ordered to cease firing, and was rebuked for having fired at all. These skirmishers soon engaged those at the right of the Second Corps, who stood their ground and were reinforced to make the line entirely secure. The Rebel skirmish line kept extending further and further to their right—toward our left. They would dash up close upon ours and sometimes drive them back a short distance, in turn to be repulsed themselves—and so they continued to do until their right was opposite the extreme left of the Third Corps. By these means they had ascertained the position and extent of our lines—but their own masses were still out of view. From the time that the firing commenced, as I have mentioned, it was kept up, among the skirmishers, until quite noon, often briskly; but with no definite results further than those mentioned, and with no considerable show of infantry on the part of the enemy to support. There was a farm house and outbuildings in front of the Third Division of the Second Corps at which the skirmishers of the enemy had made a dash, and dislodged ours posted there, and from there their sharp shooters began to annoy our line of skirmishers and even the main line, with their long range rifles. I was up to the line, and a bullet from one of the rascals hid there, hissed by my cheek so close that I felt the movement of the air distinctly. And so I was not at all displeased when I saw one of our regiments go down and attack and capture the house and buildings and several prisoners, after a spirited little fight, and, by Gen. Hays' order, burn the buildings to the ground. About noon the Signal Corps, from the top of Little Round Top, with their powerful glasses, and the cavalry at the extreme left, began to report the enemy in heavy force, making disposition of battle, to the West of Round Top, and opposite to the left of the Third Corps. Some few prisoners had been captured, some deserters from the enemy had come in, and from all sources, by this time, we had much important and reliable information of the enemy—of his disposition and apparent purposes. The Rebel infantry consisted of three Army Corps, each consisting of three Divisions, Longstreet, Ewell—the same whose leg Gibbon's shell knocked off at Gainesville on the 28th of August last year—and A. P. Hill, each in the Rebel service having the rank of Lieutenant General, were the commanders of these Corps. Longstreet's Division commanders were Hood, McLaws and Pickett; Ewell's were Rhodes, Early and Johnson, and Hill's were Pender, Heth and Anderson. Stewart and Fitzhugh Lee commanded Divisions of the Rebel cavalry. The rank of these Divisions commands, I believe, was that of Major General. The Rebels had about as much artillery as we did; but we never have thought much of this arm in the hands of our adversaries. They have courage enough, but not the skill to handle it well. They generally fire far too high, and the ammunition is usually of a very inferior quality. And, of late, we have begun to despise the enemies' cavalry too. It used to have enterprise and dash, but in the late cavalry contests ours have always been victor; and so now we think about all this *chivalry* is fit for is to steal a few of our mules occasionally, and their negro drivers. This army of the rebel infantry, however, is good— to deny this is useless. I never had any desire to—and if one should count up, it would possibly be found that they have gained more victories over us, than we have over them, and they will now, doubtless, fight well, even desperately. And it is not horses or cannon that will determine the result of this confronting of the two armies, but the men with the muskets must do it—the infantry must do the sharp work. So we watched all this posting of forces as closely as possible, for it was a matter of vital interest to us, and all information relating to it was hurried to the commander of the army. The Rebel line of battle was concave, bending around our own, with the extremities of the wings opposite to, or a little outside of ours. Longstreet's Corps was upon their right; Hill's in the center. These two Rebel

Corps occupied the second or inferior ridge to the West of our position, as I have mentioned, with Hill's left bending towards, and resting near the town, and Ewell's was upon their left, his troops being in, and to the East of the town. This last Corps confronted our Twelfth, First, and the right of the Eleventh Corps. When I have said that ours was a good *defensive* position, this is equivalent to saying that that of the enemy was not a good *offensive* one; for these are relative terms, and cannot be both predicated of the respective positions of the two armies at the same time. The reasons that this was not a good offensive position, are the same already stated in favor of ours for defense. Excepting, occasionally, for a brief time, during some movement of troops, as when advancing to attack, their men and guns were kept constantly and carefully, by woods and inequalities of ground, out of our view.

Noon is past, one o'clock is past, and, save the skirmishing that I have mentioned, and an occasional shot from our guns, at something or other, the nature of which the ones who fired it were ignorant, there was no fight yet. Our arms were still stacked, and the men were at ease. As I looked upon those interminable rows of muskets along the crests, and saw how cool and good spirited the men were, who were lounging about on the ground among them, I could not, and did not, have any fears as to the result of the battle. The storm was near, and we all knew it well enough by this time, which was to rain death upon these crests and down their slopes, and yet the men who could not, and would not escape it, were as calm and cheerful, generally, as if nothing unusual were about to happen. You see, these men were veterans, and had been in such places so often that they were accustomed to them. But I was well pleased with the tone of the men to-day—I could almost see the foreshadowing of victory upon their faces, I thought. And I thought, too, as I had seen the mighty preparations go on to completion for this great conflict—the marshaling of these two hundred thousand men and the guns of the hosts, that now but a narrow valley divided, that to have been in such a battle, and to survive on the side of the victors, would be glorious. Oh, the world is most unchristian yet!

Somewhat after one o'clock P. M.—the skirmish firing had nearly ceased now—a movement of the Third Corps occurred, which I shall describe. I cannot conjecture the reason of this movement. From the position of the Third Corps, as I have mentioned, to the second ridge West, the distance is about a thousand yards, and there the Emmetsburg road runs near the crest of the ridge. Gen. Sickles commenced to advance his whole Corps, from the general line, straight to the front, with a view to occupy this second ridge, along, and near the road. What his purpose could have been is past conjecture. It was not ordered by Gen. Meade, as I heard him say, and he disapproved of it as soon as it was made known to him. Generals Hancock and Gibbon, as they saw the move in progress, criticized its propriety sharply, as I know, and foretold quite accurately what would be the result. I suppose the truth probably is that General Sickles supposed he was doing for the best; but he was neither born nor bred a soldier. But one can scarcely tell what may have been the motives of such a man—a politician, and some other things, exclusive of the *Barton Key* affair—a man after show and notoriety, and newspaper fame, and the adulation of the mob! O, there is a grave responsibility on those in whose hands are the lives of ten thousand men; and on those who put stars upon men's shoulders, too! Bah! I kindle when I see some things that I have to see. But this move of the Third Corps was an important one—it developed the battle—the results of the move to the Corps itself we shall see. O, if this Corps had kept its strong position upon the crest, and supported by the rest of the army, had waited for the attack of the enemy!

It was magnificent to see those ten or twelve thousand men[3]— they were good men—with their batteries, and some squadrons of cavalry upon the left flank, all in battle order, in several lines, with flags streaming, sweep steadily down the slope, across the valley, and up the next ascent, toward their destined position! From our position we could see it all. In advance Sickles pushed forward his heavy line of skirmishers, who drove back those of the enemy, across the Emmetsburg road, and thus cleared the way for the main body. The Third Corps now became the absorbing object

[3] The returns give 12,630 "present for duty" in the Third Corps. See 43 War Records, 151.—T. L. L.

of interest of all eyes. The Second Corps took arms, and the 1st Division of this Corps was ordered to be in readiness to support the Third Corps, should circumstances render support necessary. As the Third Corps was the extreme left of our line, as it advanced, if the enemy was assembling to the West of Round Top with a view to turn our left, as we had heard, there would be nothing between the left flank of the Corps and the enemy, and the enemy would be square upon its flank by the time it had attained the road. So when this advance line came near the Emmetsburg road, and we saw the squadrons of cavalry mentioned, come dashing back from their position as flankers, and the smoke of some guns, and we heard the reports away to Sickles' left, anxiety became an element in our interest in these movements. The enemy opened slowly at first, and from long range; but he was square upon Sickles' left flank. General Caldwell was ordered at once to put his Division— the 1st of the Second Corps, as mentioned—in motion, and to take post in the woods at the left slope of Round Top, in such a manner as to resist the enemy should he attempt to come around Sickles' left and gain his rear. The Division moved as ordered, and disappeared from view in the woods, towards the point indicated at between two and three o'clock P. M., and the reserve brigade—the First, Col. Heath temporarily commanding—of the Second Division, was therefore moved up and occupied the position vacated by the Third Division. About the same time the Fifth Corps could be seen marching by the flank from its position on the Baltimore Pike, and in the opening of the woods heading for the same locality where the 1st Division of the Second Corps had gone. The Sixth Corps had now come up and was halted upon the Baltimore Pike. So the plot thickened. As the enemy opened upon Sickles with his batteries, some five or six in all, I suppose, firing slowly, Sickles with as many replied, and with much more spirit. The artillery fire became quite animated, soon; but the enemy was forced to withdraw his guns farther and farther away, and ours advanced upon him. It was not long before the cannonade ceased altogether, the enemy having retired out of range, and Sickles, having temporarily halted his command, pending this, moved forward again to the position he desired, or nearly that. It was now about five o'clock, and we shall soon see what Sickles gained by his move. First we hear more artillery firing upon Sickles' left—the enemy seems to be opening again, and as we watch the Rebel batteries seem to be advancing there. The cannonade is soon opened again, and with great spirit upon both sides. The enemy's batteries press those of Sickles, and pound the shot upon them, and this time they in turn begin to retire to position nearer the infantry. The enemy seems to be fearfully in earnest this time. And what is more ominous than the thunder or the shot of his advancing guns, this time, in the intervals between his batteries, far to Sickles' left, appear the long lines and the columns of the Rebel infantry, now unmistakably moving out to the attack. The position of the Third Corps becomes at once one of great peril, and it is probable that its commander by this time began to realize his true situation. All was astir now on our crest. Generals and their Staffs were galloping hither and thither—the men were all in their places, and you might have heard the rattle of ten thousand ramrods as they drove home and "thugged" upon the little globes and cones of lead. As the enemy was advancing upon Sickles' flank, he commenced a change, or at least a partial one, of front, by swinging back his left and throwing forward his right, in order that his lines might be parallel to those of his adversary, his batteries meantime doing what they could to check the enemy's advance; but this movement was not completely executed before new Rebel batteries opened upon Sickles' right flank—his former front—and in the same quarter appeared the Rebel infantry also. Now came the dreadful battle picture, of which we for a time could be but spectators. Upon the front and right flank of Sickles came sweeping the infantry of Longstreet and Hill. Hitherto there had been skirmishing and artillery practice—now the battle began; for amid the heavier smoke and larger tongues of flame of the batteries, now began to appear the countless flashes, and the long fiery sheets of the muskets, and the rattle of the volleys, mingled with the thunder of the guns. We see the long gray lines come sweeping down upon Sickles' front, and mix with the battle smoke; now the same colors emerge from the bushes and orchards upon his right, and envelope his flank in the confusion of the conflict.

O, the din and the roar, and these thirty thousand Rebel wolf cries! What a hell is there down that valley!

These ten or twelve thousand men of the Third Corps fight well, but it soon becomes apparent that they must be swept from the field, or perish there where they are doing so well, so thick and overwhelming a storm of Rebel fire involves them. It was fearful to see, but these men, such as ever escape, must come from that conflict as best they can. To move down and support them with other troops is out of the question, for this would be to do as Sickles did, to relinquish a good position, and advance to a bad one. There is no other alternative—the Third Corps must fight itself out of its position of destruction! What was it ever put there for?

In the meantime some other dispositions must be made to meet the enemy, in the event that Sickles is overpowered. With this Corps out of the way, the enemy would be in a position to advance upon the line of the Second Corps, not in a line parallel with its front, but they would come obliquely from the left. To meet this contingency the left of the Second Division of the Second Corps is thrown back slightly, and two Regiments, the 15th Mass., Col. Ward, and the 82nd N. Y., Lieut. Col. Horton, are advanced down to the Emmetsburg road, to a favorable position nearer us than the fight has yet come, and some new batteries from the artillery reserve are posted upon the crest near the left of the Second Corps. This was all Gen. Gibbon could do. Other dispositions were made or were now being made upon the field, which I shall mention presently. The enemy is still giving Sickles fierce battle—or rather the Third Corps, for Sickles has been borne from the field minus one of his legs, and Gen. Birney now commands—and we of the Second Corps, a thousand yards away, with our guns and men are, and must be, still idle spectators of the fight.

The Rebel, as anticipated, tries to gain the left of the Third Corps, and for this purpose is now moving into the woods at the west of Round Top. We knew what he would find there. No sooner had the enemy gotten a considerable force into the woods mentioned, in the attempted execution of his purpose, than the roar of the conflict was heard there also. The Fifth Corps and the First Division of the Second were there at the right time, and promptly engaged him; and there, too, the battle soon became general and obstinate. Now the roar of battle has become twice the volume that it was before, and its range extends over more than twice the space. The Third Corps has been pressed back considerably, and the wounded are streaming to the rear by hundreds, but still the battle there goes on, with no considerable abatement on our part. The field of actual conflict extends now from a point to the front of the left of the Second Corps, away down to the front of Round Top, and the fight rages with the greatest fury. The fire of artillery and infantry and the yells of the Rebels fill the air with a mixture of hideous sounds. When the First Division of the Second Corps first engaged the enemy, for a time it was pressed back somewhat, but under the able and judicious management of Gen. Caldwell, and the support of the Fifth Corps, it speedily ceased to retrograde, and stood its ground; and then there followed a time, after the Fifth Corps became well engaged, when from appearances we hoped the troops already engaged would be able to check entirely, or repulse the further assault of the enemy. But fresh bodies of the Rebels continued to advance out of the woods to the front of the position of the Third Corps, and to swell the numbers of the assailants of this already hard pressed command. The men there begin to show signs of exhaustion—their ammunition must be nearly expended—they have now been fighting more than an hour, and against greatly superior numbers. From the sound of the firing at the extreme left, and the place where the smoke rises above the tree tops there, we know that the Fifth Corps is still steady, and holding its own there; and as we see the Sixth Corps now marching and near at hand to that point, we have no fears for the left—we have more apparent reason to fear for ourselves.

The Third Corps is being overpowered—here and there its lines begin to break—the men begin to pour back to the rear in confusion—the enemy are close upon them and among them—organization is lost to a great degree—guns and caissons are abandoned and in the hands of the enemy—the Third Corps, after a heroic but unfortunate fight, is being literally swept from the field. That Corps gone, what is there between the Second Corps, and these yelling masses of the enemy? Do you not think that by this time we began to feel a personal interest in this fight? We did indeed. We had been mere observers—the time was at hand when we must be actors in this drama.

Up to this hour Gen. Gibbon had been in command of the Second Corps, since yesterday, but Gen. Hancock, relieved of his duties elsewhere, now assumed command. Five or six hundred yards away the Third Corps was making its last opposition; and the enemy was hotly pressing his advantages there, and throwing in fresh troops whose line extended still more along our front, when Generals Hancock and Gibbon rode along the lines of their troops; and at once cheer after cheer—not Rebel, mongrel cries, but genuine cheers—rang out all along the line, above the roar of battle, for "Hancock" and "Gibbon," and "our Generals." These were good. Had you heard their voices, you would have known these men would fight. Just at this time we saw another thing that made us glad:— we looked to our rear, and there, and all up the hillside which was the rear of the Third Corps before it went forward, were rapidly advancing large bodies of men from the extreme right of our line of battle, coming to the support of the part now so hotly pressed. There was the whole Twelfth Corps, with the exception of about one brigade, that is, the larger portion of the Divisions of Gens. Williams and Geary; the Third Division of the First Corps, Gen. Doubleday; and some other brigades from the same Corps—and some of them were moving at the double quick. They formed lines of battle at the foot of the Taneytown road, and when the broken fragments of the Third Corps were swarming by them towards the rear, without halting or wavering they came sweeping up, and with glorious old cheers, under fire, took their places on the crest in line of battle to the left of the Second Corps. Now Sickles' blunder is repaired. Now, Rebel chief, hurl forward your howling lines and columns! Yell out your loudest and your last, for many of your best will never yell, or wave the spurious flag again!

The battle still rages all along the left, where the Fifth Corps is, and the West slope of Round Top is the scene of the conflict; and nearer us there was but short abatement, as the last of the Third Corps retired from the field, for the enemy is flushed with his success. He has been throwing forward brigade after brigade, and Division after Division, since the battle began, and his advancing line now extends almost as far to our right as the right of the Second Division of the Second Corps. The whole slope in our front is full of them; and in various formation, in line, in column, and in masses which are neither, with yells and thick volleys, they are rushing towards our crest. The Third Corps is out of the way. Now we are in for it. The battery men are ready by their loaded guns. All along the crest is ready. Now Arnold and Brown—now Cushing, and Woodruff, and Rhorty!—you three shall survive to-day! They drew the cords that moved the friction primers, and gun after gun, along the batteries, in rapid succession, leaped where it stood and bellowed its canister upon the enemy. The enemy still advance. The infantry open fire—first the two advance regiments, the 15th Mass. and the 82d N. Y.—then here and there throughout the length of the long line, at the points where the enemy comes nearest, and soon the whole crest, artillery and infantry, is one continued sheet of fire. From Round Top to near the Cemetery stretches an uninterrupted field of conflict. There is a great army upon each side, now hotly engaged.

To see the fight, while it went on in the valley below us, was terrible,—what must it be now, when we are in it, and it is all around us, in all its fury?

All senses for the time are dead but the one of sight. The roar of the discharges and the yells of the enemy all pass unheeded; but the impassioned soul is all eyes, and sees all things, that the smoke does not hide. How madly the battery men are driving home the double charges of canister in those broad-mouthed Napoleons, whose fire seems almost to reach the enemy. How rapidly these long, blue-coated lines of infantry deliver their file fire down the slope.

But there is no faltering—the men stand nobly to their work. Men are dropping dead or wounded on all sides, by scores and by hundreds, and the poor mutilated creatures, some with an arm dangling, some with a leg broken by a bullet, are limping and crawling towards the rear. They make no sound of complaint or pain, but are as silent as if dumb and mute. A sublime heroism seems to pervade all, and the intuition that to lose that crest, all is lost. How our officers, in the work of cheering on and directing the men, are falling.

We have heard that Gen. Zook and Col. Cross, in the First Division of our Corps, are mortally wounded—they both commanded brigades,—now near us Col. Ward of the 15th Mass.—he lost a leg at Balls Bluff—and Lieut. Col. Horton of the 82d N. Y., are mortally struck while trying to hold their commands, which are being forced back; Col. Revere, 20th Mass., grandson of old Paul Revere, of the Revolution, is killed, Lieut. Col. Max Thoman, commanding 59th N. Y., is mortally wounded, and a host of others that I cannot name. These were of Gibbon's Division. Lieut. Brown is wounded among his guns—his position is a hundred yards in advance of the main line—the enemy is upon his battery, and he escapes, but leaves three of his six guns in the hands of the enemy.

The fire all along our crest is terrific, and it is a wonder how anything human could have stood before it, and yet the madness of the enemy drove them on, clear up to the muzzle of the guns, clear up to the lines of our infantry—but the lines stood right in their places. Gen. Hancock and his Aides rode up to Gibbon's Division, under the smoke. Gen. Gibbon, with myself, was near, and there was a flag dimly visible, coming towards us from the direction of the enemy. "Here, what are these men falling back for?" said Hancock. The flag was no more than fifty yards away, but it was the head of a Rebel column, which at once opened fire with a volley. Lieut. Miller, Gen. Hancock's Aide, fell, twice struck, but the General was unharmed, and he told the 1st Minn., which was near, to drive these people away. That splendid regiment, the less than three hundred that are left out of fifteen hundred that it has had, swings around upon the enemy, gives them a volley in their faces, and advances upon them with the bayonet. The Rebels fled in confusion, but Col. Colville, Lieut. Col. Adams and Major Downie, are all badly, dangerously wounded, and many of the other officers and men will never fight again. More than two-thirds fell.

Such fighting as this cannot last long. It is now near sundown, and the battle has gone on wonderfully long already. But if you will stop to notice it, a change has occurred. The Rebel cry has ceased, and the men of the Union begin to shout there, under the smoke, and their lines to advance. See, the Rebels are breaking! They are in confusion in all our front! The wave has rolled upon the rock, and the rock has smashed it. Let us shout, too!

First upon their extreme left the Rebels broke, where they had almost pierced our lines; thence the repulse extended rapidly to their right. They hung longest about Round Top, where the Fifth Corps punished them, but in a space of time incredibly short, after they first gave signs of weakness, the whole force of the Rebel assault along the whole line, in spite of waving red flags, and yells, and the entreaties of officers, and the pride of the chivalry, fled like chaff before the whirlwind, back down the slope, over the valley, across the Emmetsburg road, shattered, without organization in utter confusion, fugitive into the woods, and victory was with the arms of the Republic. The great Rebel assault, the greatest ever made upon this continent, has been made and signally repulsed, and upon this part of the field the fight of to-day is now soon over. Pursuit was made as rapidly and as far as practicable, but owing to the proximity of night, and the long distance which would have to be gone over before any of the enemy, where they would be likely to halt, could be overtaken, further success was not attainable to-day. Where the Rebel rout first commenced, a large number of prisoners, some thousands at least, were captured; almost all their dead, and such of their wounded as could not themselves get to the rear, were within our lines; several of their flags were gathered up, and a good many thousand muskets, some nine or ten guns and some caissons lost by the Third Corps, and the three of Brown's battery—these last were in Rebel hands but a few minutes—were all safe now with us, the enemy having had no time to take them off.

Not less, I estimate, than twenty thousand men were killed or wounded in this fight. Our own losses must have been nearly half this number,—about four thousand in the Third Corps, fully two thousand in the Second, and I think two thousand in the Fifth, and I think the losses of the First, Twelfth, and a little more than a brigade of the Sixth—all of that Corps which was actually engaged

—would reach nearly two thousand more.[4] Of course it will never be possible to know the numbers upon either side who fell in this particular part of the general battle, but from the position of the enemy and his numbers, and the appearance of the field, his loss must have been as heavy, or as I think much heavier than our own, and my estimates are probably short of the actual loss.

The fight done, the sudden revulsions of sense and feeling follow, which more or less characterize all similar occasions. How strange the stillness seems! The whole air roared with the conflict but a moment since—now all is silent; not a gunshot sound is heard, and the silence comes distinctly, almost painfully to the senses. And the sun purples the clouds in the West, and the sultry evening steals on as if there had been no battle, and the furious shout and the cannon's roar had never shaken the earth. And how look these fields? We may see them before dark—the ripening grain, the luxuriant corn, the orchards, the grassy meadows, and in their midst the rural cottage of brick or wood. They were beautiful this morning. They are desolate now—trampled by the countless feet of the combatants, plowed and scored by the shot and shell, the orchards splintered, the fences prostrate, the harvest trodden in the mud. And more dreadful than the sight of all this, thickly strewn over all their length and breadth, are the habiliments of the soldiers, the knapsacks cast aside in the stress of the fight, or after the fatal lead had struck; haversacks, yawning with the rations the owner will never call for; canteens of cedar of the Rebel men of Jackson, and of cloth-covered tin of the men of the Union; blankets and trowsers, and coats, and caps, and some are blue and some are gray; muskets and ramrods, and bayonets, and swords, and scabbards and belts, some bent and cut by the shot or shell; broken wheels, exploded caissons, and limber-boxes, and dismantled guns, and all these are sprinkled with blood; horses, some dead, a mangled heap of carnage, some alive, with a leg shot clear off, or other frightful wounds, appealing to you with almost more than brute gaze as

---

[4] The returns give the total loss in the battle as follows: 1,275 in First Division of Second Corps; 4,211 in Third Corps; 2,187 in Fifth Corps; 242 in Sixth Corps. Substantially all these losses were suffered July 2. See 43 War Records. The losses in the First Corps and Second Division of Second Corps on July 2 cannot be separated from those of July 1 and 3 in the War Records.—T. L. L.

you pass; and last, but not least numerous, many thousands of men—and there was no rebellion here now—the men of South Carolina were quiet by the side of those of Massachusetts, some composed, with upturned faces, sleeping the last sleep, some mutilated and frightful, some wretched, fallen, bathed in blood, survivors still and unwilling witnesses of the rage of Gettysburg.

And yet with all this before them, as darkness came on, and the dispositions were made and the outposts thrown out for the night, the Army of the Potomac was quite mad with joy. No more light-hearted guests ever graced a banquet, than were these men as they boiled their coffee and munched their soldiers' supper to-night. Is it strange?

Otherwise they would not have been soldiers. And such sights as all these, will be certain to be seen as long as war lasts in the world, and when war is done, then is the end and the days of the millenium are at hand.

The ambulances commenced their work as soon as the battle opened—the twinkling lanterns through the night, and the sun of to-morrow saw them still with the same work unfinished.

I wish that I could write, that with the coming on of darkness, ended the fight of to-day, but such was not the case. The armies have fought enough to-day and ought to sleep to-night, one would think, but not so thought the Rebel. Let us see what he gained by his opinion. When the troops, including those of the Twelfth Corps had been withdrawn from the extreme right of our line, in the afternoon, to support the left, as I have mentioned, thereby, of course, weakening that part of the line so left, the Rebel Ewell, either becoming aware of the fact, or because he thought he could carry our right at all events, late in the afternoon commenced an assault upon that part of our line. His battle had been going on there simultaneously with the fight on the left, but not with any great degree of obstinacy on his part. He had advanced his men through the woods, and in front of the formidable position lately held by the Twelfth Corps cautiously, and to his surprise, I have no doubt, found our strong defenses upon the extreme right, entirely abandoned. These he at once took possession of, and simultaneously made an attack upon our right flank, which was now near the summit of Culp's hill, and upon the front of that part of the line. That small portion of the Twelfth Corps, which had been left there, and some of the Eleventh Corps, sent to their assistance, did what they could to check the Rebels; but the Eleventh Corps men were getting shot at there, and they did not want to stay. Matters began to have a bad look in that part of the field. A portion of the First Division of the First Corps, was sent there for support—the 6th Wisconsin, among others, and this improved matters—but still, as we had but a small number of men there, all told, the enemy with their great numbers, were having too much prospect of success, and it seems that, probably emboldened by this, Ewell had resolved upon a night attack upon that wing of the army, and was making his dispositions accordingly. The enemy had not at sundown, actually carried any part of our rifle pits there, save the ones abandoned, but he was getting troops assembled upon our flank, and altogether, with our weakness there, at that time, matters did not look as we would like to have them. Such was then the posture of affairs, when the fight upon our left, that I have described, was done. Under such circumstances it is not strange that the Twelfth Corps, as soon as its work was done upon the left, was quickly ordered back to the right, to its old position. There it arrived in good time; not soon enough, of course, to avoid the mortification of finding the enemy in the possession of a part of the works the men had labored so hard to construct, but in ample time before dark to put the men well in the pits we already held, and to take up a strong defensible position, at right angles to, and in rear of the main line, in order to resist these flanking dispositions of the enemy. The army was secure again. The men in the works would be steady against all attacks in front, as long as they knew that their flank was safe. Until between ten and eleven o'clock at night, the woods upon the right, resounded with the discharges of musketry. Shortly after or about dark, the enemy made a dash upon the right of the Eleventh Corps. They crept up the windings of a valley, not in a very heavy force, but from the peculiar mode in which this Corps does outpost duty, quite unperceived in the dark until they were close upon the main line. It is said, I do not know it to be true, that they spiked two guns of one of the Eleventh Corps' batteries, and that the battery men had to drive them off with their sabres and rammers, and that there was some fearful "Dutch" swearing on the occasion, *"donner wetter"* among other similar impious oaths, having been freely used. The enemy here were finally repulsed by the assistance of Col. Correll's brigade of the Third Division of the Second Corps, and the 106th Pa., from the Second Division of the same Corps, was by Gen. Howard's request sent there to do outpost duty. It seems to have been a matter of utter madness and folly on the part of the enemy to have continued their night attack, as they did upon the right. Our men were securely covered by ample works and even in most places, a log was placed a few inches above the top of the main breastwork, as a protection to the heads of the men as they thrust out their pieces beneath it to fire. Yet in the darkness, the enemy would rush up, clambering over rocks and among trees, even to the front of the works, but only to leave their riddled bodies there upon the ground or to be swiftly repulsed headlong into the woods again. In the darkness the enemy would climb trees close to the works, and endeavor to shoot our men by the light of the flashes. When discovered, a thousand bullets would whistle after them in the dark, and some would hit, and then the Rebel would make up his mind to come down.

Our loss was light, almost nothing in this fight—the next morning the enemy's dead were thick all along this part of the line. Near eleven o'clock the enemy, wearied with his disastrous work, desisted, and thereafter until morning, not a shot was heard in all the armies.

So much for the battle. There is another thing that I wish to mention, of the matters of the 2d of July.

After evening came on, and from reports received, all was known to be going satisfactorily upon the right, Gen. Meade summoned his Corps Commanders to his Headquarters for consultation. A consultation is held upon matters of vast moment to the country, and that poor little farmhouse is honored with more distinguished guests than it ever had before, or than it will ever have again, probably.

Do you expect to see a degree of ceremony, and severe military aspect characterize this meeting, in accordance with strict military rules, and commensurate with the moment of the matters of their deliberation? Name it "Major General Meade, Commander of the Army of the Potomac, with his Corps Generals, holding a Council of War, upon the field of Gettysburg," and it would sound pretty well,—and that was what it was; and you might make a picture of it and hang it up by the side of "Napoleon and his Marshals," and "Washington and his Generals," maybe, at some future time. But for the artist to draw his picture from, I will tell how this council appeared. Meade, Sedgwick, Slocum, Howard, Hancock, Sykes, Newton, Pleasanton—commander of the cavalry—and Gibbon, were the Generals present. Hancock, now that Sickles is wounded, has charge of the Third Corps, and Gibbon again has the Second. Meade is a tall, spare man, with full beard, which with his hair, originally brown, is quite thickly sprinkled with gray—has a Roman-ish face, very large nose, and a white, large forehead, prominent and wide over the eyes, which are full and large, and quick in their movements, and he wears spectacles. His *fibres* are all of the long and sinewy kind. His habitual personal appearance is quite care-less, and it would be rather difficult to make him look well dressed. Sedgwick is quite a heavy man, short, thick-set and muscular, with florid complexion, dark, calm, straight-looking eyes, with full, heavyish features, which, with his eyes, have plenty of animation when he is aroused. He has a magnificent profile, well cut, with the nose and forehead forming almost a straight line, curly, short, chestnut hair and full beard, cut short, with a little gray in it. He dresses carelessly, but can look magnificently when he is well dressed. Like Meade, he looks and is, honest and modest. You might see at once, why his men, because they love him, call him "Uncle John," not to his face, of course, but among themselves. Slocum is small, rather spare, with black, straight hair and beard, which latter is unshaven and thin, large, full, quick, black eyes, white skin, sharp nose, wide cheek bones, and hollow cheeks and small chin. His movements are quick and angular, and he dresses with a sufficient degree of elegance. Howard is medium in size, has nothing marked about him, is the youngest of them all, I think—has lost an arm in the war, has straight brown hair and beard, shaves his short upper lip, over which his nose slants down, dim blue eyes, and on the whole, appears a very pleasant, affable, well dressed little gentleman. Hancock is the tallest and most shapely, and in many respects is the best looking officer of them all. His hair is very light brown, straight and moist, and always looks well, his beard is of the same color, of which he wears the moustache and a tuft upon the chin; complexion ruddy, features neither large nor small, but well cut, with full jaw and chin, compressed mouth, straight nose, full, deep blue eyes, and a very mobile, emotional countenance. He always dresses remarkably well, and his manner is dignified, gentlemanly and commanding. I think if he were in citizens' clothes, and should give commands in the army to those who did not know him, he would be likely to be obeyed at once, and without any question as to his right to command. Sykes is a small, rather thin man, well dressed and gentlemanly, brown hair and beard, which he wears full, with a red, pinched, rough-looking skin, feeble blue eyes, long nose, with the general air of one who is weary and a little ill-natured. Newton is a well-sized, shapely, muscular, well dressed man, with brown hair, with a very ruddy, clean-shaved, full face, blue eyes, blunt, round features, walks very erect, curbs in his chin, and has somewhat of that smart sort of swagger that people are apt to suppose characterizes soldiers. Pleasonton is quite a nice little dandy, with brown hair and beard, a straw hat with a little jockey rim, which he cocks upon one side of his head, with an unsteady eye, that looks slyly at you and then dodges. Gibbon, the youngest of them all, save Howard, is about the same size as Slocum, Howard, Sykes and Pleasonton, and there are none of these who will weigh one hundred and fifty pounds. He is compactly made, neither spare nor corpulent, with ruddy complexion, chestnut brown hair, with a clean-shaved face, except his moustache, which is decidedly reddish in color, medium-sized, well-shaped head, sharp, moderately-jutting brow, deep blue, calm eyes, sharp, slightly aquiline nose, compressed mouth, full jaws and chin, with an air of calm firmness in his manner. He always looks well dressed. I suppose Howard is about thirty-five and Meade about forty-five years of age; the rest are between these ages, but not many under forty. As they come to the council now, there is the appearance of fatigue about them, which is not customary, but is only due to the hard labors of the past few days. They all wear clothes of dark blue, some have top boots and some not, and except the two-starred straps upon the shoulders of all save Gibbon, who has but one star, there was scarcely a piece of regulation uniform about them all. They wore their swords, of various patterns, but no sashes, the Army hat, but with the crown pinched into all sorts of shapes and the rim slouched down and shorn of all its ornaments but the gilt band—except Sykes who wore a blue cap, and Pleasonton with his straw hat with broad black band. Then the mean little room where they met,—its only furniture consisted of a large, wide bed in one corner, a small pine table in the center, upon which was a wooden pail of water, with a tin cup for drinking, and a candle, stuck to the table by putting the end in tallow melted down from the wick, and five or six straight-backed rush-bottomed chairs. The Generals came in—some sat, some kept walking or standing, two lounged upon the bed, some were constantly smoking cigars. And thus disposed, they deliberated whether the army should fall back from its present position to one in rear which it was said was stronger, should attack the enemy on the morrow, wherever he could be found, or should stand there upon the horse-shoe crest, still on the defensive, and await the further movements of the enemy.

The latter proposition was unanimously agreed to. Their heads were sound. The Army of the Potomac would just halt right there, and allow the Rebel to come up and smash his head against it, to any reasonable extent he desired, as he had to-day. After some two hours the council dissolved, and the officers went their several ways.

Night, sultry and starless, droned on, and it was almost midnight that I found myself peering my way from the line of the Second Corps, back down to the General's Headquarters, which were an ambulance in the rear, in a little peach orchard. All was silent now but the sound of the ambulances, as they were bringing off the wounded, and you could hear them rattle here and there about the field, and see their lanterns. I am weary and sleepy, almost to such an extent as not to be able to sit on my horse. And my horse can hardly move—the spur will not start him—what can be the reason? I know that he has been touched by two or three bullets to-day, but not to wound or lame him to speak of. Then, in riding by a horse that is hitched, in the dark, I got kicked; had I not a very thick boot, the blow would have been likely to have broken my ankle—it did break my temper as it was—and, as if it would cure matters, I foolishly spurred my horse again. No use, he would but walk. I dismounted; I could not lead him along at all, so out of temper I rode at the slowest possible walk to the Headquarters, which I reached at last. Generals Hancock and Gibbon were asleep in the ambulance. With a light I found what was the matter with "Billy." A bullet had entered his chest just in front of my left leg," as I was mounted, and the blood was running down all his side and leg, and the air from his lungs came out of the bullet-hole. I begged his pardon mentally for my cruelty in spurring him, and should have done so in words if he could have understood me. Kind treatment as is due to the wounded he could understand and he had it. Poor Billy! He and I were first under fire together, and I rode him at the second Bull Run and the first and second Fredericksburg, and at Antietam after brave "Joe" was killed; but I shall never mount him again—Billy's battles are over.

"George, make my bed here upon the ground by the side of this ambulance. Pull off my sabre and my boots—that will do!" Was ever princely couch or softest down so soft as those rough blankets, there upon the unroofed sod? At midnight they received me for four hours delicious dreamless oblivion of weariness and of battle. So to me, ended the Second of July.

At four o'clock on the morning of the Third, I was awakened by Gen. Gibbon's pulling me by the foot and saying: "Come, don't you hear that?" I sprang up to my feet. Where was I? A moment and my dead senses and memory were alive again, and the sound of brisk firing of musketry to the front and right of the Second Corps, and over at the extreme right of our line, where we heard it last in the night, brought all back to my memory. We surely were on the field of battle, and there were palpable evidences to my reason that to-day was to be another of blood. Oh! for a moment the thought of it was sickening to every sense and feeling! But the motion of my horse as I galloped over the crest a few minutes later, and the serene splendor of the morning now breaking through rifted clouds and spreading over the landscape soon reassured me. Come day of battle! Up Rebel hosts, and thunder with your arms! We are all ready to do and to die for the Republic!

I found a sharp skirmish going on in front of the right of the Second Corps, between our outposts and those of the enemy, but save this—and none of the enemy but his outposts were in sight—all was quiet in that part of the field. On the extreme right of the line the sound of musketry was quite heavy; and this I learned was brought on by the attack of the Second Division, Twelfth Corps, Gen. Geary, upon the enemy in order to drive him out of our works which he had sneaked into yesterday, as I have mentioned. The attack was made at the earliest moment in the morning when it was light enough to discern objects to fire at. The enemy could not use the works, but was confronting Geary in woods, and had the cover of many rocks and trees, so the fight was an irregular one, now breaking out and swelling to a vigorous fight, now subsiding to a few scattering shots; and so it continued by turns until the morning was well advanced, when the enemy was finally wholly repulsed and driven from the pits, and the right of our line was again re-established in the place it first occupied. The heaviest losses the Twelfth Corps sustained in all the battle, occurred during this attack, and they were here quite severe. I heard Gen. Meade express dissatisfaction at Gen. Geary for making this attack, as a thing not ordered and not necessary, as the works of ours were of no intrinsic importance, and had not been captured from us by a fight, and Geary's position was just as good as they, where he was during the night. And I heard Gen. Meade say that he sent an order to have the fight stopped; but I believe the order was not communicated to Geary until after the repulse of the enemy. Late in the forenoon the enemy again tried to carry our right by storm. We heard that old Rebel Ewell had sworn an oath that he would break our right. He had Stonewall Jackson's Corps, and possibly imagined himself another Stonewall, but he certainly *hankered* after the right of our line—and so up through the woods, and over the rocks, and up the steeps he sent his storming parties—our men could see them now in the day time. But all the Rebel's efforts were fruitless, save in one thing, slaughter to his own men. These assaults were made with great spirit and determination, but as the enemy would come up, our men lying behind their secure defenses would just singe them with the blaze of their muskets, and riddle them, as a hail storm, the tender blades of corn. The Rebel oath was not kept any more than his former one to support the Constitution of the United States. The Rebel loss was very heavy indeed, here, ours but trifling. I regret that I cannot give more of the details of this fighting upon the right—it was so determined upon the part of the enemy, both last night and this morning—so successful to us. About all that I actually saw of it during its progress, was the smoke, and I heard the discharges. My information is derived from officers who were personally in it. Some of our heavier artillery assisted our infantry in this by firing, with the piece elevated, far from the rear, over the heads of our men, at a distance from the enemy of two miles, I suppose. Of course, they could have done no great damage. It was nearly eleven o'clock that the battle in this part of the field subsided, not to be again renewed. All the morning we felt no apprehension for this part of the line, for we knew its strength, and that our troops engaged, the Twelfth Corps and the First Division, Wadsworth's, of the First, could be trusted.

For the sake of telling one thing at a time, I have anticipated events somewhat, in writing of this fight upon the right. I shall now go back to the starting point, four o'clock this morning, and, as other events occurred during the day, second to none in the battle in importance, which I think I saw as much of as any man living, I will tell you something of them, and what I saw, and how the time moved on. The outpost skirmish that I have mentioned, soon subsided. I suppose it was the natural escape of the wrath which the men had, during the night, hoarded up against each other, and which, as soon as they could see in the morning, they could no longer contain, but must let it off through their musket barrels, at their adversaries. At the commencement of the war such firing would have awaked the whole army and roused it to its feet and to arms; not so now. The men upon the crest lay snoring in their blankets, even though some of the enemy's bullets dropped among them, as if bullets were as harmless as the drops of dew around them. As the sun arose to-day, the clouds became broken, and we had once more glimpses of sky, and fits of sunshine—a rarity, to cheer us. From the crest, save to the right of the Second Corps, no enemy, not even his outposts could be discovered, along all the position where he so thronged upon the Third Corps yesterday. All was silent there—the wounded horses were limping about the field; the ravages of the conflict were still fearfully visible—the scattered arms and the ground thickly dotted with the dead—but no hostile foe. The men were roused early, in order that the morning meal might be out of the way in time for whatever should occur. Then ensued the hum of an army, not in ranks, chatting in low tones, and running about and jostling among each other, rolling and packing their blankets and tents. They looked like an army of rag-gatherers, while shaking these very useful articles of the soldier's outfit, for you must know that rain and mud in conjunction have not had the effect to make them clean, and the wear and tear of service have not left them entirely whole. But one could not have told by the appearance of the men, that they were in battle yesterday, and were likely to be again to-day. They packed their knapsacks, boiled their coffee and munched their hard bread, just as usual—just like old soldiers who know what campaigning is; and their talk is far more concerning their present employment—some joke or drollery—than concerning what they saw or did yesterday.

As early as practicable the lines all along the left are revised and reformed, this having been rendered necessary by yesterday's battle, and also by what is anticipated to-day.

It is the opinion of many of our Generals that the Rebel will not give us battle to-day—that he had enough yesterday—that he will be heading towards the Potomac at the earliest practicable moment, if he has not already done so; but the better, and controlling judgment is, that he will make another grand effort to pierce or turn our lines—that he will either mass and attack the left again, as yesterday, or direct his operations against the left of our center, the position of the Second Corps, and try to sever our line. I infer that Gen. Meade was of the opinion that the attack to-day would be upon the left—this from the disposition he ordered, I know that Gen. Hancock anticipated the attack upon the center.

The dispositions to-day upon the left are as follows:

The Second and Third Divisions of the Second Corps are in the position of yesterday; then on the left come Doubleday's—the Third Division and Col. Stannard's brigade of the First Corps; then Colwell's—the First Division of the Second Corps; then the Third Corps, temporarily under the command of Hancock, since Sickles' wound. The Third Corps is upon the same ground in part, and on the identical line where it first formed yesterday morning, and where, had it stayed instead of moving out to the front, we should have many more men to-day, and should not have been upon the brink of disaster yesterday. On the left of the Third Corps is the Fifth Corps, with a short front and deep line; then comes the Sixth Corps, all but one brigade, which is sent over to the Twelfth. The Sixth, a splendid Corps, almost intact in the fight of yesterday, is the extreme left of our line, which terminates to the south of Round Top, and runs along its western base, in the woods, and thence to the Cemetery. This Corps is burning to pay off the old scores made on the 4th of May, there back of Fredericksburg. Note well the position of the Second and Third Divisions of the Second Corps—it will become important. There are nearly six thousand men and officers in these two Divisions here upon the field—the losses were quite heavy yesterday, some regiments are detached to other parts of the field—so all told there are less than six thousand men now in the two Divisions,[5] who occupy a line of about a thousand yards. The most of the way along this line upon the crest was a stone fence, constructed of small rough stones, a good deal of the way badly pulled down, but the men had improved it and patched it with rails from the neighboring fences, and with earth, so as to render it in many places a very passable breastwork against musketry and flying fragments of shells.

These works are so low as to compel the men to kneel or lie down generally to obtain cover. Near the right of the Second Division, and just by the little group of trees that I have mentioned there, this stone fence made a right angle, and extended thence to the front, about twenty or thirty yards, where with another less than a right angle it followed along the crest again.

[5] The returns of June 30 gave 7,546 "present for duty" in these two divisions, but five of their twenty-six regiments were not in this part of the battle. See 43 War Records, 53, 176–7, 435, 457, 462, 471.—T. L. L.

The lines were conformed to these breastworks and to the nature of the ground upon the crest, so as to occupy the most favorable places, to be covered, and still be able to deliver effective fire upon the enemy should he come there. In some places a second line was so posted as to be able to deliver its fire over the heads of the first line behind the works; but such formation was not practicable all of the way. But all the force of these two divisions was in line, in position, without reserves, and in such a manner that every man of them could have fired his piece at the same instant. The division flags, that of the Second Division, being a white trefoil upon a square blue field, and of the Third Division a blue trefoil upon a white rectangular field, waved behind the divisions at the points where the Generals of Division were supposed to be; the brigade flags, similar to these but with a triangular field, were behind the brigades; and the national flags of the regiments were in the lines of their regiments. To the left of the Second Division, and advanced something over a hundred yards, were posted a part of Stannard's Brigade two regiments or more, behind a small bush-crowned crest that ran in a direction oblique to the general line. These were well covered by the crest, and wholly concealed by the bushes, so that an advancing enemy would be close upon them before they could be seen. Other troops of Doubleday's Division were strongly posted in rear of these in the general line.

I could not help wishing all the morning that this line of the two divisions of the Second Corps was stronger; it was so far as numbers constitute strength, the weakest part of our whole line of battle. What if, I thought, the enemy should make an assault here to-day with two or three heavy lines—a great overwhelming mass; would he not sweep through that thin six thousand?

But I was not General Meade, who alone had power to send other troops there; and he was satisfied with that part of the line as it was. He was early on horseback this morning, and rode along the whole line, looking to it himself, and with glass in hand sweeping the woods and fields in the direction of the enemy, to see if aught of him could be discovered. His manner was calm and serious, but earnest. There was no arrogance of hope, or timidity of fear discernible in his face; but you would have supposed he would do his duty conscientiously and well, and would be willing to abide the result. You would have seen this in his face. He was well pleased with the left of the line to-day, it was so strong with good troops. He had no apprehension for the right where the fight now was going on, on account of the admirable position of our forces there. He was not of the opinion that the enemy would attack the center, our artillery had such sweep there, and this was not the favorite point of attack with the Rebel. Besides, should he attack the center, the General thought he could reinforce it in good season. I heard Gen. Meade speak of these matters to Hancock and some others, at about nine o'clock in the morning, while they were up by the line, near the Second Corps.

No further changes of importance except those mentioned, were made in the disposition of the troops this morning, except to replace some of the batteries that were disabled yesterday by others from the artillery reserve, and to brace up the lines well with guns wherever there were eligible places, from the same source. The line is all in good order again, and we are ready for general battle.

Save the operations upon the right, the enemy so far as we could see, was very quiet all the morning. Occasionally the outposts would fire a little, and then cease. Movements would be discovered which would indicate the attempt on the part of the enemy to post a battery. Our Parrotts would send a few shells to the spot, then silence would follow.

At one of these times a painful accident happened to us, this morning. First Lieut. Henry Ropes, 20th Mass., in Gen. Gibbon's Division, a most estimable gentleman and officer, intelligent, educated, refined, one of the noble souls that came to the country's defense, while lying at his post with his regiment, in front of one of the Batteries, which fired over the Infantry, was instantly killed by a badly made shell, which, or some portion of it, fell but a few yards in front of the muzzle of the gun. The same accident killed or wounded several others. The loss of Ropes would have pained us at any time, and in any manner; in this manner his death was doubly painful.

Between ten and eleven o'clock, over in a peach orchard in front of the position of Sickles yesterday, some little show of the enemy's infantry was discovered; a few shells scattered the gray-backs; they again appeared, and it becoming apparent that they were only posting a skirmish line, no further molestation was offered them. A little after this some of the enemy's flags could be discerned over near the same quarter, above the top and behind a small crest of a ridge. There seemed to be two or three of them—possibly they were guidons—and they moved too fast to be carried on foot. Possibly, we thought, the enemy is posting some batteries there. We knew in about two hours from this time better about the matter. Eleven o'clock came. The noise of battle has ceased upon the right; not a sound of a gun or musket can be heard on all the field; the sky is bright, with only the white fleecy clouds floating over from the West. The July sun streams down its fire upon the bright iron of the muskets in stacks upon the crest, and the dazzling brass of the Napoleons. The army lolls and longs for the shade, of which some get a hand's breadth, from a shelter tent stuck upon a ramrod. The silence and sultriness of a July noon are supreme. Now it so happened, that just about this time of day a very original and interesting thought occurred to Gen. Gibbon and several of his staff; that it would be a very good thing, and a very good time, to have something to eat. When I announce to you that I had not tasted a mouthful of food since yesterday noon, and that all I had had to drink since that time, but the most miserable muddy warm water, was a little drink of whisky that Major Biddle, General Meade's aide-de-camp, gave me last evening, and a cup of strong coffee that I gulped down as I was first mounting this morning, and further, that, save the four or five hours in the night, there was scarcely a moment since that time but that I was in the saddle, you may have some notion of the reason of my assent to this extraordinary proposition. Nor will I mention the doubts I had, as to the feasibility of the execution of this very novel proposal, except to say that I knew this morning that our larder was low; not to put too fine a point upon it, that we had nothing but some potatoes and sugar and coffee in the world. And I may as well say here, that of such, in scant proportion, would have been our repast, had it not been for the riding of miles by two persons, one an officer, to procure supplies; and they only succeeded in getting some few chickens, some butter, and one huge loaf of bread, which last was bought of a soldier, because he had grown faint in carrying it, and was afterwards rescued with much difficulty and after a long race from a four-footed hog, which had got hold of and had actually eaten a part of it. "There is a divinity," etc. Suffice it, this very ingenious and unheard of contemplated proceeding, first announced by the General, was accepted and at once undertaken by his staff. Of the absolute quality of what we had to eat, I could not pretend to judge, but I think an unprejudiced person would have said of the bread that it was good; so of the potatoes before they were boiled. Of the chickens he would have questioned their age, but they were large and in good *running* order. The toast was good and the butter. There were those who, when coffee was given them, called for tea, and vice versa, and were so ungracious as to suggest that the water that was used in both might have come from near a barn. Of course it did not. We all came down to the little peach orchard where we had stayed last night, and, wonderful to see and tell, ever mindful of our needs, had it all ready, had our faithful John. There was an enormous pan of stewed chickens, and the potatoes, and toast, all hot, and the bread and the butter, and tea and coffee. There was satisfaction derived from just naming them all over. We called John an angel, and he snickered and said he "knowed" we'd come. General Hancock is of course invited to partake, and without delay, we commence operations. Stools are not very numerous, two, in all, and these the two Generals have by common consent. Our table was the top of a mess chest. By this the Generals sat. The rest of us sat upon the ground, cross-legged, like the picture of a smoking Turk, and held our plates upon our laps. How delicious was the stewed chicken. I had a cucumber pickle in my saddle bags, the last of a lunch left there two or three days ago, which George brought, and I had half of it. We were just well at it when General Meade rode down to us from the line, accompanied by one of his staff, and by General Gibbon's invitation, they dismounted and joined us. For the General commanding the Army of the Potomac George, by an effort worthy of the person and the occasion, finds an empty cracker box for a seat. The staff officer must sit upon the ground with the rest of us. Soon Generals

Newton and Pleasonton, each with an aide, arrive. By an almost superhuman effort a roll of blankets is found, which, upon a pinch, is long enough to seat these Generals both, and room is made for them. The aides sit with us. And, fortunate to relate, there was enough cooked for us all, and from General Meade to the youngest second lieutenant we all had a most hearty and well relished dinner. Of the "past" we were "secure." The Generals ate, and after, lighted cigars, and under the flickering shade of a very small tree, discoursed of the incidents of yesterday's battle and of the probabilities of to-day. General Newton humorously spoke of General Gibbon as "this young North Carolinian," and how he was becoming arrogant and above his position, because he com· manded a corps. General Gibbon retorted by saying that General Newton had not been long enough in such a command, only since yesterday, to enable him to judge of such things. General Meade still thought that the enemy would attack his left again to-day towards evening; but he was ready for them. General Hancock thought that the attack would be upon the position of the Second Corps. It was mentioned that General Hancock would again assume command of the Second Corps from that time, so that General Gibbon would again return to the Second Division.

General Meade spoke of the Provost Guards, that they were good men, and that it would be better to-day to have them in the works[6] than to stop stragglers and skulkers, as these latter would be good for but little even in the works;[6] and so he gave the order that all the Provost Guards should at once temporarily rejoin their regiments. Then General Gibbon called up Captain Farrel, First Minnesota, who commanded the provost guard of his division, and directed him for that day to join the regiment. "Very well, sir," said the Captain, as he touched his hat and turned away. He was a quiet, excellent gentleman and thorough soldier. I knew him well and esteemed him. I never saw him again. He was killed in two or three hours from that time, and over half of his splendid company were either killed or wounded.

And so the time passed on, each General now and then dispatch-

[6] Haskell probably wrote "ranks," as there were but few "works" deserving the name on the field.—T. L. L.

ing some order or message by an officer or orderly, until about half-past twelve, when all the Generals, one by one, first General Meade, rode off their several ways, and General Gibbon and his staff alone remained.

We dozed in the heat, and lolled upon the ground, with half open eyes. Our horses were hitched to the trees munching some oats. A great lull rests upon all the field. Time was heavy, and for want of something better to do, I yawned, and looked at my watch. It was five minutes before one o'clock. I returned my watch to its pocket, and thought possibly that I might go to sleep, and stretched myself upon the ground accordingly. *Ex uno disce omnes.* My attitude and purpose were those of the General and the rest of the staff.

What sound was that? There was no mistaking it. The distinct sharp sound of one of the enemy's guns, square over to the front, caused us to open our eyes and turn them in that direction, when we saw directly above the crest the smoke of the bursting shell, and heard its noise. In an instant, before a word was spoken, as if that was the signal gun for general work, loud, startling, booming, the report of gun after gun in rapid succession smote our ears and their shells plunged down and exploded all around us. We sprang to our feet. In briefest time the whole Rebel line to the West was pouring out its thunder and its iron upon our devoted crest. The wildest confusion for a few moments obtained sway among us. The shells came bursting all about. The servants ran terror-stricken for dear life and disappeared. The horses, hitched to the trees or held by the slack hands of orderlies, neighed out in fright, and broke away and plunged riderless through the fields. The General at the first had snatched his sword, and started on foot for the front. I called for my horse; nobody responded. I found him tied to a tree, near by, eating oats, with an air of the greatest composure, which under the circumstances, even then struck me as exceedingly ridiculous. He alone, of all beasts or men near, was cool. I am not sure but that I learned a lesson then from a horse. Anxious alone for his oats, while I put on the bridle and adjusted the halter, he delayed me by keeping his head down, so I had time to see one of the horses of our mess wagon struck and torn by a shell. The pair plunge—the driver has lost the reins—horses, driver and wagon go into a heap by a tree. Two mules close at hand, packed with boxes of ammunition, are knocked all to pieces by a shell. General Gibbon's groom has just mounted his horse and is starting to take the General's horse to him, when the flying iron meets him and tears open his breast. He drops dead and the horses gallop away. No more than a minute since the first shot was fired, and I am mounted and riding after the General. The mighty din that now rises to heaven and shakes the earth is not all of it the voice of the rebellion; for our guns, the guardian lions of the crest, quick to awake when danger comes, have opened their fiery jaws and begun to roar—the great hoarse roar of battle. I overtake the General half way up to the line. Before we reach the crest his horse is brought by an orderly. Leaving our horses just behind a sharp declivity of the ridge, on foot we go up among the batteries. How the long streams of fire spout from the guns, how the rifled shells hiss, how the smoke deepens and rolls. But where is the infantry? Has it vanished in smoke? Is this a nightmare or a juggler's devilish trick? All too real. The men of the infantry have seized their arms, and behind their works, behind every rock, in every ditch, wherever there is any shelter, they hug the ground, silent, quiet, unterrified, little harmed. The enemy's guns now in action are in position at their front of the woods along the second ridge that I have before mentioned and towards their right, behind a small crest in the open field, where we saw the flags this morning. Their line is some two miles long, concave on the side towards us, and their range is from one thousand to eighteen hundred yards. A hundred and twenty-five rebel guns, we estimate, are now active, firing twenty-four pound, twenty, twelve and ten-pound projectiles, solid shot and shells, spherical, conical, spiral. The enemy's fire is chiefly concentrated upon the position of the Second Corps. From the Cemetery to Round Top, with over a hundred guns, and to all parts of the enemy's line, our batteries reply, of twenty and ten-pound Parrotts, ten-pound rifled ordnance, and twelve-pound Napoleons, using projectiles as various in shape and name as those of the enemy. Captain Hazard commanding the artillery brigade of the Second Corps was vigilant among the batteries of his command, and they were all doing

well. All was going on satisfactorily. We had nothing to do, therefore, but to be observers of the grand spectacle of battle. Captain
Wessels, Judge Advocate of the Division, now joined us, and we
sat down behind the crest, close to the left of Cushing's Battery,
to bide our time, to see, to be ready to act when the time should
come, which might be at any moment. Who can describe such a
conflict as is raging around us? To say that it was like a summer
storm, with the crash of thunder, the glare of lightning, the shrieking
of the wind, and the clatter of hailstones, would be weak. The
thunder and lightning of these two hundred and fifty guns and
their shells, whose smoke darkens the sky, are incessant, all per-
vading, in the air above our heads, on the ground at our feet, remote, near, deafening, ear-piercing, astounding; and these hailstones
are massy iron, charged with exploding fire. And there is little of
human interest in a storm; it is an absorbing element of this. You
may see flame and smoke, and hurrying men, and human passion
at a great conflagration; but they are all earthly and nothing more.
These guns are great infuriate demons, not of the earth, whose
mouths blaze with smoky tongues of living fire, and whose murky
breath, sulphur-laden, rolls around them and along the ground,
the smoke of Hades. These grimy men, rushing, shouting, their
souls in frenzy, plying the dusky globes and the igniting spark, are
in their league, and but their willing ministers. We thought that at
the second Bull Run, at the Antietam and at Fredericksburg on the
11th of December, we had heard heavy cannonading; they were but
holiday salutes compared with this. Besides the great ceaseless roar
of the guns, which was but the background of the others, a million
various minor sounds engaged the ear. The projectiles shriek long
and sharp. They hiss, they scream, they growl, they sputter; all
sounds of life and rage; and each has its different note, and all are
discordant. Was ever such a chorus of sound before? We note the
effect of the enemies' fire among the batteries and along the crest.
We see the solid shot strike axle, or pole, or wheel, and the tough
iron and heart of oak snap and fly like straws. The great oaks there
by Woodruff's guns heave down their massy branches with a crash,
as if the lightning smote them. The shells swoop down among the
battery horses standing there apart. A half a dozen horses start,

they stumble, their legs stiffen, their vitals and blood smear the ground. And these shot and shells have no respect for men either. We see the poor fellows hobbling back from the crest, or unable to do so, pale and weak, lying on the ground with the mangled stump of an arm or leg, dripping their life-blood away; or with a cheek torn open, or a shoulder mashed. And many, alas! hear not the roar as they stretch upon the ground with upturned faces and open eyes, though a shell should burst at their very ears. Their ears and their bodies this instant are only mud. We saw them but a moment since there among the flame, with brawny arms and muscles of iron wielding the rammer and pushing home the cannon's plethoric load.

Strange freaks these round shot play! We saw a man coming up from the rear with his full knapsack on, and some canteens of water held by the straps in his hands. He was walking slowly and with apparent unconcern, though the iron hailed around him. A shot struck the knapsack, and it, and its contents flew thirty yards in every direction, the knapsack disappearing like an egg, thrown spitefully against a rock. The soldier stopped and turned about in puzzled surprise, put up one hand to his back to assure himself that the knapsack was not there, and then walked slowly on again unharmed, with not even his coat torn. Near us was a man crouching behind a small disintegrated stone, which was about the size of a common water bucket. He was bent up, with his face to the ground, in the attitude of a Pagan worshipper before his idol. It looked so absurd to see him thus, that I went and said to him, "Do not lie there like a toad. Why not go to your regiment and be a man?" He turned up his face with a stupid, terrified look upon me, and then without a word turned his nose again to the ground. An orderly that was with me at the time, told me a few moments later, that a shot struck the stone, smashing it in a thousand fragments, but did not touch the man, though his head was not six inches from the stone.

All the projectiles that came near us were not so harmless. Not ten yards away from us a shell burst among some small bushes, where sat three or four orderlies holding horses. Two of the men and one horse were killed. Only a few yards off a shell exploded over an open limber box in Cushing's battery, and at the same instant, another shell over a neighboring box. In both the boxes the ammunition blew up with an explosion that shook the ground, throwing fire and splinters and shells far into the air and all around, and destroying several men. We watched the shells bursting in the air, as they came hissing in all directions. Their flash was a bright gleam of lightning radiating from a point, giving place in the thousandth part of a second to a small, white, puffy cloud, like a fleece of the lightest, whitest wool. These clouds were very numerous. We could not often see the shell before it burst; but sometimes, as we faced towards the enemy, and looked above our heads, the approach would be heralded by a prolonged hiss, which always seemed to me to be a line of something tangible, terminating in a black globe, distinct to the eye, as the sound had been to the ear. The shell would seem to stop, and hang suspended in the air an instant, and then vanish in fire and smoke and noise. We saw the missiles tear and plow the ground. All in rear of the crest for a thousand yards, as well as among the batteries, was the field of their blind fury. Ambulances, passing down the Taneytown road with wounded men, were struck. The hospitals near this road were riddled. The house which was General Meade's headquarters was shot through several times, and a great many horses of officers and orderlies were lying dead around it. Riderless horses, galloping madly through the fields, were brought up, or down rather, by these invisible horse-tamers, and they would not run any more. Mules with ammunition, pigs wallowing about, cows in the pastures, whatever was animate or inanimate, in all this broad range, were no exception to their blind havoc. The percussion shells would strike, and thunder, and scatter the earth and their whistling fragments; the Whitworth bolts would pound and ricochet, and bowl far away sputtering, with the sound of a mass of hot iron plunged in water; and the great solid shot would smite the unresisting ground with a sounding "thud," as the strong boxer crashes his iron fist into the jaws of his unguarded adversary. Such were some of the sights and sounds of this great iron battle of missiles. Our artillerymen upon the crest budged not an inch, nor intermitted, but, though caisson and limber were smashed, and the guns dismantled, and men and horses killed, there amidst smoke and sweat, they gave back, without grudge, or loss of time in the sending, in kind whatever the enemy sent, globe, and cone, and bolt, hollow or solid, an iron greeting to the rebellion, the compliments of the wrathful Republic. An hour has droned its flight since first the war began. There is no sign of weariness or abatement on either side. So long it seemed, that the din and crashing around began to appear the normal condition of nature there, and fighting man's element. The General proposed to go among the men and over to the front of the batteries, so at about two o'clock he and I started. We went along the lines of the infantry as they lay there flat upon the earth, a little to the front of the batteries. They were suffering little, and were quiet and cool. How glad we were that the enemy were no better gunners, and that they cut the shell fuses too long. To the question asked the men, "What do you think of this?" the replies would be, "O, this is bully," "We are getting to like it," "O, we don't mind this." And so they lay under the heaviest cannonade that ever shook the continent, and among them a thousand times more jokes than heads were cracked.

We went down in front of the line some two hundred yards, and as the smoke had a tendency to settle upon a higher plain than where we were, we could see near the ground distinctly all over the fields, as well back to the crest where were our own guns as to the opposite ridge where were those of the enemy. No infantry was in sight, save the skirmishers, and they stood silent and motionless—a row of gray posts through the field on one side confronted by another of blue. Under the grateful shade of some elm trees, where we could see much of the field, we made seats of the ground and sat down. Here all the more repulsive features of the fight were unseen, by reason of the smoke. Man had arranged the scenes, and for a time had taken part in the great drama; but at last, as the plot thickened, conscious of his littleness and inadequacy to the mighty part, he had stepped aside and given place to more powerful actors. So it seemed; for we could see no men about the batteries. On either crest we could see the great flaky streams of fire, and they seemed numberless, of the opposing guns, and their white banks of swift, convolving smoke; but the sound of the discharges was drowned in the universal ocean of sound. Over all the valley the smoke, a sulphury arch, stretched its lurid span; and through it always, shrieking on their unseen courses, thickly flew a myriad iron deaths. With our grim horizon on all sides round toothed thick with battery flame, under that dissonant canopy of warring shells, we sat and heard in silence. What other expression had we that was not mean, for such an awful universe of battle?

A shell struck our breastwork of rails up in sight of us, and a moment afterwards we saw the men bearing some of their wounded companions away from the same spot; and directly two men came from there down toward where we were and sought to get shelter in an excavation near by, where many dead horses, killed in yesterdays fight had been thrown. General Gibbon said to these men, more in a tone of kindly expostulation than of command "My men, do not leave your ranks to try to get shelter here. All these matters are in the hands of God, and nothing that you can do will make you safer in one place than in another." The men went quietly back to the line at once. The General then said to me: "I am not a member of any church, but I have always had a strong religious feeling; and so in all these battles I have always believed that I was in the hands of God, and that I should be unharmed or not, according to His will. For this reason, I think it is, I am always ready to go where duty calls, no matter how great the danger." Half-past two o'clock, an hour and a half since the commencement, and still the cannonade did not in the least abate; but soon thereafter some signs of weariness and a little slacking of fire began to be apparent upon both sides. First we saw Brown's battery retire from the line, too feeble for further battle. Its position was a little to the front of the line. Its commander was wounded, and many of its men were so, or worse; some of its guns had been disabled, many of its horses killed; its ammunition was nearly expended. Other batteries in similar case had been withdrawn before to be replaced by fresh ones, and some were withdrawn afterwards. Soon after the battery named had gone, the General and I started to return, passing towards the left of the division, and crossing the ground where the guns had stood. The stricken horses were numerous, and the dead and wounded men lay about, and as we passed these latter, their low, piteous call for water would invariably come to us, if they had yet any voice left. I found canteens of water near—no difficult matter where a battle has been—and held them to livid lips, and even in the faintness of death the eagerness to drink told of their terrible torture of thirst. But we must pass on. Our infantry was still unshaken, and in all the cannonade suffered very little. The batteries had been handled much more severely. I am unable to give any figures. A great number of horses had been killed, in some batteries more than half of all. Guns had been dismounted. A great many caissons, limbers and carriages had been destroyed, and usually from ten to twenty-five men to each battery had been struck, at least along our part of the crest. Altogether the fire of the enemy had injured us much, both in the modes that I have stated, and also by exhausting our ammunition and fouling our guns, so as to render our batteries unfit for further immediate use. The scenes that met our eyes on all hands among the batteries were fearful. All things must end, and the great cannonade was no exception to the general law of earth. In the number of guns active at one time, and in the duration and rapidity of their fire, this artillery engagement, up to this time, must stand alone and pre-eminent in this war. It has not been often, or many times, surpassed in the battles of the world. Two hundred and fifty guns, at least, rapidly fired for two mortal hours. Cipher out the number of tons of gunpowder and iron that made these two hours hideous.

Of the injury of our fire upon the enemy, except the facts that ours was the superior position, if not better served and constructed artillery, and that the enemy's artillery hereafter during the battle was almost silent, we know little. Of course, during the fight we often saw the enemy's caissons explode, and the trees rent by our shot crashing about his ears, but we can from these alone infer but little of general results. At three o'clock almost precisely the last shot hummed, and bounded and fell, and the cannonade was over. The purpose of General Lee in all this fire of his guns—we know it now, we did not at the time so well—was to disable our artillery and break up our infantry upon the position of the Second Corps, so as to render them less an impediment to the sweep of his own brigades and divisions over our crest and through our lines. He probably supposed our infantry was massed behind the crest and the batteries; and hence his fire was so high. and his fuses to the shells were cut so long, too long. The Rebel General failed in some of his plans in this behalf, as many generals have failed before and will again. The artillery fight over, men began to breathe more freely, and to ask, What next, I wonder? The battery men were among their guns, some leaning to rest and wipe the sweat from their sooty faces, some were handling ammunition boxes and replenishing those that were empty. Some batteries from the artillery reserve were moving up to take the places of the disabled ones; the smoke was clearing from the crests. There was a pause between acts, with the curtain down, soon to rise upon the final act, and catastrophe of Gettysburg. We have passed by the left of the Second Division, coming from the First; when we crossed the crest the enemy was not in sight, and all was still—we walked slowly along in the rear of the troops, by the ridge cut off now from a view of the enemy in his position, and were returning to the spot where we had left our horses. General Gibbon had just said that he inclined to the belief that the enemy was falling back, and that the cannonade was only one of his noisy modes of covering the movement. I said that I thought that fifteen minutes would show that, by all his bowling, the Rebel did not mean retreat. We were near our horses when we noticed Brigadier General Hunt, Chief of Artillery of the Army, near Woodruff's Battery, swiftly moving about on horseback, and apparently in a rapid manner giving some orders about the guns. Thought we, what could this mean? In a moment afterwards we met Captain Wessels and the orderlies who had our horses; they were on foot leading the horses. Captain Wessels was pale, and he said, excited: "General, they say the enemy's infantry is advancing." We sprang into our saddles, a score of bounds brought us upon the all-seeing crest. To say that men grew pale and held their breath at what we and they there saw, would not be true. Might not six thousand men be brave and without shade of fear, and yet, before a hostile eighteen thousand, armed, and not five minutes' march away, turn ashy white? None on that crest now need be told that *the enemy is advancing*. Every eye could see his legions, an overwhelming resistless tide of an ocean of armed men sweeping upon us! Regiment after regiment, and brigade after brigade, move from the woods and rapidly take their places in the lines forming the assault. Pickett's proud division, with some additional troops, hold their right; Pettigrew's (Worth's) their left. The first line at short interval is followed by a second, and that a third succeeds; and columns between, support the lines. More than half a mile their front extends; more than a thousand yards the dull gray masses deploy, man touching man, rank pressing rank, and line supporting line. The red flags wave, their horsemen gallop up and down; the arms of eighteen thousand men, barrel and bayonet, gleam in the sun, a sloping forest of flashing steel. Right on they move, as with one soul, in perfect order, without impediment of ditch, or wall or stream, over ridge and slope, through orchard and meadow, and cornfield, magnificent, grim, irresistible. All was orderly and still upon our crest; no noise and no confusion. The men had little need of commands, for the survivors of a dozen battles knew well enough what this array in front portended, and, already in their places, they would be prepared to act when the right time should come. The click of the locks as each man raised the hammer to feel with his fingers that the cap was on the nipple; the sharp jar as a musket touched a stone upon the wall when thrust in aiming over it, and the clicking of the iron axles as the guns were rolled up by hand a little further to the front, were quite all the sounds that could be heard. Cap-boxes were slid around to the front of the body; cartridge boxes opened, officers opened their pistol-holsters. Such preparations, little more was needed. The trefoil flags, colors of the brigades and divisions moved to their places in rear; but along the lines in front the grand old ensign that first waved in battle at Saratoga in 1777, and which these people coming would rob of half its stars, stood up, and the west wind kissed it as the sergeants sloped its lance towards the enemy. I believe that not one above whom it then waved but blessed his God that he was loyal to it, and whose heart did not swell with pride towards it, as the emblem of the Republic before that treason's flaunting rag in front. General Gibbon rode down the lines, cool and calm, and in an unimpassioned voice he said to the men, "Do not hurry, men, and fire too fast, let them come up close before you fire, and then aim low and steadily." The coolness of their General was reflected in the faces of his men. Five minutes has elapsed since first the enemy have emerged from the woods—no great space of time surely, if measured by the usual standard by

which men estimate duration—but it was long enough for us to
note and weigh some of the elements of mighty moment that surrounded us; the disparity of numbers between the assailants and
the assailed; that few as were our numbers we could not be supported
or reinforced until support would not be needed or would be too late;
that upon the ability of the two trefoil divisions to hold the crest and
repel the assault depended not only their own safety or destruction,
but also the honor of the Army of the Potomac and defeat or victory
at Gettysburg. Should these advancing men pierce our line and
become the entering wedge, driven home, that would sever our army
asunder, what hope would there be afterwards, and where the blood-
earned fruits of yesterday? It was long enough for the Rebel storm
to drift across more than half the space that had at first separated
it from us. None, or all, of these considerations either depressed or
elevated us. They might have done the former, had we been timid;
the latter had we been confident and vain. But, we were there waiting, and ready to do our duty—that done, results could not dishonor us.

Our skirmishers open a spattering fire along the front, and, fighting, retire upon the main line—the first drops, the heralds of the
storm, sounding on our windows. Then the thunders of our guns,
first Arnold's, then Cushing's and Woodruff's and the rest, shake
and reverberate again through the air, and their sounding shells
smite the enemy. The General said I had better go and tell General
Meade of this advance. To gallop to General Meade's headquarters,
to learn there that he had changed them to another part of the field,
to dispatch to him by the Signal Corps in General Gibbon's name
the message, "The enemy is advancing his infantry in force upon
my front," and to be again upon the crest, were but the work of a
minute. All our available guns are now active, and from the fire
of shells, as the range grows shorter and shorter, they change to
shrapnel, and from shrapnel to canister; but in spite of shells, and
shrapnel and canister, without wavering or halt, the hardy lines of
the enemy continue to move on. The Rebel guns make no reply to
ours, and no charging shout rings out to-day, as is the Rebel wont;
but the courage of these silent men amid our shots seems not to need
the stimulus of other noise. The enemy's right flank sweeps near

Stannard's bushy crest, and his concealed Vermonters rake it with a well-delivered fire of musketry. The gray lines do not halt or reply, but withdrawing a little from that extreme, they still move on. And so across all that broad open ground they have come, nearer and nearer, nearly half the way, with our guns bellowing in their faces, until now a hundred yards, no more, divide our ready left from their advancing right. The eager men there are impatient to begin. Let them. First, Harrow's breastworks flame; then Hall's; then Webb's. As if our bullets were the fire coals that touched off their muskets, the enemy in front halts, and his countless level barrels blaze back upon us. The Second Division is struggling in battle. The rattling storm soon spreads to the right, and the blue trefoils are vieing with the white. All along each hostile front, a thousand yards, with narrowest space between, the volleys blaze and roll; as thick the sound as when a summer hailstorm pelts the city roofs; as thick the fire as when the incessant lightning fringes a summer cloud. When the Rebel infantry had opened fire our batteries soon became silent, and this without their fault, for they were foul by long previous use. They were the targets of the concentrated Rebel bullets, and some of them had expended all their canister. But they were not silent before Rhorty was killed, Woodruff had fallen mortally wounded, and Cushing, firing almost his last canister, had dropped dead among his guns shot through the head by a bullet. The conflict is left to the infantry alone. Unable to find my general, when I had returned to the crest after transmitting his message to General Meade, and while riding in the search having witnessed the development of the fight, from the first fire upon the left by the main lines until all of the two divisions were furiously engaged, I gave up hunting as useless—I was convinced General Gibbon could not be on the field; I left him mounted; I could easily have found him now had he so remained—but now, save myself, there was not a mounted officer near the engaged lines—and was riding towards the right of the Second Division, with purpose to stop there, as the most eligible position to watch the further progress of the battle, there to be ready to take part according to my own notions whenever and wherever occasion was presented. The conflict was tremendous, but I had seen no wavering in all our line. Wondering how long the Rebel ranks, deep though they were, could stand our sheltered volleys, I had come near my destination, when—great heaven! were my senses mad? The larger portion of Webb's brigade—my God, it was true—there by the group of trees and the angles of the wall, was breaking from the cover of their works, and, without orders or reason, with no hand lifted to check them, was falling back, a fear-stricken flock of confusion! The fate of Gettysburg hung upon a spider's single thread! A great magnificent passion came on me at the instant, not one that overpowers and confounds, but one that blanches the face and sublimes every sense and faculty. My sword, that had always hung idle by my side, the sign of rank only in every battle, I drew, bright and gleaming, the symbol of command. Was not that a fit occasion, and these fugitives the men on whom to try the temper of the Solinzen steel? All rules and proprieties were forgotten; all considerations of person, and danger and safety despised; for, as I met the tide of these rabbits, the damned red flags of the rebellion began to thicken and flaunt along the wall they had just deserted, and one was already waving over one of the guns of the dead Cushing. I ordered these men to "halt," and "face about" and "fire," and they heard my voice and gathered my meaning, and obeyed my commands. On some unpatriotic backs of those not quick of comprehension, the flat of my sabre fell not lightly, and, at its touch their love of country returned, and, with a look at me as if I were the destroying angel, as I might have become theirs, they again faced the enemy. General Webb soon came to my assistance. He was on foot, but he was active, and did all that one could do to repair the breach, or to avert its calamity. The men that had fallen back, facing the enemy, soon regained confidence in themselves, and became steady. This portion of the wall was lost to us, and the enemy had gained the cover of the reverse side, where he now stormed with fire. But Webb's men, with their bodies in part protected by the abruptness of the crest, now sent back in the enemies' faces as fierce a storm. Some scores of venturesome Rebels, that in their first push at the wall had dared to cross at the further angle, and those that had desecrated Cushing's guns, were promptly shot down, and speedy death met him who should raise his body to cross it again. At this point little could be seen of the enemy, by reason of his cover and the smoke except the flash of his muskets and his waving flags. These red flags were accumulating at the wall every moment, and they maddened us as the same color does the bull. Webb's men are falling fast, and he is among them to direct and encourage; but, however well they may now do, with that walled enemy in front, with more than a dozen flags to Webb's three, it soon becomes apparent that in not many minutes they will be overpowered, or that there will be none alive for the enemy to overpower. Webb has but three regiments, all small, the 69th, 71st and 72nd Pennsylvania—the 106th Pennsylvania, except two companies, is not here to-day—and he must have speedy assistance, or this crest will be lost. Oh, where is Gibbon? where is Hancock?—some general—anybody with the power and the will to support that wasting, melting line? No general came, and no succor! I thought of Hayes upon the right, but from the smoke and war along his front, it was evident that he had enough upon his hands, if he stayed the inrolling tide of the Rebels there. Doubleday upon the left was too far off and too slow, and on another occasion I had begged him to send his idle regiments to support another line battling with thrice its numbers, and this "Old Sumpter Hero" had declined. As a last resort, I resolved to see if Hall and Harrow could not send some of their commands to reinforce Webb. I galloped to the left in the execution of my purpose, and as I attained the rear of Hall's line from the nature of the ground and the position of the enemy it was easy to discover the reason and the manner of this gathering of Rebel flags in front of Webb. The enemy, emboldened by his success in gaining our line by the group of trees and the angle of the wall, was concentrating all his right against and was further pressing that point. There was the stress of his assault; there would he drive his fiery wedge to split our line. In front of Harrow's and Hall's Brigades he had been able to advance no nearer than when he first halted to deliver fire, and these commands had not yielded an inch. To effect the concentration before Webb, the enemy would march the regiment on his extreme right of each of his lines by the left flank to the rear of the troops, still halted and facing to the front, and so continuing to draw in his right, when they were all massed in the position desired, he would again face them to the front, and advance to the storming. This was the way he made the wall before

Webb's line blaze red with his battle flags, and such was the purpose there of his thick-crowding battalions. Not a moment must be lost. Colonel Hall I found just in rear of his line, sword in hand, cool, vigilant, noting all that passed and directing the battle of his brigade. The fire was constantly diminishing now in his front, in the manner and by the movement of the enemy that I have mentioned, drifting to the right. "How is it going?" Colonel Hall asked me, as I rode up. "Well, but Webb is hotly pressed and must have support, or he will be overpowered. Can you assist him?" "Yes." "You cannot be too quick." "I will move my brigade at once." "Good." He gave the order, and in briefest time I saw five friendly colors hurrying to the aid of the imperilled three; and each color represented true, battle-tried men, that had not turned back from Rebel fire that day nor yesterday, though their ranks were sadly thinned, to Webb's brigade, pressed back as it had been from the wall, the distance was not great from Hall's right. The regiments marched by the right flank. Col. Hall superintended the movement in person. Col. Devereux coolly commanded the 19th Massachusetts. His major, Rice, had already been wounded and carried off. Lieut. Col. Macy, of the 20th Mass., had just had his left hand shot off, and so Capt. Abbott gallantly led over this fine regiment. The 42d New York followed their excellent Colonel Mallon. Lieut. Col. Steel, 7th Mich., had just been killed, and his regiment, and the handful of the 59th N. Y., followed their colors. The movement, as it did, attracting the enemy's fire, and executed in haste, as it must be, was difficult; but in reasonable time, and in order that is serviceable, if not regular, Hall's men are fighting gallantly side by side with Webb's before the all important point. I did not stop to see all this movement of Hall's, but from him I went at once further to the left, to the 1st brigade. Gen'l Harrow I did not see, but his fighting men would answer my purpose as well. The 19th Me., the 15th Mass., the 82d N. Y. and the shattered old thunderbolt, the 1st Minn.—poor Farrell was dying then upon the ground where he had fallen,—all men that I could find I took over to the right at the *double quick*.

As we were moving to, and near the other brigade of the division, from my position on horseback, I could see that the enemy's right, under Hall's fire, was beginning to stagger and to break. "See," I said to the men, "See the *chivalry!* See the gray-backs run!" The men saw, and as they swept to their places by the side of Hall and opened fire, they roared, and this in a manner that said more plainly than words—for the deaf could have seen it in their faces, and the blind could have heard it in their voices—*the crest is safe!*

The whole Division concentrated, and changes of position, and new phases, as well on our part as on that of the enemy, having as indicated occurred, for the purpose of showing the exact present posture of affairs, some further description is necessary. Before the 2d Division the enemy is massed, the main bulk of his force covered by the ground that slopes to his rear, with his front at the stone wall. Between his front and us extends the very apex of the crest. All there are left of the White Trefoil Division—yesterday morning there were three thousand eight hundred, this morning there were less than three thousand—at this moment there are somewhat over two thousand;—twelve regiments in three brigades are below or behind the crest, in such a position that by the exposure of the head and upper part of the body above the crest they can deliver their fire in the enemy's faces along the top of the wall. By reason of the disorganization incidental in Webb's brigade to his men's having broken and fallen back, as mentioned, in the two other brigades to their rapid and difficult change of position under fire, and in all the division in part to severe and continuous battle, formation of companies and regiments in regular ranks is lost; but commands, companies, regiments and brigades are blended and intermixed—an irregular extended mass—men enough, if in order, to form a line of four or five ranks along the whole front of the division. The twelve flags of the regiments wave defiantly at intervals along the front; at the stone wall, at unequal distances from ours of forty, fifty or sixty yards, stream nearly double this number of the battle flags of the enemy. These changes accomplished on either side, and the concentration complete, although no cessation or abatement in the general din of conflict since the commencement had at any time been appreciable, now it was as if a new battle, deadlier, stormier than before, had sprung from the body of the old—a young Phœnix of combat, whose eyes stream lightning, shaking his arrowy wings over the yet glowing ashes of his progenitor. The jostling, swaying lines on either side boil, and roar, and dash their flamy spray, two hostile billows of a fiery ocean. Thick flashes stream from the wall, thick volleys answer from the crest. No threats or expostulation now, only example and encouragement. All depths of passion are stirred, and all combatives fire, down to their deep foundations. Individuality is drowned in a sea of clamor, and timid men, breathing the breath of the multitude, are brave. The frequent dead and wounded lie where they stagger and fall—there is no humanity for them now, and none can be spared to care for them. The men do not cheer or shout; they growl, and over that uneasy sea, heard with the roar of musketry, sweeps the muttered thunder of a storm of growls. Webb, Hall, Devereux, Mallon, Abbott among the men where all are heroes, are doing deeds of note. Now the loyal wave rolls up as if it would overleap its barrier, the crest. Pistols flash with the muskets. My "Forward to the wall" is answered by the Rebel counter-command, "Steady, men!" and the wave swings back. Again it surges, and again it sinks. These men of Pennsylvania, on the soil of their own homesteads, the first and only to flee the wall, must be the first to storm it. "Major—, *lead* your men over the crest, they will follow." "By the tactics I understand my place is in rear of the men." "Your pardon, sir; I see *your* place is in rear of the men. I thought you were fit to lead." "Capt. Suplee, come on with your men." "Let me first stop this fire in the rear, or we shall be hit by our own men." "Never mind the fire in the rear; let us take care of this in front first." "Sergeant, forward with your color. Let the Rebels see it close to their eyes once before they die." The color sergeant of the 72d Pa., grasping the stump of the severed lance in both his hands, waved the flag above his head and rushed towards the wall. "Will you see your color storm the wall alone?" One man only starts to follow. Almost half way to the wall, down go color bearer and color to the ground—the gallant sergeant is dead. The line springs—the crest of the solid ground with a great roar, heaves forward its maddened load, men, arms, smoke, fire, a fighting mass. It rolls to the wall—flash meets flash, the wall is crossed—a moment ensues of thrusts, yells, blows, shots, and undistinguishable conflict, followed by a shout universal that makes the welkin ring again, and the last and bloodiest fight of the great battle of Gettysburg is ended and won.

Many things cannot be described by pen or pencil—such a fight is one. Some hints and incidents may be given, but a description or picture never. From what is told the imagination may for itself construct the scene; otherwise he who never saw can have no adequate idea of what such a battle is.

When the vortex of battle passion had subsided, hopes, fears, rage, joy, of which the maddest and the noisiest was the last, and we were calm enough to look about us, we saw that, as with us, the fight with the Third Division was ended, and that in that division was a repetition of the scenes immediately about us. In that moment the judgment almost refused to credit the senses. Are these abject wretches about us, whom our men are now disarming and driving together in flocks, the jaunty men of Pickett's Division, whose steady lines and flashing arms but a few moments since came sweeping up the slope to destroy us? Are these red cloths that our men toss about in derision the "fiery Southern crosses," thrice ardent, the battle flags of the rebellion that waved defiance at the wall? We know, but so sudden has been the transition, we yet can scarce believe.

Just as the fight was over, and the first outburst of victory had a little subsided, when all in front of the crest was noise and confusion—prisoners being collected, small parties in pursuit of them far down into the fields, flags waving, officers giving quick, sharp commands to their men—I stood apart for a few moments upon the crest, by that group of trees which ought to be historic forever, a spectator of the thrilling scene around. Some few musket shots were still heard in the Third Division; and the enemy's guns, almost silent since the advance of his infantry until the moment of his defeat, were dropping a few sullen shells among friend and foe upon the crest. Rebellion fosters such humanity. Near me, saddest sight of the many of such a field and not in keeping with all this noise, were mingled alone the thick dead of Maine and Minnesota, and Michigan and Massachusetts, and the Empire and Keystone States, who, not yet cold, with the blood still oozing from their death-wounds, had given their lives to the country upon that stormy field. So mingled upon that crest, let their honored graves be. Look with me about us. These dead have been avenged already. Where the

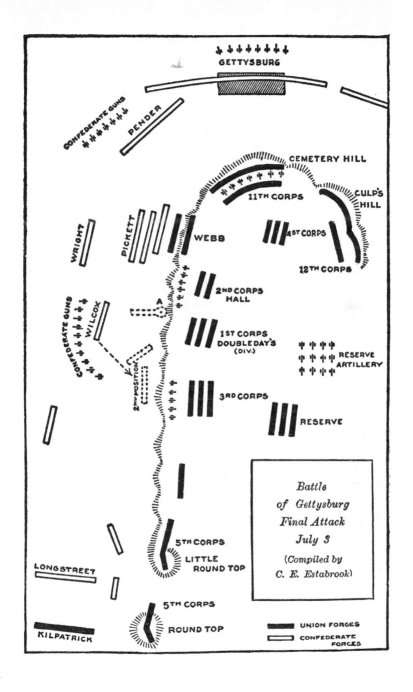

GETTYSBURG

CONFEDERATE GUNS
PENDER

CEMETERY HILL

CULP'S HILL

11TH CORPS

WRIGHT

PICKETT

WEBB

1ST CORPS

12TH CORPS

2ND CORPS
HALL

A

CONFEDERATE GUNS
WILCOX

1ST CORPS
DOUBLE DAY'S
(DIV.)

RESERVE
ARTILLERY

2ND POSITION

3RD CORPS

RESERVE

5TH CORPS
LITTLE
ROUND TOP

Battle
of Gettysburg
Final Attack
July 3
(Compiled by
C. E. Estabrook)

LONGSTREET

5TH CORPS
ROUND TOP

UNION FORCES
CONFEDERATE
FORCES

KILPATRICK

long lines of the enemy's thousands so proudly advanced, see how thick the silent men of gray are scattered. It is not an hour since these legions were sweeping along so grandly; now sixteen hundred[7] of that fiery mass are strewn among the trampled grass, dead as the clods they load; more than seven thousand, probably eight thousand, are wounded, some there with the dead, in our hands, some fugitive far towards the woods, among them Generals Pettigrew, Garnett, Kemper and Armstead, the last three mortally, and the last one in our hands. "Tell General Hancock," he said to Lieutenant Mitchell, Hancock's aide-de-camp, to whom he handed his watch, "that I know I did my country a great wrong when I took up arms against her, for which I am sorry, but for which I cannot live to atone." Four thousand, not wounded, are prisoners of war. More in number of the captured than the captors. Our men are still "gathering them in." Some hold up their hands or a handkerchief in sign of submission; some have hugged the ground to escape our bullets and so are taken; few made resistance after the first moment of our crossing the wall; some yield submissively with good grace, some with grim, dogged aspect, showing that but for the other alternative they could not submit to this. Colonels, and all less grades of officers, in the usual proportion are among them, and all are being stripped of their arms. Such of them as escaped wounds and capture are fleeing routed and panic stricken, and disappearing in the woods. Small arms, more thousands than we can count, are in our hands, scattered over the field. And these defiant battle-flags, some inscribed with "First Manassas," the numerous battles of the Peninsula, "Second Manassas," "South Mountain," "Sharpsburg," (our Antietam,) "Fredericksburg," "Chancellorsville," and many more names, our men have, and are showing about, *over thirty of them*.

Such was really the closing scene of the grand drama of Gettysburg. After repeated assaults upon the right and the left, where, and in all of which repulse had been his only success, this persistent and presuming enemy forms his chosen troops, the flower of his army, for a grand assault upon our center. The manner and result of such assault have been told—a loss to the enemy of from twelve thousand

---

[7] Final returns gave 1,653 buried by the First and Second Corps, presumably in this field. See 43 War Records, 264, 378.—T. L. L.

to fourteen thousand, killed, wounded and prisoners, and of over thirty battle-flags. This was accomplished by not over six thousand men, with a loss on our part of not over two thousand five hundred killed and wounded.

Would to Heaven Generals Hancock and Gibbon could have stood there where I did, and have looked upon that field! It would have done two men, to whom the country owes much, good to have been with their men in that moment of victory—to have seen the result of those dispositions which they had made, and of that splendid fighting which men schooled by their discipline, had executed. But they are both severely wounded and have been carried from the field. One person did come then that I was glad to see there, and that was no less than Major General Meade, whom the Army of the Potomac was fortunate enough to have at that time to command it. See how a great General looked upon the field, and what he said and did at the moment, and when he learned of his great victory. To appreciate the incident I give, it should be borne in mind that one coming up from the rear of the line, as did General Meade, could have seen very little of our own men, who had now crossed the crest, and although he could have heard the noise, he could not have told its occasion, or by whom made, until he had actually attained the crest. One who did not know results, so coming, would have been quite as likely to have supposed that our line there had been carried and captured by the enemy—so many gray Rebels were on the crest—as to have discovered the real truth. Such mistake was really made by one of our officers, as I shall relate.

General Meade rode up, accompanied alone by his son, who is his aide-de-camp, an escort, if select, not large for a commander of such an army. The principal horseman was no bedizened hero of some holiday review, but he was a plain man, dressed in a serviceable summer suit of dark blue cloth, without badge or ornament, save the shoulder-straps of his grade, and a light, straight sword of a General or General staff officer. He wore heavy, high-top boots and buff gauntlets, and his soft black felt hat was slouched down over his eyes. His face was very white, not pale, and the lines were marked and earnest and full of care. As he arrived near me, coming up the hill, he asked in a sharp, eager voice: "How is it going here?"

"I believe, General, the enemy's attack is repulsed," I answered. Still approaching, and a new light began to come in his face, of gratified surprise, with a touch of incredulity, of which his voice was also the medium, he further asked: "*What! Is the assault already repulsed?*" his voice quicker and more eager than before. "It is, sir," I replied. By this time he was on the crest, and when his eye had for an instant swept over the field, taking in just a glance of the whole—the masses of prisoners, the numerous captured flags which the men were derisively flaunting about, the fugitives of the routed enemy, disappearing with the speed of terror in the woods—partly at what I had told him, partly at what he saw, he said, impressively, and his face lighted: "Thank God." And then his right hand moved as if it would have caught off his hat and waved it; but this gesture he suppressed, and instead he waved his hand, and said "Hurrah!" The son, with more youth in his blood and less rank upon his shoulders, snatched off his cap, and roared out his three "hurrahs" right heartily. The General then surveyed the field, some minutes, in silence. He at length asked who was in command—he had heard that Hancock and Gibbon were wounded—and I told him that General Caldwell was the senior officer of the Corps and General Harrow of the Division. He asked where they were, but before I had time to answer that I did not know, he resumed: "No matter; I will give my orders to you and you will see them executed." He then gave direction that the troops should be reformed as soon as practicable, and kept in their places, as the enemy might be mad enough to attack again. He also gave directions concerning the posting of some reinforcements which he said would soon be there, adding: "If the enemy does attack, charge him in the flank and sweep him from the field; do you understand." The General then, a gratified man, galloped in the direction of his headquarters.

Then the work of the field went on. First, the prisoners were collected and sent to the rear. "There go the men," the Rebels were heard to say, by some of our surgeons who were in Gettysburg, at the time Pickett's Division marched out to take position— "There go the men that will go through your d—d Yankee lines, for you." A good many of them did "go through our lines for us," but in a very different way from the one they intended—not impetuous victors, sweeping away our thin lines with ball and bayonet, but crestfallen captives, without arms, guarded by the true bayonets of the Union, with the cheers of their conquerors ringing in their ears. There was a grim truth after all in this Rebel remark. Collected, the prisoners began their dreary march, a miserable, melancholy stream of dirty gray, to pour over the crest to our rear. Many of the officers were well dressed, fine, proud gentlemen, such men as it would be a pleasure to meet, when the war is over. I had no desire to exult over them, and pity and sympathy were the general feelings of us all upon the occasion. The cheering of our men, and the unceremonious handling of the captured flags was probably not gratifying to the prisoners, but not intended for taunt or insult to the men; they could take no exception to such practices. When the prisoners were turned to the rear and were crossing the crest, Lieut. Col. Morgan, General Hancock's Chief of Staff, was conducting a battery from the artillery reserve, towards the Second Corps. As he saw the men in gray coming over the hill, he said to the officer in command of the battery: "See up there! The enemy has carried the crest. See them come pouring over! The old Second Corps is gone, and you had better get your battery away from here as quickly as possible, or it will be captured." The officer was actually giving the order to his men to move back, when close observation discovered that the gray-backs that were coming had no arms, and then the truth flashed upon the minds of the observers. The same mistake was made by others.

In view of the results of that day—the successes of the arms of the country, would not the people of the whole country, standing there upon the crest with General Meade, have said, with him: "Thank God?"

I have no knowledge and little notion of how long a time elapsed from the moment the fire of the infantry commenced, until the enemy was entirely repulsed, in this his grand assault. I judge, from the amount of fighting and the changes of position that occurred, that probably the fight was of nearly an hour's duration, but I cannot tell, and I have seen none who knew. The time seemed but a very few minutes, when the battle was over.

When the prisoners were cleared away and order was again established upon our crest, where the conflict had impaired it, until between five and six o'clock, I remained upon the field, directing some troops to their position, in conformity to the orders of General Meade. The enemy appeared no more in front of the Second Corps; but while I was engaged as I have mentioned, farther to our left some considerable force of the enemy moved out and made show of attack. Our artillery, now in good order again, in due time opened fire, and the shells scattered the "Butternuts," as clubs do the gray snow-birds of winter, before they came within range of our infantry. This, save unimportant outpost firing, was the last of the battle.

Of the pursuit of the enemy and the movements of the army subsequent to the battle, until the crossing of the Potomac by Lee and the closing of the campaign, it is not my purpose to write. Suffice it that on the night of the 3rd of July the enemy withdrew his left, Ewell's Corps, from our front, and on the morning of the 4th we again occupied the village of Gettysburg, and on that national day victory was proclaimed to the country; that floods of rain on that day prevented army movements of any considerable magnitude, the day being passed by our army in position upon the field, in burying our dead, and some of those of the enemy, and in making the movements already indicated; that on the 5th the pursuit of the enemy was commenced—his dead were buried by us—and the corps of our army, upon various roads, moved from the battlefield.

With a statement of some of the results of the battle, as to losses and captures, and of what I saw in riding over the field, when the enemy was gone, my account is done.

Our own losses in killed, wounded and missing I estimate at *twenty-three thousand.*[8] Of the "missing" the larger proportion were prisoners, lost on the 1st of July. Our loss in prisoners, not wounded, probably was *four thousand.* The losses were distributed among the different army corps about as follows: In the Second Corps, which sustained the heaviest loss of any corps, a little over *four thousand five hundred,* of whom the missing were a mere nominal number; in the

[8] Final returns stated the loss as 23,049, as follows: First Corps, 3,897 killed and wounded, 2,162 missing; Second Corps, 3,991 and 387; Third Corps, 3,622 and 589; Fifth Corps, 1,976 and 211; Sixth Corps, 212 and 30; Eleventh Corps, 2,291 and 1,510; Twelfth Corps, 1,016 and 66; Artillery Reserve, 230 and 12; Cavalry, 445 and 407. See 43 War Records, 187.—T. L. L.

First Corps a little over *four thousand,* of whom a great many were missing; in the Third Corps *four thousand,* of whom some were missing; in the Eleventh Corps nearly *four thousand,* of whom the most were missing; and the rest of the loss, to make the aggregate mentioned, was shared by the Fifth, Sixth and Twelfth Corps and the cavalry. Among these the missing were few; and the losses of the Sixth Corps and of the cavalry were light. I do not think the official reports will show my estimate of our losses to be far from correct, for I have taken great pains to question staff officers upon the subject, and have learned approximate numbers from them. We lost no gun or flag that I have heard of in all the battle. Some small arms, I suppose, were lost on the 1st of July.

The enemy's loss in killed, wounded and prisoners I estimate at *forty thousand,* and from the following data and for the following reasons: So far as I can learn, we took *ten thousand* prisoners, who were not wounded—many more than these were captured, but several thousands of them were wounded. I have so far as practicable ascertained the number of dead the enemy left upon the field, approximately, by getting the reports of different burying parties. I think his dead upon the field were *five thousand,* almost all of whom, save those killed on the first of July, were buried by us—the enemy not having them in their possession. In looking at a great number of tables of killed and wounded in battles I have found that the proportion of the killed to the wounded is as *one* to *five,* or more than five, rarely less than five. So with the killed at the number stated, *twenty-five thousand* mentioned. I think *fourteen thousand* of the enemy, wounded and unwounded, fell into our hands. Great numbers of his small arms, two or three guns, and forty or more—was there ever such bannered harvest?—of his regimental battle-flags, were captured by us. Some day possibly we may learn the enemy's loss, but I doubt if he will ever tell truly how many flags he did not take home with him. I have great confidence however in my estimates, for they have been carefully made, and after much inquiry, and with no desire or motive to overestimate the enemy's loss.

The magnitude of the armies engaged, the number of the casualties, the object sought by the Rebel, the result, will all contribute to give Gettysburg a place among the great historic battles of the world.

That General Meade's concentration was rapid—over thirty miles a day was marched by some of the Corps—that his position was skilfully selected and his dispositions good; that he fought the battle hard and well; that his victory was brilliant and complete, I think all should admit. I cannot but regard it as highly fortunate to us and commendable in General Meade, that the enemy was allowed the initiative, the offensive, in the main battle; that it was much better to allow the Rebel, for his own destruction, to come up and smash his lines and columns upon the defensive solidity of our position, than it would have been to hunt him, for the same purpose, in the woods, or to unearth him from his rifle-pits. In this manner our losses were lighter, and his heavier, than if the case had been reversed. And whatever the books may say of troops fighting the better who make the attack, I am satisfied that in this war, Americans, the Rebels, as well as ourselves, are best on the defensive. The proposition is deducible from the battles of the war, I think, and my own observation confirms it.

But men there are who think that nothing was gained or done well in this battle, because some other general did not have the command, or because any portion of the army of the enemy was permitted to escape capture or destruction. As if one army of a hundred thousand men could encounter another of the same number of as good troops and annihilate it! Military men do not claim or expect this; but the McClellan destroyers do, the doughty knights of purchasable newspaper quills; the formidable warriors from the brothels of politics, men of much warlike experience against honesty and honor, of profound attainments in ignorance, who have the maxims of Napoleon, whose spirit they as little understand as they do most things, to quote, to prove all things; but who, unfortunately, have much influence in the country and with the Government, and so over the army. It is very pleasant for these people, no doubt, at safe distances from guns, in the enjoyment of a lucrative office, or of a fraudulently obtained government contract, surrounded by the luxuries of their own firesides, where mud and flooding storms, and utter weariness never penetrate, to discourse of battles and how campaigns should be conducted and armies of the enemy destroyed. But it should be enough, perhaps, to say that men here, or elsewhere, who have knowledge enough of military affairs to entitle them to express an opinion on such matters, and accurate information enough to realize the nature and the means of this desired destruction of Lee's army before it crossed the Potomac into Virginia, will be most likely to vindicate the Pennsylvania campaign of Gen. Meade, and to see that he accomplished all that could have been reasonably expected of any general of any army. Complaint has been, and is, made specially against Meade, that he did not attack Lee near Williamsport before he had time to withdraw across the river. These were the facts concerning this matter:

The 13th of July was the earliest day when such an attack, if practicable at all, could have been made. The time before this, since the battle, had been spent in moving the army from the vicinity of the field, finding something of the enemy and concentrating before him. On that day the army was concentrated and in order of battle near the turnpike that leads from Sharpsburg to Hagerstown, Md., the right resting at or near the latter place, the left near Jones' crossroads, some six miles in the direction of Sharpsburg, and in the following order from left to right: the 12th corps, the 2d, the 5th, the 6th, the 1st, the 11th; the 3d being in reserve behind the 2d. The mean distance to the Potomac was some six miles, and the enemy was between Meade and the river. The Potomac, swelled by the recent rain, was boiling and swift and deep, a magnificent place to have drowned all the Rebel crew. I have not the least doubt but that Gen. Meade would have liked to drown them all, if he could, but they were unwilling to be drowned, and would fight first. To drive them into the river then, they must be routed. Gen. Meade, I believe, favored an attack upon the enemy at that time, and he summoned his corps commanders to a council upon the subject. The 1st corps was represented by William Hayes, the 3d by French, the 5th by Sykes, the 6th by Sedgwick, the 11th by Howard, the 12th by Slocum, and the Cavalry by Pleasanton. Of the eight generals there, Wadsworth, Howard and Pleasanton were in favor of immediate attack, and five, Hayes, French, Sykes, Sedgwick and Slocum were not in favor of attack until better information was obtained of the position and situation of the enemy. Of the *pros* Wadsworth only temporarily represented the 1st corps in the brief absence of

Newton, who, had a battle occurred, would have commanded. Pleasanton, with his horses, would have been a spectator only, and Howard, with the *brilliant 11th corps,* would have been trusted nowhere but a safe distance from the enemy—not by Gen. Howard's fault, however, for he is a good and brave man. Such was the position of those who felt sanguinarily inclined. Of the *cons* were all of the fighting generals of the fighting corps, save the 1st. This, then, was the feeling of these generals—all who would have had no responsibility or part in all probability, *hankered* for a fight—those who would have had both part and responsibility, did not. The attack was not made. At daylight on the morning of the 14th, strong reconnaissances from the 12th, 2d and 5th corps were the means of discovering that between the enemy, except a thousand or fifteen hundred of his rear guard, who fell into our hands, and the Army of the Potomac, rolled the rapid, unbridged river. The Rebel General, Pettigrew, was here killed. The enemy had constructed bridges, had crossed during all the preceding night, but so close were our cavalry and infantry upon him in the morning, that the bridges were destroyed before his rear guard had all crossed.

Among the considerations influencing these generals against the propriety of attack at that time, were probably the following: The army was wearied and worn down by four weeks of constant forced marching or battle, in the midst of heat, mud and drenching showers, burdened with arms, accoutrements, blankets, sixty to a hundred cartridges, and five to eight days' rations. What such weariness means few save soldiers know. Since the battle, the army had been constantly diminished by sickness or prostration and by more straggling than I ever saw before. Poor fellows—they could not help it. The men were near the point when further efficient physical exertion was quite impossible. Even the sound of the skirmishing, which was almost constant, and the excitement of impending battle, had no effect to arouse for an hour the exhibition of their wonted former vigor. The enemy's loss in battle, it is true, had been far heavier than ours; but his army was less weary than ours, for in a given time since the first of the campaign, it had marched far less and with lighter loads. These Rebels are accustomed to hunger and nakedness, customs to which our men do not take readily. And the enemy had straggled less, for the men were going away from battle and towards home, and for them to straggle was to go into captivity, whose end they could not conjecture. The enemy was somewhere in position in a ridgy, wooded country, abounding in strong defensive positions, his main bodies concealed, protected by rifle-pits and epaulements, acting strictly on the defensive. His dispositions, his position even, with any considerable degree of accuracy was unknown, nor could they be known except by reconnaissances in such force, and carried to such extent, as would have constituted them attacks liable to bring on at any moment a general engagement, and at places where we were least prepared and least likely to be successful. To have had a battle there then, Gen. Meade would have had to attack a cunning enemy in the dark, where surprises, undiscovered rifle-pits and batteries, and unseen bodies of men might have met his forces at every point. With his not greatly superior numbers, under such circumstances had Gen. Meade attacked, would he have been victorious? The vote of these generals at the council shows their opinion—my own is that he would have been repulsed with heavy loss, with little damage to the enemy. Such a result might have satisfied the bloody politicians better than the end of the campaign as it was; but I think the country did not need that sacrifice of the Army of the Potomac at that time—that enough odor of sacrifice came up to its nostrils from the 1st Fredericksburg field, to stop their snuffing for some time. I felt the probability of defeat strongly at the time, when we all supposed that a conflict would certainly ensue; for always before a battle—at least it so happens to me—some dim presentiment of results, some unaccountable foreshadowing pervades the army. I never knew the result to prove it untrue, which rests with the weight of a conviction. Whether such shadows are cause or consequence, I shall not pretend to determine; but when, as they often are, they are general, I think they should not be wholly disregarded by the commander. I believe the Army of the Potomac is always willing, often eager, to fight the enemy, whenever, as it thinks, there is a fair chance for victory; that it always will fight, let come victory or defeat whenever it is ordered so to do. Of course the army, both officers and men, had very great disappointment and very great sorrow that the Rebels *escaped*—so it was called—across the river; the disappointment was genuine, at least to the extent that disappointment is like surprise; but the sorrow to judge by looks, tones and actions, rather than by words, was not of that deep, sable character for which there is no balm.

Would it be an imputation upon the courage or patriotism of this army if it was not rampant for fight at this particular time and under the existing circumstances? Had the enemy stayed upon the left bank of the Potomac twelve hours longer, there would have been a great battle there near Williamsport on the 14th of July.

After such digression, if such it is, I return to Gettysburg.

As good generalship is claimed for Gen. Meade in the battle, so was the conduct of his subordinate commanders good. I know, and have heard, of no bad conduct or blundering on the part of any officer, save that of Sickles, on the 2d of July, and that was so gross, and came so near being the cause of irreparable disaster that I cannot discuss it with moderation. I hope the man may never return to the Army of the Potomac, or elsewhere, to a position where his incapacity, or something worse, may bring fruitless destruction to thousands again. The conduct of officers and men was good. The 11th corps behaved badly; but I have yet to learn the occasion when, in the opinion of any save their own officers and themselves, the men of this corps have behaved well on the march or before the enemy, either under Siegel or any other commander. With this exception, and some minor cases of very little consequence in the general result, our troops whenever and wherever the enemy came, stood against them storms of impassable fire. Such was the infantry, such the artillery—the cavalry did less but it did all that was required.

The enemy, too, showed a determination and valor worthy of a better cause. Their conduct in this battle even makes me proud of them as Americans. They would have been victorious over any but the best of soldiers. Lee and his generals presumed too much upon some past successes, and did not estimate how much they were due on their part to position, as at Fredericksburg, or on our part to bad generalship, as at the 2d Bull Run and Chancellorsville.

The fight of the 1st of July we do not, of course, claim as a victory; but even that probably would have resulted differently had Reynolds not been struck. The success of the enemy in the battle ended with the 1st of July. The Rebels were joyous and jubilant—so said our men in their hands, and the citizens of Gettysburg—at their achievements on that day. Fredericksburg and Chancellorsville were remembered by them. They saw victory already won, or only to be snatched from the streaming coat-tails of the 11th corps, or the *"raw Pennsylvania militia"* as they thought they were, when they saw them run; and already the spires of Baltimore and the dome of the National Capitol were forecast upon their glad vision—only two or three days march away through the beautiful valleys of Pennsylvania and *"my"* Maryland. Was there ever anything so fine before? How splendid it would be to enjoy the poultry and the fruit, the meats, the cakes, the beds, the clothing, the *Whiskey,* without price in this rich land of the Yankee! It would, indeed! But on the 2d of July something of a change came over the spirit of these dreams. They were surprised at results and talked less and thought more as they prepared supper that night. After the fight of the 3d they talked only of the means of their own safety from destruction. Pickett's splendid division had been almost annihilated, they said, and they talked not of how many were lost, but of who had escaped. They talked of these "Yanks" that had *clubs* on their flags and caps, the trefoils of the 2d corps that are like *clubs* in cards.

The battle of Gettysburg is distinguished in this war, not only as by far the greatest and severest conflict that has occurred, but for some other things that I may mention. The fight of the 2d of July, on the left, which was almost a separate and complete battle, is, so far as I know, alone in the following particulars: the numbers of men actually engaged at one time, and the enormous losses that occurred in killed and wounded in the space of about two hours. If the truth could be obtained, it would probably show a much larger number of casualties in this than my estimate in a former part of these sheets. Few battles of the war that have had so many casualties altogether as those of the two hours on the 2d of July. The 3d of July is distinguished. Then occurred the "great cannonade"—so we call it, and so it would be called in any war, and in almost any battle. And besides this, the main operations that followed have few parallels in history, none in this war, of the magnitude and magnificence of the assault, single and simultaneous, the disparity of the numbers

engaged, and the brilliancy, completeness and overwhelming character of the result in favor of the side numerically the weaker. I think
I have not, in giving the results of this encounter, overestimated the
numbers or the losses of the enemy. We learned on all hands, by
prisoners and by the newspapers, that over two divisions moved up
to the assault—Pickett's and Pettigrew's—that this was the first engagement of Pickett's in the battle, and the first of Pettigrew's, save
a light participation on the 1st of July. The Rebel divisions usually
number nine or ten thousand, or did at that time, as we understood.
Then I have seen something of troops and think I can estimate their
numbers somewhat. The number of the Rebels killed here I have
estimated in this way: the 2d and 3d divisions of the 2d corps buried
the Rebel dead in their own front, and where they fought upon their
own grounds, by count they buried over *one thousand eight hundred*. I think no more than about *two hundred* of these were killed
on the 2d of July in front of the 2d division, and the rest must have
fallen upon the 3d. My estimates that depend upon this contingency
may be erroneous, but to no great extent. The rest of the particulars
of the assault, our own losses and our captures, I know are approximately accurate. Yet the whole sounds like romance, a grand stage
piece of blood.

Of all the corps d'armie, for hard fighting, severe losses and brilliant results, the palm should be, as by the army it is, awarded to the
"Old Second." It did more fighting than any other corps, inflicted
severer losses upon the enemy in killed and wounded, and sustained
a heavier life loss, and captured more flags than all the rest of the
army, and almost as many prisoners as the rest of the army. The loss
of the 2d corps in killed and wounded in this battle—there is no
other test of hard fighting—was almost as great as that of all Gen.
Grant's forces in the battle that preceded and in the siege of Vicks-
burg. Three-eighths of the whole corps were killed and wounded.
Why does the Western Army suppose that the Army of the Potomac
does not fight? Was ever a more absurd supposition? The Army
of the Potomac is grand! Give it good leadership—let it alone—and
it will not fail to accomplish all that reasonable men desire.

Of Gibbon's white trefoil division, if I am not cautious, I shall
speak too enthusiastically. This division has been accustomed to

distinguished leadership. Sumner, Sedgwick and Howard have honored, and been honored by, its command. It was repulsed under Sedgwick at Antietam and under Howard at Fredericksburg; it was victorious under Gibbon at the 2d Fredericksburg and at Gettysburg. At Gettysburg its loss in killed and wounded was over *one thousand seven hundred,* near one-half of all engaged; it captured *seventeen* battle-flags and *two thousand three hundred* prisoners. Its bullets hailed on Pickett's division, and killed or mortally wounded four Rebel generals, *Barksdale* on the 2d of July, with the three on the 3d, *Armstead, Garnett* and *Kemper.* In losses, in killed and wounded, and in captures from the enemy of prisoners and flags, it stood pre-eminent among all the divisions at Gettysburg.

Under such generals as Hancock and Gibbon, brilliant results may be expected. Will the country remember them?

It is understood in the army that the President thanked the slayer of Barton Key for *saving the day* at Gettysburg. Does the country know any better than the President, that Meade, Hancock and Gibbon were entitled to some little share of such credit?

At about six o'clock on the afternoon of the 3d of July, my duties done upon the field, I quitted it to go to the General. My brave horse *Dick*—poor creature, his good conduct in the battle that afternoon had been complimented by a Brigadier—was a sight to see. He was literally covered with blood. Struck repeatedly, his right thigh had been ripped open in a ghastly manner by a piece of shell, and three bullets were lodged deep in his body, and from his wounds the blood oozed and ran down his sides and legs and with the sweat, formed a bloody foam. Dick's was no mean part in that battle. Good conduct in men under such circumstances as he was placed in might result from a sense of duty—his was the result of his bravery. Most horses would have been unmanageable with the flash and roar of arms about and the shouting. Dick was utterly cool, and would have obeyed the rein had it been a straw. To Dick, belongs the honor of first mounting that stormy crest before the enemy, not forty yards away, whose bullets smote him, and of being the only horse there during the heat of the battle. Even the enemy noticed Dick, and one of their reports of the battle mentions the *"solitary horseman"* who rallied our wavering line. He enabled me to do twelve times as much as I could have done on foot. It would not be dignified for an officer on foot to run; it is entirely so, mounted, to gallop. I do not approve of officers dismounting in battle, which is the time of all when they most need to be mounted, for thereby they have so much greater facilities for being everywhere present. Most officers, however, in close action, dismount. Dick deserves well of his country, and one day should have a horse-monument. If there be *"ut sapientibus placit,"* and equine elysium, I will send to Charon the brass coin, the fee for Dick's passage over, and on the other side of the Styx in those shadowy clover-fields he may nibble the blossoms forever.

I had been struck upon the thigh by a bullet which I think must have glanced and partially spent its force upon my saddle. It had pierced the thick cloth of my trowsers and two thicknesses of underclothing, but had not broken the skin, leaving me with an enormous bruise that for a time benumbed the entire leg. At the time of receiving it, I heard the thump, and noticed it and the hole in the cloth into which I thrust my finger, and I experienced a feeling of relief, I am sure, when I found that my leg was not pierced. I think when I dismounted my horse after that fight that I was no very comely specimen of humanity. Drenched with sweat, the white of battle, by the reaction, now turned to burning red. I felt like a boiled man; and had it not been for the exhilaration at results I should have been miserable. This kept me up, however, and having found a man to transfer the saddle from poor Dick, who was now disposed to lie down by loss of blood and exhaustion, to another horse, I hobbled on among the hospitals in search of Gen. Gibbon.

The skulkers were about, and they were as loud as any in their rejoicings at the victory, and I took a malicious pleasure as I went along and met them, in taunting the *sneaks* with their cowardice and telling them—it was not true—that Gen. Meade had just given the order to the Provost Guard to arrest and shoot all men they could find away from their regiments who could not prove a good account of themselves. To find the General was no easy matter. I inquired for both Generals Hancock and Gibbon—I knew well enough that they would be together—and for the hospitals of the 2d corps. My search was attended with many incidents that were provokingly humorous. The stupidity of most men is amazing. I would ask of a man I met, "Do you know, sir, where the 2d corps hospitals are?" "The 12th corps hospital is there!" Then I would ask sharply, "Did you understand me to ask for the 12th corps hospital?" "No!" "Then why tell me what I do not ask or care to know?" Then stupidity would stare or mutter about the ingratitude of some people for kindness. Did I ask for the Generals I was looking for, they would announce the interesting fact, in reply, that they had seen some other generals. Some were sure that Gen. Hancock or Gibbon was dead. They had seen his dead body. This was a falsehood, and they knew it. Then it was Gen. Longstreet. This was also, as they knew, a falsehood.

Oh, sorrowful was the sight to see so many wounded! The whole neighborhood in rear of the field became one vast hospital of miles in extent. Some could walk to the hospitals; such as could not were taken upon stretchers from the places where they fell to selected points and thence the ambulances bore them, a miserable load, to their destination. Many were brought to the building, along the Taneytown road, and too badly wounded to be carried further, died and were buried there, Union and Rebel soldiers together. At every house, and barn, and shed the wounded were; by many a cooling brook, or many a shady slope or grassy glade, the red flags beckoned them to their tented asylums, and there they gathered, in numbers a great army, a mutilated, bruised mass of humanity. Men with gray hair and furrowed cheeks and soft-lipped, beardless boys were there, for these bullets have made no distinction between age and youth. Every conceivable wound that iron and lead can make, blunt or sharp, bullet, ball and shell, piercing, bruising, tearing, was there; sometimes so light that a bandage and cold water would restore the soldier to the ranks again; sometimes so severe that the poor victim in his hopeless pain, remedyless save by the only panacea for all mortal suffering, invoked that. The men are generally cheerful, and even those with frightful wounds, often are talking with animated faces of nothing but the battle and the victory. But some are downcast, their faces distorted with pain. Some have undergone the surgeon's work; some, like men at a ticket office, await impatiently their turn to have an arm or a leg cut off. Some walk about with an arm in a sling; some sit idly upon the ground; some lie at full length upon a little straw, or a blanket, with their brawny, now blood-stained, limbs bare, and you may see where the minie bullet has struck or the shell has torn. From a small round hole upon many a manly breast, the red blood trickles, but the pallid cheek, the hard-drawn breath and dim closed eyes tell how near the source of life it has gone. The surgeons, with coats off and sleeves rolled up, and the hospital attendants with green bands upon their caps, are about their work; and their faces and clothes are spattered with blood; and though they look weary and tired, their work goes systematically and steadily on. How much and how long they have worked, the piles of legs, arms, feet, hands, and fingers about partially tell. Such sounds are heard sometimes—you would not have heard them upon the field—as convince that bodies, bones, sinews and muscles are not made of insensible stone. Near by appear a row of small fresh mounds, placed side by side. They were not there day before yesterday. They will become more numerous every day.

Such things I saw as I rode along. At last I found the Generals. Gen. Gibbon was sitting on a chair that had been borrowed some-where, with his wounded shoulder bare, and an attendant was bathing it with cold water. Gen. Hancock was near by in an ambu-lance. They were at the tents of the Second Corps hospitals, which were on Rock Run. As I approached Gen. Gibbon, when he saw me, he began to hurrah and wave his right hand. He had heard the result. I said: "O, General, long and well may you wave"—and he shook me warmly by the hand. Gen. Gibbon was struck by a bullet in the left shoulder, which had passed from the front through the flesh and out behind, fracturing the shoulder blade and inflicting a severe but not dangerous wound. He thinks he was the mark of a sharpshooter of the enemy hid in the bushes, near where he and I had sat so long during the cannonade; and he was wounded and taken off the field before the fire of the main lines of infantry had commenced, he being at the time he was hit near the left of his division. Gen. Han-cock was struck a little later near the same part of the field by a bullet, piercing and almost going through his thigh, without touch-ing the bone, however. His wound was severe, also. He was carried back out of range, but before he would be carried off the field, he lay upon the ground in sight of the crest, where he could see something of the fight, until he knew what would be the result.

And then, at Gen. Gibbon's request, I had to tell him and a large voluntary crowd of the wounded who pressed around now, for the wounds they showed not rebuked for closing up to the Generals, the story of the fight. I was nothing loth; and I must say though I used sometimes before the war to make speeches, that I never had so enthusiastic an audience before. Cries of "good," "glorious," frequently interrupted me, and the storming of the wall was applauded by enthusiastic tears and the waving of battered, bloody hands.

By the custom of the service the General had the right to have me along with him, while away with his wound; but duty and inclination attracted me still to the field, and I obtained the General's consent to stay. Accompanying Gen. Gibbon to Westminster, the nearest point to which railroad trains then ran, and seeing him transferred from an ambulance to the cars for Baltimore on the 4th, the next day I returned to the field to his division, since his wounding in the command of Gen. Harrow.

On the 6th of July, while my bullet bruise was yet too inflamed and sensitive for me to be good for much in the way of duty—the division was then halted for the day some four miles from the field on the Baltimore turnpike—I could not repress the desire or omit the opportunity to see again where the battle had been. With the right stirrup strap shortened in a manner to favor the bruised leg, I could ride my horse at a walk without serious discomfort. It seemed very strange upon approaching the horse-shoe crest again, not to see it covered with the thousands of troops and horses and guns, but they were all gone—the armies, to my seeming, had vanished—and on that lovely summer morning the stillness and silence of death pervaded the localities where so recently the shouts and the cannon had thundered. The recent rains had washed out many an unsightly spot, and smoothed many a harrowed trace of the conflict; but one still needed no guide save the eyes, to follow the track of that storm, which the storms of heaven were powerless soon to entirely efface. The spade and shovel, so far as a little earth for the human bodies would render their task done, had completed their work—a great labor, that. But still might see under some concealing bush, or sheltering rock, what had once been a man, and the thousands of stricken horses still lay scattered as they had died. The scattered small arms and the accoutrements had been collected and carried away, almost all that were of any value; but great numbers of bent and splintered muskets, rent knapsacks and haversacks, bruised canteens, shreds of caps, coats, trowsers, of blue or gray cloth, worthless belts and cartridge boxes, torn blankets, ammunition boxes, broken wheels, smashed limbers, shattered gun carriages, parts of harness, of all that men or horses wear or use in battle, were scattered broadcast over miles of the field. From these one could tell where the fight had been hottest. The rifle-pits and epaulements and the trampled grass told where the lines had stood, and the batteries—the former being thicker where the enemy had been than those of our own construction. No soldier was to be seen, but numbers of civilians and boys, and some girls even, were curiously loitering about the field, and their faces showed not sadness or horror, but only staring wonder or smirking curiosity. They looked for mementoes of the battle to keep, they said; but their furtive attempts to conceal an uninjured musket or an untorn blanket— they had been told that all property left here belonged to the Government—showed that the love of gain was an ingredient at least of their motive for coming here. Of course, there was not the slightest objection to their taking anything they could find now; but their manner of doing it was the objectionable thing. I could now understand why soldiers had been asked a dollar for a small strip of old linen to bind their own wound, and not be compelled to go off to the hospitals.

Never elsewhere upon any field have I seen such abundant evidences of a terrific fire of cannon and musketry as upon this. Along the enemy's position, where our shells and shot had struck during the cannonade of the third, the trees had cast their trunks and branches as if they had been icicles shaken by a blast. And graves of the Rebels' making, and dead horses and scattered accoutrements, showed that other things besides trees had been struck by our projectiles. I must say that, having seen the work of their guns upon the same occasion, I was gratified to see these things. Along the slope of Culp's Hill, in front of the position of the 12th, and the 1st Division of the 1st Corps, the trees were almost literally peeled, from the ground up some fifteen or twenty feet, so thick upon them were the scars the bullets had made. Upon a single tree, not over a foot and a half in diameter, I actually counted as many as two hundred and fifty bullet marks. The ground was covered by the little twigs that had been cut off by the hailstorm of lead. Such were the evidences of the storm under which Ewell's bold Rebels assaulted our breastworks on the night of the 2d and the morning of the 3d of July. And those works looked formidable, zig-zaging along these rocky crests, even now when not a musket was behind them. What madness on the part of the enemy to have attacked them! All along through these bullet-stormed woods were interspersed little patches of fresh earth, raised a foot or so above the surrounding ground. Some were very near the front of the works; and near by, upon a tree whose bark had been smoothed by an axe, written in red chalk would be the words, not in fine handwriting, "75 Rebels buried here." "☞ 54 Rebs. there." And so on. Such was the burial and such the epitaph of many of those famous men, once led by the mighty Stonewall Jackson. Oh, this damned rebellion will make brutes of us all, if it is not soon quelled! Our own men were buried in graves, not trenches; and upon a piece of board, or stave of a barrel, or bit of cracker box, placed at the head, were neatly cut or penciled the name and regiment of the one buried in such. This practice was general, but of course there must be some exceptions, for sometimes the cannon's load had not left enough of a man to recognize or name. The reasons here for the more careful interment of our own dead than such as was given to the dead of the enemy are obvious and I think satisfactory. Our own dead were usually buried not long after they fell, and without any general order to that effect. It was a work that the men's hearts were in as soon as the fight was over and opportunity offered, to hunt out their dead companions, to make them a grave in some convenient spot, and decently composed with their blankets wrapped about them, to cover them tenderly with earth and mark their resting place. Such burials were not without as scalding tears as ever fell upon the face of coffined mortality. The dead of the enemy could not be buried until after the close of the whole battle. The army was about to move—some of it was already upon the march, before such burial commenced. Tools, save those carried by the pioneers, were many miles away with the train, and the burying parties were required to make all haste in their work, in order to be ready to move with their regiments. To make long shallow trenches, to collect the Rebel dead, often hundreds in one place, and to cover them hastily with a little earth, without name, number, or mark, save the shallow mound above them—their names of course they did not know—was the best that could be done. I should have been glad to have seen more formal burial, even of these men of the rebellion, both because hostilities should cease with death, and of the respect I have for them as my brave, though deluded, countrymen. I found fault with such burial at the time, though I knew that the best was done that could be under the circumstances; but it may perhaps soften somewhat the rising feelings upon this subject, of any who may be disposed to share mine, to remember that under similar circumstances—had the issue of the battle been reversed—our own dead would have had no burial at all, at the hands of the enemy, but, stripped of their clothing, their naked bodies would have been left to rot, and their bones to whiten upon the top of the ground where they fell. Plenty of such examples of Rebel magnanimity are not wanting, and one occurred on this field, too. Our dead that fell into the hands of the enemy on the 1st of July had been plundered of all their clothing, but they were left unburied until our own men buried them after the Rebels had retreated at the end of the battle.

All was bustle and noise in the little town of Gettysburg, as I entered it on my tour of the field. From the afternoon of the 1st to the morning of the 4th of July, the enemy was in possession. Very many of the inhabitants had, upon the first approach of the enemy, or upon the retirement of our troops, fled their homes and the town not to return until after the battle. Now the town was a hospital where gray and blue mingled in about equal proportion. The public buildings, the courthouse, the churches and many private dwellings were full of wounded. There had been in some of the streets a good deal of fighting, and bullets had thickly spattered the fences and walls, and shells had riddled the houses from side to side. And the Rebels had done their work of pillage there, too, in spite of the smooth-sounding general order of the Rebel commander enjoining a sacred regard for private property—the order was really good and would sound marvelously well abroad or in history. All stores of drugs and medicines, of clothing, tinware and all groceries had been rifled and emptied without pay or offer of recompense. Libraries, public and private, had been entered and the books scattered about the yards or destroyed. Great numbers of private dwellings had been entered and occupied without ceremony and whatever was liked had been appropriated or wantonly destroyed. Furniture had been smashed and beds ripped open, and apparently unlicensed pillage had reigned. Citizens and women who had remained had been kindly relieved of their money, their jewelry and their watches—all this by the high-toned chivalry, the army of the magnanimous Lee! Put these things by the side of the acts of the "vandal Yankees" in Virginia, and then let mad Rebeldom prate of honor! But the people, the women and children that had fled, were returning, or had returned to their homes—such homes—and amid the general havoc were restoring as they could order to the desecrated firesides. And the faces of them all plainly told that, with all they had lost and bad as was the condition of all things they found, they were better pleased with such homes than with wandering houseless in the fields with the Rebels there. All had treasures of incidents of the battle and of the occupation of the enemy—wonderful sights, escapes, witnessed encounters, wounds, the marvelous passage of shells or bullets which, upon the asking, or even without, they were willing to share with the stranger. I heard of no more than one or two cases of any personal injury received by any of the inhabitants. One woman was said to have been killed while at her wash-tub, sometime during the battle; but probably by a stray bullet coming a very long distance from our own men. For the next hundred years Gettysburg will be rich in legends and traditions of the battle. I rode through the Cemetery on "Cemetery Hill." How these quiet sleepers must have been astounded in their graves when the twenty-pound Parrott guns thundered above them and the solid shot crushed their gravestones! The flowers, roses and creeping vines that pious hands had planted to bloom and shed their odors over the ashes of dear ones gone, were trampled upon the ground and black with the cannon's soot. A dead horse lay by the marble shaft, and over it the marble finger pointed to the sky. The marble lamb that had slept its white sleep on the grave of a child, now lies blackened upon a broken gun-carriage. Such are the incongruities and jumblings of battle.

I looked away to *the group of trees*—the Rebel gunners know what ones I mean, and so do the survivors of Pickett's division— and a strange fascination led me thither. How thick are the marks of battle as I approach—the graves of the men of the 3d Division of the 2d Corps; the splintered oaks, the scattered horses—seventy-one dead horses were on a spot some fifty yards square near the position of Woodruff's battery, and where he fell.

I stood solitary upon the crest by *"the trees"* where, less than three days ago, I had stood before; but now how changed is all the eye beholds. Do these thick mounds cover the fiery hearts that in the battle rage swept the crest and stormed the wall? I read their names—them, alas, I do not know—but I see the regiments marked on their frail monuments—"20th Mass. Vols.," "69 P. V.," "1st Minn. Vols." and the rest—they are all represented, and as they fought commingled here. So I am not alone. These, my brethren of the fight, are with me. Sleep, noble brave! The foe shall not desecrate your sleep. Yonder thick trenches will hold them. As long as patriotism is a virtue, and treason a crime, your deeds have made this crest, your resting place, hallowed ground!

But I have seen and said enough of this battle. The unfortunate wounding of my General so early in the action of the 3d of July, leaving important duties which, in the unreasoning excitement of the moment, I in part assumed, enabled me to do for the successful issue, something which under other circumstances would not have fallen to my rank or place. Deploring the occasion for taking away from the division in that moment of its need its soldierly, appropriate head, so cool, so clear, I am yet glad, as that was to be, that his example and his tuition have not been entirely in vain to me, and that my impulses then prompted me to do somewhat as he might have done had he been on the field. The encomiums of officers, so numerous and some of so high rank, generously accorded me for my conduct upon that occasion—I am not without vanity—were gratifying. My position as a staff officer gave me an opportunity to see much, perhaps as much as any one person, of that conflict. My observations were not so particular as if I had been attached to a smaller command; not so general as may have been those of a staff officer to the General commanding the army; but of such as they were, my heart was there, and I could do no less than to write something of them, in the intervals between marches and during the subsequent repose of the army at the close of the campaign. I have put somewhat upon these pages—I make no apology for the egotism, if such there is, of this account—it is not designed to be a history, but simply *my account* of the battle. It should not be assumed, if I have told of some occurrences, that there were not other important ones. I would not have it supposed that I have attempted to do full justice to the good conduct of the fallen, or the survivors of the 1st and 12th Corps. Others must tell of them. I did not see their work. A full account of *the battle as it was* will never, can never be made. Who could sketch the changes, the constant shifting of the bloody panorama? It is not possible. The official reports may give results as to losses, with statements of attacks and repulses; they may also note the means by which results were attained, which is a statement of the number and kind of the forces employed, but the connection between means and results, the mode, the battle proper, these reports touch lightly. Two prominent reasons at least exist which go far to account for the general inadequacy of these official reports, or to account for their giving no true idea of what they assume to describe—the literary infirmity of the reporters and their not seeing themselves and their commands as others would have seen them. And factions, and parties, and politics, the curses of this Republic, are already putting in their unreasonable demands for the foremost honors of the field. "Gen. Hooker won Gettysburg." How? Not with the army in person or by infinitesimal influence—leaving it almost four days before the battle when both armies were scattered and fifty miles apart! Was ever claim so absurd? Hooker, and he alone, won the result at Chancellorsville. "Gen. Howard won Gettysburg!" "Sickles saved the day!" Just Heaven, save the poor Army of the Potomac from its friends! It has more to dread and less to hope from them than from the red bannered hosts of the rebellion. The states prefer each her claim for the sole brunt and winning of the fight. "Pennsylvania won it!" "New York won it!" "Did not Old Greece, or some tribe from about the sources of the Nile win it?" For modern Greeks—from Cork—and African Hannibals were there. Those intermingled graves along the crest bearing the names of every loyal state, save one or two, should admonish these geese to cease to cackle. One of the armies of the country won the battle, and that army supposes that Gen. Meade led it upon that occasion. If it be not one of the lessons that this war teaches, that we have a country paramount and supreme over faction, and party, and state, then was the blood of fifty thousand citizens shed on this field in vain. For the reasons mentioned, of this battle, greater than that of Waterloo, a history, just, comprehensive, complete will never be written. By-and-by, out of the chaos of trash and falsehood that the newspapers hold, out of the disjointed mass of reports, out of the traditions and tales that came down from the field some eye that never saw the battle will select, and some pen will write what will be named *the history*. With that the world will be and, if we are alive, we must be, content.

Already, as I rode down from the heights, nature's mysterious loom was at work, joining and weaving on her ceaseless web the shells had broken there. Another spring shall green these trampled slopes, and flowers, planted by unseen hands, shall bloom upon these graves; another autumn and the yellow harvest shall ripen there—all not in less, but in higher perfection for this poured out blood. In another decade of years, in another century, or age, we hope that the Union, by the same means, may repose in a securer peace and bloom in a higher civilization. Then what matters it if lame Tradition glean on this field and hand down her garbled sheaf—if deft story with furtive fingers plait her ballad wreaths, deeds of her heroes here? or if stately history fill as she list her arbitrary tablet, the sounding record of this fight? Tradition, story, history—all will not efface the true, grand epic of Gettysburg.

FRANK A. HASKELL.

To H. M. Haskell.

LINCOLN'S
GETTYSBURG ADDRESS
(1863)

[On Nov. 19, 1863, a part of the battlefield of Gettysburg was set aside as a cemetery, where monuments to the soldiers who fell there might be set up. The main oration was delivered by Edward Everett, at the conclusion of which Lincoln dedicated the field in this most pregnant and eloquent of his utterances.]

FOURSCORE and seven years ago our fathers brought forth on this continent a new nation, conceived in liberty, and dedicated to the proposition that all men are created equal. Now we are engaged in a great civil war, testing whether that nation, or any nation so conceived and so dedicated, can long endure. We are met on a great battlefield of that war. We have come to dedicate a portion of that field as a final resting-place for those who here gave their lives that the nation might live. It is altogether fitting and proper that we should do this. But, in a larger sense, we cannot dedicate—we cannot consecrate—we cannot hallow—this ground. The brave men, living and dead, who struggled here have consecrated it, far above our poor power to add or detract. The world will little note, nor long remember, what we say here, but it can never forget what they did here. It is for us the living, rather, to be dedicated here to the unfinished work which they who fought here have thus far so nobly advanced. It is rather for us to be here dedicated to the great task remaining before us—that from these honored dead we take increased devotion to that cause for which they gave the last full measure of devotion—that we here highly resolve that these dead shall not have died in vain—that this nation, under God, shall have a new birth of freedom and that government of the people, by the people, for the people, shall not perish from the earth.

PROCLAMATION OF AMNESTY

(1863)

[The Proclamation of Amnesty gives an interesting indication of the lines along which Lincoln, had he lived, would have attempted to solve the problem of reconstruction. The main idea was to create by generous treatment a party loyal to the Union in each State, in whose hands the restored state government might, as speedily as possible, be placed.]

WHEREAS, in and by the Constitution of the United States, it is provided that the President "shall have power to grant reprieves and pardons for offences against the United States, except in cases of impeachment;" and

Whereas, a rebellion now exists whereby the loyal State governments of several States have for a long time been subverted, and many persons have committed and are now guilty of treason against the United States; and

Whereas, with reference to said rebellion and treason, laws have been enacted by Congress declaring forfeitures and confiscation of property and liberation of slaves, all upon terms and conditions therein stated, and also declaring that the President was thereby authorized at any time thereafter, by proclamation, to extend to persons who may have participated in the existing rebellion of any State or part thereof, pardon and amnesty, with such exceptions and at such times and on such conditions as he may deem expedient for the public welfare; and

Whereas, the congressional declaration for limited and conditional pardon, accords with well-established judicial exposition of the pardoning power; and

Whereas, with reference to said rebellion, the President of the United States has issued several proclamations with provisions, in regard to the liberation of slaves; and

Whereas, it is now desired by some persons heretofore engaged in said rebellion to resume their allegiance to the United States, and to reinaugurate loyal State governments within and for their respective states: Therefore—

I, ABRAHAM LINCOLN, President of the United States, do proclaim, declare, and make known to all persons who have, directly or by implication, participated in the existing rebellion, except as hereinafter excepted, that a full pardon is hereby granted to them and each of them, with restoration of all rights of property, except as to slaves, and in property cases, where rights of third parties shall have intervened, and upon the condition that every such person shall take and subscribe an oath, and thenceforward keep and maintain said oath inviolate; and which oath shall be registered for permanent preservation, and shall be of the tenor and effect following, to wit:

"I, ——————— ———————, do solemnly swear, in presence of Almighty God, that I will henceforth faithfully support, protect, and defend the Constitution of the United States and the Union of the States thereunder; and that I will, in like manner, abide by and faithfully support all acts of Congress passed during the existing rebellion with reference to slaves, so long and so far as not repealed, modified, or held void by Congress, or by decision of the supreme court; and that I will, in like manner, abide by and faithfully support all proclamations of the President made during the existing rebellion having reference to slaves, so long and so far as not modified or declared void by decision of the Supreme Court. So help me God."

The persons excepted from the benefits of the foregoing provisions are all who are, or shall have been, civil or diplomatic officers or agents of the so-called Confederate government; all who have left judicial stations under the United States to aid the rebellion; all who are, or shall have been, military or naval officers of said so-called Confederate government above the rank of colonel in the army or of lieutenant in the navy; all who left seats in the United States Congress to aid the rebellion; all who resigned commissions in the army or navy of the United States and afterwards aided the rebellion; and all who have engaged in any way in treating colored persons, or white persons in charge of such, otherwise than lawfully as prisoners of war, and which persons may have been found in the United States service as soldiers, seamen, or in any other capacity.

And I do further proclaim, declare, and make known, that whenever, in any of the States of Arkansas, Texas, Louisiana, Mississippi, Tennessee, Alabama, Georgia, Florida, South Carolina, and North Carolina, a number of persons, not less than one tenth in number of the votes cast in such state at the presidential election of the year of our Lord one thousand eight hundred and sixty, each having taken the oath aforesaid, and not having since violated it, and being a qualified voter by the election laws of the state existing immediately before the so-called act of secession, and excluding all others, shall reëstablish a State government which shall be republican, and in nowise contravening said oath, such shall be recognized as the true government of the State, and the State shall receive thereunder the benefits of the constitutional provision, which declares that "the United States shall guarantee to every State in this Union a republican form of government, and shall protect each of them against invasion; and on application of the legislature, or the executive (when the legislature cannot be convened), against domestic violence."

And I do further proclaim, declare, and make known, that any provision which may be adopted by such State government in relation to the freed people of such State, which shall recognize and declare their permanent freedom, provide for their education, and which may yet be consistent as a temporary arrangement with their present condition as a laboring, landless, and homeless class, will not be objected to by the National Executive.

And it is suggested as not improper that, in constructing a loyal State government in any State, the name of the State, the boundary, the subdivisions, the constitution, and the general code of laws, as before the rebellion, be maintained, subject only to the modifications made necessary by the conditions hereinbefore stated, and such others, if any, not contravening said conditions, and which may be deemed expedient by those framing the new State government.

To avoid misunderstanding, it may be proper to say that this proclamation, so far as it relates to state governments, has no reference to states wherein loyal state governments have all the while been maintained. And, for the same reason, it may be proper to further say, that whether members sent to congress from any state shall be admitted to seats constitutionally, rests exclusively with the respective houses, and not to any extent with the Executive. And still further, that this proclamation is intended to present the people of the states wherein the national authority has been suspended, and loyal state governments have been subverted, a mode in and by which the national authority and loyal state governments may be reëstablished within said states, or in any of them; and, while the mode presented is the best the Executive can suggest, with his present impressions, it must not be understood that no other possible mode would be acceptable.

Given under my hand at the city of Washington, on the 8th day of December, A. D. 1863, and of the Independence of the United States of America the eighty-eighth.

ABRAHAM LINCOLN.

SEAL

LINCOLN'S LETTER
TO MRS. BIXBY

(1864)

Executive Mansion, Washington, November 21, 1864.

Mrs. Bixby, Boston, Massachusetts:

DEAR MADAM: I have been shown in the files of the War Department a statement of the Adjutant-General of Massachusetts that you are the mother of five sons who have died gloriously on the field of battle. I feel how weak and fruitless must be any words of mine which should attempt to beguile you from the grief of a loss so overwhelming. But I cannot refrain from tendering to you the consolation that may be found in the thanks of the Republic they died to save. I pray that our Heavenly Father may assuage the anguish of your bereavement, and leave you only the cherished memory of the loved and lost, and the solemn pride that must be yours to have laid so costly a sacrifice upon the altar of freedom.

Yours very sincerely and respectfully,

ABRAHAM LINCOLN.

TERMS OF LEE'S SURRENDER
AT APPOMATTOX

(1865)

[The following letters exchanged by Generals Grant and Lee give the terms under which the latter surrendered his army and practically brought to a close the War of Secession.]

"Appomattox Court-House, Virginia, April 9, 1865.

"GENERAL: In accordance with the substance of my letter to you of the 8th instant, I propose to receive the surrender of the army of Northern Virginia on the following terms, to wit: Rolls of all the officers and men to be made in duplicate, one copy to be given to an officer to be designated by me, the other to be retained by such officer or officers as you may designate. The officers to give their individual paroles not to take up arms against the government of the United States until properly exchanged; and each company or regimental commander to sign a like parole for the men of their commands. The arms, artillery, and public property to be parked and stacked, and turned over to the officers appointed by me to receive them. This will not embrace the side-arms of the officers nor their private horses or baggage. This done, each officer and man will be allowed to return to his home, not to be disturbed by United States authority so long as they observe their paroles and the laws in force where they may reside.

"U. S. GRANT, Lieutenant-General.

"General R. E. Lee."

"Head-Quarters, Army of Northern Virginia,

April 9, 1865.

"GENERAL: I received your letter of this date containing the terms of the surrender of the army of Northern Virginia, as proposed by you. As they are substantially the same as those expressed in your letter of the 8th instant, they are accepted. I will proceed to designate the proper officers to carry the stipulations into effect.

"R. E. LEE, General.

"Lieutenant-General U. S. Grant."

LEE'S FAREWELL
TO HIS ARMY

(1865)

"Head-Quarters, Army of Northern Virginia,

April 10, 1865.

"AFTER four years of arduous service, marked by unsurpassed courage and fortitude, the Army of Northern Virginia has been compelled to yield to overwhelming numbers and resources. I need not tell the survivors of so many hard-fought battles, who have remained steadfast to the last, that I have consented to this result from no distrust of them: but, feeling that valour and devotion could accomplish nothing that could compensate for the loss that would have attended the continuation of the contest, I have determined to avoid the useless sacrifice of those whose past services have endeared them to their countrymen. By the terms of the agreement, officers and men can return to their homes and remain there until exchanged. You will take with you the satisfaction that proceeds from the consciousness of duty faithfully performed; and I earnestly pray that a merciful God will extend to you His blessing and protection. With an increasing admiration of your constancy and devotion to your country, and a grateful remembrance of your kind and generous consideration of myself, I bid you an affectionate farewell.

"R. E. LEE, General."

LINCOLN'S SECOND
INAUGURAL ADDRESS

(1865)

[By the date of Lincoln's second inauguration, the tide of war had turned in favour of the Union, and the end was in sight. The tone of the address, however, is subdued rather than triumphant, and it rises to a rare pitch of eloquence, marked by a singular combination of tenderness and determination.]

FELLOW-COUNTRYMEN: At this second appearing to take the oath of the Presidential office, there is less occasion for an extended address than there was at first. Then, a statement, somewhat in detail, of a course to be pursued, seemed fitting and proper. Now, at the expiration of four years, during which public declarations have been constantly called forth on every point and phase of the great contest which still absorbs the attention and engrosses the energies of the nation, little that is new could be presented. The progress of our arms, upon which all else chiefly depends, is as well known to the public as to myself; and it is, I trust, reasonably satisfactory and encouraging to all. With high hope for the future, no prediction in regard to it is ventured.

On the occasion corresponding to this four years ago, all thoughts were anxiously directed to an impending civil war. All dreaded it—all sought to avert it. While the inaugural address was being delivered from this place, devoted altogether to saving the Union without war, insurgent agents were in the city seeking to destroy it without war—seeking to dissolve the Union, and divide effects, by negotiation. Both parties deprecated war; but one of them would make war rather than let the nation survive; and the other would accept war rather than let it perish. And the war came.

One-eighth of the whole population were colored slaves, not distributed generally over the Union, but localized in the Southern part of it. These slaves constituted a peculiar and powerful interest. All knew that this interest was, somehow, the cause of the war. To strengthen, perpetuate, and extend this interest was the object for which the insurgents would rend the Union, even by war; while the Government claimed no right to do more than to restrict the territorial enlargement of it. Neither party expected for the war the magnitude or the duration which it has already attained. Neither anticipated that the cause of the conflict might cease with, or even before, the conflict itself should cease. Each looked for an easier triumph, and a result less fundamental and astounding. Both read the same Bible, and pray to the same God; and each invokes His aid against the other. It may seem strange that any men should dare to ask a just God's assistance in wringing their bread from the sweat of other men's faces; but let us judge not, that we be not judged. The prayers of both could not be answered—that of neither has been answered fully. The Almighty has His own purposes. "Woe unto the world because of offenses! for it must needs be that offenses come; but woe to that man by whom the offense cometh." If we shall suppose that American slavery is one of those offenses which, in the providence of God, must needs come, but which, having continued through His appointed time, He now wills to remove, and that He gives to both North and South this terrible war, as the woe due to those by whom the offense came, shall, we discern therein, any departure from those divine attributes which the believers in a living God always ascribe to Him? Fondly do we hope—fervently do we pray—that this mighty scourge of war may speedily pass away. Yet, if God wills that it continue until all the wealth piled by the bondman's two hundred and fifty years of unrequited toil shall be sunk, and until every drop of blood drawn with the lash shall be paid by another, drawn with the sword, as was said three thousand years ago, so still it must be said: "The judgments of the Lord are true and righteous altogether."

With malice toward none; with charity for all; with firmness in the right, as God gives us to see the right, let us strive on to finish the work we are in; to bind up the nation's wounds; to care for him who shall have borne the battle, and for his widow, and his orphan—to do all which may achieve and cherish a just and lasting peace among ourselves, and with all nations.

PROCLAMATION DECLARING
THE INSURRECTION
AT AN END

(1866)

[President Johnson's proclamation of May 10, 1865, marked the actual close of hostilities; that of April 2, 1866, declared the insurrection at an end in all the States save Texas; and this of Aug. 20, 1866, gave notice of the resumption of civil government in the States which had seceded.]

WHEREAS, by proclamations of the 15th and 19th of April, 1861, the President of the United States in virtue of the power vested in him by the Constitution and the laws, declared that the laws of the United States were opposed and the execution thereof obstructed in the States of South Carolina, Georgia, Alabama, Florida, Mississippi, Louisiana, and Texas by combinations too powerful to be suppressed by the ordinary course of judicial proceedings or by the powers vested in the marshals of the law; and

Whereas, by another proclamation made on the 16th day of August, in the same year, in pursuance of an act of Congress approved July 13, 1861, the inhabitants of the States of Georgia, South Carolina, Virginia, North Carolina, Tennessee, Alabama, Louisiana, Texas, Arkansas, Mississippi, and Florida (except the inhabitants of the State of Virginia lying west of the Alleghany Mountains, and except also the inhabitants of such other parts of that State and the other States before named as might maintain a loyal adhesion to the Union and Constitution or might be from time to time occupied and controlled by forces of the United States engaged in the dispersion of the insurgents) were declared to be in a state of insurrection against the United States; and

Whereas, by another proclamation of the 1st of July, 1862, issued in pursuance of an act of Congress approved June 7, in the same year, the insurrection was declared to be still existing in the States aforesaid, with the exception of certain specified counties in the State of Virginia; and

Whereas, by another proclamation made on the second day of April, 1863, in pursuance of an act of Congress of July 13, 1861, the exceptions named in the proclamation of August 16, 1861, were revoked and the inhabitants of the States of Georgia, South Carolina, North Carolina, Tennessee, Alabama, Louisiana, Texas, Arkansas, Mississippi, Florida, and Virginia (except the forty-eight counties of Virginia designated as West Virginia and the ports of New Orleans, Key West, Port Royal, and Beaufort, in North Carolina) were declared to be still in a state of insurrection against the United States; and

Whereas, by another proclamation, of the 15th day of September, 1863, made in pursuance of the act of Congress approved March 3, 1863, the rebellion was declared to be still existing and the privilege of the writ of *habeas corpus* was in certain specified cases suspended throughout the United States, said suspension to continue throughout the duration of the rebellion or until said proclamation should, by a subsequent one to be issued by the President of the United States, be modified or revoked; and

Whereas, the House of Representatives on the 22d day of July, 1861, adopted a resolution in the following words, namely:

Resolved by the House of Representatives of the Congress of the United States, That the present deplorable civil war has been forced upon the country by the disunionists of the Southern States now in revolt against the constitutional Government, and in arms around the capitol: that in this national emergency, Congress, banishing all feelings of mere passion or resentment, will recollect only its duty to the whole country; that this war is not waged upon our part in any spirit of oppression, nor for any purpose of conquest or subjugation, nor purpose of overthrowing or interfering with the rights or established institutions of those States; but to defend and maintain the supremacy of the Constitution, and to preserve the Union, with all the dignity, equality, and rights of the several States, unimpaired; and that as soon as these objects are accomplished the war ought to cease; and

Whereas, the Senate of the United States on the 25th day of July, 1861, adopted a resolution in the words following, to wit:

Resolved, That the present deplorable civil war has been forced upon the country by the disunionists of the Southern States now in revolt against the constitutional Government and in arms around the capitol; that in this national emergency Congress, banishing all feelings of mere passion or resentment, will recollect only its own duty to the whole country; that this war is not prosecuted upon our part in any spirit of oppression, nor for any purpose of conquest or subjugation, nor purpose of overthrowing or interfering with the rights or established institutions of those States; but to defend and maintain the supremacy of the Constitution and all laws made in pursuance thereof and to preserve the Union, with all the dignity, equality, and rights of the several States unimpaired; that as soon as these objects are accomplished the war ought to cease; and

Whereas, these resolutions though not joint or concurrent in form, are substantially identical, and as such have hitherto been and yet are regarded as having expressed the sense of Congress upon the subject to which they relate; and

Whereas, the President of the United States by proclamation of the 13th of June, 1865, declared that the insurrection in the State of Tennessee had been suppressed, and that the authority of the United States therein was undisputed, and such United States officers as had been duly commissioned were in the undisturbed exercise of their official functions; and

Whereas, the President of the United States by further proclamation, issued on the 2d day of April, 1866, did promulgate and declare that there no longer existed any armed resistance of misguided citizens or others to the authority of the United States in any or in all the States before mentioned, excepting only the State of Texas, and did further promulgate and declare that the laws could be sustained and enforced in the several States before mentioned, except Texas, by the proper civil authorities, State or Federal, and that the people of the said States, except Texas, are well and loyally disposed, and have conformed or will conform in their legislation to the condition of affairs growing out of the amendment to the Constitution of the United States, prohibiting slavery within the jurisdiction of the United States;

And did further declare, in the same proclamation that it is the manifest determination of the American people that no State, of its own will, has a right or power to go out of, or separate itself from, or be separated from the American Union; and that, therefore, each State ought to remain and constitute an integral part of the United States;

And did further declare, in the same last-mentioned proclamation, that the several aforementioned States, excepting Texas, had in the manner aforesaid given satisfactory evidence that they acquiesce in this sovereign and important resolution of national unity; and

Whereas, the President of the United States in the same proclamation did further declare, that it is believed to be a fundamental principle of government that the people who have revolted and who have been overcome and subdued, must be dealt with so as to induce them voluntarily to become friends, or else they must be held by absolute military power or devastated so as to prevent them from ever again doing harm as enemies, which last-named policy is abhorrent to humanity and to freedom; and

Whereas, the President did, in the same proclamation further declare, that the Constitution of the United States provides for constituent communities only as States, and not as Territories, dependencies, provinces, or protectorates;

And further, that such constituent States must necessarily be, and by the Constitution and laws of the United States are, made equals and placed upon a like footing as to political rights, immunities, dignity, and power with the several States with which they are united;

And did further declare, that the observance of political equality, as a principle of right and justice, is well calculated to encourage the people of the before-named States, except Texas, to become more and more constant and persevering in their new allegiance; and

Whereas, the President did further declare, that standing armies, military occupation, martial law, military tribunals, and the suppression of the writ of *habeas corpus* are in times of peace dangerous to public liberty, incompatible with the individual right of the citizen, contrary to the genius and spirit of our free institutions, and exhaustive of the national resources, and ought not, therefore, to be sanctioned or allowed except in cases of actual necessity for repelling invasion and suppressing insurrection or rebellion;

And the President did further, in the same proclamation, declare that the policy of the Government of the United States from the beginning of the insurrection to its overthrow and final suppression had been conducted in conformity with the principles in the last-named proclamation recited; and

Whereas, the President, in the said proclamation, of the 13th of June, 1865, upon the grounds therein stated and hereinbefore recited, did then and thereby proclaim and declare that the insurrection which heretofore existed in the several States before named, except in Texas, was at an end, and was therefore to be so regarded; and

Whereas, subsequently to the said 2d day of April, 1866, the insurrection in the State of Texas has been completely and everywhere suppressed and ended, and the authority of the United States has been successfully and completely established in the said State of Texas and now remains therein unassisted and undisputed, and such of the proper United States officers as have been duly commissioned within the limits of the said State are now in the undisturbed exercise of their official functions; and

Whereas, the laws can now be sustained and enforced in the said State of Texas by the proper civil authority, State or Federal, and the people of the said State of Texas, like the people of the other States before named, are well and loyally disposed and have conformed or will conform in their legislation to the condition of affairs growing out of the amendment to the Constitution of the United States prohibiting slavery within the limits and jurisdiction of the United States; and

Whereas, all the reasons and conclusions set forth in regard to the several States therein especially named now apply equally and in all respects to the State of Texas, as well as to the other States which have been involved in the insurrection; and

Whereas, adequate provision has been made by military orders to enforce the execution of the acts of Congress, aid the civil authorities, and secure obedience to the Constitution and laws of the United

States within the State of Texas, if a resort to military force for such purpose should at any time be necessary:

Now therefore, I,Andrew Johnson, President of the United States, do hereby proclaim and declare that the insurrection which heretofore existed in the State of Texas is at an end, and is to be henceforth so regarded in that State as in the other States before named, in which the said insurrection was proclaimed to be at an end, by the aforesaid proclamation of the 2d of April, 1866.

And I do further proclaim, that the said insurrection is at an end, and that peace, order, and tranquility, and civil authority now exist in and throughout the whole United States of America.

In testimony whereof, I have hereunto set my hand and caused the seal of the United States to be affixed.

[Seal.]   Done at the city of Washington, this 20th day of August, A. D. 1866, and of the Independence of the United States of America the ninety-first.

ANDREW JOHNSON.

By the President:
WILLIAM H. SEWARD,
    Secretary of State.

TREATY WITH RUSSIA

(1867)

[The risk of encroachment by Russia had been one of the causes which induced President Monroe to give official utterance to the "Monroe Doctrine." After his statement, Russia ceased from attempts to increase her influence on the Pacific coast, and became willing to dispose of Alaska, regarding it as a possession difficult to defend and of little value. The territory was formally transferred on Oct. 18, 1867.]

CONVENTION between the United States of America and His Majesty the Emperor of Russia, for the Cession of the Russian Possessions in North America to the United States, Concluded at Washington, March 30, 1867; Ratification Advised by Senate, April 9, 1867; Ratified by President, May 28, 1867; Ratifications Exchanged at Washington, June 20, 1867; Proclaimed, June 20, 1867.

The United States of America and His Majesty the Emperor of all the Russias, being desirous of strengthening, if possible, the good understanding which exists between them, have, for that purpose, appointed as their Plenipotentiaries, the President of the United States, William H. Seward, Secretary of State; and His Majesty the Emperor of all the Russias, the Privy Counsellor Edward de Stoeckl, his Envoy Extraordinary and Minister Plenipotentiary to the United States;

And the said Plenipotentiaries, having exchanged their full powers, which were found to be in due form, have agreed upon and signed the following articles:

ARTICLE I

His Majesty the Emperor of all the Russias, agrees to cede to the United States, by this convention, immediately upon the exchange of the ratifications thereof, all the territory and dominion now possessed by his said Majesty on the continent of America and in adjacent islands, the same being contained within the geographical limits herein set forth, to wit: The eastern limit is the line of demarcation between the Russian and the British possessions in North America, as established by the convention between Russia and Great Britain, of February 28–16, 1825, and described in Articles III and IV of said convention, in the following terms:

"III Commencing from the southernmost point of the island called Prince of Wales Island, which point lies in the parallel of 54 degrees 40 minutes north latitude, and between the 131st and 133d degree of west longitude (meridian of Greenwich), the said line shall ascend to the north along the channel called Portland Channel, as far as the point of the continent where it strikes the 56th degree of north latitude; from this last-mentioned point, the line of demarcation shall follow the summit of the mountains situated parallel to the coast, as far as the point of intersection of the 141st degree of west longitude (of the same meridian); and finally, from the said point of intersection, the said meridian line of the 141st degree, in its prolongation as far as the Frozen Ocean.

"IV With reference to the line of demarcation laid down in the preceding article, it is understood—

"1st That the island called Prince of Wales Island shall belong wholly to Russia" (now, by this cession to the United States).

"2d That whenever the summit of the mountains which extend in a direction parallel to the coast, from the 56th degree of north latitude to the point of intersection of the 141st degree of west longitude, shall prove to be at the distance of more than ten marine leagues from the ocean, the limit between the British possessions and the line of coast which is to belong to Russia as above mentioned (that is to say, the limit to the possessions ceded by this convention), shall be formed by a line parallel to the winding of the coast, and which shall never exceed the distance of ten marine leagues therefrom."

The western limit within which the territories and dominion conveyed are contained passes through a point in Behring's Straits on the parallel of sixty-five degrees thirty minutes north latitude, at its intersection by the meridian which passes midway between the islands of Krusenstern or Ignalook, and the island of Ratmanoff, or Noonarbook, and proceeds due north without limitation, into the same Frozen Ocean. The same western limit, beginning at the same initial point, proceeds thence in a course nearly southwest, through Behring's Straits and Behring's Sea, so as to pass midway between the northwest point of the island of St. Lawrence and the southeast point of Cape Choukotski, to the meridian of one hundred and seventy-two west longitude; thence, from the intersection of that meridian, in a southwesterly direction, so as to pass midway between the island of Attou and the Copper Island of the Kormandorski couplet or group, in the North Pacific Ocean, to the meridian of one hundred and ninety-three degrees west longitude, so as to include in the territory conveyed the whole of the Aleutian Islands east of that meridian.

Article II

In the cession of territory and dominion made by the preceding article, are included the right of property in all public lots and squares, vacant lands, and all public buildings, fortifications, barracks, and other edifices which are not private individual property. It is, however, understood and agreed, that the churches which have been built in the ceded territory by the Russian Government, shall remain the property of such members of the Greek Oriental Church resident in the territory as may choose to worship therein. Any Government archives, papers, and documents relative to the territory and dominion aforesaid, which may now be existing there, will be left in the possession of the agent of the United States; but an authenticated copy of such of them as may be required, will be, at all times, given by the United States to the Russian Government, or to such Russian officers or subjects as they may apply for.

Article III

The inhabitants of the ceded territory, according to their choice, reserving their natural allegiance, may return to Russia within three years; but if they should prefer to remain in the ceded territory, they, with the exception of uncivilized native tribes, shall be admitted to the enjoyment of all the rights, advantages, and immunities of citizens of the United States, and shall be maintained and protected in the free enjoyment of their liberty, property, and religion.

The uncivilized tribes will be subject to such laws and regulations as the United States may from time to time adopt in regard to aboriginal tribes of that country.

Article IV

His Majesty, the Emperor of all the Russias, shall appoint, with convenient despatch, an agent or agents for the purpose of formally delivering to a similar agent or agents, appointed on behalf of the United States, the territory, dominion, property, dependencies, and appurtenances which are ceded as above, and for doing any other act which may be necessary in regard thereto. But the cession, with the right of immediate possession, is nevertheless to be deemed complete and absolute on the exchange of ratifications, without waiting for such formal delivery.

Article V

Immediately after the exchange of the ratifications of this convention, any fortifications or military posts which may be in the ceded territory shall be delivered to the agent of the United States, and any Russian troops which may be in the territory shall be withdrawn as soon as may be reasonably and conveniently practicable.

Article VI

In consideration of the cession aforesaid, the United States agree to pay at the Treasury in Washington, within ten months after the exchange of the ratifications of this convention, to the diplomatic representative or other agent of His Majesty the Emperor of all the Russias, duly authorized to receive the same, seven million two hundred thousand dollars in gold. The cession of territory and dominion herein made is hereby declared to be free and unincumbered by any reservations, privileges, franchises, grants, or possessions, by any associated companies, whether corporate or incorporate, Russian or any other, or by any parties, except merely private individual property-holders; and the cession hereby made conveys all the rights, franchises, and privileges now belonging to Russia in the said territory or dominion, and appurtenances thereto.

ARTICLE VII

When this convention shall have been duly ratified by the President, of the United States, by and with the advice and consent of the Senate, on the one part, and, on the other, by His Majesty the Emperor of all the Russias, the ratifications shall be exchanged at Washington within three months from the date thereof, or sooner if possible.

In faith whereof the respective Plenipotentiaries have signed this convention, and thereto affixed the seals of their arms.

Done at Washington, the thirtieth day of March, in the year of our Lord one thousand eight hundred and sixty-seven.

WILLIAM H. SEWARD [L. S.]
EDOUARD DE STOECKL [L. S.]

ANNEXATION
OF THE HAWAIIAN ISLANDS

(1898)

[Queen Liliuokalani, of the Hawaiian Islands, attempted, in 1893, to introduce a new constitution, which would place the government of the Islands much more completely in her power than it had previously been. The attempt did not succeed; the Queen was forced to abdicate; and the foreigners in Honolulu set up a provisional government with a view to negotiating for annexation to the United States. President Harrison sent an annexation treaty to the Senate, but President Cleveland, on his coming into power, withdrew it. President McKinley, in 1897, sent in a second treaty, which was passed by Congress in June and July, 1898, and the sovereignty was transferred to the United States on Aug. 12, 1898.]

JOINT Resolution To provide for annexing the Hawaiian Islands to the United States.

Whereas, the Government of the Republic of Hawaii having, in due form, signified its consent, in the manner provided by its constitution, to cede absolutely and without reserve to the United States of America, all rights of sovereignty of whatsoever kind in and over the Hawaiian Islands and their dependencies, and also to cede and transfer to the United States, the absolute fee and ownership of all public, Government, or Crown lands, public buildings or edifices, ports, harbors, military equipment, and all other public property of every kind and description belonging to the Government of the Hawaiian Islands, together with every right and appurtenance thereunto appertaining: Therefore,

Resolved by the Senate and House of Representatives of the United States of America in Congress assembled, That said cession is accepted, ratified, and confirmed, and that the said Hawaiian Islands and their dependencies be, and they are hereby, annexed as a part of the territory of the United States and are subject to the sovereign dominion thereof, and that all and singular the property and rights hereinbefore mentioned are vested in the United States of America.

The existing laws of the United States relative to public lands shall not apply to such lands in the Hawaiian Islands; but the Congress of the United States shall enact special laws for their management and disposition: *Provided,* That all revenue from or proceeds of the same, except as regards such part thereof as may be used or occupied for the civil, military, or naval purposes of the United States, or may be assigned for the use of the local government, shall be used solely for the benefit of the inhabitants of the Hawaiian Islands for educational and other public purposes.

Until Congress shall provide for the government of such islands all the civil, judicial, and military powers exercised by the officers of the existing government in said islands shall be vested in such person or persons and shall be exercised in such manner as the President of the United States shall direct; and the President shall have power to remove said officers and fill the vacancies so occasioned.

The existing treaties of the Hawaiian Islands with foreign nations shall forthwith cease and determine, being replaced by such treaties as may exist, or as may be hereafter concluded, between the United States and such foreign nations. The municipal legislation of the Hawaiian Islands, not enacted for the fulfillment of the treaties so extinguished, and not inconsistent with this joint resolution nor contrary to the Constitution of the United States nor to any existing treaty of the United States, shall remain in force until the Congress of the United States shall otherwise determine.

Until legislation shall be enacted extending the United States customs laws and regulations to the Hawaiian Islands the existing customs relations of the Hawaiian Islands with the United States and other countries shall remain unchanged.

The public debt of the Republic of Hawaii, lawfully existing at the date of the passage of this joint resolution, including the amounts due to depositors in the Hawaiian Postal Savings Bank, is hereby assumed by the Government of the United States; but the liability of the United States in this regard shall in no case exceed four million dollars. So long, however, as the existing Government and the present commercial relations of the Hawaiian Islands are continued as hereinbefore, provided said Government shall continue to pay the interest on said debt.

There shall be no further immigration of Chinese into the Hawaiian Islands, except upon such conditions as are now or may hereafter be allowed by the laws of the United States; and no Chinese, by reason of anything herein contained, shall be allowed to enter the United States from the Hawaiian Islands.

SEC. 1. The President shall appoint five commissioners, at least two of whom shall be residents of the Hawaiian Islands, who shall, as soon as reasonably practicable, recommend to Congress such legislation concerning the Hawaiian Islands as they shall deem necessary or proper.

SEC. 2. That the commissioners hereinbefore provided for shall be appointed by the President, by and with the advice and consent of the Senate.

SEC. 3. That the sum of one hundred thousand dollars, or so much thereof as may be necessary, is hereby appropriated, out of any money in the Treasury not otherwise appropriated, and to be immediately available, to be expended at the discretion of the President of the United States of America, for the purpose of carrying this joint resolution into effect.

APPROVED, July 7, 1898.

RECOGNITION OF THE INDEPENDENCE OF CUBA

(1898)

[The following resolution not only recognized the independence of Cuba, but authorized the levying of war upon Spain in order to force upon that country a similar recognition. The resolution was passed in response to a message sent to Congress by President McKinley, April 11, 1898, asking for permission to intervene in Cuba.]

JOINT Resolution for the recognition of the independence of the people of Cuba, demanding that the Government of Spain relinquish its authority and government in the Island of Cuba, and to withdraw its land and naval forces from Cuba and Cuban waters, and directing the President of the United States to use the land and naval forces of the United States to carry these resolutions into effect.

Whereas, the abhorrent conditions which have existed for more than three years in the Island of Cuba, so near our own borders, have shocked the moral sense of the people of the United States, have been a disgrace to Christian civilization, culminating, as they have, in the destruction of a United States battle-ship, with two hundred and sixty-six of its officers and crew, while on a friendly visit in the harbor of Havana, and can not longer be endured, as has been set forth by the President of the United States in his message to Congress of April eleventh, eighteen hundred and ninety-eight, upon which the action of Congress was invited: Therefore,

Resolved, by the Senate and House of Representatives of the United States of America in Congress assembled, First. That the people of the Island of Cuba are, and of right ought to be, free and independent.

Second. That it is the duty of the United States to demand, and the Government of the United States does hereby demand, that the Government of Spain at once relinquish its authority and government in the Island of Cuba, and withdraw its land and naval forces from Cuba and Cuban waters.

Third. That the President of the United States be, and he hereby is, directed and empowered to use the entire land and naval forces of the United States, and to call into the actual service of the United States, the militia of the several States, to such extent as may be necessary to carry these resolutions into effect.

Fourth. That the United States hereby disclaims any disposition or intention to exercise sovereignty, jurisdiction, or control over said Islands except for the pacification thereof, and asserts its determination, when that is accomplished, to leave the government and control of the Island to its people.

APPROVED, April 20, 1898.

TREATY WITH SPAIN

(1898)

[On July 26, 1898, nine days after the surrender of Santiago, the Spanish government opened negotiations for peace through the French ambassador at Washington. Fighting ceased on Aug. 12; and on Oct. 1, the commissioners of Spain and the United States met at Paris, where the following treaty was drawn up.]

TREATY of Peace between the United States of America and the Kingdom of Spain, Signed at Paris, December 10, 1898; ratification advised by the Senate, February 6, 1899; ratified by the President, February 6, 1899; ratified by Her Majesty the Queen Regent of Spain, March 19, 1899; ratifications exchanged at Washington, April 11, 1899; proclaimed at Washington, April 11, 1899.

THE UNITED STATES OF AMERICA AND HER MAJESTY THE QUEEN REGENT OF SPAIN, IN THE NAME OF HER AUGUST SON, DON ALFONSO XIII, desiring to end the state of war now existing between the two countries, have for that purpose appointed as Plenipotentiaries:

THE PRESIDENT OF THE UNITED STATES,

WILLIAM R. DAY, CUSHMAN K. DAVIS, WILLIAM P. FRYE, GEORGE GRAY, and WHITELAW REID, citizens of the United States;

AND HER MAJESTY THE QUEEN REGENT OF SPAIN,

DON EUGENIO MONTERO RIOS, President of the Senate,

DON BUENAVENTURA DE ABARZUZA, Senator of the Kingdom, and ex-Minister of the Crown,

DON JOSE DE GARNICA, Deputy to the Cortes and Associate Justice of the Supreme Court;

DON WENCESLAO RAMIREZ DE VILLA-URRUTIA, Envoy Extraordinary and Minister Plenipotentiary at Brussels, and

DON RAFAEL CERERO, General of Division;

Who, having assembled in Paris, and having exchanged their full powers, which were found to be in due and proper form, have, after discussion of the matters before them, agreed upon the following articles:

ARTICLE I

Spain relinquishes all claim of sovereignty over and title to Cuba.

And as the island is, upon its evacuation by Spain, to be occupied by the United States, the United States will, so long as such occupation shall last, assume and discharge the obligations that may under international law result from the fact of its occupation, for the protection of life and property.

ARTICLE II

Spain cedes to the United States, the island of Porto Rico and other islands now under Spanish sovereignty in the West Indies, and the island of Guam in the Marianas or Ladrones.

ARTICLE III

Spain cedes to the United States, the archipelago known as the Philippine Islands, and comprehending the islands lying within the following line:

A line running from west to east along or near the twentieth parallel of north latitude, and through the middle of the navigable channel of Bachi, from the one hundred and eighteenth (118th) to the one hundred and twenty-seventh (127th) degree meridian of longitude east of Greenwich, thence along the one hundred and twenty-seventh (127th) degree meridian of longitude east of Greenwich to the parallel of four degrees and forty-five minutes (4° 45′) north latitude, thence along the parallel of four degrees and forty-five minutes (4° 45′) north latitude to its intersection with the meridian of longitude one hundred and nineteen degrees and thirty-five minutes (119° 35′) east of Greenwich, thence along the meridian of longitude one hundred and nineteen degrees and thirty-five minutes (119° 35′) east of Greenwich to the parallel of latitude seven degrees and forty minutes (7° 40′) north, thence along the parallel of latitude seven degrees and forty minutes (7° 40′) north to its intersection with the one hundred and sixteenth (116th) degree meridian of longitude east of Greenwich, thence by a direct line to the intersection of the tenth (10th) degree parallel of north latitude with the one hundred and eighteenth (118th) degree meridian of longitude east of Greenwich, and thence along the one hundred and eighteenth (118th) degree meridian of longitude east of Greenwich to the point of beginning.

The United States will pay to Spain, the sum of twenty million dollars ($20,000,000) within three months after the exchange of the ratifications of the present treaty.

ARTICLE IV

The United States will, for the term of ten years from the date of the exchange of the ratifications of the present treaty, admit Spanish ships and merchandise to the ports of the Philippine Islands on the same terms as ships and merchandise of the United States.

ARTICLE V

The United States will, upon the signature of the present treaty, send back to Spain, at its own cost, the Spanish soldiers taken as prisoners of war on the capture of Manila by the American forces. The arms of the soldiers in question shall be restored to them.

Spain will, upon the exchange of the ratifications of the present treaty, proceed to evacuate the Philippines, as well as the island of Guam, on terms similar to those agreed upon by the Commissioners appointed to arrange for the evacuation of Porto Rico and other islands in the West Indies, under the Protocol of August 12, 1898, which is to continue in force till its provisions are completely executed.

The time within which the evacuation of the Philippine Islands and Guam shall be completed shall be fixed by the two Governments. Stands of colors, uncaptured war vessels, small arms, guns of all calibres, with their carriages and accessories, powder, ammunition, live stock, and materials and supplies of all kinds, belonging to the land and naval forces of Spain in the Philippines and Guam, remain the property of Spain. Pieces of heavy ordnance, exclusive of field artillery, in the fortifications and coast defences, shall remain in their emplacements for the term of six months, to be reckoned from the exchange of ratifications of the treaty; and the United States may, in the meantime, purchase such material from Spain, if a satisfactory agreement between the two Governments on the subject shall be reached.

ARTICLE VI

Spain will, upon the signature of the present treaty, release all prisoners of war, and all persons detained or imprisoned for political offences, in connection with the insurrections in Cuba and the Philippines and the war with the United States.

Reciprocally, the United States will release all persons made prisoners of war by the American forces, and will undertake to obtain the release of all Spanish prisoners in the hands of the insurgents in Cuba and the Philippines.

The Government of the United States will at its own cost, return to Spain, and the Government of Spain will at its own cost, return to the United States, Cuba, Porto Rico, and the Philippines, according to the situation of their respective homes, prisoners released or caused to be released by them, respectively, under this article.

ARTICLE VII

The United States and Spain mutually relinquish all claims for indemnity, national and individual, of every kind, of either Government, or of its citizens or subjects, against the other Government, that may have arisen since the beginning of the late insurrection in Cuba and prior to the exchange of ratifications of the present treaty, including all claims for indemnity for the cost of the war.

The United States will adjudicate and settle the claims of its citizens against Spain relinquished in this article.

ARTICLE VIII

In conformity with the provisions of Articles I, II, and III of this treaty, Spain relinquishes in Cuba, and cedes in Porto Rico and other islands in the West Indies, in the island of Guam, and in the Philippine Archipelago, all the buildings, wharves, barracks, forts, structures, public highways and other immovable property which, in conformity with law, belong to the public domain, and as such belong to the Crown of Spain.

And it is hereby declared that the relinquishment or cession, as the case may be, to which the preceding paragraph refers, cannot in any respect impair the property or rights which by law belong to the peaceful possession of property of all kinds, of provinces, municipalities, public or private establishments, ecclesiastical or civic bodies, or any other associations having legal capacity to acquire and possess property in the aforesaid territories renounced or ceded, or of private individuals, of whatsoever nationality such individuals may be.

The aforesaid relinquishment or cession, as the case may be, includes all documents exclusively referring to the sovereignty relinquished or ceded that may exist in the archives of the Peninsula. Where any document in such archives only in part relates to said sovereignty, a copy of such part will be furnished whenever it shall be requested. Like rules shall be reciprocally observed in favor of Spain in request of documents in the archives of the islands above referred to.

In the aforesaid relinquishment or cession, as the case may be, are also included such rights as the Crown of Spain and its authorities possess in respect of the official archives and records, executive as well as judicial, in the islands above referred to, which relate to said islands or the rights and property of their inhabitants. Such archives and records shall be carefully preserved, and private persons shall without distinction have the right to require, in accordance with law, authenticated copies of the contracts, wills and other instruments forming part of notarial protocols or files, or which may be contained in the executive or judicial archives, be the latter in Spain or in the islands aforesaid.

Article IX

Spanish subjects, natives of the Peninsula, residing in the territory over which Spain by the present treaty relinquishes or cedes her sovereignty, may remain in such territory or may remove therefrom, retaining in either event all their rights of property, including the right to sell or dispose of such property or of its proceeds; and they shall also have the right to carry on their industry, commerce and professions, being subject in respect thereof to such laws as are applicable to other foreigners. In case they remain in the territory they may preserve their allegiance to the Crown of Spain by making, before a court of record, within a year from the date of the exchange of ratifications of this treaty, a declaration of their decision to preserve such allegiance; in default of which declaration they shall be held to have renounced it and to have adopted the nationality of the territory in which they may reside.

The civil rights and political status of the native inhabitants of the territories hereby ceded to the United States shall be determined by the Congress.

Article X

The inhabitants of the territories over which Spain relinquishes or cedes her sovereignty shall be secured in the free exercise of their religion.

Article XI

The Spaniards residing in the territories over which Spain by this treaty cedes or relinquishes her sovereignty shall be subject in matters civil as well as criminal to the jurisdiction of the courts of the country wherein they reside, pursuant to the ordinary laws governing the same; and they shall have the right to appear before such courts, and to pursue the same course as citizens of the country to which the courts belong.

Article XII

Judicial proceedings pending at the time of the exchange of ratifications of this treaty in the territories over which Spain relinquishes or cedes her sovereignty shall be determined according to the following rules:

(1) Judgments rendered either in civil suits between private individuals, or in criminal matters, before the date mentioned, and with respect to which there is no recourse or right of review under the Spanish law, shall be deemed to be final, and shall be executed in due form by competent authority in the territory within which such judgments should be carried out.

(2) Civil suits between private individuals which may on the date mentioned be undetermined shall be prosecuted to judgment before the court in which they may then be pending or in the court that may be substituted therefor.

(3) Criminal actions pending on the date mentioned before the Supreme Court of Spain against citizens of the territory which by this treaty ceases to be Spanish shall continue under its jurisdiction until final judgment; but, such judgment having been rendered, the execution thereof shall be committed to the competent authority of the place in which the case arose.

Article XIII

The rights of property secured by copyrights and patents acquired by Spaniards in the Island of Cuba, and in Porto Rico, the Philippines and other ceded territories, at the time of the exchange of the ratifications of this treaty, shall continue to be respected. Spanish scientific, literary and artistic works, not subversive of public order in the territories in question, shall continue to be admitted free of duty into such territories, for the period of ten years, to be reckoned from the date of the exchange of the ratifications of this treaty.

Article XIV

Spain shall have the power to establish consular officers in the ports and places of the territories, the sovereignty over which has been either relinquished or ceded by the present treaty.

Article XV

The Government of each country will, for the term of ten years, accord to the merchant vessels of the other country the same treatment in respect of all port charges, including entrance and clearance dues, light dues, and tonnage duties, as it accords to its own merchant vessels, not engaged in the coastwise trade.

This article may at any time be terminated on six months' notice given by either Government to the other.

Article XVI

It is understood that any obligations assumed in this treaty by the United States with respect to Cuba are limited to the time of its occupancy thereof; but it will upon the termination of such occupancy, advise any Government established in the island to assume the same obligations.

Article XVII

The present treaty shall be ratified by the President of the United States, by and with the advice and consent of the Senate thereof, and by her Majesty the Queen Regent of Spain; and the ratifications shall be exchanged at Washington within six months from the date hereof, or earlier if possible.

In faith whereof, we, the respective Plenipotentiaries, have signed this treaty and have hereunto affixed our seals.

Done in duplicate at Paris, the tenth day of December, in the year of Our Lord one thousand eight hundred and ninety-eight.

[SEAL.]	WILLIAM R. DAY
[SEAL.]	CUSHMAN K. DAVIS
[SEAL.]	WM. P. FRYE
[SEAL.]	GEO. GRAY
[SEAL.]	WHITELAW REID

CONVENTION BETWEEN THE UNITED STATES AND THE REPUBLIC OF PANAMA

(1904)

[The attempt on the part of a French company to build a Panama canal was begun in 1879 under a concession from the Republic of Colombia, through whose territory the canal was to pass. When the enterprise was taken over by the United States in 1903, the treaty with Colombia, arranging for United States control of the canal strip, was rejected by the Congress of Colombia. The people of the isthmus, whose prosperity largely depended on the building of the canal, thereupon seceded from Colombia, set up the Republic of Panama, and agreed to the following con· vention.]

FOR the Construction of a Ship Canal to Connect the Waters of the Atlantic and Pacific Oceans. Signed at Washington, November 18, 1903. Ratification advised by the Senate, February 23, 1904. Ratified by the President, February 25, 1904. Ratified by Panama, December 2, 1903. Ratifications exchanged at Washington, February 26, 1904. Proclaimed, February 26, 1904.

By the President of the United States of America.

A Proclamation

Whereas, a Convention between the United States of America and the Republic of Panama to insure the construction of a ship canal across the Isthmus of Panama to connect the Atlantic and Pacific Oceans, was concluded and signed by their respective Plenipotentiaries at Washington, on the eighteenth day of November, one thousand nine hundred and three, the original of which Convention, being in the English language, is word for word as follows:

Isthmian Canal Convention

The United States of America and the Republic of Panama being desirous to insure the construction of a ship canal across the Isthmus of Panama to connect the Atlantic and Pacific Oceans, and the Congress of the United States of America having passed an act approved June 28, 1902, in furtherance of that object, by which the President of the United States is authorized to acquire within a reasonable time the control of the necessary territory of the Republic of Colombia, and the sovereignty of such territory being actually vested in the Republic of Panama, the high contracting parties have resolved for that purpose to conclude a convention and have accordingly appointed as their plenipotentiaries,—

The President of the United States of America, John Hay, Secretary of State, and

The Government of the Republic of Panama, Philippe Bunau-Varilla, Envoy Extraordinary and Minister Plenipotentiary of the Republic of Panama, thereunto specially empowered by said government, who after communicating with each other their respective full powers, found to be in good and due form, have agreed upon and concluded the following articles:

ARTICLE I

The United States guarantees and will maintain the independence of the Republic of Panama.

ARTICLE II

The Republic of Panama grants to the United States in perpetuity, the use, occupation and control of a zone of land and land under water for the construction, maintenance, operation, sanitation and protection of said Canal of the width of ten miles extending to the distance of five miles on each side of the center line of the route of the Canal to be constructed; the said zone beginning in the Carribbean Sea three marine miles from mean low water mark and extending to and across the Isthmus of Panama into the Pacific Ocean to a distance of three marine miles from mean low water mark with the proviso that the cities of Panama and Colon and the harbors adjacent to said cities, which are included within the boundaries of the zone above described, shall not be included within this grant. The Republic of Panama further grants to the United States in perpetuity, the use, occupation and control of any other lands and waters outside of the zone above described which may be necessary and convenient for the construction, maintenance, operation, sanitation and protection of the said Canal or of any auxiliary canals or other works necessary and convenient for the construction, maintenance, operation, sanitation and protection of the said enterprise.

The Republic of Panama further grants in like manner to the United States in perpetuity, all islands within the limits of the zone above described and in addition thereto, the group of small islands in the Bay of Panama, named Perico, Naos, Culebra and Flamenco.

Article III

The Republic of Panama grants to the United States all the rights, power and authority within the zone mentioned and described in Article II of this agreement, and within the limits of all auxiliary lands and waters mentioned and described in said Article II which the United States would possess and exercise, if it were the sovereign of the territory within which said lands and waters are located to the entire exclusion of the exercise by the Republic of Panama of any such sovereign rights, power or authority.

Article IV

As rights subsidiary to the above grants the Republic of Panama grants in perpetuity, to the United States the right to use the rivers, streams, lakes and other bodies of water within its limits for navigation, the supply of water or waterpower or other purposes, so far as the use of said rivers, streams, lakes and bodies of water and the waters thereof may be necessary and convenient for the construction, maintenance, operation, sanitation and protection of the said Canal.

Article V

The Republic of Panama grants to the United States in perpetuity, a monopoly for the construction, maintenance and operation of any system of communication by means of canal or railroad across its territory between the Caribbean Sea and the Pacific Ocean.

Article VI

The grants herein contained shall in no manner invalidate the titles or rights of private land holders or owners of private property in the said zone or in or to any of the lands or waters granted to the United States by the provisions of any Article of this treaty, nor shall they interfere with the rights of way over the public roads passing through the said zone or over any of the said lands or waters unless said rights of way or private rights shall conflict with rights herein granted to the United States in which case the rights of the United States shall be superior. All damages caused to the owners of private lands or private property of any kind by reason of the grants contained in this treaty or by reason of the operations of the United States, its agents or employees, or by reason of the construction, maintenance, operation, sanitation and protection of the said Canal or of the works of sanitation and protection herein provided for, shall be appraised and settled by a joint Commission appointed by the Governments of the United States and the Republic of Panama, whose decisions as to such damages shall be final and whose awards as to such damages shall be paid solely by the United States. No part of the work on said Canal or the Panama railroad or on any auxiliary works relating thereto and authorized by the terms of this treaty shall be prevented, delayed or impeded by or pending such proceedings to ascertain such damages. The appraisal of said private lands and private property and the assessment of damages to them shall be based upon their value before the date of this convention.

Article VII

The Republic of Panama grants to the United States within the limits of the cities of Panama and Colon and their adjacent harbors and within the territory adjacent thereto the right to acquire by purchase or by the exercise of the right of eminent domain, any lands, buildings, water rights or other properties necessary and convenient for the construction, maintenance, operation and protection of the Canal and of any works of sanitation, such as the collection and disposition of sewage and the distribution of water in the said cities of Panama and Colon, which, in the discretion of the United States may be necessary and convenient for the construction, maintenance, operation, sanitation and protection of the said Canal and railroad. All such works of sanitation, collection and disposition of sewage and distribution of water in the cities of Panama and Colon shall be made at the expense of the United States, and the Government of the United States, its agents or nominees shall be authorized to impose and collect water rates and sewage rates which shall be sufficient to provide for the payment of interest and the amortization of the principal of the cost of said works within a period of fifty years and upon the expiration of said term of fifty years the system of sewers and water works shall revert to and become the properties of the cities of Panama and Colon respectively, and the use of the water shall be free to the inhabitants of Panama and Colon, except to the extent that water rates may be necessary for the operation and maintenance of said system of sewers and water.

The Republic of Panama agrees that the cities of Panama and Colon shall comply in perpetuity, with the sanitary ordinances whether of a preventive or curative character prescribed by the United States and in case the Government of Panama is unable or fails in its duty to enforce this compliance by the cities of Panama and Colon with the sanitary ordinances of the United States the Republic of Panama grants to the United States the right and authority to enforce the same.

The same right and authority are granted to the United States for the maintenance of public order in the cities of Panama and Colon and the territories and harbors adjacent thereto in case the Republic of Panama should not be, in the judgment of the United States, able to maintain such order.

Article VIII

The Republic of Panama grants to the United States all rights which it now has or hereafter may acquire to the property of the New Panama Canal Company and the Panama Railroad Company as a result of the transfer of sovereignty from the Republic of

Columbia to the Republic of Panama over the Isthmus of Panama and authorizes the New Panama Canal Company to sell and transfer to the United States its rights, privileges, properties and concessions as well as the Panama Railroad and all the shares or part of the shares of that company; but the public lands situated outside of the zone described in Article II of this treaty now included in the concessions of both said enterprises and not required in the construction or operation of the Canal shall revert to the Republic of Panama except any property now owned by or in the possession of said companies within Panama or Colon or the ports or terminals thereof.

Article IX

The United States agrees that the ports at either entrance of the Canal and the waters thereof, and the Republic of Panama agrees that the towns of Panama and Colon shall be free for all time so that there shall not be imposed or collected custom house tolls, tonnage, anchorage, lighthouse, wharf, pilot, or quarantine dues or any other charges or taxes of any kind upon any vessel using or passing through the Canal or belonging to or employed by the United States, directly or indirectly, in connection with the construction, maintenance, operation, sanitation and protection of the main Canal, or auxiliary works, or upon the cargo, officers, crew, or passengers of any such vessels, except such tolls and charges as may be imposed by the United States for the use of the Canal and other works, and except tolls and charges imposed by the Republic of Panama upon merchandise destined to be introduced for the consumption of the rest of the Republic of Panama, and upon vessels touching at the ports of Colon and Panama and which do not cross the Canal.

The Government of the Republic of Panama shall have the right to establish in such ports and in the towns of Panama and Colon such houses and guards as it may deem necessary to collect duties on importations destined to other portions of Panama and to prevent contraband trade. The United States shall have the right to make use of the towns and harbors of Panama and Colon as places of anchorage, and for making repairs, for loading, unloading, depositing, or transshipping cargoes either in transit or destined for the service of the Canal and for other works pertaining to the Canal.

ARTICLE X

The Republic of Panama agrees that there shall not be imposed any taxes, national, municipal, departmental, or of any other class, upon the Canal, the railways and auxiliary works, tugs and other vessels employed in the service of the Canal, store houses, work shops, offices, quarters for laborers, factories of all kinds, warehouses, wharves, machinery and other works, property, and effects appertaining to the Canal or railroad and auxiliary works, or their officers or employees, situated within the cities of Panama and Colon, and that there shall not be imposed contributions or charges of a personal character of any kind upon officers, employees, laborers, and other individuals in the service of the Canal and railroad and auxiliary works.

ARTICLE XI

The United States agrees that the official dispatches of the Government of the Republic of Panama shall be transmitted over any telegraph and telephone lines established for canal purposes and used for public and private business at rates not higher than those required from officials in the service of the United States.

ARTICLE XII

The Government of the Republic of Panama shall permit the immigration and free access to the lands and workshops of the Canal and its auxiliary works of all employees and workmen of what ever nationality under contract to work upon or seeking employ- ment upon or in any wise connected with the said Canal and its auxiliary works, with their respective families, and all such persons shall be free and exempt from the military service of the Republic of Panama.

ARTICLE XIII

The United States may import at any time into the said zone and auxiliary lands, free of custom duties, imposts, taxes, or other charges, and without any restrictions, any and all vessels, dredges, engines, cars, machinery, tools, explosives, materials, supplies, and other articles necessary and convenient in the construction, maintenance, operation, sanitation and protection of the Canal and auxiliary works, and all provisions, medicines, clothing, supplies and other things necessary and convenient for the officers, employees, workmen and laborers in the service and employ of the United States and for their families. If any such articles are disposed of for use outside of the zone and auxiliary lands granted to the United States and within the territory of the Republic, they shall be subject to the same import or other duties as like articles imported under the laws of the Republic of Panama.

Article XIV

As the price or compensation for the rights, powers and privileges granted in this convention by the Republic of Panama to the United States, the Government of the United States agrees to pay to the Republic of Panama the sum of ten million dollars ($10,000,000) in gold coin of the United States on the exchange of the ratification of this convention and also an annual payment during the life of this convention of two hundred and fifty thousand dollars ($250,000) in like gold coin, beginning nine years after the date aforesaid.

The provisions of this Article shall be in addition to all other benefits assured to the Republic of Panama under this convention.

But no delay or difference of opinion under this Article or any other provisions of this treaty shall affect or interrupt the full operation and effect of this convention in all other respects.

Article XV

The joint commission referred to in Article VI shall be established as follows:

The President of the United States shall nominate two persons and the President of the Republic of Panama shall nominate two persons and they shall proceed to a decision; but in case of disagreement of the Commission (by reason of their being equally divided in conclusion), an umpire shall be appointed by the two Governments who shall render the decision. In the event of the death, absence, or incapacity of a Commissioner or Umpire, or of his omitting, declining or ceasing to act, his place shall be filled by the appointment of another person in the manner above indicated. All decisions by a majority of the Commission or by the umpire shall be final.

ARTICLE XVI

The two Governments shall make adequate provision by future agreement for the pursuit, capture, imprisonment, detention and delivery within said zone and auxiliary lands to the authorities of the Republic of Panama of persons charged with the commitment of crimes, felonies, or misdemeanors without said zone and for the pursuit, capture, imprisonment, detention and delivery without said zone to the authorities of the United States of persons charged with the commitment of crimes, felonies and misdemeanors within said zone and auxiliary lands.

ARTICLE XVII

The Republic of Panama grants to the United States the use of all the ports of the Republic open to commerce as places of refuge for any vessels employed in the Canal enterprise, and for all vessels passing or bound to pass through the Canal which may be in distress and be driven to seek refuge in said ports. Such vessels shall be exempt from anchorage and tonnage dues on the part of the Republic of Panama.

ARTICLE XVIII

The Canal, when constructed, and the entrances thereto shall be neutral in perpetuity, and shall be opened upon the terms provided for by Section I of Article three of, and in conformity with all the stipulations of, the treaty entered into by the Governments of the United States and Great Britain on November 18, 1901.

ARTICLE XIX

The Government of the Republic of Panama shall have the right to transport over the Canal, its vessels and its troops and its munitions of war in such vessels at all times without paying charges of any kind. The exemption is to be extended to the auxiliary railway for the transportation of persons in the service of the Republic of Panama, or of the police force charged with the preservation of public order outside of said zone, as well as to their baggage, munitions of war and supplies.

ARTICLE XX

If by virtue of any existing treaty in relation to the territory of the Isthmus of Panama, whereof the obligations shall descend or be assumed by the Republic of Panama, there may be any privilege or concession in favor of the Government or the citizens and subjects of a third power relative to an interoceanic means of communication which in any of its terms may be incompatible with the terms of the present convention, the Republic of Panama agrees to cancel or modify such treaty in due form, for which purpose it shall give to the said third power the requisite notification within the term of four months from the date of the present convention, and in case the existing treaty contains no clause permitting its modifications or annulment, the Republic of Panama agrees to procure its modification or annulment in such form that there shall not exist any conflict with the stipulations of the present convention.

ARTICLE XXI

The rights and privileges granted by the Republic of Panama to the United States in the preceding Articles are understood to be free of all anterior debts, liens, trusts, or liabilities, or concessions or privileges to other Governments, corporations, syndicates or individuals, and consequently, if there should arise any claims on account of the present concessions and privileges or otherwise, the claimants shall resort to the Government of the Republic of Panama, and not to the United States for any indemnity or compromise which may be required.

ARTICLE XXII

The Republic of Panama renounces and grants to the United States, the participation to which it might be entitled in the future earnings of the Canal under Article XV of the concessionary contract with Lucien N. B. Wyse, now owned by the New Panama

Canal Company and any and all other rights or claims of a pecuniary nature arising under or relating to said concession, or arising under or relating to the concessions to the Panama Railroad Company or any extension or modification thereof; and it likewise renounces, confirms and grants to the United States, now and hereafter, all the rights and property reserved in the said concessions which otherwise would belong to Panama at or before the expiration of the terms of ninety-nine years of the concessions granted to or held by the above mentioned party and companies, and all right, title and interest which it now has or may hereafter have, in and to the lands, canal, works, property and rights held by the said companies under said concessions or otherwise, and acquired or to be acquired by the United States from or through the New Panama Canal Company, including any property and rights which might or may in the future either by lapse of time, forfeiture or otherwise, revert to the Republic of Panama under any contracts or concessions, with said Wyse, the Universal Panama Canal Company, the Panama Railroad Company and the New Panama Canal Company.

The aforesaid rights and property shall be and are free and released from any present or reversionary interest in or claims of Panama and the title of the United States thereto upon consummation of the contemplated purchase by the United States from the New Panama Canal Company, shall be absolute, so far as concerns the Republic of Panama, excepting always the rights of the Republic specifically secured under this treaty.

ARTICLE XXIII

If it should become necessary at any time to employ armed forces for the safety or protection of the Canal, or of the ships that make use of the same, or the railways and auxiliary works, the United States shall have the right, at all times and in its discretion, to use its police and its land and naval forces or to establish fortifications for these purposes.

ARTICLE XXIV

No change either in the Government or in the laws and treaties of the Republic of Panama shall, without the consent of the United

States, affect any right of the United States under the present convention, or under any treaty stipulation between the two countries that now exists or may hereafter exist touching the subject matter of this convention.

If the Republic of Panama shall hereafter enter as a constituent into any other Government or into any union or confederation of states, so as to merge her sovereignty or independence in such Government, union or confederation, the rights of the United States under this convention shall not be in any respect lessened or impaired.

Article XXV

For the better performance of the engagements of this convention and to the end of the efficient protection of the Canal and the preservation of its neutrality, the Government of the Republic of Panama will sell or lease to the United States lands adequate and necessary for the naval or coaling stations on the Pacific coast and on the western Caribbean coast of the Republic at certain points to be agreed upon with the President of the United States.

Article XXVI

This convention when signed by the Plenipotentiaries of the Contracting Parties shall be ratified by the respective Governments and the ratifications shall be exchanged at Washington at the earliest date possible.

In faith whereof the respective Plenipotentiaries have signed the present convention in duplicate and have hereunto affixed their respective seals.

Done at the City of Washington, the 18th day of November in the year of our Lord, nineteen hundred and three.

JOHN HAY. [SEAL.]

P. BUNAU VARILLA. [SEAL.]

And whereas the said Convention has been duly ratified on both parts, and the ratifications of the two governments were exchanged in the City of Washington, on the twenty-sixth day of February, one thousand nine hundred and four;

Now, therefore, be it known that I, Theodore Roosevelt, President of the United States of America, have caused the said Convention to be made public, to the end that the same and every article and clause thereof, may be observed and fulfilled with good faith by the United States and the citizens thereof.

In testimony whereof, I have hereunto set my hand and caused the seal of the United States of America to be affixed.

Done at the City of Washington, this twenty-sixth day of February, in the year of our Lord one thousand nine hundred and four, and of the Independence of the United States the one hundred and twenty-eighth.

[SEAL]

THEODORE ROOSEVELT.

By the President:
JOHN HAY,
    Secretary of State.